In Defense of Free Speech in Universities

In Defense of Free Speech in Universities

A STUDY OF THREE JURISDICTIONS

Amy Lai

UNIVERSITY OF MICHIGAN PRESS
ANN ARBOR

Published in the United States of America by the
University of Michigan Press
Manufactured in the United States of America
Printed on acid-free paper
First published September 2023

A CIP catalog record for this book is available from the British Library.

Library of Congress Cataloging-in-Publication Data

Names: Lai, Amy [date] author.
Title: In defense of free speech in universities : a study of three jurisdictions / Amy Lai.
Description: Ann Arbor : University of Michigan Press, 2023. |
Includes bibliographical references.
Identifiers: LCCN 2023018060 (print) | LCCN 2023018061 (ebook) | ISBN 9780472076406 (hardcover : acid-free paper) | ISBN 9780472056408 (paper : acid-free paper) | ISBN 9780472903795 (open access ebook)
Subjects: LCSH: Academic freedom. | Education, Higher—Political aspects. | Freedom of speech. | Freedom of speech—Great Britain. | Freedom of speech—United States. | Freedom of speech—Canada. | BISAC: EDUCATION / Administration / Higher | LAW / Constitutional
Classification: LCC LC72 .L35 2023 (print) | LCC LC72 (ebook) |
DDC 371.1/04—dc23/eng/20230524
LC record available at https://lccn.loc.gov/2023018060
LC ebook record available at https://lccn.loc.gov/2023018061

DOI: https://doi.org/10.3998/mpub.11442022

The University of Michigan Press's open access publishing program is made possible thanks to additional funding from the University of Michigan Office of the Provost and the generous support of contributing libraries.

Contents

Preface and Acknowledgments vii

Introduction 1

PART ONE

Chapter 1 Free Speech in Western Universities 15

Chapter 2 Academic Freedom: History, Definitions, and Democratic Significance 30

Chapter 3 Campus Free Speech and Academic Freedom 46

PART TWO

Chapter 4 Free Speech, Compelled Speech, Fact/Falsehood/Unpopular Opinion 57

Chapter 5 Political Correctness, Harassment/Discrimination/ Hate Speech, Microaggression 81

Chapter 6 Deplatforming, Trigger Warning, Safe Space 116

PART THREE

Chapter 7 The United Kingdom: Human Rights Act, a New Bill, and the Uncertain Future of Campus Speech 155

Chapter 8 The United States: First Amendment, Speech Codes, and Promising but "Not Quite There Yet" Results 197

Chapter 9 Canada: The (Ir)relevance of the Charter to Campus Speech 238

Conclusion 283

About the Author 287

Preface and Acknowledgments

Grief is the price we pay for love.
—Queen Elizabeth II

The courtyard is lit with tiny spots—green, yellow, and orange. The scene of fireflies lighting up the countryside on a summer night fascinated me as a wide-eyed kid who had yet to venture out of her disappearing birth city. I cannot recall when I became wary of the dark and forsook the pleasure of watching fireflies, a wariness that persisted after I settled in the Western world, where I looked back with horror at a distant home sinking into chaos.

In various cultures, fireflies are believed to carry the souls of dead soldiers, heroes, and leaders. As such, they are a symbol of both death and eternity. Long gone are the days of childhood, a time when death seemed a remote idea. Every time someone dear to me or whom I respected for their courage and uprightness passed away, I imagined them, through teary eyes, becoming little souls residing in these glowing beetles. Honorable but fragile humans, very much like fundamental ideas that are prone to be forgotten in a materialistic world, are then immortalized in a vision both fleeting and eternal.

The number of fireflies, I kept getting told, has gone down in places all over the world. Despite knowing their recent comeback in many North American neighborhoods, I did not expect to see them in a suburb in Berlin—glowing and waning spots of light looked like rekindled sparks after a flame had died down. Their presence shrouded the courtyard and woodlands nearby in an eeriness that sparks longing and nostalgia.

• • •

It was a long day. I got off work and felt unusually exhausted. Thus, I took an empty seat once I got on a subway train in downtown Boston. It was a long ride. I normally would stay alert. This time I dozed off within minutes out of exhaustion. Suddenly, I felt a knock on my head. "Give the seat to the man!" I opened my eyes to find the angry face of a very fair-skinned little girl. She was very young—probably five or six. She then used her little hand that woke me up to point to a dark-skinned man in his thirties nearby who was carrying a small child.

I rose without a second thought and tried to steady myself by grabbing the nearest handrail. With my abdomen in deep throngs of pain, I closed my eyes again and pictured people on the train reprimanding me for falling asleep and not giving my seat to a poor, needy man before being told to do so by a bystander who, despite her age, had better etiquette and was more compassionate to those in need.

I finally ran off at the next station. As blood gushed out of my body, I collapsed on the nearest bench on the platform. I wept not out of pain but shame. If I had been well, I would likely have been the first person to volunteer help to the man, or any people regardless of their race, ethnicity, or even their age (imagine a teenager holding several bags or looking visibly sick!). But I felt ill and very exhausted. The little girl, no matter how noble her intention, had no right to wake up a stranger and order her to give up her seat. I could have declined. I had every right and reason to do so. Yet I did not. I felt ashamed of my weakness.

"Are you okay? Do you want some water?" I looked up to see a concerned teenaged girl. She took out a bottle of distilled water from her bag and handed it to me. What caught my attention was the school uniform she was wearing: most American high schools do not at all implement school uniforms. Her burgundy school blazer and its shiny logo dazzled my eyes, as my mind wandered back to my adolescence in Hong Kong.

The school that I went to was set up in the early 1900s by Catholic missionaries from Italy. Located in a secluded spot in West Tsimshatsui, one of the city's busiest commercial districts, it boasts of some magnificent Classical-style buildings and a serene campus, in stark contrast to the hustle-bustle of the district. While the principals were usually nuns hailing form a certain Italy-based religious institute, most teachers and students were local people. Classes were conducted in both Chinese and English. Half of the students opted to enroll in Chinese and English literature classes for the public exam. A minority studied French.

I used to detest the school for its strict regulations, stern teachers, and some snobbish and petty classmates. In recent years, I gradually came to feel grateful to it for very good reasons. It did not implement a superficial kindness that has been proven, time and again, to be a pretext for tolerance of bad conduct or plain authoritarianism. Although we had to study the Bible and attend prayer assemblies, which was reasonable as we were there by (our parents') choice, none of us was forced to convert to Catholicism, and non-Catholics were not discriminated against in any way (for example, top students, be they Catholics or not, were awarded prizes and scholarships). We were merely taught to follow the general tenets and be principled, hardworking, and respectful. We were encouraged to express ourselves. We were urged to take part in community service and be compassionate to the less fortunate. The works of Shakespeare, George Orwell, and Hsu Chih-mo nurtured in me a keen curiosity about Britain, Cambridge, and many other legendary European cities and writers from different cultures.

After so many years, I realized that this very learning environment—where one was taught morals and manners and where multiple languages were embraced and no one was persecuted for religious or political reasons—was possible only in a Hong Kong under British governance. It was the same Hong Kong that enjoyed the rule of law, tolerated schools and organizations of various political and religious affiliations, and served as a haven for refugees fleeing from Vietnam and other countries in turmoil but produced no political refugees of its own. (Things were no doubt not perfect. In employment settings, for example, there were instances where mediocre people from Britain and other British commonwealth countries were hired over better-qualified locals and succeeded by virtue of their skin color and foreign backgrounds—these were generally known as "Filth," the acronym for "Failed in London, try Hong Kong." Expatriates who were indeed capable and respectful of local culture were respected in return, while criticisms of the incapable ones were allowed in a civilized and well-governed city.)

Our school was only steps away from the world-renowned hotel, the Peninsula, which was used by the Japanese as a military headquarter during World War II. Our history teacher, reputed for her serious demeanor, candidness, and vast knowledge, revealed the likely reason why the school was left unscathed during the air raids: "We hung a huge Italian flag across our main building to warn the invaders that it was untouchable." If true, the flag literally became a giant pair of wings that shielded the school from harm while the rest of the city risked getting bombed to ruins, not unlike how the British shielded Hong Kong from the major calamities under Chinese—especially Chinese communist—governance before the city's handover in 1997.

The subway incident happened some years ago in Boston and I no longer think of it that often. Recently, though, my school memories have returned to haunt me—for very, very unfortunate reasons. Since the beginning of 2022, all public schools in Hong Kong, kindergartens included, have been required by law to display the Chinese flag on every school day. They must also conduct a flag-raising ceremony with singing of the Chinese anthem once a week. I could not picture the grotesque ritual at my school without envisaging a lovely and elegant maiden being repeatedly ravished by a brute and no bystander willing to step in or speak out, due to indifference, cowardice, or tacit approval of the atrocious act. ("Hong Kong lawyer," "Hong Kong legal scholar," and "Hong Kong academic" are now oxymorons. One has to wonder what could have motivated people born and raised in Western democracies to not only watch passively and, in some cases, to cheer on the oppressor, but to stay in this fallen city other than their prioritization of money and a false sense of superiority over fundamental freedoms and real dignity that comes along with these freedoms—the same priorities that helped contribute to the fall of the city in the first place. Alas, there are many things that money can't buy. Money can't buy class, integrity, or dignity.)

Forever gone are the good old days of British Hong Kong, which was far from perfect but civilized and prosperous especially from the 1970s to the '90s until its ill-fated handover. At one of its finest schools, I cultivated manners and a strong work ethic and learned to distinguish between right and wrong. Back then, on its idyllic campus, I was more a conformist than a rebel. To date, I still have my moments of weakness. I nonetheless attribute to my upbringing in this long-gone city my lifelong mission not to cave to pressure and to stand up for what is right.

When I am entitled to sit, don't ask me to stand; when I want to stand, I won't kneel under pressure.

• • •

Canada prides itself on its multiculturalism. Like the multilingual signs at its international airports, multiculturalism is not an inherently bad policy. In fact, it is beneficial in many ways. One rarely finds a person who does not enjoy cuisines around the world, for example. My favorite dish has always been Canton-style steamed fish. I regularly have sushi for lunch and Korean hot pot for dinner. It might even be fair to say that people from different cultures always have something to learn from one another beyond food recipes. Nevertheless, the concerted effort by leaders and scholars to gloss over potential problems created by this policy, all in the name of peace and tolerance, is unsettling.

Many Canadians endeavor to be good citizens by embracing multiculturalism, or, at least, by broadcasting to the world that they do. Some academics are great; others tend to be so driven by mainstream ideologies that they seem to have long forgotten the importance of intellectual honesty and rational debate. The latter, who otherwise appear cheerful and relaxed, are easily triggered—not by physical violence or threats of such, but by ideas and opinions. For most of Hong Kong's pro-democracy people, a "safe space" would have referred to spaces free from tear gas, bullets, surveillance, and arbitrary detention. Here, a "safe space" is generally understood as one free from offensive ideas or anything deviating from their deeply held beliefs. Deplatforming of "unsafe" opinions and ideas, sometimes in the form of penalizing "heretical" academics, by university students and staff has become a common tactic to counter unorthodox or ideologically impure opinions and views, including those expressed in the most civil manner.

Perhaps one needs to be well-versed in history, to have relatives who suffered under communism, or to have experienced firsthand the atrocities in communist countries, to be able to fully perceive how such conduct is reminiscent of the Red Guards in Mao's China or the Stasi secret police in East Germany. "Freedom of expression is not freedom from consequences," these people keep chanting, "freedom of expression is not freedom to hurt and offend." Well, if section 2(b) of the Charter does not protect offensive ideas, then what functions does it serve?

In some Canadian public schools, students are taught that privilege depends primarily on the color of a person's skin. As in many American settings, an oppression hierarchy has been established—according to which East Asians are seen as being almost as privileged as white people by virtue of their skin color (and their academic achievements)—which serves as the guidance for mitigating historical wrongs (for example, in employment and university admission). A sole focus on this hierarchy, however, oversimplifies identity politics in Canada. The city of Vancouver, for example, used to have laws discriminating against Japanese and Chinese. This is atrocious, given that people are defined not by their skin color but by their conduct. A misguided attempt to mitigate this ugly historical wrong has been underway, which is to tolerate all people in these once-oppressed groups regardless of their conduct and refuse to call out or penalize bad behaviors by these groups. Canadian universities are quick to virtue-signal on many social justice issues but would never dare to criticize the Chinese government for its genocide of minorities or punish dishonest students from China for fear of "racism" accusations. Certainly, some immigrants from China are the most honest, hardworking, and humble people I have ever met in my life. Some other immigrants, however, are to blame for the rampant money laundering and infiltration of local politics by the Chinese government, while corrupt and greedy government officials and businessmen continue to facilitate the corruption.

My readers have likely read about wealthy immigrants from China honking their Ferraris in their attempts to drown out Hong Kong pro-democracy protests in Toronto. Yes, attacks on Hongkongers by immigrants from China, generally believed to be supported or even initiated by the Chinese embassy and consulates, have often gone unpunished by Canadian law enforcement and university authorities. Personal anecdotes also reveal an overly tolerant and unsuspecting—even welcoming—attitude among the educated elites toward not only Chinese offenders but also their hostile government. I have heard of the principals of a top university's graduate student hostel, which houses many students from China, monitoring the social media postings of its residents to detect any message that may offend the Chinese students, as well as meeting and dining with members of the Chinese consulate. This is utterly unthinkable and unbecoming of these so-called educators, given the far-reaching implications of their conduct. For some Canadian academics, their fear of offending Chinese students is at times so irrational that it severely impacts their teaching. I recall a political science professor who admitted to having refrained from using the Chinese "president" as an example of a dictator in his class. Instead, he used Donald Trump, the democratically elected former president of the United States who, despite his flaws, had to work within a democratic system. Hence, the two examples of a modern dictator that he used were Adolf Hitler and Trump. How can students learn in universities full of teachers who are so cowardly, intellectually dishonest, or indoctrinated?

Come 2020. The COVID-19 virus and its variants ravaging the world also emboldened the Canadian government to unleash its authoritarian impulses. Freedom of expression was further suppressed, and many in Canada were punished for speaking their minds through words or actions. Amid the public outcry against anti-Asian racism, legitimate criticisms of the Chinese government were conflated with racism against Chinese people in an intellectually empty and overused rhetoric. Idling on the couch, I rewatched the Korean movie *Train to Busan* (2016). The scenes where human characters flee from an encroaching army of zombies to avoid being attacked and becoming zombies themselves—so surreal and yet so familiar—distracted me from the outside world that had gone mad.

If I had been born in Canada, I likely would have grown up to be happier and less cynical, and may have become an accepted, even popular, member of the "woke" crowds. The lessons that living through these trying times taught me, soul-crushing in the short term, have enabled me to better myself and to transcend them in many respects. In addition, being born in British Hong Kong might have been a blessing in disguise. Witnessing the rise and decline of my birth city, and the painful process of finding the root causes of its demise, transformed me into a more courageous and much wiser person than I otherwise would have been.

• • •

In Germany, academic freedom is protected by its very own constitution. No country is perfect: it has suffered problems very similar to those in Anglophone countries and many of its laws governing freedom of speech are known to be stricter than their American, British, and Canadian counterparts. At the same time, one is generally free to address topics within the bounds of the law and can even obtain substantial funding for projects that are considered "too controversial" and "politically incorrect" in Anglophone academia.

Yet many German academics, like their peers in Anglophone countries, have refused to fully acknowledge the harms of all extreme politics. Such a failure heralds a worrying development in German universities. Two incidents particularly irked me. Incident one: I was invited by another German university to give a guest lecture on the pro-democracy movement in Hong Kong. I endeavored to offer a realistic picture of Hong Kong under British governance and after its handover to China, detailing the accomplishments by the joint efforts of British and Hong Kong people and their destruction by China, the new colonizer. One course coordinator took issue with an initial draft of my talk, claiming that the course aimed to teach students the harms of colonialism. My account showing the prosperity of British Hong Kong as well as conveying the message that some forms of colonialism are less harmful than others therefore fell outside its paradigm. I responded that I did not aim to justify colonialism. Far from that. I aimed instead to paint a real picture of British Hong Kong, where life was not perfect but where people enjoyed the rule of law and most liberties, and to argue that the British laid down a good system of governance that Hongkongers want to retain in their fight for autonomy and self-governance. The other course coordinator admitted to knowing next to nothing about the place but said my narrative could fuel racism against the Chinese. How can embracing the rule of law, which does exist in well-developed Asian countries such as Japan, be racist? Obsessed with Hitler but oblivious to the harms of other radical politics, this German professor nevertheless kept shaking her head while hearing my lived experiences: she did not even attempt to hide the fact that she found my account of a stable and prosperous British Hong Kong, which did not align with her simplistic narrative and worldview according to which all colonized subjects are slaves without any agency, dangerous. While she approved—albeit reluctantly—a new draft of the talk, in which I kept all the substantive facts and arguments, I clearly became a sore thumb and heretic—and an irredeemable one armed with lived experiences—in their eyes.

Incident two: someone forwarded an announcement about an international bestselling author's upcoming talk in Berlin in an email group. A European recipient in the group responded in anger, claiming deep offense at the author's upcoming presence in the city because his views were "deeply offensive" and doubting that the author would be invited to any university because of his offensive and dangerous views. Ironically, though, a few months before this angered response, the author returned from his visit to one of the most prestigious universities in world. Another recipient, as if to echo the anti-Enlightenment spirit in the angered response, chimed in, "Well, you should have known that the speaker's views are far removed from what the recipients would have agreed with." (Subtext: you're asking for such a response!) Again, this incident happened in Berlin, a city that earned its fame for having witnessed two dictatorships on both ends of the political spectrum. One cannot help but wonder: in what kind of world do the offended recipient and the course coordinators—and people who think and act similarly—believe humans should live? Fortunately, local students seem to be more open to different opinions. There is hope. One can only hope that those who were shot at the Berlin Wall or otherwise perished while fighting the East German regime did not suffer in vain.

I have not wavered despite these unfortunate incidents: if anything, my convictions were strengthened. Above all, I know for a fact that Great Britain, regardless of how rotten it has become and the multiple problems that it shared with America and Canada in the twenty-first century, has been and will always be my home. My arrival at Heathrow Airport and in Cambridge and the welcoming looks and greetings on Clare Bridge years ago remain my treasured moments of homecoming.

Born British, always British.

• • •

This book was first conceived in late 2018 during a visit to my birth city. Its research and writing spanned a period from late 2018 to early 2022, interrupted multiple times due to political and social upheavals on different continents, all of which, quite sadly and ironically, testify to the erosion of our fundamental freedoms. I cannot thank enough Elizabeth Demers, the editorial director of the University of Michigan Press, as well as every member of her editorial team, for their patience, open-mindedness, and unflinching commitment to academic freedom.

My sincere gratitude also goes to my reviewers who remained anonymous until after my project had gone on to the copyediting stage. I appreciate especially one reviewer's appreciative remark that my work "does not fit neatly into a 'left'/ 'right' box." Indeed, no two persons think the same and one's worldview may shift over time. All along, I had been aiming to avoid ideologically driven and jargon-filled dialogues and instead to present well-reasoned, fact-based arguments in plain language. Upon reading this remark—albeit a generous one—I felt like my mission was complete.

Seldom do authors thank themselves and they need to do so more frequently—my last words of gratitude are reserved for myself.

I published my first book with Cambridge University Press. I almost did not make it. One reviewer identified what he considered a major "flaw" in my manuscript, which was to apply a Western Enlightenment framework of freedom of speech to the study of Hong Kong, a non-Western jurisdiction. This view, now very common in Western academia, is inherently racist by implying that people outside the Western world do not deserve the same amount or type of freedom as those in Western societies do. Cultural relativism, if taken too far, is indeed dangerous: If freedom of expression is Eurocentric and should be rewritten, does it follow that the freedom from being raped or murdered also needs to be rewritten? As luck would have it, the publisher sought feedback from a third reviewer, who approved it without reservations. The book, as well as my other writing, has already earned me four prestigious awards in the U.S., Canada, and Germany.

New York artist Ron English's parody of Vincent van Gogh's *Starry Night* was selected for its aesthetic appeal to grace the cover of my first book, which I dedicated to "all people out there who have integrity, who help to uphold the rule of law, and who stand up to evil and tyranny." The cover image took on a meaning the profundity of which I was not aware at the time. Coincidentally, American singer-songwriter Don McLean named his song after the painter, describing him as one who suffered for (because of) his sanity. I hereby dedicate this book, which can be deemed a sequel to my first, to people out there who speak truth to power, and who have suffered and will continue to suffer because of their sanity.

It is unclear whether it was W. B. Yeats who said, "There are no strangers here; only friends whom you haven't yet met." I wish many people who passed away at different points of my life and whom I still miss dearly could read this book. The living ones who read and appreciate it should see it as a token of friendship. For people who might feel offended by any part of it and want to attack its author, I have decided that I owe them no apology. To apologize for intellectually honest opinions and arguments made in good faith would be akin to kneeling on broken glass during the Cultural Revolution in China. Back then, those poor people—typically the well-educated—had no choice but to endure tortures and indignities. In civilized nations, those who can stand but choose to kneel will never be able to stand upright or walk straight again.

Throughout history, book-burning took place under different authoritarian regimes. Even today, books keep getting burned—both literally and metaphorically. As sparks fly, their ideas become the smoke that rises above the devouring flames and meanders toward the sky. I have always imagined Robert Schumann's "Träumerei" accompanying the rising smoke. This is what I have been practicing with the Yamaha digital piano that I bought with the royalties of my first book, and what I, an introvert, plan to play when that whole "party" collapses one day and crowds celebrate in the streets.

Deep down, I am still the little girl who sobbed hearing sad and nostalgic music; who waited with a dish of cat food or milk for a stray little kitten in her neighborhood; who frowned at injustices while her classmates smiled and nodded in contentment; who, walking out of an orientation meeting in early dusk and bewildered that darkness had already engulfed her new, beloved English city, panicked and struggled to find her way back to the dormitory on a wintry night.

Deep down, I am still that girl, now treading along a path often unlit by fireflies—slowly and steadily—toward the light in the distance, as countless figures and apparitions carelessly fall over or willfully succumb to the swirling abysses around them.

August 2022
Brandenburg Gate

Author's Note

The laws and materials in this book are updated to the end of April 2023.

Introduction

Freedom of expression on university campuses has become a pressing issue in many Western democratic countries in recent years. Imagine yourself in the following scenarios—

Andrew, a young professor and new hire at a well-known law school, was brimming with excitement on his way to attend a talk hosted by a student organization. Several colleagues from other Western countries had been invited to speak on the contentious but important topic of immigration. He was especially eager to exchange with his dear friend, an award-winning researcher and teacher with whom he did not always agree but whose knowledge, courage, and congeniality he had always admired. Upon arriving at the venue, he was greeted by a group of disgruntled student protesters who had congregated with their giant "f*ck bigotry" banner: fearing that the vehement protest in anticipation of his friend's arrival would escalate into violence, the university had the entire event canceled for "safety" reasons.

Beatrice, whose tenure review would be decided in the coming month, joined a campus rally organized by her Hong Kong students in support of the democracy movement and in solidarity with the arbitrarily jailed activists in their home city. What began as a peaceful assembly was soon disrupted by a counterprotest backed by the Chinese embassy. She, along with several Hongkongers, was beaten by some rabid nationalists from China. Still recovering from her broken leg, she was summoned to a disciplinary meeting where her boss told her: "We have zero tolerance for racism and hate—you must not support those racist troublemakers from Hong Kong who mock China and their fellow Chinese by claiming that their city was a better place when governed by the Brits!"

Calvin is teaching his popular course on world politics again this semester. A tenured professor, he is well versed in Chinese politics. After reviewing the name list, he decided to use Adolf Hitler and Donald Trump as examples of a dictator. He deliberately avoided mentioning Xi Jinping, head of the Chinese Communist Party (or China's "president"), like he did last time, as he noticed numerous Chinese students in his class, some of whom might have received their prior education exclusively in China and might take offense at the idea that Xi bears any semblance to a dictator. In fact, he has taken extreme care to not do anything that rabid Chinese nationalists, or the Chinese government, deem "racist": he desperately needs to improve his evaluations to remain competitive for his faculty's teaching award. The program chair and the university's president would also get upset if any "racist" remark or accusation of racism would cause a drop in student enrollment.

The foregoing episodes are by no means taken from a dystopia. Based on real incidents, they satirize the harmful politics dominating at least some Western university campuses. Few equality-loving people would deny that racism and xenophobia are social ills that need to be addressed. Society cannot find out the best ways to address evils as such without honest discussion. A healthy, functional university environment tolerates, even welcomes, opposing views on difficult but important topics. Suppressing facts, ideas, and perspectives that challenge orthodox ideas and calling people holding such ideas and perspectives "bigots," on the contrary, allows misinformation to flourish and produces echo chambers in which unchallenged members are prone to get radicalized by their preferred ideologies, even to the extent that they seek to control other people's thoughts, cry foul at sensible and well-reasoned opinions challenging their own, and create oppressive, authoritarian learning environments. Despite their good intentions, these crusaders are blindsided by their simplistic ideologies and fail to tackle the problems that they aim to solve. Worse still, their zealousness can become overtaken by greed—for money, material gain, and power. Like the professor in the last scenario who took the position that criticizing China's government, not its people, is racist, these people do not only make their universities authoritarian: while obsessing over political correctness and the avoidance of emotional harm, they continue to appease a foreign authoritarian government and enable it to infiltrate Western academia.

It would be utterly unthinkable if universities were ruled by the far right who threaten people outside of their group. It would be highly disconcerting if they were governed by right-wing academics who delegitimize viewpoints different from their own. It would be deeply concerning even if right-wingers were replaced entirely by old-school conservatives who embrace traditional ways. University campuses in general may not be hotbeds of radical left-wing activities. Nonetheless, as much as many Western societies are still threatened by the extreme right, many university campuses in Anglophone countries are currently dominated by left-wing and, in some cases, far-left politics. That left-wing academics outnumber their centrist or conservative-minded counterparts is reasonable and perhaps even desirable. It indicates not only that conservative ideas may be outdated or plain wrong but also a collective aspiration by the academic elite to help society make progress and to combat bigotry. However, the desire for social progress excuses neither the suppression and discouragement of respectful dialogues, nor the vilification and punishment of those who perform their jobs in good faith and good conscience but do not agree with or subscribe fully to the dominant ideologies. Reasonable people disagree on many issues. Tyranny, regardless of what forms it takes, is invariably evil.

Perhaps a healthy, functional university environment does not demand a balancing of liberal and conservative academics. It may only require genuine tolerance for diverse opinions and ideas, including those dissenting from mainstream or dominant politics, and respectful discussion on topics of importance. The last ten years have witnessed a rising number of incidents in which freedom of expression was threatened on Western university campuses. According to a British study, more than 80 percent of universities in the United Kingdom have restricted or actively censored free speech and expression on their campuses beyond the requirements of the law.[1] Another study found that a sizeable proportion of conservative-leaning academics in British universities were reluctant to express their views or challenge those of their left-wing colleagues, who greatly outnumbered them.[2] Evidence also indicates that speakers expressing conservative views have met with far more protests and attacks than their liberal-leaning counterparts on British campuses.[3]

---

1. Louise Tickle, *Free Speech? Not at Four in Five Universities*, The Guardian (Feb. 2, 2015), http://www.theguardian.com/education/2015/feb/02/free-speech-universities-spiked-ban-sombreros, citing Tom Slater, *Free Speech University Rankings: Exposing the Staggering Scale of Censorship on Campus*, Spiked (Feb. 3, 2015), http://www.spiked-online.com/2015/02/03/free-speech-university-rankings-exposing-the-staggering-scale-of-censorship-on-campus/
2. Remi Adekoya, Eric Kaufmann & Tom Simpson, *Academic Freedom in the UK: Protecting Viewpoint Diversity*, Policy Exchange (Aug. 3, 2020), http://policyexchange.org.uk/publication/academic-freedom-in-the-uk-2/
3. *See The Banned List*, Academics for Academic Freedom, http://www.afaf.org.uk/the-banned-list/ (last visited Dec. 21, 2021).

Across the Atlantic, similar scenarios have been common in both the United States and Canada. Although scholars, speakers, or students across the political spectrum have self-censored or had their speech rights threatened on American university campuses,[4] left-wing academics, students, and speakers have been shut down or criticized for more legitimate reasons, such as their use of expletives or calls for violence, while the suppression of their conservative counterparts has been more often than not ideologically motivated.[5] In Canada, protests against speakers holding different political views or seen as representing different ideologies have varied greatly in terms of the scale and degree of violence. A small, peaceful group of protesters appeared at the event at Dalhousie University featuring former Canadian citizen and child soldier Omar Khadr, who pled guilty to murder and other charges he committed in Afghanistan and later received a handsome compensation from the Canadian government for what it considered to be a mishandling of his case.[6] It was a far cry from the massive, at times violent, protests sparked by well-known conservative speakers and speakers who were not necessarily conservative but dared to challenge left-wing ideologies.

The prevalence of free speech battles at these places of learning is not a good sign, considering that the education system has invariably been one of the prime targets of dictatorships and authoritarian regimes. Throughout world history, these regimes have used schools and universities for indoctrination and propaganda purposes by controlling the information to which young, impressionable minds are exposed and by mobilizing indoctrinated students of different ages to participate in campaigns aimed at bolstering the ruling powers.[7] Propaganda was rife, free expression was suppressed, and teachers were

---

4. Sanford J. Ungar, *Campus Speech Protests Don't Only Target Conservatives, and When They Do, It's Often the Same Few Conservatives, Georgetown Free Speech Tracker Find*, MEDIUM (Mar. 26, 2018), https://medium.com/informed-and-engaged/campus-speech-protests-dont-only-target-conservatives-though-they-frequently-target-the-same-few-bda3105ad347

5. *See, e.g.*, Julie McMahon, *Syracuse University Chancellor Defends Prof after Tweet Sets Off Right-Wing Backlash*, SYR. UNIV. NEWS (Jan. 4, 2019), https://www.syracuse.com/su-news/2017/06/syracuse_university_chancellor_defends_prof_after_tweet_sets_off_right-wing_back.html; Maleeha Syed, *Middlebury College Cancels Talk with Conservative Speaker for Safety Purposes*, BURLINGTON FREE PRESS (Apr. 17, 2019), https://www.burlingtonfreepress.com/story/news/local/2019/04/17/campus-free-speech-middlebury-college-charles-murray-european-parliament-ryszard-legutko/3494450002/

6. Alicia Draus, *Omar Khadr Makes First Public Appearance, Delivers Keynote Address at Dalhousie University Event*, GLOBAL NEWS (Feb. 10, 2020), https://globalnews.ca/news/6534245/omar-khadr-dalhousie-university/; *e.g.*, *Key Events in the Omar Khadr Case*, CBC NEWS (Jul. 7, 2017), https://www.cbc.ca/news/canada/key-events-in-the-omar-khadr-case-1.1153759 (last visited May 5, 2020).

7. *E.g.*, Anja Neundorf & Grigore Pop-Eleches, *Dictators and Their Subjects: Authoritarian Attitudinal Effects and Legacies*, 53 COMP. POL. STUD. 1839 (2020), http://journals.sagepub.com/doi/10.1177/00

persecuted and slaughtered in schools and universities in Nazi Germany, East Germany, and Mao's China, to name just a few.[8]

It was no coincidence that book burnings were also carried out under some of these regimes. German universities and their intellectuals willingly and proudly took part in destroying "un-German" books not long after Hitler came to power, while Red Guards zealously "cleansed" school libraries during China's Cultural Revolution.[9] In the twenty-first century, book burnings have survived only in countries like China.[10] Ironically, though, this practice, as well as the spirit and the appeasement policy it entails, has continued in democratic nations, albeit in different forms. It happens, for example, when democratic governments forgo their moral duty by restraining criticism of authoritarian governments for their human rights abuses and trade their long-standing democratic values for lucrative business with these nations.[11]

The suppression of campus free speech, or what is known as the "cancel culture," in the twenty-first century is worrying as it is reminiscent of book burning[12] and, as history shows, can be an alarming symptom of rising authori-

---

1041402092 6203; D. Cantoni, Y. Chen & D. Yang, *Curriculum & Ideology*, 125(2) J. POL. ECON. 338 (2017).

8. *E.g.*, Laura Williams, *10 Terrifying Facts about the East German Secret Police*, FOUND. ECON. EDUC. (Nov. 14, 2019), http://fee.org/articles/10-terrifying-facts-about-the-east-german-secret-police/; Facing History and Ourselves, *Chapter Five: Controlling the Universities*, HOLOCAUST AND HUMAN BEHAVIOR, http://www.facinghistory.org/holocaust-and-human-behavior/chapter-5/controlling-universities (last visited Apr. 6, 2021); D. Cantoni, Y. Chen & D. Yang, *Curriculum & Ideology*, 125(2) J. POL. ECON. 338 (2017).
9. *E.g.*, Christoph Hasselbach, *When Books Were Burned in Germany*, DEUTSCHE WELLE (May 10, 2018), http://www.dw.com/en/when-books-were-burned-in-germany/a-43725960; Huizhong Wu, *In Echo of Mao Era, China's Schools in Book-Cleansing Drive*, REUTERS (Jul. 9, 2020), http://www.reuters.com/article/us-china-books-insight-idUSKBN24A1R5
10. *See, e.g.*, Christoph Hasselbach, *When Books Were Burned in Germany*, DEUTSCHE WELLE (May 10, 2018), http://www.dw.com/en/when-books-were-burned-in-germany/a-43725960; Huizhong Wu, *In Echo of Mao Era, China's Schools in Book-Cleansing Drive*, REUTERS (Jul. 9, 2020), http://www.reuters.com/article/us-china-books-insight-idUSKBN24A1R5; James Palmer, *China Brief: Why Is China Burning Books?* FOREIGN POL'Y (Dec. 11, 2019), http://foreignpolicy.com/2019/12/11/china-burning-book-censorship-online-outrage/
11. Christoph Hasselbach, *When Books Were Burned in Germany*, DEUTSCHE WELLE (May 10, 2018), http://www.dw.com/en/when-books-were-burned-in-germany/a-43725960
12. While some may challenge this analogy by arguing that the suppression of free speech has nowhere been as frequent as book burning in Nazi Germany, a single act of deplatforming (and other incidents of speech suppression) is analogous to a single episode of book burning. Other may challenge the analogy by pointing out that those who deplatform speakers likely do not want their views to gain any currency and have no issue with allowing those "dangerous" and controversial views to survive in a "safe" corner of the library. Nonetheless, the act of deplatforming (especially by such illegal means as pulling the fire alarm) reveals a similarly authoritarian mindset harboring the flawed belief that by making controversial speakers disappear from sight and hearing, their ideas and opinions would also vanish from people's minds.

tarianism. At the same time, one must not dismiss the importance of feelings in social settings. It would be unwise and insensitive to disregard sincere complaints about harmful speech and attribute all of them to the hypersensitivity of the offended, sometimes referred to disparagingly as "snowflakes."[13] More recently, quite a few scholars have argued that university officials have seldom caved in to offended students, and the instances where they seemed to do so can often been viewed in the context of a larger strategy to preserve their autonomy, power, and prestige rather than to appease or protect sensitive students. Regardless of the true reason(s) for suppressing campus speech, the question remains: Where should the line be drawn to differentiate acceptable and unacceptable speech to ensure a healthy and functional university environment? Whether or not the free speech problem has evolved into a full-blown crisis in Western universities, it is undeniably an important topic that needs to be addressed in democratic societies. This book will add to the current scholarly debate by studying the history and importance of free speech in the Western university, the philosophical foundations of free speech, and the flawed rationales and mechanisms commonly used to justify the suppression of free speech on campuses, and selected campus free speech cases in three jurisdictions: the United Kingdom, the United States, and Canada.

• • •

This book is divided into three parts. In part I, chapter 1 describes the origin of free speech in the university setting. It explains how Emperor Frederick Barbarossa's granting of the privilege of free expression to scholars in medieval Europe was an important moment in the history of free speech in the Western world, despite its limited scope according to today's standards. Chapter 2 examines the history, definitions, and significance of academic freedom—so often conflated with free speech, while chapter 3 clarifies their differences and illuminates their mutually beneficial relationship. Throughout history, erosion of these freedoms has only undermined universities' functions: without these freedoms, a university cannot be said to exist.

Any concern about what might be considered the Eurocentric assumptions of part I would be groundless.[14] Throughout history, the importance of

---

13. *Snowflakes*, SLANG DICTIONARY, http://www.dictionary.com/e/slang/snowflake/ (last visited Apr. 9, 2021).
14. For instance, Patrick Deane, president of Queen's University in Canada, believes that this freedom is "unimaginable except as facilitated by social and economic privilege" and would perpetuate "sys-

free speech has been affirmed not merely in European cultures but also in cultures widely known as oppressive.[15] Hence, comments that the idea of free speech is Eurocentric and oppressive rather than liberating is strangely reminiscent of "freedom is slavery" in George Orwell's *Nineteen Eighty-Four*, and likely have been made out of ignorance.[16] That said, this book's topic—free speech in Western universities—justifies part I's focus on the history of free speech in the Western world. Notwithstanding the fundamental value of this freedom to all humans, there is no reason why one should not draw upon Western history and philosophies if the best arguments can be made with these resources, given that the amount of relevant materials would be massive. It is with such considerations that part II turns to the Western philosophical foundations of free speech.

Chapter 4 argues that free speech is a natural right essential to the pursuit of truth, democratic governance, and self-development, and this right is nowhere more important than in the university. If the right to free speech is natural and universal and stems from freedom of thought and conscience, so is the right to silence and against being compelled to say something, whether or not one agrees with it. Compelled speech, whether it contradicts the speaker's beliefs or not, is often a symptom of authoritarianism or totalitarianism. On campus, the willful or malicious misrepresentation of facts and spread of misinformation or propaganda by academics that are found to violate academic integrity can be disciplined. However, policies banning falsehoods can discourage debates. Given that many falsehoods may be unpopular opinions, not only can distinguishing truths from falsehoods often be difficult, but blind adherence to "truth" hinders the pursuit of knowledge and can play into the hands of the powerful who weaponize their dogmas, disguised as truths, to oppress and tyrannize.

Chapter 5 turns to the origins of "political correctness." Although political correctness may help create an inclusive society, banning or discouraging facially neutral expressions with sexist or racist roots or associated with hate

---

temic oppression" if not remade according to principles of equity and diversity. Patrick Deane, *The Choices We Made*, Queen's Alumni Rev. (Mar. 2020), http://www.queensu.ca/gazette/alumnireview/stories/principal-choices-we-make

15. Examples can be found even in the history of China. Fan Zhongyan (989–1052), a nobleman and reformist in the Sung Dynasty, said it would be "better to die for speaking the truth, than to stay alive by remaining quiet."

16. *See, e.g.*, Calum Anderson, *Letter to the Editor*, Queen's J. (Oct. 13, 2020), www.queensjournal.ca/story/2020-10-13/opinions/letter-to-the-editor-october-13th/

groups would lead society down a slippery slope. Suppressing expressions for fear that they offend protected groups and individuals also frustrates the key purposes of free speech, especially given the unlikelihood that discussion of topics that are frequently considered offensive would constitute harassment, discrimination, or hate speech. The chapter further examines "microaggressions" and the idea of dignity. Acknowledging the emotional harm caused by microaggressions, it identifies the shortcomings of diversity and sensitivity training programs and suggests that recipients of microaggression should exercise their autonomy and freedom of expression—a core part of dignity—to resist lawful words or acts that they deem to have undermined their dignity.

Chapter 6 debunks numerous popular arguments in favor of deplatforming without taking the absolutist position that it should never take place. It then addresses "trigger warnings" by pointing out that the word "triggering" has become synonymous with "provocative," which need not be negative as thought-provoking ideas and methods have pedagogical value. It points to the unfortunate reality of today's campuses, where thought-provoking opinions and ideas that serve to advance knowledge, democratic governance, and personal development are regularly mistaken as personal attacks, and where personal attacks are often justified in the name of peace and harmony. Finally, the chapter explains why a safe space should be limited in scope. Turning the entire university into a "safe space," based upon an overly broad concept of violence, may justify the use of preemptive violence against perceived threats to its "safety," let alone ill prepare students for the real world.

Each chapter in part III examines campus free speech in a selected Western jurisdiction. Besides providing overviews of applicable laws and policies in the jurisdictions, the chapters apply concepts examined in part II to the study of selected case studies. They aim to argue for the equal application of the free speech principle to all expression to facilitate respectful debate and the pursuit of knowledge, and analyze whether the decisions to ban them or to penalize their speakers were justified or unfair and wrongful. Given that conservative-leaning opinions and ideas are more likely to be banned on today's campuses, the chapters feature numerous conservative speakers.[17] It must be emphasized

---

17. Some of the chapters were completed during the height of the Israel-Palestinian conflict in 2021. Antisemitism, which has been found in radical politics on both ends of the spectrum and which would present an interesting case study, is not addressed in this book due to its scope. Nonetheless, the free speech principle should apply equally to all speech, including opinions and ideas that might offend Jews and Muslims.

that the defense of speakers' right to speak is by no means a defense of their politics or vindication of their opinions. Rather, it is meant to be an impartial application of the free speech principle.

Chapter 7 studies the U.K., where freedom of expression is protected by the Human Rights Act 1998 and campus free speech is affirmed by governmental policies, but where self-censorship and suppression of free expression in universities have become increasingly concerning. The "cancel culture" that has evolved over the past decade has led to numerous attempts to deplatform speakers who dare to challenge mainstream ideologies through respectful debate. The chapter argues that British universities must avoid inconsistent application of the free speech principle to different groups, which unfairly privilege the feelings and safety of some groups over others. They must also address the Chinese Communist Party's growing threat to free speech in British academia, by ditching their passivity, complacency, and at times complicity in the continual erosion of their autonomy by this rogue state and its agents and supporters.

Chapter 8 turns to the U.S., where free speech on university campuses is protected by the First Amendment or by a "contract theory" and affirmed by the U.S. Supreme Court. Despite ample legal safeguards at both public and private universities, numerous attempts by students to deplatform or disinvite speakers have succeeded. In addition, not a few universities have terminated or considered terminating the employment of unorthodox professors, denied support to harassed academics, or penalized student for expressing nonviolent messages. American universities should be lauded for acting with courage, for the most part, to curb the attempts by both the Chinese government and their agents to exploit Western liberal concepts of free speech and diversity to ban expression challenging their pro-China narrative or to camouflage their unprofessionalism and misconduct. The same moral courage and devotion to principles need to be shown in addressing all other free speech disputes.

Chapter 9 looks at Canada, where freedom of expression is recognized as a fundamental value under section 2(b) of the Canadian Charter of Rights and Freedoms, whose application to universities nonetheless remains uncertain due to judicial deference to university administrations in formulating and applying their own free speech policies. Attacks on free speech in Canadian universities, mostly by their own professors and students, have continued to grow. The inaction and complacency of Canadian universities have also played into the hands of the agents and supporters of the Chinese government who habitually pull the race card and liberal narratives to suppress meaningful discussion of China-related topics. Canadian universities must neither concede to local extremists who seek to suppress meaningful discussion, nor surrender to tyrannical foreign governments by trading their mission, democratic values, and national sovereignty for money and "friendships."

• • •

"This was a prelude only. Wherever they burn books they will also, in the end, burn human beings," wrote German poet Heinrich Heine in 1821, well before the Nazis took over his nation.[18] A dear friend of this book's author recalled an old picture book that he found on his cousin's desk during his visit to Shanghai in 1980. It was about a little girl who was told by the Chinese Communist Party to slaughter her pet chicken. As the blood of the dying chicken came dripping down its neck, her grief turned into pride: its bright red color resembled the red scarf that she and many of her peers were wearing. The story and its gruesome message have haunted him to this day.

While this book addresses many free speech cases in Western universities, all chapters in part III conclude by discussing the serious threat posed by the Chinese government and by its agents and supporters to campus free speech in these Western jurisdictions. They end by emphasizing that even if "every man has his price,"[19] and student tuition and funding from hostile foreign nations help to keep universities running, university administrators and educators must strive to raise their prices and not surrender to hostile foreign forces for financial gain. Sacrificing cherished democratic values for foreign money is far worse than willingly prostituting oneself despite claiming to believe in the sanctity of sex.[20] In fact, given that some universities might prioritize money over free speech, it is more akin to serving as mistresses to enrich oneself at the expense of other people's marriages. This is pure hypocrisy and a gross betrayal of what are important and fundamental principles, which is likewise done by self-proclaimed patriots who swear their love for the authoritarian governments of their home countries, but for whatever reasons emigrate to Western democracies while exporting authoritarianism to their new homes. Just as

18. This line is taken from Heine's famous tragic play *Almansor* (1821) ("Dort, wo man Bücher verbrennt, verbrennt man am Ende auch Menschen"). Heine was Jewish by birth, and his books were notably among those burned by the Nazis.
19. Richard Rich's famous line in Robert Bolt, *A Man for All Seasons* (1954).
20. In fact, the author harbors tremendous respect and sympathy for women who, due to poverty, entered the sex trade to feed their families. It is hypocrisy and greed that she abhors and detests.

those who willingly trade sex with people other than their partners or spouses for material gain have no claim to chastity, universities cannot claim to embrace free speech while trading this fundamental value for money.

This pattern of similar chapter endings is hardly coincidental. The resemblance between the aggressive Chinese state and the creeping authoritarian tendencies on some of today's Western university campuses is uncanny enough. In addition, considering the fact that blind, uncritical adherence to certain ideologies can distract the educated elites from more pressing concerns of society and real threats by foreign dictators, empower hostile foreign states, and enable them to suppress academic speech and undermine Western democracy (for example, by shamelessly weaponizing anti-Asian racism due to the spread of COVID-19 to quash legitimate criticisms of the Chinese government[21]), there may not be a better way to spell out the parallel and causality between authoritarian foreign states and authoritarian tendencies on campuses. Indeed, such endings are one of the coherent ways to hold up a mirror to the extreme ideologies and excessive actions at some universities. They issue the warning that extreme ideologies embraced with the best intentions and excessive actions undertaken in the name of the greater good are nothing but dangerous and will only undermine our long-standing and deeply held democratic values.

---

21. Tenzin Dorjee, *Anti-China Is Not Anti-Asian*, WASH. P. (Apr. 6, 2021), http://www.washingtonpost.com/opinions/2021/04/06/anti-china-is-not-anti-asian/?fbclid=IwAR0PguPpgfS_FM2bsA-tgkK9iqAiS4yfDfD8b98FPAi-EKF8aL46y49c1r8

Part One

The new Nazi commissar wasted no time on the amenities. He immediately announced that Jews would be forbidden to enter university premises and would be dismissed without salary on March 15; this was something that no one had thought possible despite the Nazis' loud antisemitism. Then he launched into a tirade of abuse, filth, and four-letter words such as had been heard rarely even in the barracks and never before in academia. . . . [He] pointed his finger at one department chairman after another and said, "You either do what I tell you or we'll put you into a concentration camp."

—*Facing History and Ourselves*,
Holocaust and Human Behavior (2017)

"On August 19, I organized a meeting to criticize the leaders of the Beijing education system," Chen, now 67, recalls. "A rather serious armed struggle broke out. At the end, some students rushed onstage and used leather belts to whip some of the education officials, including the party secretary of my school."

. . . The same summer, Chairman Mao met with crowds of frenzied Red Guards in Beijing's Tiananmen Square. He endorsed their violent tactics—consisting mainly of beatings with fists, clubs and other blunt instruments. In August and September 1966, a total of 1,772 people were killed in Beijing, according to the *Beijing Daily* newspaper.

—Anthony Kuhn, *Chinese Red Guards Apologize, Reopening a Dark Chapter*, NPR (Feb. 4, 2014)

CHAPTER ONE
Free Speech in Western Universities

Who needs the atrocities and mass persecutions—even murders—of academics and students in Nazi Germany and Mao's China to serve as a reminder that freedom of speech is important to the existence of universities? Probably not many. Yet people who know the full history of free speech in Western universities may be far fewer. Free speech in the Western university originated in *Authentica Habita*, a decree issued around November 1158 by Emperor Frederick Barbarossa (Frederick I) to protect traveling scholars who helped to advance knowledge in the Holy Roman Empire. The *Habita* and the freedom enjoyed by scholars in medieval Europe were crucial to the development of free speech in Western history. Nonetheless, over the past centuries, the pursuit of freedom of expression to foster learning and the creation of new knowledge in Western universities has continued to be fraught with obstacles.

I. The Origin of Campus Free Speech

Although free speech on campus has become a hot topic globally, most books examining this topic were authored by American scholars. Unsurprisingly, they tend to locate the American civil rights movement of the 1960s as the pivotal moment—if not the origin—of the history of free speech in Western universities. Erwin Chemerinsky and Howard Gillman describe the Berkeley Free Speech Movement in the 1964–65 academic year, when a group of students at Berkeley protested against the ban of political activities on campus and advocated for students' free speech rights.[1] Sigal R. Ben-Porath likewise mentions the long-term impact of nationwide civil rights struggles on American university campuses. She uses as an example the student protests against the Vietnam War in the 1960s, crediting it as a time when the University of Pennsylvania, where she now works as a professor, first developed its free speech guidelines to ensure that no views are supressed on campus based on their content.[2] Keith Whittington explains that the fight for free speech at the time was not entirely a left-wing movement in America as it is widely believed to be, by drawing attention to conservative student protests against what they considered to be overwhelmingly left-wing faculties and liberal agendas served by university administrators.[3] Whittington also identifies Yale University's defense of freedom of expression in the aftermath of the Schockley incident in the mid-1970s as an important moment in the free speech movement in American universities.[4]

The focus upon the civil rights movement of the 1960s by these American scholars aligns with the general understanding of campus free speech in American journalism and popular media. Describing college and universities as "hubs of free speech" and "hotbeds of protest," CNN (Cable News Network) begins its official chronicle of campus free speech with episodes of protests and demonstrations by university students in the 1960s. Its highlights include not only the Berkeley Free Speech Movement but also protests against Alabama governor George Wallace's denunciation of a civil rights law in 1963, Boston students' demonstrations against U.S. involvement in the Vietnam War in 1968, and Columbia University's student uprising in the same year against its plan to construct a segregated gymnasium in the city-owned Morningside Park.[5]

---

1. Erwin Chemerinsky & Howard Gillman, Free Speech on Campus 75–78 (2017).
2. Sigal R. Ben-Porath, Free Speech on Campus 9 (2017).
3. Keith Whittington, Speak Freely: Why Universities Must Defend Free Speech 23 (2019).
4. Keith Whittington, Speak Freely: Why Universities Must Defend Free Speech 54–55 (2019). In spring 1974, Stanford physicist William Shockley, a believer in the voluntary sterilization of low-IQ individuals, was invited by the student chapter of Young Americans for Freedom to Yale to debate *National Review*'s publisher, William Rusher, on the proposition: "Resolved: That society has a moral obligation to diagnose and treat tragic racial IQ inferiority." The Woodward report—named after eminent historian C. Vann Woodward who chaired the committee investigating the uproar caused by the event—concluded that while certain speech might cause "shock, hurt, and anger," nothing could supersede the right to free expression if the university was to serve its central purpose of fostering "free access of knowledge." Eliana Johnson, *The Road to Yale's Free-Speech Crisis*, Nat'l Rev. (Jul. 5, 2016), http://www.nationalreview.com/2016/07/yale-free-speech/
5. *See* CNN, *A History of Free Speech on Campus* (Apr. 19, 2017), http://edition.cnn.com/2017/04/18/us/gallery/college-campus-protests/index.html

The origin of free speech in the university can nonetheless be traced to *Authentica Habita*, a decree issued around November 1158 by Frederick Barbarossa (Frederick I), emperor of the Holy Roman Empire, notwithstanding that none of the privileges that it granted to scholars at the time is equivalent to the free speech enjoyed on campus today. While in Italy to receive his crown, the emperor invited four doctors of law (Italian jurists) as well as masters and students of the University of Bologna's school of law to the Diet of Roncaglia, a general assembly of the nobles and ecclesiasts in the empire, to express their opinions on the laws of the empire.[6] There, the doctors implored the emperor to forbid the exercise of the right of reprisal against foreign scholars and to grant all scholars freedom of movement, considering that similar privileges had been granted to teachers and scholars by various emperors.[7]

Frederick I likely issued the *Habita* in connection with the edict for the maintenance of the public peace, a general edict also issued at this Roncaglian Diet. There is no doubt, however, that he singled out the scholars as particularly worthy of protection and favor, noting that "the whole world is illuminated by their learning," and affirmed the significance of the scientific knowledge that scholars brought to the empire.[8] Also known as "Privilegium Scholasticum," the *Habita* aimed to protect "those who exile themselves through love of learning, those who prefer to wear themselves out in poverty rather than to enjoy riches, and those who expose their lives to every peril, so that, defenseless, they must often suffer bodily injury from the vilest of men."[9]

The *Habita*, later confirmed by Pope Alexander III and incorporated by Frederick I into the *Codex Justinianus*, granted several imperial rights and protections to scholars, including freedom of movement and travel and the right to

---

6. *E.g.*, Pearl Kibre, *Scholarly Privileges: Their Roman Origins and Medieval Expression*, 59 Am. Hist. Rev. 549 (1954); Nichole Slack, *Authentica Habita and the Protection of Medieval Roman Scholars*, The Thin Tweed Line: The History and Practice of Higher Education (Mar. 17, 2012).
7. By then, some of these privileges had been preserved in the *Codex Justinianus*, or *Code of Justinian*, a collection of Roman laws codified and published in AD 529 at the order of Justinian I, an Eastern Roman emperor in Constantinople. Pearl Kibre, *Scholarly Privileges: Their Roman Origins and Medieval Expression*, 59 Am. Hist. Rev. 545–46 (1954); Nichole Slack, *Authentica Habita and the Protection of Medieval Roman Scholars*, The Thin Tweed Line: The History and Practice of Higher Education (Mar. 17, 2012); *Authentica Habita*, Encyclopaedia Britannica, http://www.britannica.com/topic/Authentica-Habita (last visited May 16, 2021)
8. *See* Pearl Kibre, *Scholarly Privileges: Their Roman Origins and Medieval Expression*, 59 Am. Hist. Rev. 549 (1954).
9. Nichole Slack, *Authentica Habita and the Protection of Medieval Roman Scholars*, The Thin Tweed Line: The History and Practice of Higher Education (Mar. 17, 2012).

safe residence in the imperial lands for the purposes of study.[10] Another protection was immunity from reprisal, so that debtors could not recover from scholars debts incurred in provinces or cities in which they resided.[11] They also included the right to decline the ordinary jurisdictions for offenses that scholars committed against others and to choose as judges their own masters at schools or the bishop of the diocese, so that plaintiffs applying to other judges could lose the cases even if they stood on legally sufficient ground; and where scholars were the plaintiffs, the right to be tried before judges of their choice and at their schools.[12]

Although the *Habita* did not expressly provide for the right to free speech, its grant of various imperial rights to scholars to protect their comfort and safety during their studies put them in a privileged position. These scholarly privileges might have been a source of empowerment for students, considering that university student movements could already be found in medieval Europe. One instance occurred in the Italian Università di Bologna, recognized as the first university in Europe. In 1284, its students, mostly foreign, banded together to pressure their teachers, mainly citizens, to commit to their teaching jobs at the university and not sell their expertise on the more lucrative open market, threatening to migrate elsewhere if they did not comply.[13] Soon, protest migrations from Bologna inspired similar movements in such cities as Reggio, Vicenza, Arezzo, Padua, Vercelli, Siena, Pisa, and Florence.[14]

The privileged position of scholars also led to more freedoms, freedom of expression included, than for nonscholars in ways that were perhaps not expected by Frederick I. Due to the *Habita*'s open-endedness, its provisions were analyzed, annotated, and expanded by jurists to represent much more

---

10. Pearl Kibre, *Scholarly Privileges: Their Roman Origins and Medieval Expression*, 59 AM. HIST. REV. 560 (1954); Paolo Nardi, Chapter 3: Relations with Authority, *in* A HISTORY OF THE UNIVERSITY IN EUROPE: VOL 1: UNIVERSITIES IN THE MIDDLE AGES 78 (Hilde de Ridder-Symoens ed., 1991).
11. Pearl Kibre, *Scholarly Privileges: Their Roman Origins and Medieval Expression*, 59 AM. HIST. REV. 550 (1954); Paolo Nardi, Chapter 3: Relations with Authority, *in* A HISTORY OF THE UNIVERSITY IN EUROPE: VOL 1: UNIVERSITIES IN THE MIDDLE AGES 78 (Hilde de Ridder-Symoens ed., 1991).
12. Pearl Kibre, *Scholarly Privileges: Their Roman Origins and Medieval Expression*, 59 AM. HIST. REV. 550 (1954); Aleksander Gieysztor, Chapter 4: Management and Resources, *in* A HISTORY OF THE UNIVERSITY IN EUROPE: VOL 1: UNIVERSITIES IN THE MIDDLE AGES 124 (Hilde de Ridder-Symoens ed., 1991).
13. James S. Preus, *Coercion in the University: Historical Reflections on the Current Crisis*, 19 CROSSCURRENTS 297, 301 (1969); *see* PEARL KIBRE, SCHOLARLY PRIVILEGES IN THE MIDDLE AGES: THE RIGHTS, PRIVILEGES, AND IMMUNITIES OF SCHOLARS AND UNIVERSITIES AT BOLOGNA, PADUA, PARIS, AND OXFORD 27 (1961).
14. James S. Preus, *Coercion in the University: Historical Reflections on the Current Crisis*, 19 CROSSCURRENTS 297, 301 (1969).

than was present in the text and to allow for students to take advantage of their newfound freedom and security, depending on the circumstances of individual cases, even to the detriment of other residents in the same university towns.[15] Certainly, the *Habita* did not entitle scholars to criticize the Church or the emperor due to their supremacy, and despite few formal restrictions on speech, prosecutions of scholars for heresy in the medieval period by the Inquisition—an ecclesiastical tribunal established by Pope Gregory IX in 1232 for the suppression of heresy—are well documented.[16] Nevertheless, their scholarly privileges, which were a source of conflicts between town and gown, were expanded to shield them from liabilities—civil and criminal—for their disorderly, unruly, and sometimes verbally abusive conduct toward other residents, and even arrests by the order of municipal magistrates, except in the commission of the most serious crimes.[17]

Hence, it can be argued that despite its lack of a speech-related provision, the *Habita* emboldened scholars of the time to exploit their speech freedom, often without legal ramifications, as long as their expressions did not target the Church or the emperor. First applied to the university in Bologna, the *Habita* was later adopted by other universities in Italy, and its provisions were either directly followed or emulated by other European universities as they enacted their own charters in the following centuries.[18]

---

15. Nichole Slack, *Authentica Habita and the Protection of Medieval Roman Scholars*, The Thin Tweed Line: The History and Practice of Higher Education (Mar. 17, 2012). For example, students were often able to evade taxes or tolls on various items related to their studies, and to commandeer housing and horses even if the owners of houses and horses disapproved.
16. *See, e.g.*, William J. Courtenay, *Inquiry and Inquisition: Academic Freedom in Medieval Universities*, 58 Church History 168 (1989); Jennifer Kolpacoff Deane, A History of Medieval Heresy and Inquisition (2011). Some nonetheless pointed out that the Roman Empire had few formal legal restrictions on speech and social pressures did much more than the law to limit what people said and wrote. Edward Watts, *Introduction: Freedom of Speech and Self-Censorship in the Roman Empire*, 92 Revue Belge de Philologie et d'Histoire (special issue) 1 (2014).
17. *E.g.*, Pearl Kibre, *Scholarly Privileges: Their Roman Origins and Medieval Expression*, 59 Am. Hist. Rev. 552 (1954); *see* Paolo Nardi, Chapter 3: Relations with Authority, *in* A History of the University in Europe: Vol 1: Universities in the Middle Ages 86 (Hilde de Ridder-Symoens ed., 1991).
18. One example was "Cessatio," conferred by Pope Gregory IX for Paris in 1231, which enabled scholars to suspend lectures in cases of unredressed grievances against ecclesiastical and especially civil authorities. Those dissatisfied with the ways the authorities addressed their grievances also migrated to other universities. After the cessation in Paris in 1229, the king of England invited Parisian scholars to migrate to Oxford, where royal privileges were increasingly granted to scholars as they engaged in unruly or even violent conduct in town-gown conflicts. An example was the St. Scholastica Day riot on February 10, 1355. King Edward III defended the students who caused the riot, which led to several murders, by reiterating that scholars and universities were under royal protection and by pardoning the scholars for any offenses they were accused of in connection with the violence. *See, e.g.*, Charles E. Mallet, A History of the University of Oxford (vol. 1) 35, 151 (1934); Steph-

One may, however, argue that the freedoms and privileges enjoyed by students in medieval Europe, whether it took the form of organized protests against their teachers or civil or ecclesiastical authorities, or abusive expressions targeting other residents of university towns, did not truly originate in the *Habita*. Their exercises of this freedom instead can be deemed as part of the evolution of free speech in Western history.

II. Western History of Free Speech and Universities' Contributions

In Western history, freedom of speech has its origin in ancient Greece, as Athens, its capital city, was the first society in recorded history to embrace freedom and democracy.[19] "Democracy" originated from the Greek word "dēmokratía," meaning the "rule of the people."[20] The right to parrhesia, open and candid speech in private and public life, empowered early Athenians to participate in their government,[21] and to free themselves from social hierarchy and reverence for the past.[22] Without referring to an inalienable right to free speech as it is understood today, the word therefore captured the freedom enabling Athenians to choose their governments, and represented the egalitarian foundation and participatory principle of the ancient regime.[23]

Parrhesia and its significance were affirmed by ancient Greek philoso-

---

anie Jenkins, *St Scholastica's Day Riot, Oxford, 1355*, Oxford History: Mayors and Lord Mayors, http://www.oxfordhistory.org.uk/mayors/government/scholastica.html (last visited May 18, 2021).

19. Kurt A. Raaflaub, Aristocracy and Freedom of Speech in the Greco-Roman World, *in* Free Speech in Classical Antiquity 58 (I. Sluiter & Ralph Mark Rosen eds., 2004).

20. The Western history of free speech in this section draws extensively upon a relevant chapter in the author's other book, *The Right to Parody: Comparative Analysis of Copyright and Free Speech* (2018). Robert Hargreaves, The first freedom: a history of free speech 5 (2002); Robert W. Wallace, Power to Speak—and Not to Listen—in Ancient Athens, *in* Free Speech in Classical Antiquity 221 (I. Sluiter & Ralph Mark Rosen eds., 2004).

21. Robert Hargreaves, The first freedom: a history of free speech 5 (2002); Robert W. Wallace, Power to Speak—and Not to Listen—in Ancient Athens, *in* Free Speech in Classical Antiquity 221 (I. Sluiter & Ralph Mark Rosen eds., 2004).

22. Arlene W. Saxonhouse, Free speech and democracy in ancient Athens 40, 86 (2008).

23. Moses Finley, in *Democracy: Ancient and Modern* (1988, 116), contends that in ancient Athens there were "no theoretical limits to the power of the state, no activity . . . in which the state could not legitimately intervene provided that decision was taken properly. . . . Freedom meant the rule of law and participation in decision making process, not the possession of inalienable rights." Robert Hargreaves, The first freedom: a history of free speech 5–6 (2002); Robert W. Wallace, Power to Speak—and Not to Listen—in Ancient Athens, *in* Free Speech in Classical Antiquity 227 (I. Sluiter & Ralph Mark Rosen eds., 2004); Arlene W. Saxonhouse, Free speech and democracy in ancient Athens 23, 131 (2008).

phers. Socrates describes the Assembly, the primary venue for political decisions at the time, as the site where all citizens, whatever their social and economic statuses, could "deliberate on something concerning the governance of the city (poleos dioikeseos)," and where "carpenter, bronze worker, shoemaker, merchant, shop-owner, rich, poor, noble, lowly born" participated in the deliberations.[24] Socratic parrhesia, or the freedom to say whatever one wants so long as it aligns with truth, became an important component of Plato's political ideals.[25] Aristotle, a student of Plato, compared the Assembly to a potluck dinner, where participants both contributed to and benefited from the wisdom of many.[26]

In the Roman Republic, no word carried the same meaning as parrhesia did. "Libertas," the Latin word for liberty, did not refer to freedom of speech in the way Athenians understood it.[27] The Roman Senate and senior statesmen were the only citizens to whom the right to political discussion was formally granted.[28] While ordinary citizens could vote in the Roman assemblies, they had no formal right to make their voices heard.[29] This, however, did not stop them from finding ways and opportunities to express their opinions and even to influence those of the Senate.[30]

As Europe entered the medieval period, which lasted from the fifth to the fifteenth centuries, dissent, especially religious divisions, was largely outlawed among fragile alliances in the empire under the overarching goal of nation-

---

24. Arlene W. Saxonhouse, Free speech and democracy in ancient Athens 94 (2008), citing Cynthia Farrar, The Origins of Democratic Thinking: The. Invention of Politics in Classical Athens (1988). For many generations, the trial of Socrates, who was charged with "corrupting the young" and impiety, has served as a symbol of free speech violation. Some affirm that Athens was a fundamentally tolerant regime and that the trial was an aberration. Hargreaves, however, contends that the death of Socrates is "the first and plainest example of how a democracy may be diminished when it dispenses with the freedom of expression," and how a "truly free spirit is likely to fall victim to the tyranny of the majority as he is of a single dictator." Robert Hargreaves, The first freedom: a history of free speech 21 (2002).
25. Marlein van Raalte, Socratic Parrhesia and Its Afterlife in Plato's Laws, *in* Free Speech in Classical Antiquity 305, 310 (I. Sluiter & Ralph Mark Rosen eds., 2004).
26. Arlene W. Saxonhouse, Free speech and democracy in ancient Athens 150 (2008), citing Aristotle, Politics, bk. 3, ch. 2.
27. Kurt A. Raaflaub, Aristocracy and Freedom of Speech in the Greco-Roman World, *in* Free Speech in Classical Antiquity 54 (I. Sluiter & Ralph Mark Rosen eds., 2004); Robert Hargreaves, The first freedom: a history of free speech 22 (2002).
28. Kurt A. Raaflaub, Aristocracy and Freedom of Speech in the Greco-Roman World, *in* Free Speech in Classical Antiquity 55 (I. Sluiter & Ralph Mark Rosen eds., 2004); Robert Hargreaves, The first freedom: a history of free speech 23 (2002).
29. Susan Wiltshire, Greece, Rome and the Bill of Rights 116 (1992).
30. Kurt A. Raaflaub, Aristocracy and Freedom of Speech in the Greco-Roman World, *in* Free Speech in Classical Antiquity 55–56 (I. Sluiter & Ralph Mark Rosen eds., 2004).

building.[31] Christianity, which began to transition to the dominant religion of the Western Roman Empire during the reign of Constantine the Great (AD 306–337), continued to be the state religion of medieval Europe. Because salvation is to be found exclusively in the Christian Church, heresy was punished as if it were one of the most heinous crimes.[32]

Hence, when Frederick I issued the *Habita* in 1158, heresy was strictly forbidden. Unsurprisingly, the *Habita*, while providing for numerous scholarly privileges, did not contain any provision pertaining to freedom of expression. Neither did the *Code of Justinian*, in which it was incorporated during his reign. During this period, interest in Roman law revived, and so the content of this *Code* was quarried for arguments by both secular and ecclesiastical authorities, and the revived Roman law in turn became the foundation of law in all civil law jurisdictions.[33] Nonetheless, many laws in the *Code* were aimed at legitimizing Christianity and securing its status as the state religion of the empire, rather than establishing the rule of law as it is understood today.[34]

As explained, the *Habita* nevertheless emboldened scholars to exercise their freedom of expression in rather unexpected ways. It also empowered scholars to resist their authorities and encouraged them to travel around Europe, leading to the establishment of new universities, including Oxford and Cambridge.[35] These new seats of learning in turn became the breeding grounds for philosophers who advanced the idea of freedom of speech in the Renaissance and Enlightenment periods. The two most remarkable examples were John Milton and John Locke, both outspoken students at Cambridge and Oxford, respectively.[36]

---

31. John B. Bury, A History of Freedom of Thought 57–63 (1913); John D. Stevens, Shaping the First Amendment 22–23 (1982).
32. John B. Bury, A History of Freedom of Thought 57–63 (1913); John D. Stevens, Shaping the First Amendment 22–23 (1982).
33. *The Justinian Code*, Western Civilization, https://courses.lumenlearning.com/suny-hccc-worldhistory/chapter/the-justinian-code/ (last visited May 19, 2021).
34. *See The Justinian Code*, Western Civilization, https://courses.lumenlearning.com/suny-hccc-worldhistory/chapter/the-justinian-code/ (last visited May 19, 2021).
35. *E.g.*, Gordon Leff, Paris and Oxford Universities in the Thirteenth and Fourteenth Centuries: An Institutional and Intellectual History (1968); *The Medieval University*, University of Cambridge, https://www.cam.ac.uk/about-the-university/history/the-medieval-university (last visited May 21, 2021).
36. There were stories about Milton's open disputes with his Cambridge tutor, Bishop William Chappell, which may have led to his suspension from school, and Locke's dissatisfaction with Oxford's undergraduate teaching, which he found dull and unstimulating, and his preference for modern philosophers to classical materials in its curriculum. *E.g.*, C. V. Wedgwood, Thomas Wentworth, First Earl of Strafford 1593–1641 (1961); Donald Lemen Clark, *John Milton and William Chappell*, 18 Huntington Library Q. 329 (1955); *John Locke: English Philosopher*, Encyclopedia Britannica, http://www.britannica.com/biography/John-Locke (last visited May 21, 2021).

Milton authored *Areopagitica: A Speech for the Liberty of Unlicenc'd Printing* (1644), now considered "the most eloquent plea for a free press ever penned"[37] and "the foundational essay of the free speech tradition."[38] He addressed it to the English Parliament, which, at the height of the English Civil War, instituted a regime of prior censorship through the Licensing Order of 1643 requiring all books, pamphlets, and other written materials to be approved by the government before being printed.[39] Published without official approval, *Areopagitica* argues that the regime of his time dampened one's reasoning ability and pursuit of knowledge.[40] It should learn from ancient Greeks and Romans who, despite punishing blasphemous and libelous writing, never required prior approval for published writing, and should punish only those who abuse this freedom.[41]

After Milton's *Areopagitica*, Locke's *A Letter Concerning Toleration* (1689) is considered to provide "the seventeenth century's most intellectually persuasive justification for the right to free speech."[42] It argues that the liberty of conscience is an inalienable right, and the power of the government, which "consists only in outward force," cannot compel moral behavior, which "consists in the inward persuasion of the mind."[43] *An Essay Concerning Human Understanding* (1689) further affirms the role of reason in finding the truth.[44] Both freedom of conscience and the liberty to reason and pursue the truth imply the right to speak freely.[45] Locke's embrace of free speech is also indicated in his *Second Treatise of Government* (1689) through his endorsement of a limited

---

37. Robert Hargreaves, The first freedom: a history of free speech 100 (2002).
38. Vincent Blasi, *Milton's Areopagitica and the Modern First Amendment*, Yale Law School Legal Scholarship Repository Occasional Papers, no. 6 (1995), at 1, http://digitalcommons.law.yale.edu/cgi/viewcontent.cgi?article=1007&context=ylsop_papers (last visited Oct. 10, 2021).
39. John Milton, Areopagitica (1644), https://www.saylor.org/site/wp-content/uploads/2012/08/ENGL402-Milton-Aeropagitica.pdf
40. Milton argued that reading impious material is not dangerous because "[t]o the pure, all things are pure." He further contrasts the classical, enlightened tradition of the Greeks and Romans with the censorship tradition imposed by the Catholic Church and the Spanish Inquisition. Although Greece and Rome condemned libelous materials, neither embraced censorship. It was not until after the year 800 that the Roman Catholic Church implemented a censorship policy, which became increasingly stringent in Spain and Italy during the fifteenth century and was endorsed by the Council of Trent that ended in 1563. By then, "no Book, pamphlet, or paper" could be printed unless "approv'd and licenc't under the hands of 2 or 3 glutton Friers." John Milton, Areopagitica (1644), https://www.saylor.org/site/wp-content/uploads/2012/08/ENGL402-Milton-Aeropagitica.pdf
41. John Milton, Areopagitica (1644), https://www.saylor.org/site/wp-content/uploads/2012/08/ENGL402-Milton-Aeropagitica.pdf
42. Robert Hargreaves, The first freedom: a history of free speech 104 (2002).
43. John Locke, A Letter Concerning Toleration (1689), https://socserv2.socsci.mcmaster.ca/econ/ugcm/3ll3/locke/toleration.pdf
44. John Locke, An Essay Concerning Human Understanding, ch. XVII (1689), http://enlightenment.supersaturated.com/johnlocke/BOOKIVChapterXVII.html
45. Robert Hargreaves, The first freedom: a history of free speech 109 (2002).

government. People, he argues, should readily overthrow their government when it becomes unjust or authoritarian so as to preserve their rights to life, liberty, and property.[46] For this to happen, freedom of speech, as well as freedom of action, need to be granted to people for them to speak out against their government when it acts contrary to their welfare.[47] These works became crucial to the establishment of the English Bill of Rights, which secured freedom of speech and elections for members of the English Parliament.[48]

The ideas of speech freedom conceptualized by ancient Athenians and scholars in medieval Europe, though limited in scope according to today's standards, therefore led to the formation of the first universities and were pivotal to the development of free speech during the Enlightenment. Unfortunately, this freedom, the importance of which was affirmed at different points in history, has continued to be eroded in different universities from the Renaissance to the present.

III. Campus Free Speech from the Renaissance to the Present

The fact that some of these European universities produced philosophers who advanced the notion of freedoms of conscience and of expression should not detract from the problem of censorship, mostly on religious grounds, across different universities during the Renaissance. In Renaissance Italy, professors and students enjoyed different levels of intellectual and religious freedom and freedom of expression.[49] While Italian governments allowed neither Italian professors nor students to profess non-Catholic views, they were more tolerant of dissent among foreign scholars. Hence, these governments did not attempt to enforce religious orthodoxy on Protestant scholars from other parts of Europe until the latter half of the sixteenth century, and even then, only forbade these foreign students from practicing their religion openly.[50] Criticism of the Catholic Church and expression challenging its

46. John Locke, Second Treatise of Government, ch. XVII–XVIX (1689), http://www.earlymoderntexts.com/assets/pdfs/locke1689a.pdf
47. Arlene W. Saxonhouse, Free speech and democracy in ancient Athens 22 (2008).
48. Robert Hargreaves, The first freedom: a history of free speech 110 (2002).
49. Paul F. Grendler, The Universities of the Italian Renaissance 193–94 (2002).
50. When Protestant students from Germany transgressed, for example, by posting anonymous notices attacking Catholicism, the Venetian government would not permit the Venetian Inquisition to make any arrests due to the uncertain identities of culprits and the hearsay nature of the charges. Bologna was similarly tolerant of such transgressions, and the only known trial by the Bolognian Inquisition

orthodoxy were also suppressed in France during the same period. The most well-known and extreme example involved Étienne Dolet, a law student at Toulouse University and later a translator, who was convicted of heresy for questioning the Catholic belief in immortality in his work and executed in 1546, through the joint effort of the Parlement of Paris, the Inquisition, and the theological faculty of Sorbonne University.[51]

Protestant universities in the Renaissance were at least as intolerant of dissent as their Catholic counterparts. After becoming Protestant, the University of Heidelberg imposed Calvinist or Lutheran oaths, depending on the religion of the presiding ruler, on its professors and students.[52] In England, the governments of Edward VI (1547–53) and Elizabeth I (1558–1603) expelled and compelled to resign many officers and students from Oxford who held or were suspected of holding Catholic views.[53] Later, the power shifted. In 1559, the latter further imposed an oath accepting royal supremacy over the Anglican Church and renouncing papal authority as a condition for students to receive degrees from Oxford.[54] New statutes of 1581 required that that all students sixteen or older subscribe to the royal supremacy over the Church and the English articles of religion as a condition of matriculation into any college or residence hall.[55] Nearly seventy English Catholics who were connected to Oxford University were executed by the Tudor and Stuart governments from the late fifteenth through the early eighteenth centuries.[56]

The nineteenth century saw the secularization of European universities in general, and criticisms of religions were more tolerated than before. After the unification of Italy (1860–70), its liberal governments began secularizing institutions and public life.[57] Likewise, reforms of Oxford and Cambridge, largely initiated by the British government and carried out between the 1850s and 1880s, both modernized their curricula and diminished their connections with

---

of students was that of five Spanish students in 1553–54, which led to one abjuration and light penances for the rest. PAUL F. GRENDLER, THE UNIVERSITIES OF THE ITALIAN RENAISSANCE 192, 194 (2002).

51. His blasphemy charge apparently rested on his adding the phrase *rien du tout* ("nothing at all") in one of Plato's dialogues about what existed after death. JEREMY MUNDAY, INTRODUCING TRANSLATION STUDIES: THEORIES AND APPLICATIONS 23 (2008).
52. PAUL F. GRENDLER, THE UNIVERSITIES OF THE ITALIAN RENAISSANCE 194 (2002).
53. PAUL F. GRENDLER, THE UNIVERSITIES OF THE ITALIAN RENAISSANCE 194–95 (2002).
54. PAUL F. GRENDLER, THE UNIVERSITIES OF THE ITALIAN RENAISSANCE 195 (2002).
55. PAUL F. GRENDLER, THE UNIVERSITIES OF THE ITALIAN RENAISSANCE 195 (2002).
56. PAUL F. GRENDLER, THE UNIVERSITIES OF THE ITALIAN RENAISSANCE 195 (2002).
57. Alessandro Ferrari Silvio Ferrari, Religion and the Secular State: The Italian Case, *in* RELIGION AND THE SECULAR STATE 452 (Javier Martinez-Torron & W. Cole Durham, Jr. eds., 2014).

the Anglican Church.[58] Yet free speech battles continued to be forged in many places on political grounds. For example, following Napoleon I's 1802 reform of the French education system, political authorities exerted tight control over institutions of higher learning and shut down faculties where professors and students opposed the French government.[59] After the Congress of Vienna in 1815, the states of the German Confederation suppressed dissenting voices to stabilize their governments. As a result, professors who were believed to cause social unrest through criticizing the government were blacklisted by universities or put under constant police supervision and censorship.[60]

In America, freedom of speech was not in fact encouraged on university campuses until the latter half of the nineteenth century.[61] Before then, freedom of inquiry or expression on campuses was restricted by the prevailing theory of "doctrinal moralism," according to which the worth or legitimacy of an idea is judged by the moral standards of the institution's leaders.[62] For example, during the Civil War, professors or students in the Northern states who defended slavery, or their counterparts in the Southern states who challenged slavery, could be dismissed, disciplined, or expelled.[63] American higher education underwent a revolution between 1870 and 1900, so that more room was then provided for freedom of expression: during that time, both criticizing and preserving traditional moral values and understandings became accepted activities on campuses.[64]

The winds continued to shift from the late nineteenth to the early twentieth century, when an increasing number of American universities were sup-

---

58. Lawrence Goldman, *Oxford and the Idea of a University in Nineteenth Century Britain*, 30 Oxford Rev. Educ. 575, 582 (2004).
59. Emmanuelle Picard, *Recovering the History of the French University*, 5(3) Studium 156, 158 (2012).
60. Matthew Bunn, *Civility and Speech in the Modern University, 200 Years Ago in Germany*, Not Even Past, http://notevenpast.org/civility-and-speech-in-the-modern-university-200-years-ago-in-germany/ (last visited May 21, 2021).
61. Geoffrey R. Stone, *Prof. Geoffrey Stone Discusses Free Speech on Campus at the American Law Institute*, University of Chicago School of Law: News (Jun. 6, 2016), http://www.law.uchicago.edu/news/prof-geoffrey-stone-discusses-free-speech-campus-american-law-institute
62. Geoffrey R. Stone, *Prof. Geoffrey Stone Discusses Free Speech on Campus at the American Law Institute*, University of Chicago School of Law: News (Jun. 6, 2016), http://www.law.uchicago.edu/news/prof-geoffrey-stone-discusses-free-speech-campus-american-law-institute
63. Geoffrey R. Stone, *Prof. Geoffrey Stone Discusses Free Speech on Campus at the American Law Institute*, University of Chicago School of Law: News (Jun. 6, 2016), http://www.law.uchicago.edu/news/prof-geoffrey-stone-discusses-free-speech-campus-american-law-institute
64. In 1892, William Rainey Harper, the first president of the University of Chicago, asserted: "When for any reason the administration of a university attempts to dislodge a professor or punish a student because of his political or religious sentiments, at that moment the institution has ceased to be a university."

ported by conservative business owners. Pro-labor scholars who offended these wealthy trustees and donors by criticizing the ethics or legitimacy of their business practices risked getting dismissed from their universities.[65] During World War I, students and professors who questioned the morality or wisdom of the war, or merely showed "indifference" toward the war, were persecuted, expelled, or fired at such famous institutions as the universities of Columbia, Virginia, and Nebraska.[66] During the age of McCarthy in the late 1940s and the 1950s, suspected Communist sympathizers and Communist apologists were expelled.[67]

The Berkeley Free Speech Movement, described at the beginning of this chapter, can be deemed part of a global phenomenon in the 1960s and early 1970s.[68] The continuous boom in industrial capitalism and the large-scale expansion of postsecondary education in many nations after World War II created favorable conditions for the spread of student movements protesting regulations, policies, and actions by their universities.[69] Politicians, senior administrators, and academics tried to curb on-campus activism in the U.S. and other Western nations, and political expression—both left- and right-wing—became the target of suppression depending on the political climate of the time. Yet committees on free expression were also formed at various universities by academics, alumni, and trustees to address the free speech issue and defend free expression on campuses.[70]

Since the 1980s, freedom of speech has undergone further challenges across many Western campuses. Increasingly heterogeneous and ideologically diverse student bodies and a globalized environment more generally have fostered a

---

65. Geoffrey R. Stone, *Prof. Geoffrey Stone Discusses Free Speech on Campus at the American Law Institute*, University of Chicago School of Law: News (Jun. 6, 2016), http://www.law.uchicago.edu/news/prof-geoffrey-stone-discusses-free-speech-campus-american-law-institute
66. Geoffrey R. Stone, *Political Conservatives Suddenly Embrace Free Speech on Campus*, Huffington P. (May 1, 2017), http://www.huffpost.com/entry/political-conservatives-suddenly-embrace-free-speech_b_590745dee4b084f59b49fb07
67. Geoffrey R. Stone, *Political Conservatives Suddenly Embrace Free Speech on Campus*, Huffington P. (May 1, 2017), http://www.huffpost.com/entry/political-conservatives-suddenly-embrace-free-speech_b_590745dee4b084f59b49fb07
68. Colin Barker, *Some Reflections on Student Movements of the 1960s and Early 1970s*, 81 Revista Crítica de Ciências Sociais 43, 48 (2008).
69. Colin Barker, *Some Reflections on Student Movements of the 1960s and Early 1970s*, 81 Revista Crítica de Ciências Sociais 43, 48 (2008).
70. *E.g.*, Bettina Aptheker, *FSM: The Free Speech Movement at Berkeley*, Calisphere, http://content.cdlib.org/view?docId=kt709nb23t;NAAN=13030&doc.view=frames&chunk.id=d0e77&toc.depth=1&toc.id=&brand=calisphere (last visited May 22, 2021); Natalie Schoen, *Unbuckling Expression: A History of Free Speech Policies at Yale*, The Politic (Dec. 14, 2016), http://thepolitic.org/unbuckling-expression-a-history-of-free-speech-policies-at-yale/

culture of "political correctness" in universities and colleges that, accordingly to many, have become predominately liberal.[71] As the incidents described in this book's introduction show, balancing freedom of speech on campuses with the need to be sensitive to all members of academic communities is not easy: concern for sensitivity, when taken too far, stifles free speech.

The importance of fighting discrimination is not to be doubted. In extreme cases, however, this political correctness narrative is allowed to dominate campuses, where certain individuals in what are deemed marginalized groups use it to indulge in their sensitivities and vulnerabilities and to shield themselves from expression that they deem offensive.[72] When this happens, little room is allowed for free and vigorous intellectual enquiries within the law.[73] Considering that "victims" of verbal offenses—some of which may be more imagined than real—may even gain a higher moral status relative to nonvictims, and paramount concerns about "safety" and "sensitivity" for such "victims" may smother freedom of speech, the disastrous impact of this "victimhood culture" on free speech on campus may not have been overstated.[74]

The Enlightenment philosophers, if they were still alive, would frown on how free speech—and the very existence of universities—is being threatened today despite the decline in the importance of religion and the democratization of the Western world. Not a few scholars deem that the university, estranged from its ideals of freedom of inquiry and tolerance of different opinions, has now turned into a conformist, paternalistic institution with such infantilizing practices as "trigger warnings," "safe spaces," and "mandatory sensitivity training."[75] Worse still, when it is indeed a crime to express ideas—or entertain thoughts—that run contrary to the "social justice" dogma, or not to embrace correct thoughts or make correct expressions in accordance with its mandate, the university, once a bastion of free speech and thought, has devolved into nothing more than an institute of indoctrination.[76] The obsession over political

71. *E.g.*, Peter Scott, *"Free Speech" and "Political Correctness,"* 6 Eur. J. Higher Educ. 417 (2016); Chris Mooney, *Does College Make You Liberal—or Do Liberals Make Colleges?*, Huffington P. (Mar. 1, 2012), http://www.huffpost.com/entry/does-college-make-you-lib_b_1312889
72. Peter Scott, *"Free Speech" and "Political Correctness,"* 6 Eur. J. Higher Educ. 417 (2016).
73. Peter Scott, *"Free Speech" and "Political Correctness,"* 6 Eur. J. Higher Educ. 417 (2016).
74. *E.g.*, Bradley Campbell & Jason Manning, The Rise of Victimhood Culture: Microaggressions, Safe Spaces, and the New Culture War (2018).
75. *See, e.g.*, Greg Lukianoff & Jonathan Haidt, The Coddling of the American Mind: How Good Intentions and Bad Ideas Are Setting Up a Generation for Failure (2018); Frank Furedi, What Has Happened to the University? A Sociological Exploration of Its Infantilization (2016).
76. *See, e.g.*, Michael Rectenwald, Springtime for Snowflakes: "Social Justice" and Its Post-

correctness also diverts attention from more pressing social problems and emboldens the real evils lurking out there.

• • •

The Nazi regime has long since collapsed and China's Cultural Revolution ended more than four decades ago. Sadly, their deadly spirits cannot be said to have vanished. Assuming different shapes, they continued to ravage universities in different countries. When free speech is threatened, universities' very existence is at stake. Indeed, as free speech is suppressed, academic freedom is also undermined. The next chapter will turn to the history, definitions, and significance of academic freedom, which shares the same origin with campus free speech, and is therefore often conflated with freedom of expression. While this confusion is both common and understandable, the rest of part I will both clarify their differences and illuminate how they benefit each other.

MODERN PARENTAGE (2018); Cathy Young, *The Totalitarian Doctrine of "Social Justice Warriors,"* OBSERVER (Feb. 2, 2016), https://observer.com/2016/02/the-totalitarian-doctrine-of-social-justice-warriors/

CHAPTER TWO

Academic Freedom

History, Definitions, and Democratic Significance

Who would even doubt that academic freedom, like free speech, was nonexistent in Nazi Germany and Mao's China? In fact, academic freedom, like free speech, also found its origin in *Authentica Habita* in medieval Europe. This freedom continued to evolve in the nineteenth and early twentieth centuries before gaining recognition and protection in many Western nations in the mid to late twentieth century. Among the most thorough discussions of academic freedom is Stanley Fish's 2014 book, *Versions of Academic Freedom*. Fish's preferred model according to which scholars should not engage in politics in their pursuit of knowledge is nonetheless rife with internal inconsistencies. Examples from the Renaissance to the modern period also show that a distinction between academics and politics cannot and should not be made, in legal as well as in other disciplines, and that academic freedom should serve the common good and help realize democratic principles.

I. A Brief History

Essential to the mission of the academy, academic freedom is generally defined as the freedom to engage in an entire range of activities involved in the production of knowledge,[1] without unreasonable interference or restric-

1. *Academic Freedom*, New World Encyclopedia, http://www.newworldencyclopedia.org/entry/Academic_freedom (last visited May 24, 2021).

tion from law, institutional regulations, or public pressure.[2] Arguably, it is a freedom enjoyed by all members of the academic community. For teachers, it is the freedom to research any subject that they consider to be of value, to present and publish their findings without control or censorship, and to teach in a manner they consider professionally appropriate.[3] For students, it is the freedom to study subjects that concern them, to form their own conclusions, and to express their opinions.[4] Academic freedom is subject to a number of constraints, including the professional standards of relevant disciplines and the legitimate and nondiscriminatory requirements of individual institutions to fulfill their academic missions.[5]

Some argue that ancient Greece, where freedom of thought and expression originated, was also the breeding ground for academic freedom.[6] Hence, academic freedom can be known as a modern term for an ancient idea.[7] However, because this freedom is located in academia, like campus free speech, its origin is more properly located in *Authentica Habita*, the decree that was issued in Bologna and applied to the first European universities.[8] Among the imperial rights and protections that the *Habita* conferred on scholars, including freedom of travel and safe residence, immunity from reprisal, the right to choose as judges their own masters at schools or the bishop of the diocese, none of them expressly protected their freedom in teaching and research. Yet an idea of academic freedom, albeit one that is more restrained than is commonly understood and practiced today, is implicitly recognized in the security that scholars in medieval Europe enjoyed through these rights and protections. Such security—physical, mental, and economic—empowered scholars of that time

2. *Academic Freedom*, Britannica, http://www.britannica.com/topic/academic-freedom (last visited May 24, 2021).
3. *Academic Freedom*, Britannica, http://www.britannica.com/topic/academic-freedom (last visited May 24, 2021).
4. *Academic Freedom*, Britannica, http://www.britannica.com/topic/academic-freedom (last visited May 24, 2021).
5. Peter MacKinnon, *What Do We Mean When We Talk about Academic Freedom*, University Affairs (Sep. 12, 2011), https://www.universityaffairs.ca/opinion/in-my-opinion/what-do-we-mean-when-we-talk-about-academic-freedom/
6. *See, e.g.*, Michiel Horn suggests that the struggle for freedom in teaching can be traced as far back as Socrates's eloquent self-defense against the charge of corrupting Athenian youth. Academic Freedom in Canada: A History 4 (1999); *see also* William J. Hoye, The Religious Roots of Academic Freedom, Theological Studies 58 (1997).
7. *See* William J. Hoye, The Religious Roots of Academic Freedom, Theological Studies 58 (1997).
8. *E.g.*, William J. Hoye, The Religious Roots of Academic Freedom, Theological Studies 58 (1997); Kemal Gürüz, Global: University Autonomy and Academic Freedom: A Historical Perspective, International Higher Education 63 (2011).

to teach, learn, research, publish, and produce knowledge so long as no heresy was involved.

Privileges provided by the *Habita*, as explained, also led to the formation of more universities throughout Europe, which modeled their own charters upon it. Further, *Parens Scientiarum*, a papal bull issued by Pope Gregory IX on April 13, 1231, first recognized the right of the university as a corporate body to award degrees.[9] The papal bulls and imperial edicts that followed, while providing privileges and support to institutions and scholars, stipulated detailed conditions under which institutions operated and functioned—including syllabi, graduation, and promotion requirements, libraries, facilities, and codes of conduct.[10] Medieval scholars thus benefited from the autonomy of their institutions to pursue knowledge, subject to the oversight of the Catholic Church.[11]

The idea of academic freedom further took shape in the nineteenth century, which witnessed the slow decline of religion and its impact on universities. Napoleon I reformed French national education by replacing all universities in France and the occupied lands by l'Université de France, a highly centralized state educational institution.[12] After Napoleon's defeat, Prussian philosopher and linguist Wilhelm von Humboldt was put in charge of reviving German universities.[13] Humboldt had contended that education serves both individual and social purposes, and that "self-education can only be continued [. . .] in the wider context of development of the world."[14] His views on the structure of the university can be collectively expressed as the freedom to teach and publish (*Lehrfreiheit*), the freedom to learn (*Lernfreiheit*), and the unity of teaching and

9. Kemal Gürüz, Global: University Autonomy and Academic Freedom: A Historical Perspective, International Higher Education 63 (2011).
10. Kemal Gürüz, Global: University Autonomy and Academic Freedom: A Historical Perspective, International Higher Education 63 (2011).
11. Kemal Gürüz, Global: University Autonomy and Academic Freedom: A Historical Perspective, International Higher Education 63 (2011); *Academic Freedom*, New World Encyclopedia, http://www.newworldencyclopedia.org/entry/Academic_freedom (last visited May 24, 2021).
12. Kemal Gürüz, Global: University Autonomy and Academic Freedom: A Historical Perspective, International Higher Education 63 (2011).
13. Kemal Gürüz, Global: University Autonomy and Academic Freedom: A Historical Perspective, International Higher Education 63 (2011).
14. Wilhelm von Humboldt, Gesammelte Schriften: Ausgabe Der Preussischen Akademie Der Wissenschaften Book 7: 33 (1968). Individuals must "absorb the great mass of material offered to him by the world around him and by his inner existence . . . then reshape that material with all the energies of his own activity and appropriate it to himself so as to create an interaction between his own personality and nature in a most general, active and harmonious form." Wilhelm von Humboldt, Gesammelte Schriften: Ausgabe Der Preussischen Akademie Der Wissenschaften, bk. 2: 117.

research (*Einheit von Forschungund Lehre*).[15] These views, though neither clearly nor fully articulated, formed the basis for the modern research university and the modern concept of academic freedom.[16] Inspired by this model, German universities, particularly those in the Protestant states, emphasized *Lehrfreiheit*, the freedom of professors to determine the content of their teaching and to publish the results of their research without prior approval by their institutions.[17]

In the 1940s, the concept of academic freedom further evolved in response to the encroachments of totalitarian states on science and academia for the furtherance of their own goals. In the Soviet Union and Nazi Germany, for example, scientific research was brought under the control of the state. Hungarian-British scientist Michael Polanyi argued against Marxist John Desmond Bernal's instrumentalist view in *The Social Function of Science* (1938) that science exists primarily to serve the needs of society.[18] Demands in Britain for centrally planned scientific research finally prompted Polanyi, together with John Baker, to found the Society for Freedom in Science in 1940, which promoted a liberal conception of science as a discipline pursued freely for the sake of truth through peer review and the scientific method.[19]

In the United States, the first university to incorporate the Humboldtian ideal was Johns Hopkins University, founded in 1876, which made the needs of its professors, many having studied in Germany, central to its enterprise.[20] Academic freedom came to be further defined, first through the "1915 Declaration of Principles on Academic Freedom and Academic Tenure," authored by the American Association of University Professors (AAUP), and then through the "1940 Statement of Principles on Academic Freedom and Tenure," jointly authored by the AAUP and the Association of American Colleges (now the Association of American Colleges and Universities). The former affirms that

15. Wilhelm von Humboldt, Gesammelte Schriften: Ausgabe Der Preussischen Akademie Der Wissenschaften, bk. 2: 117.
16. Kemal Gürüz, Global: University Autonomy and Academic Freedom: A Historical Perspective, International Higher Education 63 (2011).
17. Michiel Horn, Academic Freedom in Canada: A History 7 (1999).
18. William McGucken, On Freedom and Planning in Science: The Society for Freedom in Science 1940–1946 (1978).
19. William McGucken, On Freedom and Planning in Science: The Society for Freedom in Science 1940–1946 (1978). In *The Contempt of Freedom* (1940) and *The Logic of Liberty* (1951), Polanyi claimed that co-operation among scientists is analogous to the coordination among agents within a free market. Just as consumers in a free market determine the value of products, scientists should freely pursue truth as an end through open debate with fellow specialists.
20. Michiel Horn, Academic Freedom in Canada: A History 7 (1999).

"academic freedom" applies to both academics and students, and that scholars should not be "debarred from giving expression to their judgments upon controversial questions," nor should their freedom of speech, outside the university, "be limited to questions falling within their own specialties."[21] The latter states that "[t]eachers are entitled to full freedom in research and in the publication of the results, subject to the adequate performance of their other academic duties," and "are entitled to freedom in the classroom in discussing their subject," but "should be careful not to introduce into their teaching controversial matter which has no relation to their subject."[22] In the years that followed, the U.S. Supreme Court further held that "[i]n a university knowledge is its own end, not merely a means to an end," and thus a university "is characterized by the spirit of free inquiry, its ideal being the ideal of Socrates—'to follow the argument where it leads.'"[23] Just as freedom of speech in America is guaranteed as a fundamental right by the First Amendment, the Supreme Court identified academic freedom as "a special concern of the First Amendment, which does not tolerate laws that cast a pall of orthodoxy over the classroom."[24]

There is no protection of academic freedom in the British constitution, whether through direct mention of the concept or indirectly under freedom of expression. To date British courts have not applied freedom of expression under Article 10 of the Human Rights Act 1998 to academic freedom like the American court interpreted the First Amendment to include this freedom. The 1988 Education Reform Act nonetheless established the legal right of academics in the U.K. "to question and test received wisdom and to put forward new ideas and controversial or unpopular opinions without placing themselves in jeopardy of losing their jobs or the privileges they may have."[25] According to the statement published by the University and College Union, formed in 2006 through the merger of the Association of University Teachers and the University and College Lecturers' Union, academic freedom includes the right to

---

21. *The 1915 Declaration of Principles on Academic Freedom and Academic Tenure*, American Association of University Professors, https://www.aaup.org/NR/rdonlyres/A6520A9D-0A9A-47B3-B550-C006B5B224E7/0/1915Declaration.pdf/

22. Seven regional accreditors worked with American colleges and universities to implement these principles. The AAUP, which is not an accrediting body and works with these same institutions, does not always agree with the regional accrediting bodies on these principles. *The 1940 Statement of Principles on Academic Freedom and Tenure*, AAUP, https://www.aaup.org/report/1940-statement-principles-academic-freedom-and-tenure

23. Sweezy v. N.H., 354 U.S. 234, 262–63 (1958).

24. Keyishian v. Bd. of Regents, 385 U.S. 589, 603 (1967).

25. Education Reform Act 1988, § 202(2)(a).

"freedom in teaching and discussion; freedom in carrying out research without commercial or political interference; freedom to disseminate and publish one's research findings; freedom from institutional censorship, [. . .] and freedom to participate in professional and representative academic bodies, including trade unions."[26] Academic freedom is also "bound up with broader civil liberties and human rights," and carries with it "the responsibility to respect the democratic rights and freedoms of others."[27]

Academic freedom was not unheard of in nineteenth- and early twentieth-century Canada.[28] Yet it was not until the Great Depression of the 1930s, when academic freedom was severely restricted, that academics claimed it as a professorial right—even the "essence of university life" and a "sacred privilege"—a trend that continued into World War II and the postwar period.[29] The 1950s, with the boom in the academic labor market, saw the establishment of the Canadian Association of University Teachers (CAUT), which, in fighting for stronger protection of academic freedom, confronted numerous prominent cases.[30] The CAUT defines academic freedom as "the right, without restriction by prescribed doctrine, to freedom to teach and discuss; freedom to carry out research and disseminate and publish the results thereof; [. . .] freedom to express one's opinion about the institution, its administration, and the system in which one works," among other freedoms.[31]

The significance of academic freedom has been recognized on a global level. The most symbolic event was the signing of the *Magna Charta Universitatum* at the European Rectors' conference on September 18, 1988 by universities from all over the world, both to commemorate the 900th anniversary of the

26. *UCU Statement on Academic Freedom*, University and College Union, https://www.ucu.org.uk/academicfreedom
27. *UCU Statement on Academic Freedom*, University and College Union, https://www.ucu.org.uk/academicfreedom
28. Michiel Horn, Academic Freedom in Canada: A History 15–61 (1999).
29. Sir Robert Falconer, addressing alumni of the University of Toronto on February 14, 1922, gave academic freedom a certain degree of public exposure by noting that "[t]he freedom to investigate and evaluate new truth was of the essence of university life," that the academic freedom enjoyed by professors was "one of the most sacred privileges of a university," and that the information that they provide would be "intelligible to [students] and will equip them to fulfil their duties as citizens and as searchers for the truth." Michiel Horn, Academic Freedom in Canada: A History 69 (1999).
30. One such case involved the dismissal of Professor Harry S. Crowe by the Board of Regents of Winnipeg's United College for a letter he wrote to a colleague that criticized the college administration and disparaged religious influence over the institution. The case led to the establishment of a permanent CAUT office in Ottawa.
31. *Policy Statement on Academic Freedom*, Canadian Association of University Teachers, https://www.caut.ca/about-us/caut-policy/lists/caut-policy-statements/policy-statement-on-academic-freedom

founding of the University of Bologna and to celebrate university traditions.[32] The *Universitatum* provides for an international standard for the fundamental values and principles of the university, in particular institutional autonomy and academic freedom.[33] It describes "freedom in research and training" as "the fundamental principle of university life," which enables an "independent search for truth" and serves as a "barrier against undue intervention by both government and interest groups."[34] Referencing the mobility that the *Habita* ensured for both teachers and students in the twelfth century, the *Universitatum* stresses that the freedoms of students—and not only of teachers—must be safeguarded, and that "instruments appropriate to realise that freedom must be made available to all members of the university community."[35]

II. *Why an Academic Job Isn't "Just a Job"*

Certainly, the idea of academic freedom has matured through the centuries and its significance is now widely recognized and protected in many countries. The exact scope of this freedom nonetheless has remained highly contested. Neither the *Habita* nor the Humboldtian ideal delineates the scope of academic freedom. Polanyi's notion of science, liberal in his time and a reaction against totalitarianism, did not require that scientific knowledge fulfill any critical purpose with regard to society. If anything, his conceptualization of science aimed to sever science from the state. It was in the second half of the twentieth century that academic freedom came to be expressly associated with freedom of expression, civil liberties, and democracy in Western societies.

This section and the next examine in detail Stanley Fish's 2014 book *Versions of Academic Freedom: From Professionalism to Revolution*, which is one of the most comprehensive studies of this topic particularly with regard to how academic freedom has been defined and ought to be defined. Fish espouses what he calls the "It's just a job" school of academic freedom. Academic freedom, according to this school of thought, is a mere subset of "professionalism" and rests upon a deflationary view of higher education as a service that offers

32. In 1988, 318 universities signed the *Universitatum*, and the number later increased to 805. *Magna Charta Universitatum*, http://www.magna-chata.org

33. *Magna Charta Universitatum*, http://www.magna-chata.org

34. *Magna Charta Universitatum*, http://www.magna-chata.org

35. *Magna Charta Universitatum*, http://www.magna-chata.org

knowledge and skills to students who wish to receive them.[36] Because the obligations and aspirations of college and university professors are defined by the sole task of advancing their field of knowledge, any latitude or freedom they enjoy does not include performing other tasks, no matter how worthy they might be.[37]

Both research and teaching are accordingly circumscribed in Fish's preferred school of academic freedom. For example, legal scholars should commit to the "inquiry into the intellectual coherence of rules and doctrines," not to higher goals such as "justice," "political desirability," or "cost-effectiveness," even where these might be identified as aspirations for the law.[38] Fish quotes Ernest Weinrib, who asserts that to understand tort law from the vantage point of wealth maximization would be to regard it as a branch of economics, and thereby to distort tort law as a practice informed by the goal of redressing wrongs suffered by an individual due to another person's negligent actions.[39] Weinrib's reasoning applies to other disciplines. Performing solely as academics rather than as political agents in the classroom, teachers should base their judgment of a text upon its own merit, so that any partisan implications that it might contain should not occupy the foreground or even the surface of the discussion.[40] In sum, while debating political issues is a valuable activity in a democracy, it is not an academic activity and does not deserve protection under the doctrine of academic freedom.[41]

Fish distinguishes his preferred school of academic freedom from the "For the common good" and the "Academic exceptionalism or uncommon beings" schools. The former shares some arguments with the "It's just a job" school, especially the argument that the academic job is distinctive and involves a transaction between academics and students.[42] Yet the "For the common good"

---

36. Stanley Fish, Versions of Academic Freedom: From Professionalism to Revolution 22–23, 34 (2014).
37. Stanley Fish, Versions of Academic Freedom: From Professionalism to Revolution 22–23, 34 (2014).
38. Stanley Fish, Versions of Academic Freedom: From Professionalism to Revolution 22–23, 34 (2014).
39. Stanley Fish, Versions of Academic Freedom: From Professionalism to Revolution 22–23 (2014); citing Ernest Weinrib, *Legal Formalism: On the Immanent Rationality of Law*, 97 Yale L.J. 949 (1988).
40. Stanley Fish, Versions of Academic Freedom: From Professionalism to Revolution 34 (2014).
41. Stanley Fish, Versions of Academic Freedom: From Professionalism to Revolution 35 (2014).
42. Stanley Fish, Versions of Academic Freedom: From Professionalism to Revolution 35 (2014).

school also contends that academia produces experts to advise both legislators and administrators and to make public opinions more self-critical and circumspect.[43] Academics armed with this freedom help to further the realization of democratic principles.[44] The latter can be seen as a logical extension of the former, seeing academics as "men of high gift and character" and uncommon or exceptional both intellectually and morally.[45] Hence, they not only correct the errors of popular opinion, but are entitled to the privilege of unaccountability to the same laws and restrictions that constrain ordinary citizens.[46]

Fish also introduces the "Academic freedom as critique" school, which holds that academics, possessing the special capacity to expose the weaknesses and contradictions of public opinions, are obliged to interrogate and revise the professional norms and standards of the current academy's practices rather than accepting them complacently.[47] In his view, this school represents "the very antithesis of academic freedom" by challenging the legitimizing authority of the academy itself and, in doing so, it turns this freedom into an engine for social progress.[48] Lastly, the "Academic freedom as revolution" school further radicalizes this idea of social progress. Rather than a mere offer of critique, fighting for an inclusive and radical democracy and standing in solidarity with other academics in the same fight becomes a responsibility that comes along with teaching.[49] "A passion for justice is of course a good thing," Fish admits, but emphasizes that "it's just not an academic good thing."[50]

Obviously, Fish's view is that there are only two competing versions of aca-

---

43. Stanley Fish, Versions of Academic Freedom: From Professionalism to Revolution 35 (2014).
44. Stanley Fish, Versions of Academic Freedom: From Professionalism to Revolution 35 (2014).
45. Stanley Fish, Versions of Academic Freedom: From Professionalism to Revolution 36 (2014).
46. This is found in the plaintiffs' argument in *Urofsky v. Gilmore* (2000), a decision by the Court of Appeals for the Four Circuit of the U.S., which involved Virginia's law forbidding state employees from accessing sexually explicit material on state-owned computers without their supervisors' permission. The plaintiffs argued that professors in the state university system claimed a special status: while the act was valid to most state employees, it violated the academic freedom of professors and did not apply to them.
47. Stanley Fish, Versions of Academic Freedom: From Professionalism to Revolution 36 (2014).
48. Stanley Fish, Versions of Academic Freedom: From Professionalism to Revolution 69 (2014).
49. Stanley Fish, Versions of Academic Freedom: From Professionalism to Revolution 69 (2014).
50. Stanley Fish, Versions of Academic Freedom: From Professionalism to Revolution 17 (2014).

demic freedom among the five: the "It's just a job" and the "For the common good" schools.[51] Because, as Fish argues, "parents, churches, free libraries, political discussion groups, newspapers, high-level journals, the internet, public television, National Public Radio, documentaries, popular culture, folk wisdom, common sense" can all enlighten and empower a political citizenry, the academy should not appeal to the claim of a larger common good to justify its privileges.[52] This, in his words, is his position's "greatest strength because, in refusing the challenge of public/political justification, it reaffirms the independent value of what academics do, and provides a secure, because wholly internal, justification of allowing them to do it freely."[53] Ole W. Pedersen, an academic, contends that in this day and age, an increasing value is being attached to academic research on account of its societal benefit as opposed to its intrinsic value and, in some cases, even to the extent that the academic research enterprise is shaped in accordance with researchers' desired social objectives and detracts from the core purpose of inquiry.[54] Fish's assertion of the importance of the intrinsic value of the academy is important, as any social value that it may produce would be seen as an unintended consequence rather than a deliberate, calculated attempt to influence matters external to it (which, though Pederson does not expressly state it, may compromise the integrity of the research process).[55] Fellow academic Evan Kindley, on the other hand, believes that Fish's arguments will only speed up the eradication of the professional academy by preventing new entrants from invoking the spiritual or social value(s) of the academic profession, which is already deprived of many worldly benefits commonly enjoyed in other professions.[56]

Both Pedersen and Kindley argue from the perspective of academics who are deeply concerned about the intrinsic value and existence of the academy, respectively—concerns that are both timely and legitimate. On the contrary, law professor Robert Post compellingly exposes the weaknesses of Fish's argu-

---

51. *E.g.*, Evan Kindley, *The Calling*, DISSENT (2015), https://www.dissentmagazine.org/article/the-calling-academic-freedom-stanley-fish
52. STANLEY FISH, VERSIONS OF ACADEMIC FREEDOM: FROM PROFESSIONALISM TO REVOLUTION 47 (2014).
53. STANLEY FISH, VERSIONS OF ACADEMIC FREEDOM: FROM PROFESSIONALISM TO REVOLUTION 49 (2014).
54. Ole W. Pedersen, *Review of: Versions of Academic Freedom, by Stanley Fish*, 35 LEG. STUD. 551 (2015).
55. Ole W. Pedersen, *Review of: Versions of Academic Freedom, by Stanley Fish*, 35 LEG. STUD. 551 (2015).
56. *E.g.*, Evan Kindley, *The Calling*, DISSENT (2015), https://www.dissentmagazine.org/article/the-calling-academic-freedom-stanley-fish

ment for the "It's just a job" school by targeting its internal inconsistencies.[57] Agreeing with the thrust of Fish's thesis, Post rightly contends that his efforts to distinguish "It's just a job" and "For the common good" schools were misplaced. First, Fish is wrong in saying that justifying academic freedom in terms of external goods would corrupt the academy, because this freedom is primarily a value empowering scholars to defend the autonomy of the scholarly enterprise, and it would be more effective to appeal to the common good outside of the academy to persuade nonscholars to respect the profession's autonomy.[58] Second, by arguing that academic freedom cannot be justified in terms of values external to the academic enterprise, Fish effectively denies all constitutional underpinnings of this freedom, including democracy's need for the creation and distribution of expert knowledge.[59] Third, because the disciplinary norms defining and constituting legitimate scholarship are not unitary and shared by all scholarly fields, his criteria for distinguishing scholarship from politics fail to account for the breadth and diversity of scholarly practices that characterize the modern university.[60]

Michael Robertson, also a law professor, adds to Post's robust criticism of Fish's opinion that the refusal to consider external values and goals is the best and most principled way to defend the academy. As Robertson wisely argues, citing Larry Alexander, good academic works do tend to produce great social benefits even if scholars do not aim to do so, and benefits completely different from the original goals can justify the academic enterprise to outsiders.[61] In fact, such collateral or even random social benefits will be valuable ammunition to use against those who seek to dismiss and undermine the work of universities.[62]

The following section will further the arguments of Fish's reviewers by justifying the role of the academy in serving the common good and realizing democratic principles. Examples from the Renaissance and Enlightenment periods

57. Robert Post, *Why Bother with Academic Freedom?* 9 FIU L. Rev. 9 (2013).
58. Robert Post, *Why Bother with Academic Freedom?* 9 FIU L. Rev. 9, 9 (2013).
59. Robert Post, *Why Bother with Academic Freedom?* 9 FIU L. Rev. 9, 9 (2013).
60. Post points out that Fish's method applies more readily to fields like literature. Academic disciplines like political theory, on the contrary, commonly require political theorists to take positions on real-life political events. It is merely one of the practical disciplines that study and analyze the world to effect changes. Robert Post, *Why Bother with Academic Freedom?* 9 FIU L. Rev. 9, 20 (2013).
61. Michael Robertson, *Book Review on Stanley Fish, Versions of Academic Freedom*, 65(3) J. Leg. Educ. 672, 700 (2016); citing Larry Alexander, *Fish on Academic Freedom: A Merited Assault on Nonsense, but Perhaps a Bridge Too Far*, 9 Fla. Int'l U. L. Rev. 1, 8 (2013).
62. Michael Robertson, *Book Review on Stanley Fish, Versions of Academic Freedom*, 65(3) J. Leg. Educ. 672, 700 (2016).

and from totalitarian regimes in the twentieth century will be used to illuminate the flaws and impracticality of the "It's just a job" school and to justify the democratic function of academic freedom. The chapter will end by discussing the statement by the United Nations Education, Scientific, and Cultural Organization (UNESCO) on academic freedom, the first successful international attempt to articulate in a single major UN document the rights and responsibilities of postsecondary faculties and the democratic implications of the academy.

III. Why Academic Freedom Is Important to Democracy

Robertson correctly identifies one common criticism of Fish's "It's just a job" school—that it would be difficult for scholars to compartmentalize academics from politics while they are on the job.[63] Indeed, compartmentalization is not only impractical but may also be self-defeating. While certain scholars were victimized by the circumstances of their times, others benefited from them. The greatest philosophies, inventions, and discoveries cannot be isolated from the social and political circumstances that gave rise to them. Chapter 1 has already described the stories of Milton and Locke, who benefited from the intellectual atmosphere at their respective universities and later advanced their theories of freedom of expression. Similarly, one would be hard pressed to isolate Nicolaus Copernicus's heliocentric theory and Galileo Galilei's invention of his telescope and support for the Copernican view of the universe from the Renaissance, which saw the decline of the Church's influence, the resurrection of the ancient Greek tradition of law and reasoning, the reform of the educational curriculum, and the rise in the study of mathematics and astronomy.[64] The same goes for Isaac Newton's discovery of gravity, the laws of motion, and calculus, which, being products of the late Renaissance, hugely impacted the Enlightenment period that followed it.[65]

Yet Fish's preferred model is inadequate for a related reason. In his earlier works, Fish expresses views similar to those in his work on academic freedom,

63. *See* Michael Robertson, *Book Review on Stanley Fish, Versions of Academic Freedom*, 65(3) J. Leg. Educ. 672, 700 (2016).

64. *See, e.g.*, Allen George Debut, Man and Nature in the Renaissance (Cambridge Studies in the History of Science) (1978).

65. *See* Allen George Debut, Man and Nature in the Renaissance (1978).

by arguing that making partisan politics part of the academic job could expose the university to hostile political actors. To protect their pursuit of disciplinary truths from interference by legislators and political activists, he argues, academics should stay away from politics.[66] Legislators and activists who want to usurp the role of academics then "would have no traction or point of polemical entry because politics, or religion, or ethics would enter the classroom only as objects of analysis and not as candidates for approval or rejection. The culture wars, at least in the classroom, would be over."[67] This interestingly echoes Polanyi's argument back in the 1930s against the instrumentalist view of science and his promotion of a liberal view of science and knowledge to be pursued for its own sake. What Fish may have overlooked is that despite any attempt to shield the academy from politics, the academic profession may—and likely still will—become infiltrated or usurped by nonscholars and politicians to further their agendas. A better and more sensible approach, therefore, would be not to stay within the confines of one's disciplinary expertise, but to aspire to loftier goals like democracy and justice while drawing upon one's expertise in pursuing knowledge. This approach would entail following the "For the common good" school, meaning scholars should actively communicate knowledge produced in the academy to the public and feed the input from the public back into the academy to produce more knowledge.

Throughout Western history, not only have universities not been immune to political forces, but they were exploited and weaponized to serve totalitarian agendas during different periods. This happened in Germany in the 1930s, when the Humboldtian model was said to have inspired many universities by the time Hitler took power. *Lehrfreiheit*, or the freedom to teach, research, and publish, which had been the foundation of many German universities, was not enough to shield them from the Nazis. While many German scholars who opposed Hitler or expressed anti–National Socialist sentiments were expelled from the Nazi-controlled universities along with their Jewish counterparts, those who stayed either openly supported the regime or did not defy it and so were complicit in the Holocaust.[68]

That the German academy could do little to resist the Nazis was due to many factors, one being that German universities themselves had served on different occasions as a breeding ground of nationalism. There were other reasons. Curi-

66. Fish, Professional Correctness 96 (1995).
67. Fish, Save the World on Our Own Time 169–70 (2008).
68. *See, e.g.*, Robert P. Ericksen, Complicity in the Holocaust: Churches and Universities in Nazi Germany (2012).

ously enough, neither Post nor Robertson, both legal academics, questions Fish's reliance on Weinrib's argument that academics should study law purely from a legal, rather than interdisciplinary, perspective to bolster his preferred model of academic freedom. Neither do they draw examples to show that studying law without reference to democratic or justice principles could pose problems to society. In fact, another reason that the German academy was unable to resist the Nazis could have been due to the rise of legal positivism in Germany, which treats law as a construct dependent on social facts rather than as something that is driven by universal principles. Although there is nothing inherently authoritarian about legal positivism per se,[69] the common good or justice, as in the natural law tradition, arguably offers an intellectual defense and moral safeguard against arbitrary state power and unjust laws.[70] Unsurprisingly, not a few have attributed Nazism in part to the belief in legal positivism—that law bears no relation to morality or justice—among German academics of that time.[71]

The mere belief in the role that higher moral principles play in law, or even an entire academy that actively resisted the Nazi regime, may not have helped rewrite the modern history of Germany. Yet in the aftermath of World War II, Germany and the world realized the dangers of excluding ethics and metaphysics from the understanding of law. One of the Nuremberg Principles, created by the UN's International Law Commission to codify the legal principles underlying the Nuremberg Trials of Nazi party members following World War II, states that individuals have "a duty to disobey laws which are clearly recognizable as violating higher moral principles."[72] If law should be understood and studied with respect to justice, morality, and democratic principles, there is no reason why this idea should not also apply to other disciplines. Fish's view that an academic position is "just a job" turns out to be too restrictive and regressive.

Nazi Germany is long gone. As the previous chapter has explained, however, campus speech is not free, in part because extreme political correctness

---

69. *See, e.g.*, Brian Leiter, *The Radicalism of Legal Positivism*, University of Chicago Public Law Working Paper, no. 303 (Mar. 12, 2010), http://papers.ssrn.com/sol3/papers.cfm?abstract_id=1568333

70. *E.g.*, Kenny Yang, *The Rise of Legal Positivism in Germany: A Prelude to Nazi Arbitrariness?* 3 W. Aus. Jurist 245 (2012).

71. Kenny Yang, *The Rise of Legal Positivism in Germany: A Prelude to Nazi Arbitrariness?* 3 W. Aus. Jurist 245, 253–54 (2012); Oren Gross disagrees, arguing that the Nazis adopted a perverted version of natural law to support their actions, and "it was not inattention to values that marred the post-WWII reputation of the German legal profession, but it was rather devotion to a base and odious set of values"—the "Nazi morality." 11 Wake Forest L. Rev. Online 54 (2021), http://wakeforestlawreview.com/2021/05/what-both-hart-and-fuller-got-wrong/

72. Kenny Yang, *The Rise of Legal Positivism in Germany: A Prelude to Nazi Arbitrariness?* 3 W. Aus. Jurist 245, 253–54 (2012).

has stifled freedom of speech and discussion on many campuses. This culture of conformity and censorship, unfortunately born out of a globalized and heterogeneous environment, can be challenged through academic freedom, which enables existing knowledge to be evaluated and new knowledge to be created.[73] The defense and exercise of this broadly conceived freedom will ideally help to thwart despotic tendencies that ruin our democracies.

Unsurprisingly, the importance of academic freedom came to be affirmed by the UN. UNESCO recognizes this freedom as a right to which all academic staff should be entitled and which should be protected by the tenure system. On November 11, 1997, it issued a statement titled *Recommendation concerning the Status of Higher-Education Teaching Personnel*. According to this statement, "the right to education, teaching and research can only be fully enjoyed in an atmosphere of academic freedom," and "open communication of findings, hypotheses and opinions lies at the very heart of higher education and provides the strongest guarantee of the accuracy and objectivity of scholarship and research."[74]

Among the main components of academic freedom, according to the UNESCO's statement, are "Institutional autonomy," "Individual rights and freedoms," "Self governance and collegiality," and "Tenure."[75] Regarding the second item in particular, it stipulates that "[h]igher-education teaching personnel are entitled to the maintaining of academic freedom, that is to say, the right, without constriction by prescribed doctrine, to freedom of teaching and discussion, freedom in carrying out research and disseminating and publishing the results thereof, freedom to express freely their opinion about the institution or system in which they work, freedom from institutional censorship and freedom to participate in professional or representative academic bodies."[76] "Tenure," which serves to protect the freedom of academic staff, "should be safeguarded as far as possible even when changes in the organization of or within a higher education institution or system are made, and should be granted, after a reasonable period of probation, to those who meet stated objective criteria in teaching, and/or scholarship, and/or research to the satisfaction of an academic body."[77]

---

73. *See* JOANNA WILLIAMS, ACADEMIC FREEDOM IN AN AGE OF CONFORMITY: CONFRONTING THE FEAR OF KNOWLEDGE (2016).
74. *Recommendation concerning the Status of Higher-Education Teaching Personnel*, UNESCO (1997), http://www.gdrc.org/doyourbit/113234mb.pdf
75. *Recommendation concerning the Status of Higher-Education Teaching Personnel* § 5, UNESCO (1997), http://www.gdrc.org/doyourbit/113234mb.pdf
76. *Recommendation concerning the Status of Higher-Education Teaching Personnel* § 27, UNESCO (1997), http://www.gdrc.org/doyourbit/113234mb.pdf
77. *Recommendation concerning the Status of Higher-Education Teaching Personnel* § 46, UNESCO (1997), http://www.gdrc.org/doyourbit/113234mb.pdf

UNESCO's *Recommendation concerning the Status of Higher-Education Teaching Personnel* is not a treaty and is aimed to set a standard rather than to stand as formal legislation. Yet it was the first successful international attempt to articulate in a single major UN document the rights and responsibilities of postsecondary faculties.[78] Compared to the *Magna Charta Universitatum* described earlier, it is lacking in the sense that it fails to address the freedom of students. In addition, it has low compliance among many nations, including European states.[79] Nonetheless, as a UN document, it has been drawn upon in different countrywide protests over violations of academic freedom, including those that occurred under authoritarian regimes.[80] In sum, it sets out an important freedom—one that has been violated or compromised in many nations, but to which postsecondary institutions and faculty associations in many of these nations have continued to aspire.[81]

• • •

It was hardly surprising that some of the worst dictators like Hitler and Mao sought to usurp intellectuals' academic freedom through their ministers of education and Red Guards. Academic freedom, taken broadly, is a form of free expression and the freedom to teach and research plays an important role in democracies. Yet this chapter has also indicated that free speech and academic freedom, often conflated and used interchangeably, are not the same. The next chapter will explicate the relationship between campus free speech and academic freedom. In light of the democratic function of academic freedom, it will also examine the proper role of academics as instructors and discuss the measures they may take to safeguard students' freedom of speech while exercising their academic freedom in the classroom.

---

78. Donald C. Savage & Patricia A. Finn, *The Road to the 1997 UNESCO Statement on Academic Freedom*, CAUT (Sep. 2017), at 5, http://www.caut.ca/sites/default/files/unesco_en_insidepages_final2017-09-11.pdf
79. Terence Karran, *Academic Freedom in Europe: Reviewing UNESCO's Recommendations*, 57 Brit. J. Educ. Stud. 191 (2009).
80. Donald C. Savage & Patricia A. Finn, *The Road to the 1997 UNESCO Statement on Academic Freedom*, CAUT (Sep. 2017), at 5, http://www.caut.ca/sites/default/files/unesco_en_insidepages_final2017-09-11.pdf
81. Donald C. Savage & Patricia A. Finn, *The Road to the 1997 UNESCO Statement on Academic Freedom*, CAUT (Sep. 2017), at 5, http://www.caut.ca/sites/default/files/unesco_en_insidepages_final2017-09-11.pdf

CHAPTER THREE

Campus Free Speech and Academic Freedom

Could either free speech or academic freedom have existed in Nazi Germany and Mao's China without the other? This chapter will clarify the meanings of the two concepts and explain how they benefit each other in the university setting. Free speech is a precondition for academic freedom, as shown by the dearth of the freedom of inquiry along with campus free speech under authoritarian regimes. Academic freedom empowers and even obligates academics to inform free expression in universities to help advance knowledge and better serve the needs of democratic societies. Examples will be given to illuminate how academics, equipped with their disciplinary knowledge and expertise acquired through freedom of inquiry, can inform campus free expression to serve the needs of academia and society.

I. Two Conflated Concepts

Free speech on campus and academic freedom are frequently—though carelessly and mistakenly—considered synonymous. The former, which originated in the *Habita*, was part of the freedom that found its roots in ancient Greece and was further recognized as a fundamental, inalienable right by Enlightenment thinkers. The latter, though it can be said to have similar origins, refers to the freedom of all members of the academic community to engage in the production of knowledge. These two freedoms are therefore subject to different constraints. Now recognized as a fundamental right in most national constitutions and as a universal right by different international conventions, free speech is subject to some restrictions including laws on obscenity, defamation, and national security. Depending on the university, free speech on campus may be restricted by further regulations. Academic freedom, on the other hand, is subject to not only speech regulations but also the professional standards of relevant disciplines.

In the news media, the differences between free expression and academic freedom are typically glossed over and the two terms are regularly used interchangeably.[1] Even where the differences are noted, they are often only implied but seldom sufficiently examined.[2] On the contrary, Keith Whittington in his book *Speak Freely* correctly points out that the scope of free speech is wider than that of academic freedom: "Scholarly speech is not 'free' in the sense of anything goes, but the ideal of academic freedom emphasizes that members of the faculty should have the independence to exercise their professional judgment and not be constrained by social, political, or financial pressure to shade how they teach or what they write."[3] Nonscholarly speech on campuses, "home to more than the work of scholars," is necessarily freer and has a broader scope than that of scholarly speech.[4] Sigal Ben-Porath goes further than Whittington to explain their different constraints. While the law prohibits or regulates various types of speech both on and off campus, academic freedom, aimed at protecting researchers who contribute to the advancement of knowledge from political, institutional, and other pressures, precludes certain forms of speech, for example, plagiarism or mischaracterization of the results of research even if they are protected by free speech norms.[5] Erwin Chemerinsky adds to the ideas of Whittington and Ben-Porath by stating that colleges and universities "are properly expected to recognize both a professional zone, which requires standards of peer review, scholarly norms, teaching excellence, and appropriate

---

1. *See, e.g.*, Kristin Nelson & Willow Smith, *Where's the Line between Free Expression and Protecting Students from Hate Speech*, CBC (Dec. 1, 2017), www.cbc.ca/radio/thecurrent/the-current-for-december-1-2017-1.4426944/where-s-the-line-between-free-expression-and-protecting-students-from-hate-speech-1.4427115; Timothy Ash, *Safe Spaces Are Not the Only Threat to Free Speech*, THE GUARDIAN (Sep. 16, 2016, https://www.theguardian.com/commentisfree/2016/sep/16/safe-spaces-free-speech-university-prevent-no-platforming-academic-freedom
2. E.g., *Free Speech IS Not the Campus Problem You Think It Is*, CBC (Apr. 21, 2017), https://www.cbc.ca/radio/the180/the-not-so-great-trans-canada-trail-it-s-ok-to-be-grumpy-at-work-policing-free-speech-on-campus-1.4078755/free-speech-is-not-the-campus-problem-you-think-it-is-1.4080033; Hannah Richardson, *Terror Plans "Threaten Academic Freedom,"* BBC (Jan. 12, 2015), https://www.bbc.com/news/education-30776946
3. KEITH WHITTINGTON, SPEAK FREELY: WHY UNIVERSITIES MUST DEFEND FREE SPEECH 9 (2018).
4. *See* KEITH WHITTINGTON, SPEAK FREELY: WHY UNIVERSITIES MUST DEFEND FREE SPEECH 9 (2018).
5. SIGAL R. BEN-PORATH, FREE SPEECH ON CAMPUS 20 (2017).

conduct in the work environment, and a free speech zone, which explicitly rejects professional educational standards in order to allow for a more raucous space of expression."[6]

The conflation of campus free speech and academic freedom likely has been due to the fact that both are freedoms in the academy. In fact, their boundary is not at all clear in some cases. As UNESCO recommends as part of academic freedom the "freedom to express freely their opinion about the institution or system in which they work,"[7] such opinions are often not subject to scholarly review like academic works are. For example, writing opinion pieces for the media is a concurrent exercise of both freedom of speech and academic freedom. Hence, the following section will explain how one freedom contributes to the other.

II. How Campus Speech and Academic Freedom Are Interdependent

The academic freedom enjoyed by German universities during the 1930s failed to shield them from Nazism and, as chapter 2 has explained, the rise of legal positivism in the academy may have played a role in facilitating the spread of this extreme ideology. The chapter nonetheless has also acknowledged that a strong belief in higher moral principles in law, or even an academy that more actively resisted the Nazi regime, may not have enabled the nation to avoid this calamity. Indeed, evidence throughout Western history provides ample support for the view that free speech in universities is only possible in democratic societies where this freedom is legally protected. Free speech on campus is in turn a necessary condition for academic freedom. Without free speech, academic freedom cannot truly flourish.

Although the medieval period turned out to play a significant part in the Western history of free speech, speech freedom was not widely enjoyed back then. As the Roman Catholic Church dominated everyday life and heresy was severely punished, academic freedom was also circumscribed and scholars who dared to challenge the Church were punished. John Wycliffe (1330–84), Oxford's leading philosopher and theologian, was put under house arrest for his criti-

6. Erwin Chemerinsky, Free Speech on Campus 112–13 (2017).
7. *Recommendation concerning the Status of Higher-Education Teaching Personnel* § 27, UNESCO.

cism of the wealth of the Church and how its teachings conflicted with scripture.[8] The persecution of academics, or the fear of persecution, continued well into the Renaissance, even as the power of the Church declined. Among the well-known academics was French philosopher René Descartes (1596–1650), who, fearing persecution due to what could be considered his atheist beliefs, left his native country and fled to the Netherlands.[9] The less remembered ones included Kazimierz Lyszczynski (1634–89), Poland's first atheist who was executed and whose writings were burned along with him.[10]

Free speech died in Germany after Hitler rose to power. The Law for the Restoration of the Professional Civil Service, passed in 1933, two months after Hitler attained power, was an antisemitic law targeting Jews as well as civil servants who did not "support the national state at all times and without reservation."[11] Hence, this law enabled the Nazis to root out any dissent to their policies and ideology in Germany's state-run higher education.[12] It was welcomed by some professors, who promoted state ideology through their works and facilitated the death of academic freedom in Nazi Germany, while leading to the dismissal of others.[13] One-third of them were dismissed due to their Jewish identity; many more were dismissed or left their positions due to their political beliefs or fear of persecution.[14]

---

8. Andrew E. Larsen, The School of Heretics: Academic Condemnation at the University of Oxford, 1277–1409 241 (2011).
9. *E.g.*, *René Descartes*, Strange Science Net, https://www.strangescience.net/descartes.htm (last visited May 29, 2021).
10. Marek Łyszczyński, *Our Foundation Is Named after the First Polish Atheist Kazimierz Łyszczyński*, Kazimierz Łyszczyński Foundation (Mar. 14, 2016), https://lyszczynski.com.pl/index.php/en/2016/03/14/our-foundation-is-named-after-the-first-polish-atheist-kazimierz-lyszczynski/ (last visited May 29, 2021).
11. Facing History and Ourselves, *Chapter Five: A Test of Loyalty*, Holocaust and Human Behavior (2017), https://www.facinghistory.org/holocaust-and-human-behavior/chapter-5/test-loyalty (last visited May 29, 2021).
12. Frankfurt, among the most liberal of major German universities and with a faculty that prided itself on its allegiance to scholarship, freedom of conscience, and democracy, was the first university targeted by the Nazis. Facing History and Ourselves, *Chapter Five: Controlling the Universities*, Holocaust and Human Behavior (2017), https://www.facinghistory.org/holocaust-and-human-behavior/chapter-5/controlling-universities (last visited May 29, 2021).
13. The most notable example was philosopher Martin Heidegger, who said that freedom of inquiry and free expression were negative and selfish ideas. His fellow professors at Freiburg University voted him head of the university in April 1933. Facing History and Ourselves, *Chapter Five: Controlling the Universities*, Holocaust and Human Behavior (2017), https://www.facinghistory.org/holocaust-and-human-behavior/chapter-5/controlling-universities (last visited May 29, 2021).
14. Albert Einstein was among the world-famous scientists who were fired or who left their positions at universities across Germany. Facing History and Ourselves, *Chapter Five: Controlling the Universities*, Holocaust and Human Behavior (2017), https://www.facinghistory.org/holocaust-and-human-behavior/chapter-5/controlling-universities (last visited May 29, 2021).

A more recent example in the Western world of how academic freedom perished with campus free speech as the government turned authoritarian can be found in Turkey. Never a beacon of free speech, the Turkish state tightened its grip on expressive freedom as its democracy broke down over the past decade.[15] In particular, the failed coup attempt in 2016 to overthrow an increasingly authoritarian government was followed by a precipitous decline in media freedom, as hundreds of journalists were imprisoned or lost their jobs and dozens of critical media outlets were taken over by the state.[16] As in other dictatorships and authoritarian regimes, the academy became a key target in the state's attempt to eradicate dissent. Under a string of emergency decrees issued since July 2016, more than 150,000 public officials were fired—some jailed—without due process, among them more than 5,800 academics.[17] Campus activities, especially those related to activism and rights struggles, came under intense pressure from both private actors and university administrations.[18] Students were prohibited from participating in peaceful political protests, while academics who remained in their positions were warned to "be cautious" in choosing research topics and to avoid those there were "too sensitive at the moment."[19]

If campus free speech, or free speech more generally, is a precondition for academic freedom, what can academic freedom bring to free speech? Academics, equipped with the freedom to research and publish in their disciplines, can bring their expertise to inform free—sometimes uneducated—expression to advance knowledge to the benefit of democratic societies. This view is supported by Robert Post's *Democracy, Expertise, and Academic Freedom* (2012), which argues that the free and open exchange of opinions and ideas must be complemented by professional standards of competence and practice.

15. *E.g.*, Murat Somer, *Understanding Turkey's Democratic Breakdown: Old vs. New and Indigenous vs. Global Authoritarianism*, 16 S.E. Euro. & Black Sea Stud. 481 (2016); Kerem Öktem, *The Rise and Fall of Free Speech under Turkey's Islamists*, Free Speech Debate (Feb. 12, 2016), http://freespeechdebate.com/discuss/the-rise-and-fall-of-free-speech-under-turkeys-islamists/ (last visited Dec. 23, 2021).
16. *Turkey: Journalism Is Not a Crime*, Amnesty International (Feb. 2017), https://www.amnesty.org/en/latest/campaigns/2017/02/free-turkey-media/ (last visited Dec. 23, 2021).
17. *Turkey: Government Targeting Academics: Dismissals, Prosecutions Create Campus Climate of Fear*, Human Rights Watch (May 14, 2018), https://www.hrw.org/news/2018/05/14/turkey-government-targeting-academics (last visited May 29, 2021).
18. *Turkey: Government Targeting Academics: Dismissals, Prosecutions Create Campus Climate of Fear*, Human Rights Watch (May 14, 2018), https://www.hrw.org/news/2018/05/14/turkey-government-targeting-academics (last visited May 29, 2021).
19. *Turkey: Government Targeting Academics: Dismissals, Prosecutions Create Campus Climate of Fear*, Human Rights Watch (May 14, 2018), https://www.hrw.org/news/2018/05/14/turkey-government-targeting-academics (last visited May 29, 2021).

Post explains that the free speech paradigm of the First Amendment of the U.S. Constitution is committed to the egalitarian premise that every person is entitled to communicate his or her own opinion in a "marketplace of ideas."[20] An "uninhibited marketplace of ideas" alone,[21] however, would not produce knowledge and lead us to the truth. As expert knowledge depends on the preservation and nurturing of disciplines, the egalitarian principle, or what he calls "democratic legitimation," must be complemented by "democratic competence," defined by reference to scholarly or disciplinary standards and not public opinion.[22] Post thereby advances a theory of First Amendment rights and academic freedom that reconciles the need for the free formation of public opinions and for the distribution and creation of expertise. Furthermore, because universities are essential institutions for nurturing disciplines and creating disciplinary knowledge by discriminating between good and bad ideas, the state must not intervene by enforcing the views of some members against those of others.[23] Ultimately, it is not the state or even the appointing authorities but faculty members who, as appointees rather than mere employees of universities, must make "informed and educated public opinion[s]" by clarifying "matter[s] . . . of public concern."[24]

Undoubtedly, Post's critique of Fish's "It's just a job" school, discussed in chapter 2, to a great extent echoes and reaffirms his argument in this book by emphasizing that academic freedom should serve the common good through contributing to democratic governance. Although Post's argument in this book is contextualized in America, where academic freedom is part of its First Amendment tradition, the previous chapter has explained the superiority of the "for the common good" school and its democratic and human rights impli-

---

20. Robert Post, Democracy, Expertise, and Academic Freedom: A First Amendment Jurisprudence for the Modern State 62 (2012) (citing Justice Holmes, "[W]hen men have realized that time has upset many fighting faiths, they may come to believe even more than they believe the very foundations of their own conduct that the ultimate good desired is better reached by free trade in ideas—that the best test of truth is the power of the thought to get itself accepted in the competition of the market, and that truth is the only ground upon which their wishes safely can be carried out." Abrams v. United States, 250 U.S. 616, 630 (Holmes, J., dissenting).) This conception of a marketplace resonates throughout U.S. Supreme Court jurisprudence to this day. *See, e.g.*, McConnell v. FEC, 124 S. Ct. 619, 729 (2003); Red Lion Broad. Co. v. FCC, 3995 U.S. 367, 390 (1969).

21. McConnell v. FEC, 124 S. Ct. 619, 729 (2003).

22. Robert Post, Democracy, Expertise, and Academic Freedom: A First Amendment Jurisprudence for the Modern State 34 (2012).

23. Robert Post, Democracy, Expertise, and Academic Freedom: A First Amendment Jurisprudence for the Modern State 91 (2012).

24. Robert Post, Democracy, Expertise, and Academic Freedom: A First Amendment Jurisprudence for the Modern State 14 (2012).

cations with reference to the UNESCO statement and in different Western nations. Post's idea of democratic competence therefore applies to other nations, including those where academic freedom has not attained a constitutional status. Unsurprisingly, other scholars, without citing the idea of "democratic competence," also allude to the freedom and even moral obligation of academics to draw upon their expertise to counter the culture of conformity and censorship prevalent on many Western campuses.[25] While Post's theory of academic freedom is compelling and well-received,[26] his analysis mainly focuses on research in higher educational institutions. It does not examine at great length how academics can and should use this competence to inform free speech on university campuses, particularly in the classroom setting.

III. How Academic Freedom Informs Free Speech: Some Examples

To continue the discussion of Nazi Germany, a good example of how academics should exercise their professional judgment to inform free speech in the classroom is the case of Holocaust denial. In European civil law countries such as Germany, France, and Austria, the denial of the Holocaust is a crime and considered an example of antisemitism and hate speech against Jewish people.[27] This is not the case in the United States, while other common law countries like the United Kingdom and Canada do not have laws that specifically outlaw the denial of the Holocaust. Students in the latter countries have the right to say that the mass killings of Jews under the Nazi regime did not happen without getting prosecuted for making these ill-informed assertions. However, historical inquiries lead to truth or knowledge only if they are informed by facts rather than false premises. Equipped with their expertise and training in history or related disciplines, or what Post calls "democratic competence," professors

25. *See, e.g.*, JOANNA WILLIAMS, ACADEMIC FREEDOM IN AN AGE OF CONFORMITY: CONFRONTING THE FEAR OF KNOWLEDGE (2016).

26. *See, e.g.*, Rachel Levinson-Waldman, *Review of Robert C. Post's Democracy, Expertise, and Academic Freedom: A First Amendment Jurisprudence for the Modern State*, 48 TULSA L. REV. 245 (2012); David M. Skover & Ronald K.L. Collins, *The Guardians of Knowledge in the Modern State: Post's Republic and the First Amendment*, 87 WASH. L. REV. 369 (2012); Scott McLemee, *Ideas of Academic Freedom*, INSIDE HIGHER EDUC. (Jan. 18, 2012), https://www.insidehighered.com/views/2012/01/18/review-robert-posts-democracy-expertise-academic-freedom

27. *E.g.*, Deborah Lipstadt, *The Denial of Holocaust*, BBC (Feb. 17, 2011), http://www.bbc.co.uk/history/worldwars/genocide/deniers_01.shtml

should guide students to see the real picture by offering them facts and ensuring that their inquiries are educated and informed.

The example of Holocaust denial may be too straightforward, given that what the Nazis did is well documented and almost universally agreed upon. A more challenging example of how academic freedom may benefit unfettered and sometimes biased or ill-informed expression is a class discussion on the immigration policies of Western liberal countries. Students in the anti-immigration camp may refer to high-profile crimes committed by migrants and refugees—for example, from war-torn Islamic countries—and even rely upon racial and religious stereotypes to bolster their arguments.[28] Students who are pro-immigration may draw upon reports indicating that migrants and refugees from these countries commit fewer crimes than the general population does on average, and conclude that they in fact make better citizens than the local people in their host countries.[29] Academics in disciplines such as law and political science, while engaging their students in this challenging topic, should draw upon knowledge in human rights law and statistics to help them address problems caused by mass immigration.

An even more challenging and timely example would be whether Western countries such as the U.S. and Canada should sanction China for its thefts of intellectual property, abysmal human rights record, and, more recently, its spread of COVID-19. Unfettered and ill-informed expression from students may include statements that China has not stolen Western technologies, that America and Canada are far worse than China when it comes to their treatment of Indigenous peoples, or that the pandemic did not originate in China. Academics can fulfill their proper role by referring to records, substantial though often shamelessly dismissed or even censored for diplomatic and economic reasons, of the Chinese government's intellectual property thefts and severe human rights violations, the latter continuing from the establishment of the People's Republic of China to the present, which stand in stark contrast to the

---

28. *E.g.*, Peter Hasson, *Canadian Schools Struggling to Integrate Violent Syrian Migrants*, DAILY CALLER (Oct. 5, 2016), https://dailycaller.com/2016/10/05/canadian-schools-struggling-to-integrate-violent-syrian-migrants-documents-show-video/

29. *E.g.*, Andrew Russell & Ryan Rocca, *Canadians Are Concerned Refugees Pose a Terror Threat: Should They Be Worried?* GLOBAL NEWS (Jul. 6, 2017), https://globalnews.ca/news/3568629/canadians-are-concerned-refugees-pose-a-terror-threat-should-they-be-worried/; Alan Anderson, *Popular Misconceptions about Canadian Immigration and Refugees*, CANADIAN INTERNATIONAL COUNCIL (Jun. 28, 2018), https://thecic.org/popular-misconceptions-about-canadian-immigration-and-refugees/ (last visited May 31, 2021).

record of human rights abuses on American and Canadian soils.[30] Undoubtedly, the overwhelming and scientifically credible evidence that COVID-19, be it natural or manmade, indeed originated in China is something that no moral and intellectually honest people would and could dismiss without offending their consciences.[31] Professors can also steer the students toward even more important issues, such as whether punishing China through trade sanctions would be effective in combating intellectual property thefts and protecting their own industries, what countries can serve as alternative and far more ethical trade partners and friends, and whether disentangling themselves from this rogue state is both moral and strategically wise and the best way to help safeguard their own democracies and protect the safety of their citizens.

• • •

Campus free speech or academic freedom alone could not have existed without the other in Nazi Germany and Mao's China: in fact, either one could not have existed meaningfully without the other anywhere. While free speech is a necessary condition for academic freedom, the latter enables and even obligates academics to inform campus free expression and steer classroom discussions in proper directions to advance knowledge and better serve society. The foregoing discussion has merely scraped the surface of political correctness and the difference between facts and opinions. The next part of the book will examine the scope of campus free speech. It will delve into the fundamental nature of free speech, look at the murky boundary between facts, falsehoods, and opinions, and explore numerous concepts in the campus free speech debate. Through exploring these concepts, it will also suggest measures that members of academia should implement to protect campus free speech.

---

30. *See, e.g.*, *China: Events of 2020*, HUMAN RIGHTS WATCH, http://www.hrw.org/world-report/2021/country-chapters/china-and-tibet (last visited May 31, 2021); *Canada: Events of 2020*, HUMAN RIGHTS WATCH, https://www.hrw.org/world-report/2021/country-chapters/canada (last visited May 31, 2021); *United States: Events of 2020*, HUMAN RIGHTS WATCH, https://www.hrw.org/world-report/2021/country-chapters/united-states (last visited May 31, 2021).

31. *E.g.*, Joel Achenbach, *Prominent Scientist Who Said Lab-Leak Theory of Covid-19 Origin Should Be Probed Now Believes Evidence Points to Wuhan Market*, WASH. P. (Nov. 18, 2021), http://www.washingtonpost.com/health/2021/11/18/coronavirus-origins-wuhan-market-animals-science-journal/; Amy Maxmen & Smriti Mallapaty, *The Covid Lab-Leak Hypothesis: What Scientists Do and Don't Know*, NATURE (Jun. 8, 2021), http://www.nature.com/articles/d41586-021-01529-3

Part Two

No one is more dangerous than he who imagines himself pure in heart; for his purity, by definition, is unassailable.

—James Baldwin,
The Black Boy Looks at the White Boy,
Esquire (May 1961)

KING LEAR: To thee and thine hereditary ever Remain this ample third of our fair kingdom; No less in space, validity, and pleasure, Than that conferr'd on Goneril. Now, our joy, Although the last, not least; to whose young love The vines of France and milk of Burgundy Strive to be interess'd; what can you say to draw A third more opulent than your sisters? Speak.

CORDELIA: Nothing, my lord.

KING LEAR: Nothing!

CORDELIA: Nothing.

KING LEAR: Nothing will come of nothing: speak again.

CORDELIA: Unhappy that I am, I cannot heave My heart into my mouth: I love your majesty According to my bond; nor more nor less.

—Shakespeare,
King Lear, 1.1.88–102

CHAPTER FOUR

Free Speech, Compelled Speech, Fact/Falsehood/Unpopular Opinion

Is suppressing free speech ever justified if the suppressor is "pure in heart," and are compelled expressions of love, for instance, to one's beloved parents, still a violation of freedom, assuming that they align with the feeling of the compelled person?[1] This chapter attempts to tackle these difficult questions by looking at the nature of free speech. It draws upon the writings of natural law philosophers to argue that the right to free speech is a natural right essential to the pursuit of truth, democratic governance, and self-development. Utilitarianism, which aims for the maximization of pleasure, justifies free speech also on these grounds. The law and economics rationale for free speech, however, should remain subordinate to natural law arguments. Free speech is nowhere more important than in the university.

If the right to free speech is natural and universal and stems from freedom of thought and conscience, so is the right to silence and against being compelled, by law or otherwise, to speak, regardless of whether the person being compelled agrees with the expression. Compelled speech, save for very few exceptions, obstructs truth-seeking, undermines democratic principles, and thwarts self-development. As numerous modern and contemporary examples show, compelled expressions, whether they contradict the speaker's beliefs or not, are often a symptom of authoritarianism regimes.

Given that compelled speech is often authoritarian in nature, even statements proven to be false should not be outlawed or prohibited, or else people are compelled to state the truth or remain silent when asked to comment on

1. James Baldwin, *The Black Boy Looks at the White Boy*, ESQUIRE (May 1961).

related topics. In addition, it would be impractical and coercive to outlaw or prohibit all expression of falsehoods. Some "truths" may have derived their legitimacy in part from their endorsement by authorities, while certain "falsehoods" may be valuable opinions that have become unpopular or unfashionable. On campus, willful or malicious misrepresentation of facts or the spread of propaganda that is found to violate academic integrity arguably can be disciplined. Outright banning falsehoods nonetheless discourages debate. Unquestioningly upholding "truths" not only prevents the pursuit of knowledge but can also play into the hands of the powerful who weaponize their dogmas, disguised as truths, to oppress and tyrannize.

I. Free Speech as a Natural Right

Chapter 1 traced the origin of free speech in ancient Greece, the general awareness among Roman citizens of the importance of conveying their messages to the Senate, and the dearth of this freedom during the medieval period. By the fifteenth century, the authority of the Roman Catholic Church, which curbed free expression in medieval Europe, was partially undermined by Renaissance humanists critical of repressive church power.[2] The struggle for freedom of speech continued throughout the Enlightenment period despite continued control of the press by both the Church and the state. In England, freedom of speech was secured in Parliament through the Bill of Rights in 1689,[3] while press freedom was broadened by the Commons' rejection of the Licensing of the Press Act, a law enabling the Crown to exert its prerogative power to control the press.[4] Britain's attempt to impose stamp duties on printed materials in the American colonies in part triggered the American Revolution.[5] Although the U.S. Constitution of 1789 made no mention of free speech, the Bill of Rights was ratified in 1791 in response to calls for greater constitutional protection for indi-

2. This section borrows extensively from a relevant chapter in the author's book *The Right to Parody*. These Renaissance humanists included Desiderius Erasmus, a Dutch Catholic priest and theologian who satirized the corrupt practices of the Catholic Church; Niccolò Machiavelli, an Italian historian and philosopher who developed a theory of free speech based on the dangers of repression; and Martin Luther, a German priest and key figure in the Protestant Reformation. The spread of heresy was facilitated by the invention of the printing press. Arlene W. Saxonhouse, Free Speech and Democracy in Ancient Athens 31–32 (2008); Robert Hargreaves, The First Freedom: A History of Free Speech 39–53 (2002).
3. Robert Hargreaves, The First Freedom: A History of Free Speech 111 (2002); Bill of Rights (Act) 1689 (England) 1688 c.2.
4. Robert Hargreaves, The First Freedom: A History of Free Speech 113–17 (2002).
5. Robert Hargreaves, The First Freedom: A History of Free Speech 115 (2002).

vidual liberties. Its First Amendment states: "Congress shall make no law . . . abridging the freedom of speech, or of the press."[6] The ideals of the American Revolution further inspired the Declaration of the Rights of Man and of the Citizen (1789) in France, where, until the revolution, censorship was universal and freedom of speech was granted at the discretion of the monarch.[7] Its Article XI identifies free speech and liberty of the press as the most precious rights.[8]

Free speech, recognized as a fundamental right in most—if not all—national jurisdictions, is what is known as a natural right. According to the natural law tradition, the enactment of laws should be guided by universal and immutable principles that are discoverable by reason.[9] While the origins of natural law theory are secular and, like free speech, also originated in ancient Athens,[10] this tradition was appropriated by the medieval Catholic Church for Christian purposes.[11] It was resecularized by the Enlightenment humanists in the seventeenth century who, claiming that the laws of nature are discernible by human reason and do not require any God or gods to confirm their validity,[12] used their beliefs to justify the toppling of oppressive regimes.[13] Whereas ethics based upon the natural law tradition provide guidance for one's actions, they also determine what rights people possess within a moral space so that others may not interfere with their actions.[14]

---

6. Robert Hargreaves, The First Freedom: A History of Free Speech 175 (2002); U.S. Const. amend. I.
7. Robert Hargreaves, The First Freedom: A History of Free Speech 154 (2002); citing Déclaration des Droits de l'Homme et du Citoyen de 1789 [*Declaration of the Rights of Man and of the Citizen* (August 1789)] (Fr.).
8. These freedoms died with the Reign of Terror four years later and were not revived until after the overthrow of Napoleon. Robert Hargreaves, The First Freedom: A History of Free Speech 167 (2002).
9. Raymond Wacks, Philosophy of Law: A Very Short Introduction 15, 22 (2006). According to natural law legal theory, "the authority of legal standards necessarily derives, at least in part, from considerations having to do with the moral merit of those standards." Natural law legal theory is to be distinguished from (though not independent of) natural law moral theory, according to which "the moral standards that govern human behavior are, in some sense, objectively derived from the nature of human beings and the nature of the world." Kenneth Einar Himma, *Natural Law*, Internet Encyclopedia of Philosophy, http://www.iep.utm.edu/natlaw/ (last visited March 30, 2018).
10. Plato and Aristotle demanded that human laws conform to a natural and rationally discernable standard of justice transcending local customs or conventions. Raymond Wacks, Philosophy of Law: A Very Short Introduction 11 (2006).
11. St. Thomas Aquinas, the Dominican scholar who reconciled Aristotelian with Christian views of life, contended that the Eternal Law is known only to God, while men can discover and participate in the Eternal Law through the light of reason. Raymond Wacks, Philosophy of Law: A Very Short Introduction 12, 13 (2006).
12. Raymond Wacks, Philosophy of Law: A Very Short Introduction 16 (2006).
13. Raymond Wacks, Philosophy of Law: A Very Short Introduction 17 (2006).
14. Randy E. Barnett, *A Law Professor's Guide to Natural Law and Natural Rights*, 20 Harv. J.L. & Pub. Pol'y 655, 668–69 (1997).

Chapter 1 has described John Milton's *Areopagitica*, a landmark essay explaining how prepublication censorship curbs the pursuit of truth. In fact, Milton's work uses ancient Athens as its model for free speech by making frequent allusions to this city and its authors. Derived from Areopagus, where the Athenian council gathered to give their advice to the polis,[15] "Areopagitica" was also the title of ancient Greek orator Isocrates' speech invoking virtues embodied in the judges sitting on the Areopagus in the early fifth century BC—virtues he found lacking among Athenians in his own time.[16] By naming his essay after Isocrates' speech, Milton insinuated that those virtues would flourish only when people are free to offer their views in print.[17] In addition, its epigraph originated from Greek playwright Euripides' *Suppliant Women*, which states that "this is true liberty where free born men, having to advise the people, may speak free."[18] Hence, Milton's work indicates that free speech is a right to which all people are naturally entitled.[19] Unsurprisingly, *Areopagitica* inspired numerous writers, John Locke among them, who proved to be an even more ardent supporter of free expression and conscience.[20]

If Milton's advocacy for free speech mainly relies on its truth-seeking function,[21] then Locke's espousal of free speech focuses as much on individual autonomy and self-government as on the "marketplace of ideas" rationale implied in Milton's work.[22] His *Two Treatises on Government*, *An Essay Concerning Human Understanding*, and *A Letter Concerning Toleration* all indicate that freedom of conscience and freedom of expression are not granted by any superior authority, but are inalienable rights with which all individuals are naturally endowed.[23] Liberty of conscience is expressly affirmed as an inalienable right.[24] Furthermore, reason can guide an individual's conscience toward the

---

15. Robert Hargreaves, The First Freedom: A History of Free Speech 99 (2002).
16. Arlene W. Saxonhouse, Free Speech and Democracy in Ancient Athens 20 (2008).
17. Arlene W. Saxonhouse, Free Speech and Democracy in Ancient Athens 20 (2008).
18. Arlene W. Saxonhouse, Free Speech and Democracy in Ancient Athens 20 (2008); Robert Hargreaves, The First Freedom: A History of Free Speech 99 (2002); citing John Milton, Areopagitica (1644), https://www.saylor.org/site/wp-content/uploads/2012/08/ENGL402-Milton-Aeropagitica.pdf
19. Robert Hargreaves, The First Freedom: A History of Free Speech 99 (2002); Arlene W. Saxonhouse, Free Speech and Democracy in Ancient Athens 20 (2008).
20. Robert Hargreaves, The First Freedom: A History of Free Speech 111 (2002).
21. Alon Harel, Freedom of Speech, *in* The Routledge Companion to the Philosophy of Law 601–2 (Andrei Marmor ed., 2015).
22. Alon Harel, Freedom of Speech, *in* The Routledge Companion to the Philosophy of Law 603 (Andrei Marmor ed., 2015).
23. Susan Wiltshire, Greece, Rome and the Bill of Rights 76, 79 (1992).
24. John Locke, A Letter Concerning Toleration (1689), https://socserv2.socsci.mcmaster.ca/econ/ugcm/3ll3/locke/toleration.pdf

truth[25] without interference by political and religious leaders.[26] This, and the fact that people have the right to overthrow their government that they have formed by a social contract,[27] imply that free speech is also an inalienable right.[28] The influence of these works, all published in 1689, was far-reaching. They were not only crucial to the establishment of the English Bill of Rights.[29] Many have traced the phrase "Life, Liberty, and the pursuit of Happiness" in the American Declaration of Independence to Locke's assertion that every person has a natural right to defend his "Life, Health, Liberty, or Possessions."[30]

Twentieth-century philosopher John Rawls more directly connects free speech with democracy.[31] His book *A Theory of Justice* takes up the Lockean idea of social contract by setting up a hypothetical situation, the "original position," in which "free and equal" people come together to agree on the moral principles of justice regulating their social and political relations.[32] "Freedom of speech and assembly" is one of the "basic liberties" under his first principle, the "Principle of Equal Liberty."[33] Further, freedom of conscience, the "religious and moral freedom" or the freedom to honor one's "religious or moral obligations," is another, and all people enjoy "the equal liberty of conscience" with regard to their fundamental, religious, moral, and philosophical interests.[34] Freedom of conscience and of speech and assembly are subsumed under a "principle of (equal) participation," which grants all citizens an equal right to take part in and determine the laws of their society.[35] In the preface to the revised edition of *A Theory of Justice*, Rawls argues further that these basic rights and liberties "guarantee equally for all citizens the social conditions

---

25. John Locke, An Essay Concerning Human Understanding, ch. XVII (1689), http://enlightenment.supersaturated.com/johnlocke/BOOKIVChapterXVII.html
26. "For there being but one truth . . . what hope is there that more men would be led into it if they had no rule but the religion of the court and were put under the necessity to quit the light of their own reason, and oppose the dictates of their own consciences, and blindly to resign themselves up to the will of their governors and to the religion which either ignorance, ambition, or superstition had chanced to establish in the countries where they were born?" John Locke, A Letter Concerning Toleration (1689), https://socserv2.socsci.mcmaster.ca/econ/ugcm/3ll3/locke/toleration.pdf
27. John Locke, Second Treatise of Government, ch. XVII–XVIX (1689), http://www.earlymoderntexts.com/assets/pdfs/locke1689a.pdf
28. Robert Hargreaves, The First Freedom: A History of Free Speech 109 (2002).
29. Robert Hargreaves, The First Freedom: A History of Free Speech 110 (2002).
30. *See, e.g.*, Ross J. Corbett, The Lockean Commonwealth (2009); Michael P. Zuckert, The Natural Rights Republic (1996); Thomas L. Pangle, The Spirit of Modern Republicanism (1988).
31. *See* Alon Harel, Freedom of Speech, *in* The Routledge Companion to the Philosophy of Law 607–8 (Andrei Marmor ed., 2015).
32. John Rawls, A Theory of Justice 11, 13 (1971).
33. John Rawls, A Theory of Justice 61, 225 (1971).
34. John Rawls, A Theory of Justice 205–7 (1971).
35. John Rawls, A Theory of Justice 221–22 (1971).

essential for the adequate development and the full and informed exercise of their two moral powers—their capacity for a sense of justice and their capacity for a conception of the good."[36]

The ideas of self-development and self-realization in Rawls's writing are far more prominent in Immanuel Kant's theory of free speech. Though generally considered a moral theorist, Kant is rightly deemed "the most forceful exponent of natural law theory in modern days" for upholding the objective validity of fundamental moral and political principles.[37] His free speech theory was informed by his strong conviction in its importance to an individual's autonomy, self-development, and self-realization.[38] His essay *What is Enlightenment?* notes that for "enlightenment," or "a human being's emergence from his self-incurred minority [or childhood]," to take place, "nothing is required but freedom . . . namely, freedom to make public use of one's reason in all matters," meaning "that use which someone makes of it as a scholar before the entire public of the world of readers."[39] The formation and expression of beliefs, insofar as they do not hinder others' freedom, do not legitimize public regulation or coercive laws, especially speech laws that would makes enlightenment impossible.[40] In addition, enlightenment also takes place on the state level. Kant's *Theory and Practice* defends freedom of the press, stating that "freedom of the pen" empowers people to speak out against unjust or defective laws and poli-

36. John Rawls, A Theory of Justice vii (revised ed., 1999).
37. A. P. d'Entrèves, Natural Law: An Introduction to Legal Philosophy 110 (2nd ed. 1970); John Ladd's Introduction *in* Immanuel Kant, The Metaphysical Elements of Justice: Part I of the Metaphysics of Morals xviii (2nd ed. 1965). A prime example is his "Categorical Imperative," which identifies objectively justifiable moral principles that must apply in the same way to all rational beings without exception. Immanuel Kant, Grounding for the Metaphysics of Morals: With on a Supposed Right to Lie Because of Philanthropic Concerns 30 (James Ellington, trans., 3rd ed., 1993). It should be noted that Kant's writings, which hold that rightness comes before goodness, does not completely adhere to what is known as the "paradigmatic natural law view," according to which "(1) the natural law is given by God; (2) it is naturally authoritative over all human beings; and (3) it is naturally knowable by all human beings"; "(4) the good is prior to the right, that (5) right action is action that responds nondefectively to the good." To Mark Murphy, the views of many writers are readily known as natural law views, even though they do not share all of these paradigmatic positions, and there is "no clear answer to the question of when a view ceases to be a natural law theory, though a nonparadigmatic one, and becomes no natural law theory at all." *The Natural Law Tradition in Ethics*, Stanford Encyclopedia of Philosophy, https://plato.stanford.edu/entries/natural-law-ethics/ (last visited March 30, 2018).
38. Alon Harel, Freedom of Speech, *in* The Routledge Companion to the Philosophy of Law 606 (Andrei Marmor ed., 2015).
39. Kant, An Answer to the Question: What is Enlightenment? (1798), *in* Immanuel Kant, Practical Philosophy 17–19.
40. Kant, An Answer to the Question: What is Enlightenment? (1798), *in* Immanuel Kant, Practical Philosophy 17–19; Immanuel Kant, Kant: The Metaphysics of Morals 30 (Mary Gregor, trans. & ed., 1996).

cies. Outlawing this freedom would deny the ruler the information he needs to govern his people and bring him "in contradiction with himself."[41]

The foregoing justifications for free speech find their echoes in the writing of eighteenth-century French Enlightenment thinker Voltaire (François-Marie Arouet) on human law and religious freedom. In his *Treatise on Toleration*, Voltaire argues that "human law must in every case be based on . . . natural law," which he defines as "the law indicated to all men by nature."[42] Religious intolerance is "absurd and barbaric" and worse than the "law of the tigers; except that it is even more horrible, because tigers tear and mangle only so as to have food, whereas we wipe each other out over paragraphs."[43] Reserving the right to disagree with this position, he argues against tolerance of religious fanaticism and criminal acts in the name of religion.[44] Unsurprisingly, Voltaire's English biographer Evelyn Beatrice Hall formulated his "attitude" as "I disagree with what you say, but I will defend to the death your right to say it" in her 1906 biography, *The Friends of Voltaire*—a formulation often misattributed to Voltaire himself.[45] Voltaire's writing, along with the writings of other Enlightenment thinkers, inspired the 1789 Declaration of the Rights of Man and the Citizen that protects the "natural and imprescriptible rights" to "Liberty, Property, Security, and Resistance to Oppression," although the modern concept of free speech as a right to which all people are entitled in pursuing knowledge did not emerge until some years after the French Revolution.[46]

---

41. "[F]reedom of the pen," Kant writes, is "the sole palladium of the people's rights. For to want to deny them this freedom is not only tantamount to taking from them any claim to a right with respect to the supreme commander (according to Hobbes), but is also to withhold from the latter—whose will gives order to the subjects as citizens only by representing the general will of the people—all knowledge of matters that he himself would change if he knew about them and to put him in contradiction with himself." IMMANUEL KANT, THEORY AND PRACTICE (1793), http://users.sussex.ac.uk/~sefd0/tx/tp2.htm
42. VOLTAIRE, TREATISE OF TOLERATION 13 (1763) (Jonathan Bennett, trans., 2017), https://www.earlymoderntexts.com/assets/pdfs/voltaire1763.pdf
43. VOLTAIRE, TREATISE OF TOLERATION 13 (1763) (Jonathan Bennett, trans., 2017), https://www.earlymoderntexts.com/assets/pdfs/voltaire1763.pdf
44. VOLTAIRE, TREATISE OF TOLERATION 39–40 (1763) (Jonathan Bennett, trans., 2017), https://www.earlymoderntexts.com/assets/pdfs/voltaire1763.pdf
45. Steven Poole, *A Beginner's Guide to Voltaire, the Philosopher of Free Speech and Tolerance*, THE GUARDIAN (Jan. 18, 2015, https://www.theguardian.com/books/shortcuts/2015/jan/18/beginners-guide-voltaire-philosopher-free-speech-tolerance
46. Déclaration des Droits de l'Homme et du Citoyen de 1789, arts. 1 & 2, http://www.conseil-constitutionnel.fr/conseil-constitutionnel/english/constitution/declaration-of-human-and-civic-rights-of-26-august-1789.105305.html. Scholars like Helena Rosenblatt argue that Voltaire (as well as another French philosopher, Jean-Jacques Rousseau) in fact favored a two-tiered policy of censorship, under which the rights of the educated and the elite to freedom of expression were prioritized over those of the masses, whose expression should be suppressed in the interest of peace and security. Immediately

Utilitarians, who do not offer rights-based arguments but aim for the maximization of pleasure for the greatest number of people, also justify free speech on the same grounds of knowledge, democracy, and individual development. In fact, it is in the writings of Locke and Milton that the roots of the concept of the marketplace of ideas, often attributed to utilitarian John Stuart Mill, can be found. While his predecessor Jeremy Bentham advocated for liberty of the press to keep a check on government's arbitrary powers,[47] Mill goes further in his book *On Liberty* by stating that freedom of speech is necessary for truth-seeking and self-realization. The fullest liberty of expression should exist within every subject matter, he argues, so that all people have "absolute freedom of opinion and sentiment on all subjects, practical or speculative, scientific, moral or theological."[48] Such freedom is "absolute" so that if all mankind "minus one were of one opinion, and only one person were of the contrary opinion, mankind would be no more justified in silencing that one person, than he, if he had the power would be justified in silencing mankind."[49] The price of stifling this liberty would be "a sort of intellectual pacification" that sacrifices "the entire moral courage of the human mind."[50]

Law and economics arguments for the right to free speech should remain subordinate to natural law perspectives. American legal scholar Richard Posner builds upon the free-speech formula that Judge Learned Hand used in *United States v. Dennis*.[51] Judge Hand's formula determines the constitutionality of regulations limiting freedom of speech by asking "whether the gravity of the 'evil' [i.e., if the instigation sought to be prevented or punished succeeds], discounted by its improbability, justifies such invasion of free speech

following the French Revolution, the National Constituent Assembly took over the royal government's responsibilities to suppress ideas in the marketplace. It was not until the early 1800s that the modern concept of free speech began to emerge through such thinkers as Benjamin Constant. Helena Rosenblatt, Rousseau, Constant, and the Emergence of the Modern Notion of Freedom of Speech, *in* ELIZABETH POWERS, FREEDOM OF SPEECH: THE HISTORY OF AN IDEA 133–64 (2011); Lyombe Eko, *New Medium, Old Free Speech Regimes: The Historical and Ideological Foundations of French and American Regulation of Bias-Motivated Speech and Symbolic Expression on the Internet*, 28 LOY. L.A. INT'L & COMP. L. REV. 69, 99 (2006).

47. James E. Crimmins, *Jeremy Bentham*, STANFORD ENCYCLOPEDIA OF PHILOSOPHY, https://plato.stanford.edu/entries/natural-law-ethics/ (last visited Oct. 10, 2019), citing JEREMY BENTHAM, THE WORKS OF JEREMY BENTHAM, PUBLISHED UNDER THE SUPERINTENDENCE OF HIS EXECUTOR, JOHN BOWRING, 11 VOLS. (1838–43) AND ON THE LIBERTY OF THE PRESS, AND PUBLIC DISCUSSION, AND OTHER LEGAL AND POLITICAL WRITINGS FOR SPAIN AND PORTUGAL (C. Pease-Watkin and P. Schofield eds., 2012).
48. JOHN STUART MILL, ON LIBERTY 11 (1978).
49. JOHN STUART MILL, ON LIBERTY 16 (1978).
50. JOHN STUART MILL, ON LIBERTY 31 (1978).
51. Richard Posner, *Free Speech in an Economics Perspective*, 20 SUFFOLK U. L. REV. 1 (1986).

as is necessary to avoid the danger."[52] Posner decomposes the cost of regulation into two components: value, or the social loss from suppressing valuable information, and error, or the legal-error costs in trying to distinguish the information that society desires to suppress from valuable information.[53] He further discounts value to present value, to properly compare with the harm, the dollar cost of which is also discounted to its present dollar cost, from allowing dangerous speech to continue that may not be incurred for some years.[54] Above all, he challenges the common perception that political speech has more value than other forms of speech such as economic speech, "broadly defined to include all speech that enhances individual welfare and therefore embracing artistic expression (including even the most vulgar entertainment) and scientific inquiry."[55]

Posner's economic perspective nonetheless should remain subordinate to natural law perspectives for two major reasons. First, one needs to appeal to not only economics but also to reason in seeking to identify what is beneficial to society. Demands for equality, liberty, truth, knowledge, and autonomy, which are natural law principles, are at least as compelling reasons as efficient governance, an economic rationale, for protecting speech rights. Second, by defining value as the social loss from suppressing valuable information, Posner sees speech as primarily social while overlooking its related role in safeguarding individual autonomy and encouraging self-development.

The last chapter has already described the importance of free speech in the history and development of the university and the mutually beneficial relationship between free speech and academic freedom in contemporary universities. If free speech is a natural right essential to the pursuit of truth, democratic governance, and self-development, then it is nowhere more

---

52. United States v. Dennis, 183 F.2d 201, 212 (2d Cir. 1950), aff'd, 341 U.S. 494 (1951). In symbols, the speech should be regulated only if $B < PL$, where B is the cost of the regulation (including any loss from suppressing valuable information), P is the probability that the speech sought to be suppressed will do harm, and L is the magnitude (social cost) of the harm.

53. Posner adds that value is a function of the size of the actual and potential audiences for the speech in question and of the decrease in audience brought about by the challenged regulation.

54. With these adjustments, the *Dennis* formula becomes $V + E < P \times L/(1 + i)^n$, where V stands for "value," E for "error," n for the number of periods between the utterance of the speech and the resulting harm, and i for the interest or discount rate that translates a future dollar of social cost into a present dollar. In the case of national security laws, subversive ideas will not likely do great harm to nations with stable political institutions, which therefore have less need to regulate subversive speech than relatively unstable institutions do. Richard Posner, *Free Speech in an Economics Perspective*, 20 SUFFOLK U. L. REV. 1, 8, 42–45 (1986).

55. Richard Posner, *Free Speech in an Economics Perspective*, 20 SUFFOLK U. L. REV. 1, 10 (1986).

important than in the university, whose role is to promote knowledge and educate its members. Arguably, it can be morally and ethically questionable for profit-oriented companies to suppress lawful expressions that go against their narrow missions or that are perceived to harm their businesses, or both. The university plays a broader, more socially significant role than an average business does. Hence, it would be downright unthinkable for universities to suppress free speech that serves the purposes of truth-seeking, democratic governance, and self-development: doing so arguably contravenes the very purpose of their existence.

II. Compelled Speech and Symptoms of Authoritarianism

If the right to free speech is natural and universal for all and stems from freedom of thought and conscience, then shouldn't people be entitled to remain silent and to not be compelled, by law or otherwise, to speak, regardless of whether they agree with the expression? Compelled speech, save for certain exceptions, impedes truth-seeking, contravenes democratic principles, and obstructs self-development. As history shows, compelled expression, whether it aligns with the speaker's beliefs or not, is often a symptom of authoritarian regimes.

If compelled silence is bad, then compelled speech is perhaps worse. Compelled speech is worse than prepublication censorship in Milton's *Areopagitica*: rather than seeking approval from the authorities before speaking, one's speech is dictated by the authorities. Whereas prepublication censorship would impede truth-seeking as it would not "[let] her [Truth] and Falsehood grapple" in "a free and open encounter,"[56] compelled expression would overwhelm a public sphere to the extent of clouding (if not crowding out) the truth. In Lockean terms, having one's expression dictated by authorities who may have no better grasp of the truth than one does—whether those expressions turn out to contain any truth at all—would also violate one's liberty of conscience and obstructs reasoning and the pursuit of truth.

Compelled speech, which often promotes certain doctrines while discrediting others, undermines democratic governance. By violating what Rawls calls

56. *See* JOHN MILTON, AREOPAGITICA (1644), https://www.saylor.org/site/wp-content/uploads/2012/08/ENGL402-Milton-Aeropagitica.pdf

the equal liberty of conscience and the liberty of speech,[57] it enables authorities to uphold certain political, religious, or moral doctrines at the expense of people who have no choice but to speak as they are dictated.[58] Hence, even if all citizens are formally given an equal right to participate in law-making, the outcomes would be skewed in favor of the authorities or those with the power to impose their favored doctrines upon those without.[59]

Compelled speech obstructs self-development. Arguably, despite being forced to speak certain words, people may still harbor different thoughts. Yet when they are deprived of the "freedom to make public use of one's reason in all matters," personal enlightenment or even adulthood, in Kant's understanding, would be far more difficult than if they can speak freely.[60] When the "freedom of the pen" is also frustrated and the media are filled with prescribed narratives, the ruler would remain uninformed about his governance.[61] While Bentham would have bemoaned an unfree press, filled with compelled narratives, which failed to keep arbitrary governmental powers in check,[62] Mill would no doubt have frowned upon the drowning of liberty of expression and "moral courage" due to compelled expression.[63]

Certain forms of compelled speech are nonetheless considered lawful in many jurisdictions and even widely accepted as part of everyday life. The most common examples include health warnings on cigarette packages and food labels indicating the nutritional makeup of food products or the presence of allergens.[64] Another example is the oath of allegiance sworn by would-be citizens at citizenship ceremonies.[65] Salutes to the national flag, however, are not

57. *See* John Rawls, A Theory of Justice 205–7 (1971).
58. *See* John Rawls, A Theory of Justice 207 (1971).
59. *See* John Rawls, A Theory of Justice 221–22 (1971).
60. Kant, An Answer to the Question: What is Enlightenment? (1798), *in* Immanuel Kant, Practical Philosophy 17–19.
61. *See* Immanuel Kant, Theory and Practice (1793), http://users.sussex.ac.uk/~sefd0/tx/tp2.htm
62. *See* James E. Crimmins, *Jeremy Bentham*, Stanford Encyclopedia of Philosophy, https://plato.stanford.edu/entries/natural-law-ethics/ (last visited Oct. 10, 2019).
63. *See* John Stuart Mill, On Liberty 11 (1978).
64. *See, e.g.*, *The United States*, Tobacco Labelling Resource Centre, https://tobaccolabels.ca/countries/united-states/ (last visited Oct. 15, 2019); *Food Labelling for Industry*, Canadian Food Inspection Agency, http://www.inspection.gc.ca/food/requirements-and-guidance/labelling/industry/eng/1383607266489/1383607344939 (last visited Oct. 15, 2019); *Food Labelling Guide*, Food and Drug Administration, https://www.fda.gov/regulatory-information/search-fda-guidance-documents/guidance-industry-food-labeling-guide (last visited Oct. 15, 2019).
65. *See, e.g.*, Oaths of Allegiance Act, R.S.C., 1985, c. O-1 (Can.); *Naturalization Oath of Allegiance to the United States of America*, U.S. Citizenship and Immigration Services, https://www.uscis.gov/us-citizenship/naturalization-test/naturalization-oath-allegiance-united-states-america (last visited Oct. 15, 2019).

compelled by laws or policies in many jurisdictions; in some jurisdictions, where citizens were once compelled to stand to the flag, such laws or policies were held unconstitutional by courts.[66]

The acceptance of certain forms of compelled speech is not without dispute. From a philosophical point of view, cigarette package warnings and food labels can be justified for the purpose of protecting consumer health. None of the foregoing philosophers makes any explicit mention of health. Both Locke and Rawls affirm the importance of the body. In his *Second Treatise of Government*, Locke holds not only that every person has a natural right to defend his "Life, Health, Liberty, or Possessions," but also that people have a natural right of property in their bodies.[67] Kant unambiguously affirms the body's role as the "visible" house of the "invisible" soul, which serves to "recall and connect" external impressions and is therefore "indispensable for thinking" and cognition.[68] While Rawls makes no explicit statements about health or the body in his writing, numerous critics have argued that his justice principles can be extended to justify a human right to health care.[69] A universal right to health care is a stronger, though subtler, affirmation of the importance of the body and its well-being than a mere endorsement of the importance of the body or its role.

Philosophically, oaths of allegiance can be justified for national security reasons, as they ensure loyalty from swearers to the nations of which they desire to become citizens. Locke, Rawls, and Kant, for example, all indicate the importance of national security and, in doing so, impliedly justify it as a free speech restriction. Locke argues that people have to give up part of their natural freedom and commit to a majority-rule society that provides a law, a judge, and an executive working "to no other end, but the peace, safety, and public good of the people."[70] Rawls contends that "an effective sovereign, or even the general belief in his efficacy, has a crucial role" in society to protect the people's liber-

66. West Virginia v. Barnette, 319 U.S. 624 (1943); *also* Holloman ex rel. Holloman v. Harland, 370 F.3d 1252 (11th Cir. 2004).

67. John Locke, Second Treatise of Government, ch. XVII–XVIX (1689), http://www.earlymoderntexts.com/assets/pdfs/locke1689a.pdf

68. Andrew N. Carpenter, Kant, the Body, and Knowledge (Twentieth World Congress of Philosophy, Boston, Massachusetts, Aug. 10–15, 1998), citing Kant, Universal Natural History 186 (1755), https://www.bu.edu/wcp/Papers/TKno/TKnoCarp.htm (last visited Oct. 15, 2019).

69. *See, e.g.*, Perihan E. Ekmekci & Berna Arda, *Enhancing John Rawls's Theory of Justice to Cover Health and Social Determinants of Health*, 21 Acta Bioethics 227 (2015); J. C. Moskop, *Rawlsian Justice and a Human Right to Health Care*, 8 J. Med. Philos 329 (1983).

70. John Locke, Second Treatise of Government, ch. XI (1689), http://www.earlymoderntexts.com/assets/pdfs/locke1689a.pdf

ties, to assign them duties, and to "guide men's conduct for mutual advantage."[71] Kant stresses the significance of the legal system in constraining both the sovereign's power and citizens' unruly desires.[72] Even engaging in civil disobedience with the aim of changing policies or laws does not undermine the importance of national security.[73] Hence, the requirement that would-be citizens pledge allegiance to the nation does not conflict with outlawing compelled expressions such as saluting national symbols and permitting citizens to express their discontent with their governments by refusing to salute these symbols.

The costs of compelled commercial speech and oaths of allegiance are minimal, as they would not likely frustrate truth-seeking, democratic participation, or self-development. Compelling tobacco companies to issue warnings that smoking is hazardous to health, for example, does not affect the operation of the marketplace of ideas because ample scientific evidence exists backing this statement. Rather than clouding or crowding out facts, these statements would help consumers make informed decisions. As well, because companies are entities rather than actual people, and commercial speech is protected primarily for the sake of audiences rather than speakers, compelling largely factual and uncontroversial expressions about their products would also do far less to violate speakers' liberty of conscience or frustrate their democratic participation than compelling people to make expressions about personal beliefs or values.[74] Oaths of allegiance hardly have any adverse impact on truth-seeking or democratic governance. For people who have decided to become citizens of foreign countries, which in many cases means forgoing their original citizenship and leaving their home country, pledging allegiance to the new country's constitution and laws is only reasonably expected of them and can do little to violate their liberty of conscience or frustrate their self-development. Arguably, these oaths should be sincere, heartfelt expressions for those who are not welfare-seeking opportunists but who willingly and eagerly embrace the new country of their choice.

---

71. John Rawls, A Theory of Justice 238 (1971).
72. Roger J. Sullivan, An Introduction to Kant's Ethics 11–12 (3rd ed. 1997).
73. For Locke, a government failing to discharge its fundamental duties loses its legitimacy and justifies people's rebellion against it. According to Rawls, protesters are entitled to break the law when policymakers no longer respect the principles of justice. John Rawls, A Theory of Justice vii 364–65 (revised ed., 1999). Scholars generally agree that Kant at least supports a passive form of civil disobedience. *See, e.g.*, Michael Allen, Civil Disobedience in Global Perspective: Decency and Dissent over Borders 108, 110 (2017); David Cummiskey, Justice and Revolution in Kant's Political Philosophy, *in* Rethinking Kant Volume I 217–40 (Pablo Muchnik ed., 2008).
74. *E.g.*, Caroline Mala Corbin, *Compelled Disclosures*, 65 Alabama L. Rev. 1278, 1314 (2014).

The law and economics formula also justifies compelled commercial speech and oaths of allegiance. Regardless of the size of potential or actual audiences, the costs of compelling cigarette warnings and food labels are relatively low, given that the compelled statements are largely factual and uncontroversial and alternative expressions likely contain little value.[75] The "gravity of evil" avoided—in this case, purchasing potentially hazardous or non-nutritious food or food that the consumers deem not to contain proper nutrition—is tremendous and justifies compelling warnings and factual information.[76] Oaths of allegiance, though not factual or uncontroversial information, are also a low-cost form of compelled speech for would-be citizens that is relatively cheap and easy to enforce. The values lost by compelling the oaths are the value of keeping allegiances private or the value of making statements that contravene the oaths. Although these oaths cannot rule out the possibility that would-be citizens betray their adopted countries at a later time, they arguably help reduce the likelihood of this grave harm by making those seeking citizenship declare their allegiance in full solemnity.[77] On the contrary, the social (and individual) costs of compelled salutes to the flag or other national symbols are likely high, as citizens may not feel any loyalty for what they stand for or may want to express a variety of messages by refusing to salute, relative to the potential harm that may be avoided by compelling the salutes—if there is any harm at all.[78]

The above is by no means an exhaustive list of common examples of compelled speech in democratic nations.[79] While compelled speech may be justified in some cases, it is something to beware of. As the following examples will show, compelled expression has proven to be a symptom of authoritarian states, which legislate speech to reinforce submission to governmental power. As such, they may signify the creeping influence of authoritarian control over otherwise free societies.

Although one might suspect that state-enforced compelled speech may be most prevalent in North Korea, because the nation is very much closed off to the world, reports about what its citizens are compelled by law to say or do

75. *See* Richard Posner, *Free Speech in an Economics Perspective*, 20 SUFFOLK U. L. REV. 1, 8 (1986).
76. *See* Richard Posner, *Free Speech in an Economics Perspective*, 20 SUFFOLK U. L. REV. 1, 8 (1986).
77. Richard Posner, *Free Speech in an Economics Perspective*, 20 SUFFOLK U. L. REV. 1, 8 (1986).
78. Richard Posner, *Free Speech in an Economics Perspective*, 20 SUFFOLK U. L. REV. 1, 8 (1986).
79. *E.g.*, Caroline Mala Corbin, *Compelled Disclosures*, 65 ALABAMA L. REV. 1278, 1324–50 (2014). More controversial examples in the U.S. include compelled medical advice in the form of abortion counseling. Many states, for example, dictate the content of informed consent that abortion centers obtain from women seeking abortion by requiring centers to inform these women of all the known risks of abortion including increased risk of suicide ideation and suicide.

remain unsubstantiated. In modern times, the Hitler salute in Nazi Germany remains one of the best-known examples of compelled speech under a dictatorial regime. Also called *deutscher Gruß* (German greeting) and performed by raising the right arm into the air at eye level with a straightened hand and open palm, it was adopted in the 1930s by the Nazi Party to signal obedience to Adolf Hitler and to glorify the German nation.[80] Although the decree issued on July 13, 1933, one day before the ban on all other parties, stipulated that all German public employees use the salute, it soon became mandatory for all citizens.[81] By the end of 1934, special courts were established to punish offenders, and even foreigners who refused to salute were subjected to punishment.[82] Perhaps less known and talked about in the Western world are the compelled expressions in Mao's China. One good example was the loyal dance, known as *zhongzi wu* in Mandarin, which became a state-enforced daily ritual in the late 1960s, not long after the unfolding of the Great Proletarian Cultural Revolution (1966–76), both to reinforce total submission to the Communist Party and to inspire "a spirit of collective worship."[83] The dance, performed both at home and in public, was often accompanied by the singing of these revolutionary lyrics: "No matter how close our parents are to us, they are not as close as our relationship with Mao."[84] These compelled expressions exemplify the power of puppetry, according to which the best way of controlling people's minds is by turning them into puppets, in other words, by seizing control over their bodies and speech.[85]

Come the twenty-first century, China has evolved into a so-called global economic superpower, albeit one with an abysmal human rights record in comparison to other superpowers and especially to Germany, which has turned

80. *E.g.*, Tilman Allert, The Hitler Salute: On the Meaning of a Gesture 6 (2009); Richard Grunberger, The 12-Year Reich: A Social History of Nazi Germany, 1933–1945 (1995).
81. Tilman Allert, The Hitler Salute: On the Meaning of a Gesture 33 (2009); Jack Knight, *Didn't Know This: Giving the Nazi Salute in Modern Day Germany Is Punishable for Up to 3 Yrs in Prison*, War History Online (Oct. 17, 2015), https://www.warhistoryonline.com/world-war-ii/didnt-know-this-giving-the-nazi-salute-in-modern-day-germany-is-punishable-for-up-to-3-yrs-in-prison.html (last visited Oct. 19, 2019).
82. Tilman Allert, The Hitler Salute: On the Meaning of a Gesture 61 (2009); Zachary Shore, What Hitler Knew: The Battle for Information in Nazi Foreign Policy 33 (2003).
83. Leslie Nguyen-Okwu, *Hitler Had a Salute, Mao Had a Dance*, Daily Dose (Dec. 12, 2016), https://www.ozy.com/flashback/hitler-had-a-salute-mao-had-a-dance/74076/ (last visited Oct. 19, 2019); *also* Andrew Walson, China under Mao: A Revolution Derailed 12, 281 (2015).
84. Leslie Nguyen-Okwu, *Hitler Had a Salute, Mao Had a Dance*, Daily Dose (Dec. 12, 2016), https://www.ozy.com/flashback/hitler-had-a-salute-mao-had-a-dance/74076/ (last visited Oct. 19, 2019).
85. Leslie Nguyen-Okwu, *Hitler Had a Salute, Mao Had a Dance*, Daily Dose (Dec. 12, 2016), https://www.ozy.com/flashback/hitler-had-a-salute-mao-had-a-dance/74076/ (last visited Oct. 19, 2019).

into a full-fledged democracy since the end of World War II. While the Cultural Revolution is long over, its tradition of compelled speech, as well as the Communist Party that has backed it, still flourishes. One widely reported example, which is as prominent as ever during current Chinese "President" Xi Jinping's reign, is the practice of forced confessions. Detainees, including human rights activists, are coerced into delivering scripted confessions before their convictions by courts—confessions that are then televised by China Central Television.[86] There are also far more insidious forms of compelled speech affecting the lives of all Chinese citizens. Not only does the Chinese government suppress religious speech, for example, by removing crosses and other identifiers from Christian churches and demolishing some of them. It also requires that all state-sanctioned religious groups fly the national flag at their places of worship, and, in some cases, also a banner proclaiming patriotism and love for the Communist Party.[87] In 2017, the National Anthem Law was enacted, which, among other things, requires attendees at events to stand "solemnly" when the anthem is being played.[88] Those violating the law, which embodies citizens' "constitutional obligation to respect the national anthem unconditionally as they do the national flag and national emblem" and which essentially compels visible gestures of respect for the anthem, could be detained for up to fifteen days or face criminal prosecution.[89]

As China has continued to stretch its claws and tighten its grip over Hong Kong, a former British colony that once enjoyed many freedoms, compelled speech was introduced into its legal system. According to the Sino-British

86. Guardian Staff, *"My Hair Turned White": Report Lifts Lid on China's Forced Confessions*, THE GUARDIAN (Apr. 12, 2018), https://www.theguardian.com/world/2018/apr/12/china-forced-confessions-report, citing a report by Safeguard Defenders, a human rights nongovernmental organization in Asia. In fact, this practice can also be traced to the days of the Cultural Revolution in Mao's China, during which "counterrevolutionaries" were frequently paraded through the streets and forced to confess to their alleged crimes.

87. *E.g.*, *China Promoting Flying of State Flags at Religious Events*, AP NEWS (Aug. 1, 2018), https://www.apnews.com/313ddb922a4b4d58b3fcce9c4a55c981 (last visited Oct. 19, 2019); Kelsey Cheng, *All Religious Buildings in China Are Forced to Fly Communist Flag as Beijing Is Accused of Ethnic Cleansing*, DAILY MAIL (Aug. 3, 2018), https://www.dailymail.co.uk/news/china/article-6022933/Religious-buildings-China-forced-fly-Communist-flag-Beijing-accused-ethnic-cleansing.html

88. *E.g.*, Jeffie Lam, *Explainer: What Will China's National Anthem Law Mean for Hong Kong?* S. CHINA MORNING P. (Aug. 30, 2017), https://www.scmp.com/news/hong-kong/politics/article/2108834/explainer-what-will-chinas-national-anthem-law-mean-hong (last visited Oct. 19, 2019).

89. *E.g.*, C. Y. Yeung, *Why the National Anthem Law Is a Matter of Concern*, EJINSIGHT (Aug. 30, 2017), http://www.ejinsight.com/20170830-why-the-national-anthem-law-is-a-matter-of-concern/ (last visited Oct. 19, 2019); Staff writer, *National Dignity at Heart of Anthem Bill*, CHINA DAILY (Jan. 10, 2019), https://www.chinadailyhk.com/articles/121/3/163/1547088346609.html (last visited Oct. 19, 2019).

Joint Declaration of 1984, Hong Kong shall retain its autonomy as a special administrative region with an independent legal system after its handover to China, except in matters of national defense and foreign affairs.[90] Rather than honoring the Joint Declaration, China declared it void after the handover and has since then chipped away at Hongkongers' freedom of speech and press freedom, eagerly embraced since the British colonial era and enshrined in Hong Kong's current mini-constitution.[91] Unsurprisingly, the pro-China Hong Kong government introduced China's National Anthem Law into Hong Kong, which, like its Chinese counterpart, requires Hongkongers to stand "solemnly" to signal their respect for China when the anthem is played.[92] The public announcement about this law, which could only have been born of an authoritarian regime, was one of the things that triggered massive protests in the territory in 2019.

III. Banning Falsehoods and Unpopular Ideas

The right to freedom of expression, one would argue, includes the right not to be compelled to make statements even if they are true or generally accepted as true. Should people only be allowed to state the truth, or should statements proven to be false be allowed by law or in universities? If the expression of falsehoods is outlawed, does it not follow that one would be compelled to state the facts, or else remain silent, when asked to address a topic? Is it always possible to draw a line separating falsehoods from unpopular opinions, or even facts, that are considered false or harmful, or both, by the state or those in power?

---

90. Joint Declaration of the Government of the United Kingdom of Great Britain and Northern Ireland and the Government of the People's Republic of China on the Question of Hong Kong, 1984.

91. *See, e.g.*, Amy Lai, *June 4—Reminiscences of a Hongkonger in Canada*, MacDonald Laurier Institute (Jun. 3, 2019), https://www.macdonaldlaurier.ca/june-4-reminiscences-hongkonger-canada-amy-lai-inside-policy/ (last visited Oct. 19, 2019).

92. *E.g.*, Kimmy Chung, *How National Anthem Law Is Being Applied More Strictly in Hong Kong Than in Beijing*, S. China Morning Post (Jun. 7, 2019), https://www.scmp.com/news/hong-kong/politics/article/3013586/how-national-anthem-law-being-applied-more-strictly-hong (last visited Oct. 19, 2019). Interestingly, this authoritarian law was mirrored by the uncivil and coercive behavior of some Chinese nationals on foreign soils. In 2019, when Hong Kong students rallied in solidarity with protesters in their home city on a Canadian university campus on October 1—China's national day—a large group of students from China, possibly emboldened by the National Anthem Law and believing that compelled respect for the government is acceptable, coaxed the Hong Kong students for not joining them in the singing of the anthem. *E.g., Hong Kong Protesters Physically Assaulted by Chinese Students on the University of British Columbia's Vancouver Campus*, YouTube (Oct. 2, 2019), https://www.youtube.com/watch?v=CUA1I_jJkjc (last visited Oct. 19, 2019).

Laws against Holocaust denial are a good example of outlawing the expression of falsehoods deemed harmful to society. In European civil law countries including Germany, France, and Austria, the denial of the systemic murder of Jews in Nazi Germany is considered antisemitism and hate speech against the Jews.[93] For example, a German court ruled that a man's statements, made after Holocaust Remembrance Day in 2010, that the "the so-called Holocaust is being used for political and commercial purposes" and a "barrage of criticism and propagandistic lies" and "Auschwitz projections," violated the country's laws against the intentional defamation of Jewish people.[94] The European Court of Human Rights upheld the German court's decision, finding the German man's argument that his statements were protected by Article 10 of the European Convention on Human Rights safeguarding freedom of expression "manifestly ill-founded."[95] Common law countries like the United Kingdom, the United States, and Canada do not have specific Holocaust denial legislation.[96]

Laws criminalizing Holocaust denial have been justified on several grounds. One rationale is to prevent the negation of historical facts established at the Nuremburg trials in 1946.[97] Another rationale is to prohibit extremists from using its denial to rehabilitate Nazism.[98] The United Nations in 2007 adopted a resolution condemning the denial of the Holocaust as "tantamount to approval of genocide in all its forms."[99] The European Union adopted a Framework Decision in 2008 requiring that all European states criminalize denials when such conduct is tantamount to "publicly inciting to violence or hatred directed against a group of persons or a member of such a group defined by reference to

---

93. *E.g.*, Deborah Lipstadt, *Denying the Holocaust*, BBC (Feb. 17, 2011), http://www.bbc.co.uk/history/worldwars/genocide/deniers_01.shtml

94. Pastörs v. Germany, ECHR 331 (2019), application no. 55225/14.

95. Pastörs v. Germany, ECHR 331 (2019), application no. 55225/14.

96. In Canada, for example, denying the Holocaust may indeed be held to violate s. 319(2) of the Canadian Criminal Code, which outlaws public statements that "willfully (promote) hatred against any identifiable group." Hence, the court may determine that the denial is illegal if it has the effect of promoting hatred against the Jews, such as by playing on negative Jewish stereotypes. In countries like Germany, statements denying the Holocaust are illegal per se. Doug Beazley, *Can Holocaust Denial Legally Be Considered Hate Speech?* CAN. BAR ASS'N (Aug. 10, 2018), http://nationalmagazine.ca/en-ca/articles/law/hot-topics-in-law/2019/can-holocaust-denial-legally-be-considered-hate-sp (last visited Jun. 11, 2021).

97. *E.g.*, Michael Whine, *Expanding Holocaust Denial and Legislation Against It*, 20 (1–2) JEWISH POL. STUD. REV. (2008).

98. Michael Whine, *Expanding Holocaust Denial and Legislation Against It*, 20(1–2) JEWISH POL. STUD. REV. (2008).

99. United Nations General Assembly, Resolution No. A/RES/61/255 (GA/10569) condemning any denial of the Holocaust (Jan. 26, 2007).

race, colour, religion, descent or national or ethnic origin."[100] This view has found support among scholars. One argues that Holocaust denial can inspire violence against Jews, whose rights are best protected in "open and tolerant democracies that actively prosecute all forms of racial and religious hatred."[101]

Despite the ruling by the European Court of Human Rights, the strongest argument against Holocaust denial laws remains that it violates the universal right to free speech.[102] Noam Chomsky considers it a "scandal" to have to debate the legitimacy of criminalizing Holocaust denial in light of the importance of freedom of expression, and "a poor service to the memory of the victims of the holocaust to adopt a central doctrine of their murderers."[103] Even Holocaust historian Deborah E. Lipstadt doubts the efficacy of such laws, which she considers would only "turn whatever is being outlawed into forbidden fruit," let alone give enormous power to politicians to decide what can and cannot be said.[104] Others consider education to be more effective than legislation at combating Holocaust denial.[105]

Apparently, Holocaust denial laws, like many limits placed upon free speech, may impede the pursuit of truth, democratic governance, and self-development, and therefore would have been deemed undesirable by the natural law thinkers discussed in previous sections. Nevertheless, given that the Holocaust has been

---

100. European Union, Acts Adopted Under Title VI of the EU Treaty Council Framework Decision No. 2008/913/JHA on combating certain forms and expressions of racism and xenophobia by means of criminal law (Nov. 28, 2008).

101. Michael Whine, *Expanding Holocaust Denial and Legislation Against It*, 20(1–2) Jewish Pol. Stud. Rev. (2008).

102. For instance, the Hungarian Constitutional Court struck down a law against Holocaust denial in 1992 on free speech grounds. Decision 30/1992 (V.26), The Constitutional Court of the Republic of Hungary, http://www.mkab.hu/content/en/en3/30_1992.pdf. However, on February 22, 2010, the Hungarian Parliament again passed a bill criminalizing the minimization or denial of the Holocaust, which was signed into law on March 3, 2010. Jacqueline Lechtholz-Zey, *The Laws Banning Holocaust Denial—Revised from GPN Issue* 3, 9 Genocide Prevention Now (Winter 2012), http://www.ihgjlm.com/wp-content/uploads/2016/01/Laws-Banning-Holocaust_Denial.pdf (last visited Nov. 12, 2019).

103. Noam Chomsky, *His Right to Say It*, The Nation (Feb. 28, 1981), archived on the Noam Chomsky website, https://chomsky.info/19810228/ (last visited Nov. 12, 2019).

104. Isaac Chotiner, *Looking at Ant-Semitism on the Left and the Right: An Interview with Deborah E. Lipstadt*, The New Yorker (Jan. 24, 2019), https://www.newyorker.com/news/the-new-yorker-interview/looking-at-anti-semitism-on-the-left-and-the-right-an-interview-with-deborah-e-lipstadt

105. *E.g.*, Jacqueline Lechtholz-Zey, *The Laws Banning Holocaust Denial—Revised from GPN Issue* 3, 9 Genocide Prevention Now (Winter 2012), http://www.ihgjlm.com/wp-content/uploads/2016/01/Laws-Banning-Holocaust_Denial.pdf (last visited Nov. 12, 2019); Adam Lebor, *A Bad Law against Holocaust Denial*, Jewish Chronicle (Mar. 25, 2010), https://www.thejc.com/comment/comment/a-bad-law-against-holocaust-denial-1.14690 (last visited Nov. 12, 2019); *Why Hungary Is Wrong to Criminalize Holocaust Denial*, Dissent (Mar. 30, 2010), https://www.dissentmagazine.org/blog/why-hungary-is-wrong-to-criminalize-holocaust-denial (last visited Nov. 12, 2019).

established as a historical fact by substantial records and evidence,[106] it is morally unsound to allow its denial, especially in countries where it happened. In addition, the argument that laws prohibiting Holocaust denial discourage truth-seeking is less convincing than if it were not backed by a large amount of evidence. Likewise, due to its objectivity, arguing that such laws would impose state-sanctioned ideologies or prevent an individual's enlightenment is less persuasive than if it is an opinion or a belief that is being suppressed. However, outlawing false statements to prevent the spread of misinformation, or the promotion of hate, may lead us down different slippery slopes.

First, it would be impractical and coercive to outlaw all expression of falsehoods. If laws on Holocaust denial are justified on the grounds that the Holocaust is a historical fact and denying that it happened is tantamount to the approval of genocide, many more examples of negationist historical revisionism should also be criminalized. It follows, for example, that the denial of the Armenian Genocide, the systemic killing of Armenians during World War I by the Ottoman government, can be seen as promoting hatred against Armenians, and should be outlawed not only in Switzerland, Greece, Cyprus, and Slovakia but also in other nations.[107] The denial of the Nanking Massacre during World War II can be considered hate speech against the Chinese. To take this logic further, the denial of the June 4 Massacre that took place on June 4, 1989 may be regarded as promoting hatred against Chinese students who dared to resist their authoritarian government. Ironically enough, to this day, the Chinese government has used a number of terms, including "riot," "political storm," or the more neutral "political turmoil between the Spring and Summer of 1989," to refer to the massacre and to deny the mass killing that happened in order to lay blame on the "rioters" and "trouble-makers" and to prevent similar protests from happening again.[108] While denying such atrocities is morally injurious, outlawing their denials would be coercive and indicates that all examples of negationist historical revisionism also need to be prohibited by law.

---

106. *E.g.*, Mark Oliver, *10 Facts That Conclusively Prove The Holocaust Really Happened*, ListVerse (Jan. 10, 2017), https://listverse.com/2017/01/10/10-facts-that-conclusively-prove-the-holocaust-really-happened/ (last visited Nov. 12, 2019); Heather Murphy, *Ancestry Digitalizes Millions of Holocaust Records*, N.Y. Times (Aug. 2, 2019), https://www.nytimes.com/2019/08/02/us/ancestry-holocaust-records.html

107. *See, e.g.*, Don Melvin, *8 Things to Know about the Mass Killings of Armenians 100 Years Ago*, CNN (Apr. 23, 2015), https://www.cnn.com/2015/04/23/world/armenian-mass-killings/index.html (last visited Nov. 15, 2019); *Genocide*, Genocide and Holocaust Studies, https://cla.umn.edu/chgs/holocaust-genocide-education/resource-guides/armenia (last visited Nov. 15, 2019).

108. *See, e.g.*, Ezra F. Vogel, Deng Xiaoping and the Transformation of China 634 (2011).

Second, outlawing false statements about a topic means that disagreements about certain aspects of it may easily get outlawed or discouraged along the way. Rather than denying that the Holocaust happened, historians dispute the number of Jews (and non-Jews) who were killed.[109] In the case of the June 4 Massacre, people have disagreed about the number of people who were massacred and where most killings happened, on Tiananmen Square or in other places in its vicinity, such as Chang'an Avenue.[110] Whereas negationist historical revisionism is abhorrent, people often have different versions of and opinions about historical incidents, the outlawing, or even discouragement, of which would impede the pursuit of knowledge.

Finally, distinguishing truths from falsehoods can be difficult. Some "truths" or "facts" may have derived their legitimacy in part from their endorsement by authorities and have not been proven to be completely correct and beyond dispute. Certain "falsehoods," which have been abandoned by authorities or have simply gone out of fashion, may contain value. Suppressing such ideas, no matter how unorthodox or unpopular, would curb honest, productive debate and therefore frustrate the pursuit of knowledge and harm democratic governance. One example is global climate change. Despite the consensus among many scientific authorities that global climate change is happening and that humans should take responsibility in circumventing it,[111] skepticism has been raised concerning the role of humans in this phenomenon and whether it is necessarily disastrous.[112] Another example is multiculturalism. Although multiculturalism is embraced as a laudable tradition or even upheld as an official policy in some Western nations,[113] social scientists note that multicultural-

---

109. *E.g.*, *Holocaust Facts: Where Does the Figure of 6 Million Victims Come From?* HAARETZ.COM (May 1, 2019), https://www.haaretz.com/jewish/holocaust-remembrance-day/6-million-where-is-the-figure-from-1.5319546 (last visited Nov. 15, 2019).

110. *E.g.*, RICHARD BAUM, BURYING MAO: CHINESE POLITICS IN THE AGE OF DENG XIAOPING 283 (1996); *"No One Expected AK-47s": Journalist Jan Wong on Reporting from the Tiananmen Square Massacre*, CBC (Jun. 4, 2019), https://www.cbc.ca/news/canada/british-columbia/jen-wong-tiananmen-square-remembers-1.5161847 (last visited Nov. 15, 2019).

111. *E.g.*, *Global Climate Change: Vital Signs of the Planet*, NATIONAL AERONAUTICS AND SPACE ADMINISTRATION, https://climate.nasa.gov/ (last visited Nov. 15, 2019); *Climate Change*, UNION OF CONCERNED SCIENTISTS, https://www.ucsusa.org/climate (last visited Nov. 15, 2019).

112. *E.g.*, Denis Rancourt, *Denis Rancourt on Climate*, http://climateguy.blogspot.com (last visited Nov. 15, 2019); Tom Harris & Richard S. Courtney, *Batten Down the Hatches: Climate Change Fear-Mongering to Get Worse*, CAN. FREE PRESS (Nov. 27, 2007), https://canadafreepress.com/article/batten-down-the-hatches-climate-fear-mongering-to-get-worse (last visited Nov. 15, 2019).

113. *E.g.*, Canadian Multiculturalism Act, c. 1988; *Multiculturalism*, GOVERNMENT OF CANADA, https://www.canada.ca/en/services/culture/canadian-identity-society/multiculturalism.html (last visited Nov. 15, 2019); Elsa Koleth, *Multiculturalism: A Review of Australian Policy Statements and Recent Debates in Australia and Overseas* (Research Paper no. 6 2010–11), PARLIAMENT OF AUSTRALIA (Oct.

ism alone, unaccompanied by unity, can lead to distrust and reduce social cohesion, and that a culturally diverse society whose members are not united by common values can easily sink into chaos and fall apart.[114]

In some circles, typically found in Western countries, global climate change and the merits of multiculturalism are indisputable facts and therefore not up for debate. A non-Western example may help Western readers to step back and perceive the perils of unquestioningly believing in orthodoxies and not tolerating alternative opinions. According to the Chinese government, Hong Kong is historically an inalienable part of China's territory and rightfully belongs to China.[115] In recent years, an increasing number of Hongkongers, especially those advocating for Hong Kong independence, embrace an alternative narrative. Many places throughout Europe, North Africa, and the Middle East that once fell within the expansive territory of the Roman Empire are now sovereign nations.[116] Thus, there is no reason why Hong Kong, which happened to be part of China's changing territory when it was ceded by the Qing Dynasty's imperial government to the British Crown, should not achieve sovereignty after the British withdrawal in 1997 and be governed by Hong Kong people who embrace democracy, rather than becoming part of an oppressive one-party state ruled by the Chinese Communist Party—a state that has a shorter history than Hong Kong and is, moreover, legally, politically, and culturally distinct from it.[117] The suppression of this compelling analogy (or other "heretical" views) challenging the official narrative of the Chinese state has enabled the Chinese Communist Party to use the latter to usurp Hongkongers' right to self-governance.[118] While

---

8, 2010), https://www.aph.gov.au/About_Parliament/Parliamentary_Departments/Parliamentary_Library/pubs/rp/rp1011/11rp06 (last visited Nov. 15, 2019).

114. *E.g.*, Robert D. Putnam, *E Pluribus Unum: Diversity and Community in the Twenty-First Century*, 30 Scandinavian Pol. Stud. 137–74 (2007); Frank Knopfelmacher, The Case against Multiculturalism, *in* Robert Manne, The New Conservatism in Australia 40–66 (1982).

115. The preamble of the Hong Kong Basic Law, the constitution of Hong Kong, says that "Hong Kong has been part of the territory of China since ancient times." Hong Kong Basic Law, c. 1997, Apr. 2017; Yi-Zheng Lian, *Is Hong Kong Really Part of China?* N.Y. Times (Jan. 1, 2018), https://www.nytimes.com/2018/01/01/opinion/hong-kong-china.html

116. *See, e.g.*, LadyKylie, *If Hong Kong "Is" a Part of China Because It "Was" a Part of the So-Called China, Should England Be "Returned" to Italy (Roman Empire?)*, https://medium.com/@kyliecthapthong/if-hongkong-is-a-part-of-china-because-it-was-a-part-of-china-should-england-be-returned-to-8e279c31ce7f (last visited Nov. 15, 2019); Amy Lai, *In Hong Kong, Colonialism Isn't a Bad Word—It's a Legacy Worth Fighting For*, Globe and Mail (Jul. 4, 2019), https://www.theglobeandmail.com/opinion/article-in-hong-kong-colonialism-isnt-a-bad-word-its-a-legacy-worth/

117. Amy Lai, *In Hong Kong, Colonialism Isn't a Bad Word—It's a Legacy Worth Fighting For*, Globe and Mail (Jul. 4, 2019), https://www.theglobeandmail.com/opinion/article-in-hong-kong-colonialism-isnt-a-bad-word-its-a-legacy-worth/

118. Hong Kong Basic Law, c. 1997, Apr. 2017; Legislative Council Ordinance, Cap. 542 § 40(1)(b) (re-

few existing states are as oppressive as China and few leaders can even compare to the current head of the Chinese Communist Party, this example shows that letting orthodoxies go unchallenged can play into the hands of those with power, who then weaponize these dogmas to oppress and tyrannize.

Although the forgoing discussion has explained how expression of falsehoods should be regulated by law, it has not touched upon its regulation on campus. The prohibition of fake news by media outlets can be justified on the grounds that readers likely do not have time to fact-check and so can easily be misled by misinformation and propaganda. Even so, checking facts can be challenging and the neutrality and credibility of fact-checking machines can often be disputable. On university campuses, there is much less reason to prohibit what are considered "falsehoods" and "misinformation."

As chapter 2 has explained, academic freedom does have a narrower scope than freedom of expression in part because it is subject to professional and disciplinary standards. Policies banning falsehoods nonetheless can harm the role of the university in pursuing and promoting knowledge. Academics, let alone students, should not be prohibited from expressing what may be considered falsehoods or unpopular opinions in dominant, mainstream ideologies, let alone be compelled to state orthodox or popular views. Blatantly false statements and propaganda would be readily discredited, as in the case of Holocaust denial, and those making the statements would suffer tremendous harm to their reputation for their ignorance, be it willful or not, or for their malicious intentions, if present. Arguably, if the willful or malicious misrepresentation of established facts or the spread of propaganda indeed are found to violate academic integrity, as in the case of some pro-China professors willfully serving as "useful idiots" of the Chinese government by denying the genocide of Uyghurs in Xinjiang despite well-documented evidence, they can be disciplined under professional codes of conduct. At the very least, however, unpopular opinions and unorthodox arguments should not be presumed to be expressed in bad faith or to violate academic integrity. Statements that have not been proven to

---

quiring all candidates of the Legislative Council to uphold the Basic Law and pledge allegiance to the Hong Kong Special Administrative Region); *see, e.g.*, Owen Fung & Tony Cheung, *HKU Student Magazine Says Hong Kong Should Become Independent from China after 2047*, S. CHINA MORNING P. (Mar. 15, 2016), https://www.scmp.com/news/hong-kong/politics/article/1925691/hku-student-magazine-says-hong-kong-should-become (last visited Nov. 15, 2019); Joyce Ng et al., *Hong Kong Court Rules Localist Lawmakers Must Vacate LegCo Seats*, S. CHINA MORNING P. (Nov. 15, 2016), https://www.scmp.com/news/hong-kong/politics/article/2046162/hong-kong-court-rules-localist-lawmakers-must-vacate-legco

be false and arguments that are backed by facts and sound reason more often than not contribute to debates. Hence, they should be assessed in the marketplace of ideas through respectful debate and scrutinized according to relevant standards.

• • •

Suppressing free expression, even with the best intentions, is not justified. Compelled expression is still a violation of freedom of speech even if it aligns with the feelings of the people being compelled to make it. Nonetheless, in the current political climate, radicals may feel ready to decry and ban lawful expression and civil discussion that run contrary to their ideologies. Attempts by the "purest in heart" to police free expression may be the most insidious. The next chapter will examine political correctness, harassment/discrimination/hate speech, and microaggression in the university context, as it seeks to draw the difficult boundaries between speech that should be allowed on university campuses and those that should be discouraged or prohibited.

CHAPTER FIVE

Political Correctness, Harassment/Discrimination/Hate Speech, Microaggression

Perhaps the desire to create a world that is free from harassment, discrimination, hate speech, improper language, and ill feeling has often been motivated by the best intentions and has come from the purest of heart. This chapter begins by examining the origins of "political correctness" and its different examples in today's universities and media. To the extent that language shapes the perception and interpretation of reality, politically correct language may help create an inclusive and equal society. Given the arbitrary association between words and meanings, prohibiting facially neutral expressions with sexist or racist roots or associated with hate groups nonetheless would lead society down a slippery slope, let alone encourage people to "virtue-signal" and show how correct their thoughts and words are. Suppressing lectures, debates, and discussions for fear that they offend certain protected groups and individuals causes even greater harm than banning facially harmless "non-PC" language. Doing so impedes the pursuit of truth, personal development, and democratic governance by favoring information and perspectives confirming or aligning with orthodoxies over those challenging them.

In Western universities, many academics and students have been shut down by their peers due to accusations, often wrongful, that they incited hatred or violence toward minority groups. Without delving into the laws of different jurisdictions, section II explains why lectures, debates, and discussions on contentious topics generally would not constitute harassment, discrimination, or hate speech. Given that there are already laws prohibiting these offenses, shutting down these topics for fear that they offend the feelings of some people is not only unnecessary but also inhibits learning and research.

Feelings do matter. The last section turns to microaggression and the idea of dignity, which is vaguely defined in legal and philosophical discourses. Although policies and measures aimed to deter microaggression, which harms one's dignity, seem reasonable, the shortcomings of diversity/sensitivity training programs, which are especially designed for such purposes, are often overlooked. Without discrediting the idea of microaggression, this section argues that recipients of microaggression should exercise their agency and freedom of expression—a core part of dignity—to resist words or acts that undermine their self-worth.

I. *Political Correctness*

The term "political correctness" did not originate in the 1960s and 1970s as some believe it did.[1] In the United States, the term "politically correct" first appeared in a U.S. Supreme Court decision, *Chisholm v. Georgia* (1793), where Justice James Wilson used it in the literal sense.[2] The ideological use of "political correctness" was bound up with the communist doctrine and refers to "doing the right thing" and "thinking the right thoughts."[3] Such a use first appeared in the Marxist-Leninist vocabulary to describe strict adherence to the dogmas of the Communist Party of the Soviet Union.[4] Professor Frank Ellis at the University of Sheffield, for instance, noted that the term was first used in the late nineteenth and early twentieth centuries when Vladimir Lenin rose to power.[5] In China, Maoists also emphasized the importance of ideological cor-

1. *E.g.*, Clive Hamilton, *Political Correctness: Its Origins and the Backlash against It*, THE CONVERSATION (Aug. 30, 2015), http://theconversation.com/political-correctness-its-origins-and-the-backlash-against-it-46862; Adam Geller & Bryna Godar, *"No More Political Correctness" for Trump Supporters*, ASSOCIATED PRESS (Apr. 10, 2016), https://www.pbs.org/newshour/politics/no-more-political-correctness-for-trump-supporters
2. *E.g.*, Chisholm v. Georgia, 2 U.S. 419, 463 (1793) ("The mode of expression, which I would substitute in the place of that generally used, is not only politically, but also (for between true liberty and true taste there is a close alliance) classically more correct."); Joshua Florence. *A Phrase in Flux: The History of Political Correctness*, HARV. POL. REV. (Oct. 30, 2015); GEOFFREY HUGHES, POLITICAL CORRECTNESS: A HISTORY OF SEMANTICS 61–62 (2009).
3. GEOFFREY HUGHES, POLITICAL CORRECTNESS: A HISTORY OF SEMANTICS 62 (2009).
4. GEOFFREY HUGHES, POLITICAL CORRECTNESS: A HISTORY OF SEMANTICS 62–63 (2009); Cynthia Roper, *Political Correctness*, ENCYCLOPAEDIA BRITANNICA, https://www.britannica.com/topic/political-correctness (last visited Nov. 20, 2019).
5. GEOFFREY HUGHES, POLITICAL CORRECTNESS: A HISTORY OF SEMANTICS 62–63 (2009); Ziyard Rahaman Azeez, *Why the Origins of Political Correctness Should Frighten You*, WASH. EXAMR. (Feb. 12, 2018), https://www.washingtonexaminer.com/why-the-origins-of-political-correctness-should-frighten-you (last visited Nov. 20, 2019).

rectness. One of revolutionary leader Mao's edicts was "On Correcting Mistaken Ideas in the Party" (December 1929), which, together with its better known *Little Red Book* (its official name was *Quotations of Mao Tse Tung*), laid out the strict teachings of the Chinese Communist Party.[6] Nonetheless, political correctness was by no means dictated only by the Communists or the left. Far less mentioned was the dictatorial regime of Nazi Germany, where being politically correct and having the "right opinions" was one of the requirements for obtaining a permit to practice journalism.[7]

It was indeed in the 1970s, in the wake of the American civil rights movements of the 1960s, when "political correctness" entered the public lexicon. It was used by social activists on American campuses as self-critical satire, a self-parody, or an "in-joke," to dismiss views that they considered too rigid, as well as to poke fun at themselves for the care they took not to say or do anything that others might find offensive.[8] They did so by telling others that they were "so PC."[9] At other times, however, they mimicked the tone of the Red Guards of China's Cultural Revolution as they called out the "politically incorrect"—meaning glaringly sexist or racist—beliefs and expressions of their fellow students ("comrades").[10] It was also during this period that British comic artists Bobby London and Borin Van Loon appropriated the term satirically in their underground comic strips to mock the excessive efforts of progressives to advance their activist agendas.[11]

From the late 1980s through the early 1990s, "political correctness" was

---

6. Geoffrey Hughes, Political Correctness: A History of Semantics 62–63 (2009) (Oct. 10, 2016), https://medium.com/@mickdanahy/political-correctness-history-future-and-consequences-da50a8967b26 (last visited Nov. 20, 2019).
7. Caitlin Gibson, *How "Politically Correct" Went from Compliment to Insult*, Wash. Post (Jan. 13, 2016), https://www.washingtonpost.com/lifestyle/style/how-politically-correct-went-from-compliment-to-insult/2016/01/13/b1cf5918-b61a-11e5-a76a-0b5145e8679a_story.html
8. *E.g.*, Joel Bleifuss, *A Politically Correct Lexicon: Your "How-to" Guide to Avoid Offending Anyone*, In These Times (Feb. 21, 2007), http://inthesetimes.com/article/3027/a_politically_correct_lexicon (last visited Nov. 20, 2019); Stuart Hall, Some "Politically Incorrect" Pathways through PC, *in* The War of the Words: The Political Correctness Debate 164–84 (S. Dunant ed., 1994); Ruth Perry, A Short History of the Term "Politically Correct," *in* Beyond PC: Toward a Politics of Understanding (Patricia Aufderheide ed., 1992).
9. Joel Bleifuss, *A Politically Correct Lexicon: Your "How-to" Guide to Avoid Offending Anyone*, In These Times (Feb. 21, 2007), http://inthesetimes.com/article/3027/a_politically_correct_lexicon (last visited Nov. 20, 2019).
10. Stuart Hall, Some "Politically Incorrect" Pathways through PC, *in* The War of the Words: The Political Correctness Debate 164–84 (S. Dunant ed., 1994).
11. Bobby Sibley, *Blame the Intellectuals for Our Politically Correct Language Conflicts*, Ottawa Citizen (Oct. 24, 2016), https://ottawacitizen.com/opinion/columnists/sibley-blame-the-intellectuals-for-our-politically-correct-language-conflicts; Ruth Perry, A Short History of the Term "Politically Correct," *in* Beyond PC: Toward a Politics of Understanding (Patricia Aufderheide ed., 1992).

made popular again, this time by conservative intellectuals. Making a sarcastic reference to Stalinist and Maoist thought police, they questioned the rise of a left-wing curriculum, such as feminism, queer politics, and postcolonial history, in universities and colleges, and criticized attempts by liberal academics to impose their orthodoxies and to prohibit what they considered bigotry and racism.[12] Richard Bernstein's 1990 *New York Times* article was credited for popularizing "political correctness," a time when the term was primarily used within academia and concerned with what should be taught on campuses.[13] In May 1991, the *New York Times* published a follow-up article by Robert D. McFadden, which explains that the term was extending its influence beyond academia and becoming "the focus of an angry national debate, mainly on campuses, but also in the larger arenas of American life."[14] On May 4 1991, at the University of Michigan's commencement ceremony, President George H. W. Bush said to the graduating class: "The notion of political correctness has ignited controversy across the land. And although the movement arises from the laudable desire to sweep away the debris of racism and sexism and hatred, it replaces old prejudice with new ones. It declares certain topics off-limits, certain expression off-limits, even certain gestures off-limits."[15]

Come the twenty-first century, political correctness policies are increasingly implemented in Western universities and outside academia.[16] To a certain extent, this phenomenon on campus has been due to increasingly heterogeneous and diverse student bodies in terms of race, sex, and ideology in an era

12. *E.g.*, Clive Hamilton, *Political Correctness: Its Origins and the Backlash against It*, THE CONVERSATION (Aug. 30, 2015), http://theconversation.com/political-correctness-its-origins-and-the-backlash-against-it-46862; Cynthia Roper, *Political Correctness*, ENCYCLOPAEDIA BRITANNICA, https://www.britannica.com/topic/political-correctness (last visited Nov. 20, 2019). Some critics attributed the rise of PC controversies among American conservatives to the fall of their familiar Soviet adversary, and the need for them to redirect their anxieties toward the post-1960s left-wingers. "'Now that the other 'Cold War' is over,' wrote neoconservative godfather Irving Kristol in 1993, 'the real cold war has begun.' The new enemy was a "liberal ethos" that had "ruthlessly corrupted" almost every "sector of American life."" Peter Beinart, *Political Correctness Is Back*, ATLANTIC (Oct. 31, 2014), https://www.theatlantic.com/politics/archive/2014/10/the-campus-free-speech-debates-of-the-1990s-are-back-unfortunately/382173/
13. Robert Bernstein, *Ideas & Trends: The Rising Hegemony of the Politically Correct*, N.Y. TIMES (Oct. 28, 1990); *see, e.g.*, PAUL BERMAN, DEBATING P.C.: THE CONTROVERSY OVER POLITICAL CORRECTNESS ON COLLEGE CAMPUSES (2011).
14. Robert D. McFadden, *Political Correctness: New Bias Test?* N.Y. TIMES (May 5, 1991).
15. President George H. W. Bush, *Remarks at the University of Michigan Commencement Ceremony in Ann Arbor, 4 May 1991*, GEORGE BUSH PRESIDENTIAL LIBRARY, https://www.presidency.ucsb.edu/documents/remarks-the-university-michigan-commencement-ceremony-ann-arbor
16. *E.g.*, Neil Howe, *Why Do Millennials Love Political Correctness? Generational Values*, FORBES (Nov. 16, 2016), https://www.forbes.com/sites/neilhowe/2015/11/16/america-revisits-political-correctness/#6bfeb4342de7

of globalization.[17] Yet some have noted that the rise of PC policies has been less often about alleviating oppression or enforcing equality than about protecting individuals from emotional distress.[18] This paternalistic trend might in turn be attributed to the rise of social media, which have facilitated the spread of the most controversial ideas that offend many.[19] It might also be explained by the outgrowth of a growing therapeutic culture, in which people are increasingly encouraged to use psychological tools to alleviate emotional and mental suffering.[20] In extreme cases, individuals are encouraged to indulge in their sensitivities and vulnerabilities and to shield themselves from expression that they deem offensive.[21]

Despite the Communist origins of "political correctness" and its pejorative uses and negative criticisms, it is defined in relatively neutral terms by dictionaries as the avoidance of language and action that could offend, insult, and exclude socially disadvantaged groups.[22] Indeed, the promotion of equality, inclusion, and sensitivity, which is nothing short of laudable, is what many PC advocates have aimed for. Many people remain skeptical of political cor-

---

17. *E.g.*, Peter Scott, *"Free Speech" and "Political Correctness,"* 6 EUR. J. HIGHER EDUC. 417 (2016); Chris Mooney, *Does College Make You Liberal—or Do Liberals Make Colleges?*, HUFFINGTON POST (Mar. 1, 2012, 8:56 AM), https://www.huffpost.com/entry/does-college-make-you-lib_b_1312889
18. *E.g.*, Neil Howe, *Why Do Millennials Love Political Correctness? Generational Values*, FORBES (Nov. 16, 2016), https://www.forbes.com/sites/neilhowe/2015/11/16/america-revisits-political-correctnes s/#6bfeb4342de7 (last visited Nov. 20, 2019); GREG LUKIANOFF & JONATHAN HAIDT, THE CODDLING OF THE AMERICAN MIND: HOW GOOD INTENTIONS AND BAD IDEAS ARE SETTING UP A GENERATION FOR FAILURE (2018); FRANK FUREDI, WHAT HAS HAPPENED TO THE UNIVERSITY? A SOCIOLOGICAL EXPLORATION OF ITS INFANTILIZATION (2016).
19. Neil Howe, *Why Do Millennials Love Political Correctness? Generational Values*, FORBES (Nov. 16, 2016), https://www.forbes.com/sites/neilhowe/2015/11/16/america-revisits-political-correctness/ #6bfeb4342de7 (last visited Nov. 20, 2019), *citing* Judith Shulevitz, *In College and Hiding from Scary Ideas*, N.Y. TIMES (Mar. 22, 2015), https://www.nytimes.com/2015/03/22/opinion/sunday/judith-sh ulevitz-hiding-from-scary-ideas.html
20. Neil Howe, *Why Do Millennials Love Political Correctness? Generational Values*, FORBES (Nov. 16, 2016), https://www.forbes.com/sites/neilhowe/2015/11/16/america-revisits-political-correctness/ #6bfeb4342de7, *citing* Jeet Heer, *Generation PTSD: What the "Trigger Warning" Debate Is Really About*, THE NEW REPUBLIC (May 20, 2015), https://newrepublic.com/article/121866/history-ptsd -and-evolution-trigger-warnings
21. *See, e.g.*, Neil Howe, *Why Do Millennials Love Political Correctness? Generational Values*, FORBES (Nov. 16, 2016), https://www.forbes.com/sites/neilhowe/2015/11/16/america-revisits-political-corre ctness/#6bfeb4342de7; GREG LUKIANOFF & JONATHAN HAIDT, THE CODDLING OF THE AMERICAN MIND: HOW GOOD INTENTIONS AND BAD IDEAS ARE SETTING UP A GENERATION FOR FAILURE (2018).
22. E.g., *Political Correctness*, CAMBRIDGE DICTIONARY, https://dictionary.cambridge.org/dictionary/en glish/political-correctness (last visited Mar. 17, 2022); *Political Correctness*, MERRIAM-WEBSTER DICTIONARY, https://www.merriam-webster.com/dictionary/politically%20correct (last visited Mar. 17, 2022).

rectness, while others contend that PC is bad when taken too far.[23] Different examples of political correctness in today's universities and media are worth examining.

A. Examples: PC Language and PC-Driven Omissions

Some of the most common everyday examples of political correctness in English-speaking countries can be found in the everyday use of language. Many changes or usages have been sex/gender-related and made to avoid the appearance of sexism. When referring to a person whose sex/gender is unknown and unspecific, it is common to use the singular pronoun "one" or the plural pronoun "they" rather than "he" (or "she"). For a long time, job titles, for example, "chairman," "fireman," and "policeman," often have been replaced by their gender-neutral alternatives "chair" (or "chairperson"), "firefighter," and "police officer."[24] It is also not uncommon to find words like "mankind" replaced by "humankind" or "humanity." It is now common to ask people about their "partner," rather than "girlfriend/boyfriend" or "husband/wife," to avoid assuming people's sexual orientation or gender or implying that heterosexuality is the norm, and to dispel any notion of traditional gender roles and inequality in a relationship.[25]

Regarding race, "people of color" is at present the politically correct term for nonwhites in the U.S., the United Kingdom, and Canada.[26] In the U.S., it

23. *E.g.*, Anna Mikhailova, *Political Correctness Has Gone Too Far and "Exceeds Common Sense," Three Quarters of Britons Say*, THE TELEGRAPH (Aug. 23, 2019), https://www.telegraph.co.uk/politics/2019/08/23/political-correctness-has-gone-far-exceeds-common-sense-three/; Ryan Maloney, *Most Canadians Say Political Correctness Has Gone Too Far: Anna Reid Institute Poll*, HUFFINGTON POST (Aug. 29, 2016), https://www.huffingtonpost.ca/2016/08/29/canada-political-correctness-poll-angus-reid_n_11761738.html

24. *E.g.*, *Political Correctness*, CAMBRIDGE DICTIONARY, https://dictionary.cambridge.org/dictionary/english/political-correctness (last visited Mar. 17, 2022); *Politically Correct (PC) Language—Used to Practice*, USING ENGLISH, https://www.usingenglish.com/files/pdf/used-to-politically-correct-language.pdf (last visited Nov. 22, 2019).

25. *E.g.*, Katherine Timpf, *Op Ed: Use "Partner" Instead of "Boyfriend" or "Girlfriend" to Be "Politically Correct,"* NAT'L REV. (Feb 25, 2019), https://www.nationalreview.com/2019/02/op-ed-use-partner-instead-of-boyfriend-or-girlfriend-to-be-politically-correct/

26. *E.g.*, Javahir, Askari, *The Political Correctness of People of Color*, POL. ANIMAL MAG. (Oct. 10, 2019), https://www.politicalanimalmagazine.com/2019/10/10/the-political-correctness-of-people-of-colour/; Varaidzo, *Why We Can't Say Coloured, and Other Questions about Race . . . Answered*, RIFE MAG. (Jan. 29, 2015), https://www.rifemagazine.co.uk/2015/01/cant-say-coloured-questions-race-answered/. "Nigger," often used as an ethnic slur directed at black people, is widely considered to be unacceptable. Places that have banned it (even when not used as a slur) have used as a substitute the "N-word." *E.g.*, Steven A. Holmes, *Why the N-word Doesn't Go Away*, CNN (Jul. 16, 2018), https://www.cnn.com/2018/07/16/opinions/papa-johns-n-word-wont-go-away-holmes/index.html (last visited Nov. 22, 2019).

is politically incorrect to call people "illegal immigrants" who crossed the national borders illegally, on the rationale that illegal acts do not make people themselves illegal.[27] Hence, "undocumented immigrants" became the PC alternative.[28] In Canada, even calling such acts of border-crossing "illegal" may be deemed politically incorrect—under its Liberal government, headed by one of the most zealous PC advocates, "irregular" has long been substituted for "illegal."[29]

In medical settings, "people with (physical) disabilities" or "people who are physically challenged" are the politically correct alternatives to using adjectives such as "crippled" or "handicapped" to describe individuals.[30] Not only are the former more neutrally worded than the latter, the use of people-first terminology indicates that the person is more important than the disability.[31] Similarly, language indicating intellectual and learning disabilities continues to evolve. "Moron," "idiot," "retard," which began as medical terms, had long been unacceptable.[32] Today, "people with intellectual/learning disabilities" and "people with mental conditions" are the PC alternatives to "mentally handicapped," "mad," or "schizo," which are still pejorative and stigmatizing.[33] "Fat" is now seldom used by doctors to describe their patients because of the stigma associated with the word. Even "overweight" and "obese" are considered insensitive by some professionals, who propose using "unhealthy weight" instead.[34]

---

27. *E.g.*, *Drop the I-Word: Journalist Stylebook Reference Guide: Offensive Terms to Avoid*, RACE FORWARD, https://www.raceforward.org/sites/default/files/DTIW_Stylebook.pdf (last visited Nov. 22, 2019).
28. *E.g.*, *Drop the I-Word: Journalist Stylebook Reference Guide: Offensive Terms to Avoid*, RACE FORWARD, https://www.raceforward.org/sites/default/files/DTIW_Stylebook.pdf (last visited Nov. 22, 2019).
29. Oliver Chandler, *Immigration Department Changed "Illegal" to "Irregular" on Webpage about Asylum Seekers as Debate Flared*, CBC (Oct. 4, 2018), https://www.cbc.ca/news/politics/asylum-seekers-immigration-illegal-irregular-federal-government-1.4847571 (last visited Nov. 22, 2019).
30. *E.g.*, *Politically Correct (PC) Language—Used to Practice*, USING ENGLISH, https://www.usingenglish.com/files/pdf/used-to-politically-correct-language.pdf (last visited Nov. 22, 2019); *Communicating with and about People with Disabilities*, CENTERS FOR DISEASE CONTROL, https://www.cdc.gov/ncbddd/disabilityandhealth/pdf/disabilityposter_photos.pdf (last visited Nov. 22, 2019).
31. *E.g.*, *Communicating with and about People with Disabilities*, CENTERS FOR DISEASE CONTROL, https://www.cdc.gov/ncbddd/disabilityandhealth/pdf/disabilityposter_photos.pdf (last visited Nov. 22, 2019).
32. *E.g.*, Ben O'Neill, *A Critique of Politically Correct Language*, 16 INDEPENDENT REV. 279 (2011).
33. *E.g.*, *Communicating with and about People with Disabilities*, CENTERS FOR DISEASE CONTROL, https://www.cdc.gov/ncbddd/disabilityandhealth/pdf/disabilityposter_photos.pdf (last visited Nov. 22, 2019); *Appropriate Terms to Use*, NATIONAL DISABILITY AUTHORITY, http://nda.ie/Publications/Attitudes/Appropriate-Terms-to-Use-about-Disability/ (last visited Nov. 22, 2019).
34. *E.g.*, Roger Collier, *Who You Calling Obese, Doc?*, 182 CMAJ 1161 (2010); Mark Santore, *Choosing Words Wisely When Talking to Patients about Weight*, YALE SCHOOL OF MEDICINE (Jul. 1, 2012), https://medicine.yale.edu/news-article/6382/ (last visited Nov. 22, 2019).

In recent years, a growing number of words, terms, and gestures have been banned or discouraged in some communities because they are now considered racist, sexist, and classist and therefore run contrary to the PC mandate. One example is the "OK hand gesture," performed by connecting the thumb and index finger into a circle, while holding the other three fingers straight away from the palm. Generally used to denote approval and "everything is fine," it is now considered a hate symbol loaded with racist overtones by people who read the three upheld fingers in the gesture to resemble a "W," and the circle made with the thumb and forefinger to mimic the head of a "P"—which, taken together, stand for "white power."[35] The use of this gesture by some members on the far right of the political spectrum helped to bolster its interpretation as a hate symbol.[36] A history lecturer at Cambridge University warned against using innocuous words like "genius," "brilliant," and "flair" on the grounds that they "have long been associated with qualities culturally assumed to be male," and therefore carry "assumptions of gender inequality and also of class and ethnicity."[37]

In addition, there has been a trend for liberal-leaning Western media not only to adopt language policies that are sensitive to race, ethnicity, and religion,[38] but in more extreme cases to omit details about race, ethnicity, and religion, or to not report stories that they think may offend certain minority groups or may lead the public to form negative impressions of those groups.[39] On some cam-

---

35. *Okay Hand Gesture*, Anti-Defamation League, https://www.adl.org/education/references/hate-symbols/okay-hand-gesture (last visited Nov. 22, 2019).

36. The Anti-Defamation League, a U.S.-based international Jewish nongovernmental organization, added it to its hate symbols list after some members of the far right made this gesture on various occasions. In September 2018, a member of the Coast Guard of the U.S. got expelled from the emergency team he was serving for flashing an "OK" gesture during a live TV interview featuring his boss. J. D. Simkins, *Coastie Allegedly Flashes White Power Gesture on Live TV, Gets Kicked Off Hurricane Response Team*, Navy Times (Sep. 15, 2018), https://www.navytimes.com/news/your-navy/2018/09/15/coastie-flashes-ok-white-power-gesture-gets-kicked-off-hurricane-response-team/ (last visited Nov. 22, 2019). In May 2019, Chicago's Oak Park and River Forest High School reprinted its yearbook after eighteen students playing the circle game showed the OK sign in pictures, fearing that the sign's association with white supremacy could jeopardize the students' reputations and future college and job prospects. Stefano Esposito, *Suburban High School Will Reprint Yearbooks after White Nationalism Controversy*, Chi. Sun Times (May 21, 2019), https://chicago.suntimes.com/2019/5/21/18633900/oak-park-river-forest-high-school-students-yearbooks-white-nationalism-controversy

37. Katherine Timph, *Cambridge University to Examiners: Don't Use the Words "Flair" or "Genius" Because of "Gender Inequality,"* Nat'l Rev. (Jun. 13, 2017), https://www.nationalreview.com/2017/06/cambridge-examiners-dont-use-words-flair-or-genius-because-gender-inequality/

38. Robert Novak, *Political Correctness Has No Place in the Newsroom*, USA Today (Mar. 15, 1995).

39. *See, e.g.*, Jorg Luyken, *When Should the Media Report on Murders by Refugees?*, The Local (Aug. 27, 2018), https://www.thelocal.de/20180827/when-should-the-media-report-on-murders-by-refugees; Elisabeth Braw, *European Media Face New Scrutiny of Reporting on Immigration and Crime*, Chris-

puses, attempts by PC advocates and minority groups to cancel talks and deplatform speakers whose views they considered offensive and politically incorrect have sometimes succeeded.[40] As the number of students from China continues to increase in Western universities, instances of self-censorship have been reported concerning policies instituted by university administrations and student clubs to prohibit or discourage China-related current affair discussions that might offend these students.[41] Although such policies might have been driven by profit-seeking motives, the PC culture—its emphasis on sensitivity to minorities as well as the need to shield these people from emotional harm caused by meaningful but potentially offensive discussions—has certainly played a role.[42]

B. How Political Correctness Can Become Excessive

To the extent that language shapes the perception and interpretation of reality, politically correct language arguably helps to create an inclusive and equal society and to promote civil and respectful learning and work environments, while discriminatory language indeed reinforces existing inequalities, although it does not necessarily create them.[43] It was for this reason that Nazi propaganda seized upon language to dehumanize the Jews: calling them rats, cockroaches, and pigs served to embed in the national psyche the frightening message that these despicable and parasitical beings were not worthy of human rights or

---

TIAN SCI. MONITOR (Feb. 5, 2016), https://www.csmonitor.com/World/Europe/2016/0205/European-media-face-new-scrutiny-of-reporting-on-immigration-and-crime

40. It has become common for universities to justify canceling talks and deplatforming speakers based on public safety concerns raised by the controversial topics and speakers. *E.g.*, Jack Hauen, *Facing Pushback, Ryerson University Cancels Panel Discussion on Campus Free Speech*, NAT'L POST (Aug. 16, 2017), https://nationalpost.com/news/canada/facing-pushback-ryerson-cancels-panel-discussion-on-campus-free-speech

41. *E.g.*, Steven Chase, *Student Group Warns Members to Avoid Upsetting Chinese Officials in Upcoming Embassy Visit*, GLOBE & MAIL (Nov. 19, 2019), https://www.theglobeandmail.com/politics/article-carleton-student-group-warns-members-to-avoid-upsetting-chinese/; Amy Lai, *June 4—Reminiscences of a Hongkonger in Canada*, MACDONALD LAURIER INSTITUTE (Jun. 3, 2019), https://www.macdonaldlaurier.ca/june-4-reminiscences-hongkonger-canada-amy-lai-inside-policy/ (last visited Oct. 19, 2019).

42. *E.g.*, Amy Lai, *June 4—Reminiscences of a Hongkonger in Canada*, MACDONALD LAURIER INSTITUTE (Jun. 3, 2019), https://www.macdonaldlaurier.ca/june-4-reminiscences-hongkonger-canada-amy-lai-inside-policy/ (last visited Oct. 19, 2019).

43. *See, e.g.*, Sandra Dzenis & Filipe Nobre Faria, *Political Correctness: The Twofold Protection of Liberalism*, 48 PHILOSOPHIA 95–114 (2019); Dale Spender, Language and Reality: Who Made the World?, *in* DALE SPENDER, MAN MADE LANGUAGE (1990).

dignity and deserved to be exterminated.[44] Gender-neutral job titles such as "chair" (or "chairperson"), "firefighter," and "police officer" not only more accurately describe people holding these jobs, who include people of different genders, but also help promote gender equality by conveying the message that people of any gender can hold these jobs. Likewise, people-first terminologies like "people with disabilities" convey that, whether disabled or not, people deserve the same amount of respect and dignity. "Mentally handicapped," "mad," or "schizo" may be as stigmatizing as "moron," "idiot," and "retard," and they may increase discrimination against people with disabilities.

Prohibiting certain words or phrases, however, does not make the meanings associated with them disappear.[45] Due to the endless interplay between denotation (what words literally mean) and connotation (what words imply), new words and phrases can readily replace the prohibited ones to fulfill their semantic functions.[46] On the other hand, pejorative expressions might lose some of their connotations over time; used in different contexts, these expressions might completely lose their negative connotations or even take on entirely different connotations.[47]

Here, one needs to be reminded that "PC" was once used by civil rights activists to keep their dogmatic tendencies in check. Without intending to "drive a wedge" between the oppressed and those trumpeting their rights,[48] it must be pointed out that banning or discouraging expressions—especially apparently innocuous ones—for the sake of equality and inclusion can indeed go too far. One argument for prohibiting even facially innocuous language is that what appear to be natural and ahistorical expressions may have cultural, historical, or contextual biases embedded in them, and so the cultural meanings of these expressions may be harmful even though their literal meanings are not.[49] Given the arbitrary association between words and meanings, however,

---

44. *E.g.*, *Vocabulary of the Holocaust*, BREMAN MUSEUM, https://www.thebreman.org/Portals/0/VOCABULARY%20OF%20THE%20HOLOCAUST.pdf (last visited Nov. 22, 2019); *"Less Than Human": The Psychology of Cruelty (Interview with David Livingstone Smith)*, NATIONAL PUBLIC RADIO (Mar. 29, 2011), https://www.npr.org/2011/03/29/134956180/criminals-see-their-victims-as-less-than-human (last visited Nov. 22, 2019).
45. *E.g.*, Cordula Simon, *How Language Works and Why Political Correctness Doesn't*, AREO MAG. (Feb. 14, 2019).
46. *E.g.*, Simon, *How Language Works and Why Political Correctness Doesn't*.
47. Simon, *How Language Works and Why Political Correctness Doesn't*.
48. Moira Weigel, *Political Correctness: How the Right Invented a Phantom Enemy*, THE GUARDIAN (Nov. 30, 2016), https://www.theguardian.com/us-news/2016/nov/30/political-correctness-how-the-right-invented-phantom-enemy-donald-trump
49. *E.g.*, Matthew Flisfeder, *The Trouble with Saying "It's Okay to Be White,"* THE CONVERSATION (Nov. 19, 2018), https://theconversation.com/the-trouble-with-saying-its-okay-to-be-white-106929

statements considered culturally biased may not—and often do not—contain biases in different contexts. The "OK" hand gesture is a great example. Despite its more recent use by members of the far right, it conveys nothing other than approval and "everything is fine" in most other contexts. While "genius," "brilliant," and "flair" may be "associated with qualities culturally assumed to be male" in the distant past, they need not—and most likely do not—carry "assumptions of gender inequality and of class and ethnicity"[50] in most contexts. Hence, banning or discouraging facially neutral expressions that may have sexist or racist roots or may have been used by hate groups would lead society down a slippery slope. To promote civility, equality, and inclusion, one instead needs to look at whether the expressions are being used in a discriminatory manner—and this can often be determined from the context.

Suppressing news stories and canceling lectures, debates, or discussions due to concerns that they offend certain protected groups and individuals arguably causes more harm than benefit. Such measures shield people from meaningful discussions that they find offensive and thereby encourage them to indulge in their sensitivities and vulnerabilities.[51] They also frustrate honest, free inquiries crucial to the pursuit of knowledge, democratic governance, and self-development—all key purposes of freedom of expression identified by Enlightenment thinkers in the last chapter. It is no wonder that many have bemoaned how political correctness, even though not harmful per se, stifles reasoning, truth-seeking, and social progress when taken too far.[52]

While PC policies aim to promote equality and inclusion of marginalized groups, shielding these groups from "un-PC" ideas can eventually lead to the prioritization of their rights over those of unprotected groups. In the worst-case scenario, such policies empower oppressed and protected groups to become the newly privileged, when some of their members or PC advocates weaponize the PC mandate to tyrannize unprotected groups or people who dare to side with these "oppressors." An everyday example of weaponization happens when some

---

50. *See* Katherine Timph, *Cambridge University to Examiners: Don't Use the Words "Flair" or "Genius" Because of "Gender Inequality,"* NAT'L REV. (Jun. 13, 2017), https://www.nationalreview.com/2017/06/cambridge-examiners-dont-use-words-flair-or-genius-because-gender-inequality/

51. *See, e.g.*, Neil Howe, *Why Do Millennials Love Political Correctness? Generational Values*, FORBES (Nov. 16, 2016), https://www.forbes.com/sites/neilhowe/2015/11/16/america-revisits-political-correctness/#6bfeb4342de7; GREG LUKIANOFF & JONATHAN HAIDT, THE CODDLING OF THE AMERICAN MIND: HOW GOOD INTENTIONS AND BAD IDEAS ARE SETTING UP A GENERATION FOR FAILURE (2018).

52. *See, e.g.*, STEPHEN PINKER, ENLIGHTENMENT NOW: A MANIFESTO FOR SCIENCE, REASON, HUMANISM, AND PROGRESS (2018); FRANK FUREDI, WHAT'S HAPPENED TO THE UNIVERSITY? A SOCIOLOGICAL EXPLORATION OF ITS INFANTILIZATION (2016); JONATHAN RAUCH, KINDLY INQUISITORS: THE NEW ATTACKS ON FREE THOUGHT (2013).

overweight people, who are shielded by the PC mandate from what they consider to be pejorative terms, insult, bully, or harass physically fit, slim, or underweight people, whom they consider "privileged" for not having suffered weight-based oppression and therefore do not deserve the same protection as the overweight do (this phenomenon might also have been bolstered by envy and insecurity, in which case those bullyish overweight people should seek the help of psychiatrists).[53] More sinister examples involve members of protected groups or their advocates issuing death threats or threats of severe violence to public figures and speakers who challenge their ideologies through respectful dialogue.[54] To the extent that political correctness can indeed become excessive and some PC policies stifle free speech and hinder truth-seeking, democratic governance, and self-realization, the historical associations between political correctness and dictatorships do not seem to be pure coincidences.

Excessive PC policies have no place in journalism and academia. The importance of respectful language in news reporting cannot be overstated. Yet the practice by some left-wing media outlets of not covering stories or important details due to concerns that doing so would lead to biases against certain groups violates the public's right to access information. In criminal cases where those details bear relevance to the crimes, such omissions compromise the security of citizens.[55] A more recent and one of the most outrageous examples (so outrageous that it made many a sane person's blood boil) arose during the early days of the coronavirus pandemic, which concerns the left-wing media's underreporting of, if not turning a blind eye to, the incompetence and alleged corruption of the World Health Organization's director-general, who is from Ethiopia, was part of his home nation's dictatorial regime, has never obtained a

---

53. *E.g.*, Melissa A. Fabello, *Skinny Shaming Is Not the Same as Fat Phobia*, SELF.COM (Jun. 26, 2018), https://www.self.com/story/skinny-shaming-is-not-the-same-as-fat-phobia (last visited Dec. 1, 2019).

54. One example is Meghan Murphy, a Canadian feminist, who has become the target of death threats for criticizing far left ideologies especially regarding transgender rights. Sue-Ann Levy, *The Intolerance Radicals and Their Meghan Murphy Circus*, TOR. SUN (Oct. 30, 2019), https://torontosun.com/news/local-news/levy-the-intolerant-radicals-and-their-meghan-murphy-circus

55. For example, it would have been a bad idea for reporters not to report the murder of teenaged girl Marrisa Shen by a twenty-eight-year-old Syrian refugee, or to omit details about his country of origin or the fact that he committed the crime only three months after his arrival in Vancouver, Canada. Although some feared that the story would cause a backlash against the Syrian community and unfairly stigmatize its members, it did raise legitimate concerns about potential problems that mass immigration may pose to the host nation, and the importance of carefully vetting applicants and helping them to integrate into the host community. *E.g.*, Jon Aspiri, *Protests outside Vancouver Court ahead of Marrisa Shen Murder Suspect Appearance*, GLOBAL NEWS (Sep. 14, 2018), https://globalnews.ca/news/4449879/marrisa-shen-murder-suspect-ibrahim-ali/

medical degree, and cried "racism" when called out for his misdeeds.[56] Universities are places for critical thinking and rational debate. Where policies are implemented to police thoughts and actions, academics and students may be tempted to channel their time and resources into virtue-signaling[57] to show how "correct" and "pure" both their thoughts and actions are. They may forget that the pursuit of knowledge, contingent on freedom of information, critical thinking, and rational debate, is the primary goal of universities. They may also forget that the knowledge pursued is necessary to democratic governance. Finally, they may forget that self-realization and self-development can only be fostered by freedom of speech and thought rather than by following the dictates of orthodoxies.

PC advocates, after all, aim to promote an inclusive environment. The next section examines concepts of harassment, discrimination, and hate speech to show how scholarly lectures, debates, and discussions generally amount to none of them. Suppressing potentially controversial or even offensive topics is therefore unnecessary to provide an environment free of hate speech, discrimination, and harassment.

II. Harassment/Discrimination/Hate Speech

According to a recent study, the "free speech crisis" in American universities is overblown.[58] The study indicates that protests and disinvitations do not only happen to conservative-leaning speakers, and points to the left-wing scholars, speakers, and students who have been shut down.[59] One example was Princeton professor Keeanga-Yamahtta Taylor, who canceled her commencement speech at the University of California at San Diego after receiving death threats

56. *E.g.*, *Coronavirus: WHO Chief and Taiwan in Row over "Racist" Comments*, BBC (Apr. 9, 2020), https://www.bbc.com/news/world-asia-52230833 (last visited Mar. 19, 2022).
57. *Virtue Signaling*, Cambridge Dictionary, https://dictionary.cambridge.org/dictionary/english/virtue-signalling (last visited Dec. 1, 2019).
58. Sanford J. Ungar, *Campus Speech Protests Don't Only Target Conservatives, and When They Do, It's Often the Same Few Conservatives, Georgetown Free Speech Tracker Finds*, Medium (Mar. 26, 2018), https://medium.com/informed-and-engaged/campus-speech-protests-dont-only-target-conservatives-though-they-frequently-target-the-same-few-bda3105ad347
59. Sanford J. Ungar, *Campus Speech Protests Don't Only Target Conservatives, and When They Do, It's Often the Same Few Conservatives, Georgetown Free Speech Tracker Finds*, Medium (Mar. 26, 2018), https://medium.com/informed-and-engaged/campus-speech-protests-dont-only-target-conservatives-though-they-frequently-target-the-same-few-bda3105ad347

and threats of physical violence for her criticism of President Donald Trump.[60] Another example was the president of Sonoma State University who issued an open apology for allowing a black student to read a poem critical of police violence and President Trump at the commencement.[61] Dana Cloud, a left-wing professor at Syracuse University, was severely criticized after she labeled protesters in the "March Against Sharia" rally "fascists" on Twitter and called upon "Syracuse people" to "come down to the federal building to finish them off."[62]

Undoubtedly, scholars and students, regardless of their political leanings, are entitled to exercise their freedom of expression on campus, and the death threats to the professor must be condemned. Yet the above examples illustrate that left-wing academics and students have had their speech shut down or criticized for reasons quite different from those of their conservative counterparts. Taylor was not disinvited by university authorities or pressured by students who found fault with her political views: she canceled her own talk after receiving death threats and slurs from email-senders with extreme right-wing views who might not be affiliated with any university.[63] The president of Sonoma State University apologized for the expletives in the poem that offended some parents attending the ceremony, rather than for its ideology, to which no one objected.[64] The Syracuse professor's call to "finish [. . .] off" her opponents could rightly be interpreted as a call for violence and criticisms of her tweet were not ideologically based.[65] On the contrary, disinvitations of

60. Sanford J. Ungar, *Campus Speech Protests Don't Only Target Conservatives, and When They Do, It's Often the Same Few Conservatives, Georgetown Free Speech Tracker Finds*, MEDIUM (Mar. 26, 2018), https://medium.com/informed-and-engaged/campus-speech-protests-dont-only-target-conservatives-though-they-frequently-target-the-same-few-bda3105ad347

61. Sanford J. Ungar, *Campus Speech Protests Don't Only Target Conservatives, and When They Do, It's Often the Same Few Conservatives, Georgetown Free Speech Tracker Finds*, MEDIUM (Mar. 26, 2018), https://medium.com/informed-and-engaged/campus-speech-protests-dont-only-target-conservatives-though-they-frequently-target-the-same-few-bda3105ad347

62. Sanford J. Ungar, *Campus Speech Protests Don't Only Target Conservatives, and When They Do, It's Often the Same Few Conservatives, Georgetown Free Speech Tracker Finds*, MEDIUM (Mar. 26, 2018), https://medium.com/informed-and-engaged/campus-speech-protests-dont-only-target-conservatives-though-they-frequently-target-the-same-few-bda3105ad347; Julie McMahon, *Syracuse University Chancellor Defends Prof after Tweet Sets Off Right-Wing Backlash*, SYRACUSE UNIV. NEWS (Jun. 26, 2017), https://www.syracuse.com/su-news/2017/06/syracuse_university_chancellor_defends_prof_after_tweet_sets_off_right-wing_back.html

63. Paige Cornwell, *Princeton Professor Cancels Seattle Talk after Fox News Segment, Death Threats*, SEATTLE TIMES (Jun. 1, 2017), https://www.seattletimes.com/seattle-news/princeton-professor-cancels-seattle-talk-after-fox-news-segment-death-threats/

64. Scott Jaschik, *Anger over Poem and Apology at Sonoma State*, INSIDE HIGHER EDUC. (Jun. 9, 2017), https://www.insidehighered.com/quicktakes/2017/06/09/anger-over-poem-and-apology-sonoma-state

65. *See* Julie McMahon, *Syracuse University Chancellor Defends Prof after Tweet Sets Off Right-Wing*

conservative speakers by university authorities and attempts to censor conservative speech by academics or students, or both, were almost always rationalized on ideological grounds, and often made after accusations—both vague and unfounded—that their speech incited violence or hate speech, or both, against minority groups.[66]

Shutting down expression on ideological grounds violates speakers' freedom of expression, unless the expression violates laws on harassment, discrimination, or hate speech. Without delving into legal cases or offering detailed statutory analyses, this section explains why lectures, debates, or discussions on what are generally known as controversial topics do not cause harassment or discrimination or constitute hate speech.

A. Harassment

In many jurisdictions, harassment refers generally to a course of uninvited and unwelcome conduct that annoys, threatens, alarms, or otherwise puts a person in fear of their safety.[67] Conduct can be physical, verbal, or nonverbal, and the perpetrator can be a stranger or someone known to the victim.[68] It may take the form of stalking, unwanted phone calls, unwelcome physical contact, inappropriate comments, threatening gestures, impediment of a person's movement, or interference with a person's work.[69] In some jurisdictions, where harassment is a civil—in addition to a criminal—offense, it covers a wider spectrum of behaviors, and may include those that merely distress or humiliate a person, quite often on account of race, religion, sex, age, disability, or any other grounds of

Backlash, SYRACUSE UNIV. NEWS (Jun. 26, 2017), https://www.syracuse.com/su-news/2017/06/syracuse_university_chancellor_defends_prof_after_tweet_sets_off_right-wing_back.html

66. *E.g.*, Maleeha Syed, *Middlebury College Cancels Talk with Conservative Speaker for Safety Purposes*, BURLINGTON FREE PRESS (Apr. 17, 2019), https://www.burlingtonfreepress.com/story/news/local/2019/04/17/campus-free-speech-middlebury-college-charles-murray-european-parliament-ryszard-legutko/3494450002/; Tristin Hopper, *"Not Every Opinion Is Valid": Carleton University Free Speech Wall Torn Down within Hours*, NAT'L POST (Jan. 22, 2013), https://nationalpost.com/news/canada/not-every-opinion-is-valid-activist-censors-peers-by-tearing-down-universitys-free-speech-wall
67. *See, e.g.*, Criminal Code, s. 264(1) (R.S.C., 1985, c. C-46) (Can.); N.Y. Penal Code, s. 240.25–26, 30–31.
68. *See, e.g.*, Criminal Code, s. 264(2) (Can.); N.Y. Penal Code, s. 240.25–26, 30–31; *A Handbook for Police and Crown Prosecutors on Criminal Harassment*, DEPARTMENT OF JUSTICE OF CANADA, https://www.justice.gc.ca/eng/rp-pr/cj-jp/fv-vf/har/part1.html (last accessed Dec. 20, 2019).
69. *See, e.g.*, Criminal Code, s. 264(2) (Can.); N.Y. Penal Code, s. 240.25–26, 30–31; *A Handbook for Police and Crown Prosecutors on Criminal Harassment*, DEPARTMENT OF JUSTICE OF CANADA, https://www.justice.gc.ca/eng/rp-pr/cj-jp/fv-vf/har/part1.html (last accessed Dec. 20, 2019).

discrimination in residential or commercial premises or employment settings.[70] These may include, but are by no means limited to, regular and repeated slurs, epithets, lewd propositions, and insults.[71] Generally, the harassing conduct persists over time or occurs at least once, although one-time incidents, if serious and egregious enough, can be considered harassment.[72]

If the right to free speech is universal and fundamental, so is the right to be free from harassment and threats to one's safety due to speech. Locke's idea of freedom of speech is tied to his belief in individual autonomy. He also contends that the government should protect people's "Life, Health, Liberty, or Possessions."[73] It follows that harassing speech, which threatens the life, health, liberty, or autonomy of one's fellows, must be prohibited. Likewise, Rawls's basic liberties includes the "integrity of the person," which covers "freedom from psychological oppression and physical assault."[74] From Kant's moralistic perspective, all free and equal members of a community should act in such a way that they would be willing for that way to become a universal law.[75] They also have the "perfect duty" not to use themselves or others "merely as a means to an end."[76] Harassing others to satisfy one's desires—whatever they may be—is exploiting others merely as a means to a selfish end. Free speech has limits, one of which is that people have no right to use their speech to harass others, to threaten them, or to put them in fear of their safety.

---

70. *See, e.g.*, Canadian Human Rights Act, s. 14(1)(2) (R.S.C., 1985, c. H-6) (Can.); Ontario Human Rights Code, ss. 10(1) (Can.).
71. *E.g.*, *Racial Harassment and Poisoned Environments (Fact Sheet)*, ONTARIO HUMAN RIGHTS COMMISSION, http://www.ohrc.on.ca/en/racial-harassment-and-poisoned-environments-fact-sheet (last visited Dec. 20, 2019).
72. *E.g.*, *Is It Harassment? A Tool to Guide Employees*, CANADIAN GOVERNMENT, https://www.canada.ca/en/government/publicservice/wellness-inclusion-diversity-public-service/harassment-conflict-resolution/harassment-tool-employees.html (last visited Dec. 20, 2019); *Attention New York Employers: When It Comes to Workplace Harassment, Times Are Changing*, NAT'L L. REV. (Aug. 20, 2019), https://www.natlawreview.com/article/attention-new-york-employers-when-it-comes-to-workplace-harassment-times-are
73. JOHN LOCKE, SECOND TREATISE OF GOVERNMENT, ch. XVII–XVIX (1689), http://www.earlymoderntexts.com/assets/pdfs/locke1689a.pdf
74. JOHN RAWLS, A THEORY OF JUSTICE 53 (1971).
75. This is Kant's first formulation of the Categorical Imperative: "The first principle of morality is, therefore, act according to a maxim which can, at the same time, be valid as universal law.—Any maxim which does not so qualify is contrary to morality." IMMANUEL KANT, GROUNDING FOR THE METAPHYSICS OF MORALS: WITH ON A SUPPOSED RIGHT TO LIE BECAUSE OF PHILANTHROPIC CONCERNS 30 (James Ellington, trans., 3rd ed., 1993).
76. Kant's second formulation of the Categorical Imperative is as follows: "Act in such a way that you always treat humanity, whether in your own person or in the person of any other, never simply as a means, but always at the same time as an end." IMMANUEL KANT, GROUNDING FOR THE METAPHYSICS OF MORALS: WITH ON A SUPPOSED RIGHT TO LIE BECAUSE OF PHILANTHROPIC CONCERNS 36 (James Ellington, trans., 3d ed., 1993).

Reports indicate that all forms of harassment have happened in Western universities. According to one U.K.-based report, racial harassment of both students and staff is rampant in universities.[77] Victims, more likely than not ethno-racial minorities and those of foreign origins, are subjected to physical attacks, verbal death threats, name-calling, insults, and jokes.[78] Sexual harassment and harassment targeting gender minorities, which take the form of stalking, groping, texting, and other forms of assault, are also widespread in some North American universities.[79]

Because harassment takes the form of physical, verbal, or nonverbal threats, or in its milder form repeated slurs and insults targeting individuals, academic lectures, discussions, and scholarly debates, even on the most contentious and potentially offensive topics, generally do not constitute harassment. Just as talks advancing the "Black Lives Matter" movement do not constitute harassment of white people, discussing whether New York's law on gender pronouns compels speech by no means harasses gender minorities. Neither do debates on the merits of affirmative action or multiculturalism policies amount to harassment of ethno-racial minorities, immigrants, and refugees. Clearly, discussing China's attempts to infiltrate Western governments, or whether Western nations should attempt to curb the Chinese government's human rights violations in Hong Kong, Tibet, and Xinjiang, cannot by any logic (or any stretch of the imagination) be understood as harassment of its nationalistic Chinese natives studying or working at universities where such discussions take place—unless causing offense or disagreement is considered harassment, a "logic" that might be valued under totalitarian and authoritarian regimes that habitually pull the race card and cry "racism" when criticized, but does not hold in the free world.

Harassment of speakers and participants, however, has frequently occurred

---

77. Judith Burns, *Universities "Oblivious" to Campus Racial Abuse*, BBC (Oct. 23, 2019), https://www.bbc.com/news/education-50123697 (last visited Dec. 20, 2019).

78. Judith Burns, *Universities "Oblivious" to Campus Racial Abuse*, BBC (Oct. 23, 2019), https://www.bbc.com/news/education-50123697 (last visited Dec. 20, 2019).

79. Jeff Outhit, *Stalking, Harassment, Unwanted Sex Widespread on Campuses, Survey Suggests*, THE RECORD (Mar. 20, 2019), https://www.therecord.com/news-story/9231431-stalking-harassment-unwanted-sex-widespread-on-campuses-survey-suggests/; *This Prof Put out a Call for Stories of Harassment on Campus—and Received Hundreds of Responses*, CBC (Dec. 5, 2017), https://www.cbc.ca/radio/asithappens/as-it-happens-tuesday-edition-1.4433699/this-prof-put-out-a-call-for-stories-of-harassment-on-campus-and-received-hundreds-of-responses-1.4433721 (last visited Dec. 20, 2019); Adrienne Green & Alia Wong, *Stalking, Harassment, Unwanted Sex Widespread on Campuses, Survey Suggests*, ATLANTIC (Sep. 22, 2015), https://www.theatlantic.com/education/archive/2015/09/campus-sexual-assault-lgbt-students/406684/

and has been instigated by those who disagreed with the contents of the discussions or simply took offense at the topics. Outside of liberal campuses, activists for left-wing causes occasionally receive death threats from extremists campaigning against their activism.[80] On some liberal campuses, however, conservative speakers are more likely the victims. For example, speakers criticizing transgender politics and laws on gender pronouns have been harassed by trans activists.[81] In addition, Tibetan and Uyghur student activists addressing the Chinese government's human rights violations have been harassed by nationalistic students from China.[82] Evidence indicated that their actions were backed by the Chinese government.[83]

B. Discrimination

Lectures, debates, and discussions on controversial topics generally would not lead to discrimination or violate relevant laws. Discrimination generally refers to the unfair treatment of people based on their membership or perceived membership in certain groups. The prohibited grounds of discrimination usually include race, national or ethnic origin, religion, sex, marital status, family status, and disability.[84] Some added grounds in recent years include gender

80. Paige Cornwell, *Princeton Professor Cancels Seattle Talk after Fox News Segment, Death Threats*, SEATTLE TIMES (Jun. 1, 2017), https://www.seattletimes.com/seattle-news/princeton-professor-cancels-seattle-talk-after-fox-news-segment-death-threats/; Oliver Milman, *Climate Scientists Face Harassment, Threats and Fears of "McCarthyist Attacks,"* THE GUARDIAN, Feb. 22, 2017, https://www.theguardian.com/environment/2017/feb/22/climate-change-science-attacks-threats-trump
81. *E.g.*, Camille Bains, *B.C. Event Featuring Meghan Murphy Moved to New Venue over Security Concerns*, CANADIAN PRESS (Nov. 1, 2019), https://bc.ctvnews.ca/b-c-event-featuring-meghan-murphy-moved-to-new-venue-over-security-concerns-1.4667130; Karen Yossman, *Meet Meghan Murphy, the "Transphobic" Feminist Booted off Twitter . . . but Who Won't Be Silenced*, THE TELEGRAPH (May 22, 2019), https://www.telegraph.co.uk/women/life/meet-meghan-murphy-transphobic-feminist-booted-twitter-wont/; Sarina Grewal, *University, Kingston Police Respond to Jordan Peterson Protests*, QUEENS J. (Mar. 7, 2018), https://www.queensjournal.ca/story/2018-03-07/news/university-kingston-police-respond-to-jordan-peterson-protests/
82. *E.g.*, Tom Blackwell, *Student Groups Call for Ottawa to Investigate Alleged Interference by Chinese Officials on Canadian Campuses*, NAT'L POST (Feb. 21, 2019), https://nationalpost.com/news/student-groups-call-for-ottawa-to-investigate-alleged-interference-by-chinese-officials-on-canadian-campuses
83. Tom Blackwell, *Student Groups Call for Ottawa to Investigate Alleged Interference by Chinese Officials on Canadian Campuses*, NAT'L POST (Feb. 21, 2019), https://nationalpost.com/news/student-groups-call-for-ottawa-to-investigate-alleged-interference-by-chinese-officials-on-canadian-campuses
84. *See, e.g.*, Civil Rights Act of 1964, s. 201(a) (Pub. L. 88–352, 78 Stat. 241); Americans with Disabilities Act of 1990 (42 U.S.C. § 12101); Canadian Human Rights Act, ss. 3(1), 5, 7 (R.S.C., 1985, c. H-6) (Can.).

identity and expression.[85] Denying people goods, services, facilities, accommodations, and employment on these grounds amounts to discrimination.[86]

The right to free speech does not extend to the right to discriminate against others through speech, and it can be argued that the right not to be discriminated against as a human being is also fundamental to all. Locke and Kant, who lived several centuries ago, have been criticized by contemporary critics for what they consider racism and sexism in their writings.[87] Regardless of what Locke thought about other races than his own, the right against discriminatory treatment is implied in his belief in the equal right to life, liberty and property for all.[88] It is also a logical extension of Kant's argument that all human beings are free and equal members of society, and that they should treat others the way they want to be treated.[89] While freedom of expression is a fundamental liberty under Rawls's first principle, this freedom does not extend to advocacy against the fundamentals of justice, including the exclusion or subordination of certain groups.[90]

Like harassment, discrimination happens in universities despite laws and policies against it. In one case, a U.S. court held that an American academic was denied tenure and promotion due to her transgender identity.[91] In another case, an African American professor won his discrimination claim against the university, which was found to create a hostile work environment for him based on his race.[92] More recently, a black student was found to be subject to dispropor-

85. *E.g.*, *Gender Expression Non-Discrimination Act (GENDA) Takes Effect in New York*, NAT'L L. REV. (Feb. 28, 2019), https://www.natlawreview.com/article/gender-expression-non-discrimination-act-genda-takes-effect-new-york; Marie-Philippe Lavoie, *Canada: Senate Passes Landmark Transgender Rights Bill*, GLOBAL LEG. MONITOR (Sep. 11, 2017), https://www.loc.gov/law/foreign-news/article/canada-senate-passes-landmark-transgender-rights-bill/

86. *E.g.*, Civil Rights Act of 1964, s. 201(a); Canadian Human Rights Act, ss. 5–7.

87. *E.g.*, Julie K. Ward, *The Roots of Modern Racism*, THE CRITIQUE (Sept.–Oct. 2016), http://www.thecritique.com/articles/the-roots-of-modern-racism/ (last visited Dec. 28, 2019).

88. JOHN LOCKE, SECOND TREATISE OF GOVERNMENT, ch. XVII–XVIX (1689), http://www.earlymoderntexts.com/assets/pdfs/locke1689a.pdf

89. IMMANUEL KANT, GROUNDING FOR THE METAPHYSICS OF MORALS: WITH ON A SUPPOSED RIGHT TO LIE BECAUSE OF PHILANTHROPIC CONCERNS 30 (James Ellington, trans., 3d ed., 1993).

90. Jeremy Waldron, *What Does a Well-Ordered Society Look Like?*, 2009 HOLMES LECTURES AT HARVARD LAW SCHOOL (Oct. 5–7, 2009), at 4, http://www.law.nyu.edu/sites/default/files/ECM_PRO_063313.pdf

91. John Paul Brammer, *Jury Awards Transgender Professor $1.1 Million in Discrimination Case*, NBC NEWS (Nov. 20, 2017), https://www.nbcnews.com/feature/nbc-out/jury-awards-transgender-professor-1-1-million-discrimination-case-n822646 (last visited Dec. 28, 2019).

92. Jayati Ramakrishnan, *Eugene Professor Awarded $127,000 in Racial Discrimination Case against University*, OREGONIAN (May 6, 2019), https://www.oregonlive.com/pacific-northwest-news/2019/05/eugene-professor-awarded-127000-in-racial-discrimination-case-against-university.html

tionate and unreasonable response by campus police at a Canadian university because of his race.[93]

Lectures, debates, and discussions on contentious topics generally do not amount to discrimination. Merely arguing that requiring the use of preferred pronouns is a form of compelled speech and legislating their use is an illegitimate intrusion of freedom of speech, for example, does not amount to discrimination against gender minorities who are in favor of the law on pronoun use, even if the law states that refusal to use such pronouns is discrimination against gender minorities. Similarly, debating the pros and cons of affirmative action or multiculturalism policies has no bearing on how participants in the debates treat ethno-racial minorities, immigrants, refugees, or any groups who benefit from these policies. Thus, regardless of one's position, it does not amount to favoritism toward, or discrimination against, these groups. There is no doubt that the severest criticism of the Chinese government and its dark record of mass murders and other human rights violations and urging sanctions against it do not amount to discrimination against Chinese natives at universities, unless these individuals and their government are taken as the same entity. Although certain nationalistic individuals indeed might have been taught to identify strongly with their government, individuals, save some exceptions, are generally not held responsible for the crimes of their governments.

It is indeed possible for discussions such as the above to contain biased remarks and to promote discrimination based on stereotypes. Discussion on affirmative action and multiculturalism policies, for example, can contain generalizations about races that might contribute to racial discrimination. Yet such concerns only bolster the case for promoting—rather than banning—discussion of these topics. Speakers who are unaware of the discriminatory messages in their talks may then be made aware of them through engaging with their audiences, while those knowingly making discriminatory remarks can get exposed. In addition, well-informed and well-reasoned discussion can be misquoted or completely taken out of context by some people to further their discriminatory agendas. Speakers are nonetheless responsible only for the content of their speech and not for the ways in which it may be used by others—although they may seek to reduce the chances of misappropriation, for instance, through clarification and denouncement of discriminatory acts perceived to have resulted

93. Christopher Whan, *Black Student Carded on UOttawa's Campus in June Was the Subject of Discrimination: Report*, GLOBAL NEWS (Oct. 1, 2019), https://globalnews.ca/news/5975870/black-student-uottawa-carded/

from their speech. On the other hand, prohibiting speakers or participants from discussing certain topics merely on the grounds of their group memberships—examples include the banning of discussions on Black Lives Matter by speakers who are not African Americans or the prohibition of criticism of Islam by non-Muslims—on the presumption that any such discussions must be biased or discriminatory and that the views arising from those discussions should be outright invalidated, is arguably a very self-righteous form of discrimination under the pretext of diversity.

C. Hate Speech

Hate speech can generally be understood as "public speech that expresses hate or encourages violence towards a person or group based on something such as race, religion, sex, or sexual orientation."[94] In the U.S., what is known as "hate speech" is constitutionally protected and only speech that calls for imminent lawless action upon a person or group and is likely to lead to such action is prohibited.[95] In countries like Canada and the U.K., hate speech legislation forbids expression that threatens, advocates the genocide of, or incites hatred against any people on account of identifiable characteristics such as color, race, religion, national or ethnic origin, age, sex, sexual orientation, or gender identity and expression.[96] In some other countries, where hate speech legislation also aims to protect human dignity, the offense has a much lower legal threshold and includes expression that insults, humiliates, and maliciously slurs members for identifiable characteristics in ways that violate their human dignity.[97]

Although many philosophers would have agreed that people have a natural right against harassment and discrimination, whether they would have agreed that one also has a natural right against hate speech may depend on how hate speech is defined.[98] If hate speech is defined as speech that threatens safety or

---

94. *Hate Speech*, Cambridge Dictionary, https://dictionary.cambridge.org/us/dictionary/english/hate-speech (last visited Dec. 28, 2019).
95. Brandenberg v. Ohio, 395 U.S. 444, 447 (1969).
96. *E.g.*, Criminal Code, S.C. 1985, c C-46, s. 319 (1) & (2) (Can.); Public Order Act, 1986, c. 4, s. 18(1) (U.K.); Racial and Religious Hatred Act, 2006, c. 1, s. 29(A) (U.K.); Criminal Justice and Immigration Act, 2008, c. 4, s. 74 (U.K.).
97. *E.g.*, Strafgesetzbuch, s. 130 (1) & (2) (Germany).
98. This paragraph provides a more nuanced discussion than the subsection in chapter 1 of the author's previous work *The Right to Parody*, which explains very generally why hate speech is a natural limit on the fundamental right to free speech.

incites violence or genocide, then they likely would have agreed that hate speech should be prohibited along with harassment and discrimination. The answer is not that certain if hate speech is defined more broadly to include speech that offends human dignity. It is uncertain whether the equal rights to life, liberty, and property in Locke's writing imply that people are also entitled to human dignity and that this dignity must be defended at the expense of free speech.[99] Rawls would have argued against the exclusion or subordination of certain groups because it is against his principles of liberty and justice, but it is unclear whether his ideas of inclusion and equality preclude offending the dignity of individuals by free expression.[100] Kant did recognize human dignity in his work. He states that a human being is not a means but an end in itself, and "humanity . . . alone has dignity."[101] Human dignity is related to "free will" and human agency—the human dignity to act freely and choose your own actions.[102] However, with this definition, only expression interfering with the human agency to act freely would be hate speech, such as incitement of violence, hatred, and genocide prohibited under American, British, and Canadian laws. Expression that merely humiliates or insults, which are prohibited under German law, may not fit the bill, as feelings of humiliation and insult can be subjective. The concept of dignity will be examined further later in this chapter.

Would lectures, discussions, and debates amount to hate speech? If hate speech is defined as expression that threatens the safety of or incites violence or hate against certain groups, respectful discussions and debates on controversial topics would be unlikely to constitute hate speech. As the previous subsections have explained, discussions on topics like gender pronouns, affirmative action, multiculturalism, and China generally would not constitute harassment, incite violence, or promote discrimination. What if hate speech is more broadly defined to include expression that offends human dignity? There is no reason why discussion of these topics would reasonably be considered hate speech. For example, the argument that gender pronoun laws violate freedom of speech targets the government, not the gender nonbinary people who might or might

---

99. *See* John Locke, Second Treatise of Government, ch. XVII–XVIX (1689), http://www.earlymoderntexts.com/assets/pdfs/locke1689a.pdf

100. *See* Jeremy Waldron, *What Does a Well-Ordered Society Look Like?*, 2009 Holmes Lectures at Harvard Law School (Oct. 5–7, 2009), at 4, http://www.law.nyu.edu/sites/default/files/ECM_PRO_063313.pdf

101. Immanuel Kant, *Groundwork of the Metaphysics of Morals* 4: 434–435, *in* Immanuel Kant, Practical Philosophy 84–85 (Mary J. Gregor, trans. & ed., 1996).

102. Phillip Anthony O'Hara, Encyclopedia of Political Economy 471 (1999).

not benefit from such laws. If anything, it is the former, not the latter, whose dignity is offended: this is especially true given that people making this argument may object to the legislation only and not the use of the pronouns. Well-reasoned arguments for and against affirmative action and multiculturalism policies can be made without offending ethno-racial and religious minority—or majority—groups by avoiding harmful stereotypes. Likewise, criticisms of hostile authoritarian governments are not criticisms of their people and therefore cannot be said to offend their dignity, except those secret agents or rabid nationalists who hopelessly identify with these governments, which might not truly care about them and might see them merely as disposable tools.

While academics or students were very rarely, if ever, convicted for hate speech in Western universities,[103] "hate speech" and related catchphrases have been frequently and even mindlessly used by certain campus groups to label speakers or contents that they find objectionable and attempt to shut down. In most cases, the expression in question was not remotely hate speech and, in many cases, cannot reasonably be considered hateful. For instance, a free speech wall at a Canadian university was torn down within hours after it was erected, by a student who labeled the wall an "act of violence" and an "expression of hate" against the gay community, even though no hate speech against gay people was found on the wall.[104] On an American university campus, students protested to shut down a public lecture by Polish politician and academic Ryszard Legutko for his "inflammatory" views, including for his often-cited statement that he did not understand "why anyone should want to be proud of being a homosexual," and that people should be proud of their conduct—what they do—instead.[105] That university finally canceled, for "safety" reasons, his lecture, which aimed to examine a different topic.[106] In the U.K. and the U.S.,

103. Among the relatively few examples include an incident in which an eighteen-year-old student was charged with aggravated harassment, a hate crime in which someone "etches, paints, draws upon or otherwise places a swastika, commonly exhibited as the emblem of Nazi Germany, on any building or other real property," for hanging posters featuring Nazi symbols in parts of the campus "frequented and utilized by members of the Jewish community." Emanuella Grinberg, *Student Faces Hate Crime Charge for Nazi-Themed Posters on SUNY Campus*, CNN (Dec. 11, 2018), https://www.cnn.com/2018/12/10/us/nazi-posters-suny-purchase/index.html (last visited Dec. 28, 2019).

104. Tristin Hopper, *"Not Every Opinion Is Valid": Carleton University Free Speech Wall Torn Down within Hours*, NAT'L POST (Jan. 22, 2013), https://nationalpost.com/news/canada/not-every-opinion-is-valid-activist-censors-peers-by-tearing-down-universitys-free-speech-wall

105. Maleeha Syed, *Middlebury College Cancels Talk with Conservative Speaker for Safety Purposes*, BURLINGTON FREE PRESS (Apr. 17, 2019), https://www.burlingtonfreepress.com/story/news/local/2019/04/17/campus-free-speech-middlebury-college-charles-murray-european-parliament-ryszard-legutko/3494450002/

106. Entitled "The Demon in Democracy: Totalitarian Temptations in Free Societies," the lecture argued

renowned feminist scholars who challenged mainstream Western transgender ideologies by offering their personal or scholarly views, or both, on womanhood were sometimes deplatformed by students who called their views "hate speech" against trans women.[107]

Many scholars contend that not only hate speech, but racist speech, should be prohibited on campus. Interestingly, not a few of these scholars are from the U.S., which has the most permissive law with regard to hateful expression and where hate speech is constitutionally protected unless it passes the imminent lawless action test. Charles Lawrence's well-cited article, for instance, argues that the American Constitution in fact supports the regulation of racist speech despite the First Amendment.[108] The history of racism in America, and the Framers' exclusion of black people from First Amendment protections, and the continued injuries inflicted upon minorities, also support such regulations.[109] Richard Delgado similarly points out that free speech throughout American history has never been "minorities' best friend," as it is often considered to be, and that the First Amendment has favored the powerful and not the underprivileged.[110] Hate-speech regulations on campus, rather than encouraging minorities to wallow in victimhood, provide an additional avenue for them to fight back and take charge of their lives.[111] Emphasizing the lasting injuries of racist speech on minorities, and equating tolerance of racist speech with tolerance of racism, Mari Matsuda likewise calls for regulation of racist speech to send the message that all members of society are equally valued.[112]

---

that Western democracy "has over time crept towards the same goals as communism, albeit without Soviet-style brutality." Maleeha Syed, *Middlebury College Cancels Talk with Conservative Speaker for Safety Purposes*, Burlington Free Press (Apr. 17, 2019), https://www.burlingtonfreepress.com/story/news/local/2019/04/17/campus-free-speech-middlebury-college-charles-murray-european-parliament-ryszard-legutko/3494450002/

107. *E.g.*, Conor Friedersdorf, *Camille Paglia Can't Say That*, Atlantic (May 1, 2019), https://www.theatlantic.com/ideas/archive/2019/05/camille-paglia-uarts-left-deplatform/587125/; Frank Furedi, *The Death of Free Speech*, Daily Mail (Oct. 31, 2015), http://www.frankfuredi.com/article/the_death_of_free_speech

108. Charles R. Lawrence III, *If He Hollers Let Him Go: Regulating Racist Speech on Campus*, 43 Duke L. J. 431, 439 (1990). Lawrence uses the U.S. Supreme Court's landmark decision *Brown v. Bd of Education* to make a case for regulating racist speech on campus, as the court held that segregated schools were unconstitutional "primarily because of the message segregation conveys—the message that Black children are an untouchable caste, unfit to be educated with white children."

109. Charles R. Lawrence III, *If He Hollers Let Him Go: Regulating Racist Speech on Campus*, 43 Duke L. J. 431, 457–66 (1990).

110. Richard Delgado, *Legal Realism and the Controversy over Campus Speech Codes*, 69 Case W. Res. L. Rev. 275, 283–84 (2018).

111. Richard Delgado, *Legal Realism and the Controversy over Campus Speech Codes*, 69 Case W. Res. L. Rev. 275, 291 (2018).

112. Mari J. Matsuda, *Public Response to Racist Speech: Considering the Victim's Story*, 87 Mich. L. Rev. 2320 (1989).

Advocacy for prohibiting hate speech on campus is reasonable, especially from a jurisdiction like the U.S. where hate speech is generally protected by its constitution. One must however be careful to distinguish among hate speech, racial harassment, and racist speech. Racial harassment is a form of harassment outlawed in most states in America and other Western jurisdictions, and any race-based harassment on campus meeting the corresponding legal thresholds are already prohibited by law. Well-informed lectures and debates and discussions inspired by these lectures in an academic setting generally can take place without anyone resorting to any form of racial harassment. It might be risky to outlaw expression that some consider racist but do not meet the legal standards because "racist" can have a loose definition: this concept, if expanded indefinitely, becomes void of meaning. This is an issue that will be examined in the next chapter.

Arguably, given that laws prohibiting harassment, discrimination, and hate speech also apply to universities within the same jurisdictions, there is no need for universities to set up additional policies regulating speech on campus. Content amounting to any of these offenses are already prohibited by law. Otherwise, they are lawful and should not be subjected to additional rules that may stifle the free exchange of ideas. The only exception is perhaps policies requesting that lectures and discussions be conducted in a civil manner—but these are not a real exception as such policies regulate not so much the content as the manner of expression.

III. Microaggression

To the extent that a respectful environment is essential to learning, feelings should not be dismissed. Expression that does not target individuals and is lawful nevertheless may harm the feelings of recipients, who find themselves disrespected and trapped in a hostile environment unconducive to learning. An environment that is free from harassment and hate speech may still be full of instances of "microaggression," which refers to small acts or remarks, be they intentional or not, that express harmful stereotypes about certain groups of people or prejudicial attitudes toward those groups and make them feel insulted or slighted.[113]

113. *E.g.*, *Microaggression*, CAMBRIDGE DICTIONARY, https://dictionary.cambridge.org/dictionary/english/microaggression (last visited Jan. 4, 2020); *Microaggression*, MERRIAM-WEBSTER DICTIONARY, https://www.merriam-webster.com/dictionary/microaggression (last visited Jan. 4, 2020).

The term "microaggression" was first introduced in 1970 by Chester M. Pierce, a psychiatrist and Harvard University professor, to describe insults, slights, and dismissals that he frequently observed being inflicted on African Americans by non-black Americans.[114] Pierce distinguished these from what he referred to as "macroaggressions," more overt or violent forms of racism, by emphasizing the former's ambiguity and presence in everyday life.[115] Since then, the term has expanded and now applies to degrading remarks or behavioral communications, often subtle and casual, directed toward other socially marginalized groups, including other racial and ethnic minorities, gender minorities, and the disabled.[116] Psychologist Derald Wing Sue, for instance, now defines microaggressions as "brief, everyday exchanges that send denigrating messages to certain individuals because of their group membership," adding that people making the comments may be well-intentioned and therefore unaware of the potential impact of their words.[117] Identified as "the new face of racism," they may have led to the impression that racism no longer exists as its nature has shifted over time from overt, blatant expressions of racial hatred and hate crimes toward much more subtle, ambiguous—and sometimes unintentional—expression of biases.[118]

Microaggressions are thus characterized by their subtlety, ambiguity, and commonality. Unsurprisingly, scholars and commentators have criticized the very concept for its lack of scientific basis and overreliance on subjective evidence, and attributed the negative impacts of microaggressions on some people to their personalities and propensity to see negativity in what are harmless remarks.[119] Some argue that avoiding microaggressions or situations that give rise to them can inhibit one's freedom and personal growth.[120] Relying on

114. DERALD WING SUE, MICROAGGRESSIONS IN EVERYDAY LIFE: RACE, GENDER, AND SEXUAL ORIENTATION xvi (2010).

115. Chester M. Pierce, Offensive Mechanisms, *in* THE BLACK SEVENTIES 265–82 (Floyd B. Barbour ed., 1970).

116. *E.g.*, DERALD WING SUE, MICROAGGRESSIONS IN EVERYDAY LIFE: RACE, GENDER, AND SEXUAL ORIENTATION xvi (2010); MICHELE A. PALUDI, MANAGING DIVERSITY IN TODAY'S WORKPLACE: STRATEGIES FOR EMPLOYEES AND EMPLOYERS (2012).

117. DERALD WING SUE, MICROAGGRESSIONS IN EVERYDAY LIFE: RACE, GENDER, AND SEXUAL ORIENTATION xvi (2010).

118. DERALD WING SUE, et al., RACIAL MICROAGGRESSIONS AGAINST BLACK AMERICANS: IMPLICATIONS FOR COUNSELING 330 (2007).

119. Alex Fradera, *The Scientific Evidence for Microaggressions Is Weak and We Should Drop the Term, Argues Review Author*, RES. DIGEST (Mar. 16, 2017), https://digest.bps.org.uk/2017/03/16/the-scientific-evidence-for-microaggressions-is-weak-and-we-should-drop-the-term-argues-review-author/

120. *E.g.*, Greg Lukianoff & Jonathan Haidt, *The Coddling of the American Mind*, ATLANTIC (Sep. 2015), https://www.theatlantic.com/magazine/archive/2015/09/the-coddling-of-the-american-mind/399356/

authority figures to address microaggressions may also discourage people from developing the skills useful in mediating conflicts caused by such conduct.[121] In addition, using a term connoting violence to describe minor, albeit objectionable, slights is an overstatement, and can be used to exaggerate the emotional harm they cause and elevate victimhood among recipients.[122] In extreme cases, the term may even be used by "victims" to justify retributive violence toward their "aggressors."[123] Nonetheless, to the extent that microaggressions affirm stereotypes about minority groups, they can be stressful and frustrating for recipients who perceive them.[124] Over time, stress and frustration may lead to diminished self-confidence and poor self-esteem, or even more severe mental health problems such as depression and trauma.[125] In universities, they are associated with "lower feelings of belonging," poorer academic performances, and poorer retention and graduation rates.[126] Microaggressions can be more damaging than overt, violent expressions of discrimination because their seemingly benign nature means that they tend to be ignored or downplayed.[127]

A. Examples: Insults and Invalidations Do Hurt

Microaggressions, according to Sue and his team of psychologists, can be divided into three types: "microassault," "microinsult," and "microinvalidation." Microassaults, the most obvious type, refer to subtle but purposeful discrimi-

121. Greg Lukianoff & Jonathan Haidt, *The Coddling of the American Mind*, Atlantic (Sep. 2015), https://www.theatlantic.com/magazine/archive/2015/09/the-coddling-of-the-american-mind/399356/

122. *E.g.*, Conor Friedersdorf, *Why Critics of the "Microaggressions" Framework Are Skeptical*, Atlantic (Sep. 14, 2015), https://www.theatlantic.com/politics/archive/2015/09/why-critics-of-the-microaggressions-framework-are-skeptical/405106/

123. Conor Friedersdorf, *Why Critics of the "Microaggressions" Framework Are Skeptical*, Atlantic (Sep. 14, 2015), https://www.theatlantic.com/politics/archive/2015/09/why-critics-of-the-microaggressions-framework-are-skeptical/405106/

124. *E.g.*, Alia E. Dastagir, *Microaggressions Don't Just "Hurt Your Feelings,"* USA Today (Feb. 28, 2018), https://www.usatoday.com/story/news/2018/02/28/what-microaggressions-small-slights-serious-consequences/362754002/

125. *E.g.*, Alia E. Dastagir, *Microaggressions Don't Just "Hurt Your Feelings,"* USA Today (Feb. 28, 2018), https://www.usatoday.com/story/news/2018/02/28/what-microaggressions-small-slights-serious-consequences/362754002/

126. *E.g.*, S.A. Harwood, et al., Racial Microaggressions at the University of Illinois at Urbana-Champaign: Voices of Students of Color in the Classroom (2015), https://www.racialmicroaggressions.illinois.edu/files/2015/03/RMA-Classroom-Report.pdf (last visited Jan. 20, 2020).

127. *E.g.*, Derald Wing Sue, et al., *Racial Microaggressions in Everyday Life: Implications for Clinical Practice*, 62 American Psychologist 271 (2007); Kristen P. Jones, et al., *Not So Subtle: A Meta-Analytic Investigation of the Correlates of Subtle and Overt Discrimination*, 42 J. Management 1588 (2013).

natory actions such as verbal attacks or avoidant behaviors.[128] They can take the form of sexist language and racial epithets and deliberately serving a white person before a person of color in a restaurant.[129]

Sue focuses on microinsults and microinvalidations, which make the recipient feel offended without knowing the exact reason, and which the perpetrator may be unwilling to acknowledge when confronted.[130] Microinvalidations refer to "communications that subtly exclude, negate, or nullify the thoughts, feelings or experiential reality of a person of color," and by this logic, a person of any other group.[131] The most cited example is asking people of Asian ethnicities where they were born or where they are "originally from," which carries the assumption that they were not born in the white-majority country or sends the message that they are not real citizens and are perpetual foreigners in their own land.[132] Related examples include expecting people of East Asian descent to speak Mandarin Chinese and adhering to certain cultural and behavioral norms, and dismissing the fact that people of Chinese/East Asian descents often have different upbringings and experiences and embrace distinct beliefs and value systems (and, yes, they may embrace Western democratic values more than many white, "Western-looking" people do, and therefore are far more willing and ready to defend those values when they are under attack!).

Microinsults are verbal and nonverbal communications that demean people on the basis of their race, ethnicity, gender, or other group identities.[133] An example is asking colleagues in racial or ethnic minority groups how they obtained their jobs, thus implying they may have landed their jobs through affirmative action or quota systems.[134] So is congratulating students of color on

---

128. Derald Wing Sue, et al., Racial Microaggressions Against Black Americans: Implications for Counseling 330 (2007).
129. Derald Wing Sue, et al., Racial Microaggressions Against Black Americans: Implications for Counseling 330 (2007).
130. Derald Wing Sue, et al., Racial Microaggressions against Black Americans: Implications for Counseling 330 (2007); *also* Tori DeAngelis, *Unmasking "Racial Microaggressions,"* 40 Monitor on Psychol. 42, https://www.apa.org/monitor/2009/02/microaggression (last visited Jan. 15, 2020).
131. Derald Wing Sue, et al., Racial Microaggressions against Black Americans: Implications for Counseling 330 (2007).
132. *See* Derald Wing Sue, et al., Racial Microaggressions against Black Americans: Implications for Counseling 330 (2007).
133. Derald Wing Sue, et al., Racial Microaggressions against Black Americans: Implications for Counseling 330 (2007).
134. Derald Wing Sue, et al., Racial Microaggressions Against Black Americans: Implications for Counseling 330 (2007); *also* Tori DeAngelis, *Unmasking "Racial Microaggressions,"* 40 Monitor on Psychol. 42, https://www.apa.org/monitor/2009/02/microaggression (last visited Jan. 15, 2020).

their admission to competitive programs and attributing their success to their schools' diversity initiatives, because such a "congratulatory" remark insinuates that they would not have qualified for the programs on their academic credentials alone. Although some programs might prioritize diversity of skin color over anything else (which is no doubt a sad reality), assuming that random members of minority groups have succeeded due to the color of their skin and stating this assumption in their presence is unfair and rude. Asking a foreign student enrolled at an American or Canadian law school (except where the language of instruction is French) whether the school waived the LSAT requirement for that student is equally if not more insulting, because it makes assumptions about the student's ability by inventing a privilege that is unheard of. Where a decent LSAT score is already sufficient to gain admission to the law school, this question is especially demeaning; however, it may not have intended to offend as it likely reflects on the ability and abysmal intellectual standard (let alone propriety and decency) of the person asking it rather than the person being asked. Quite ironically, however, microinsults and microinvalidations may come from people in traditionally marginalized groups.[135] Apparently, there is also nothing that stops people who take pride in their progressive beliefs from becoming offenders—not even their own progressivism. None of these scholars seems to have probed the question of whether only members of traditionally marginalized groups can be recipients of microinsults or microaggressions. One cannot help but wonder: Should remarking or insinuating that a white male stranger is privileged by virtue of his skin color be considered a microinsult?

A common and noteworthy example of what may be considered gender microaggression is asking a woman to smile or commenting that she should smile more. It has been observed that women get told to smile far more often than men do by strangers or colleagues even in workplaces where smiling is not a job requirement.[136] The "smile request" is now widely interpreted as having stemmed from the societal expectation that women display stereotypically feminine emotions or make themselves pleasing to the public eye no matter how they feel (even when they may be feeling tired, depressed, or recovering from

135. The foregoing question about LSAT was posed by a former colleague of the author. This woman, a Taiwanese American, went to a law school that closed in 2017 due to its extremely low student achievement.

136. *E.g.*, Rosa Inocencio Smith, *The Sexism of Telling Women to Smile: What It's Like When a Coworker Tells You to Smile*, ATLANTIC (Oct. 27, 2016), https://www.theatlantic.com/business/archive/2016/10/what-its-like-when-a-coworker-tells-you-to-smile/622972/

the death of a loved one).[137] Requests and remarks as such, regardless of the gender of those making them, are often found to be annoying, condescending, and disruptive by recipients who feel entitled to carry whatever facial expressions they want, are merely trying to focus on their lives and jobs, and would appreciate more genuine expressions of care (such as "How are you doing?" and "Are you okay?") when their expressions—be they angry, grim, or simply neutral—become discomforting to onlookers and the "smile police."[138] In the workplace, such remarks and requests coming from colleagues or superiors can take a toll on recipients' emotional well-being and sense of autonomy.[139]

Like other examples of microaggression, complaints about "smile requests" tend to get dismissed. Yet, at times, seemingly harmless—some say good-humored and well-intentioned—requests and remarks can escalate into criminal harassment and full-blown physical assault. In one case, a woman was told by her supervisor: "If you don't put a smile on your face, I'll shove my dick so far down your throat, it will make you smile."[140] In another case, a woman was grabbed, yelled at, and almost hit by a male acquaintance for refusing to smile at his command.[141] (By the same token, annoyances and indignities of a similar nature that happen to other genders may also be considered gender microaggressions.)

B. Reexamining "Dignity" and Its Implications

Microaggressions, generally not as harmful as harassment and hate speech, can be distressing to recipients. Even policies on civility and respectful learning environments mentioned in the "hate speech" subsection may not deter the subtler forms of microaggression as perpetrators may not be aware of their own incivility. To the extent that recipients' well-being does impact their ability to

137. *E.g.*, Rosa Inocencio Smith, *The Sexism of Telling Women to Smile: Your Stories: Do Strangers Ever Tell Men to Smile?*, ATLANTIC (Oct. 19, 2016), https://www.theatlantic.com/culture/archive/2016/10/do-strangers-ever-tell-men-to-smile/623011/

138. *See, e.g.*, Rosa Inocencio Smith, *The Sexism of Telling Women to Smile: Your Stories: Do Strangers Ever Tell Men to Smile?*, ATLANTIC (Oct. 19, 2016), https://www.theatlantic.com/culture/archive/2016/10/do-strangers-ever-tell-men-to-smile/623011/

139. *See, e.g.*, Rosa Inocencio Smith, *The Sexism of Telling Women to Smile: What It's Like When a Coworker Tells You to Smile*, ATLANTIC (Oct. 27, 2016), https://www.theatlantic.com/business/archive/2016/10/what-its-like-when-a-coworker-tells-you-to-smile/622972/

140. Rosa Inocencio Smith, *The Sexism of Telling Women to Smile: What It's Like When a Coworker Tells You to Smile*, ATLANTIC (Oct. 27, 2016), https://www.theatlantic.com/business/archive/2016/10/what-its-like-when-a-coworker-tells-you-to-smile/622972/

141. Rosa Inocencio Smith, *The Sexism of Telling Women to Smile: Your Stories: "I Will Not Smile, I Am Not Your Monkey,"* ATLANTIC (Oct. 12, 2016), https://www.theatlantic.com/culture/archive/2016/10/women-respond-to-the-men-who-told-them-to-smile/623044/

learn and that these everyday communications arguably play a much lesser role in the pursuit of knowledge and democratic governance than lectures, debates, and discussions do, policies and measures aimed at deterring such casual but harmful attacks on one's well-being—or dignity—may seem reasonable. This subsection picks up where the discussion on hate speech left off by taking another look at the various meanings of dignity.

Although human dignity appears in legal documents and philosophical discourses, its meaning is often left undefined or remains obscure.[142] The Universal Declaration of Human Rights of 1948 mentions dignity without defining it: "All human beings are born free and equal in dignity and rights. They are endowed with reason and conscience and should act towards one another in a spirit of brotherhood."[143] The Preamble to the International Covenant on Civil and Political Rights of 1966 (ICCPR) states that the rights proclaimed by the Universal Declaration of Human Rights "derive from the inherent dignity of the human person."[144] The Universal Declaration's mention of "brotherhood," whose meaning is unclear, could possibly be inspired by contemporary American philosopher Alan Gewirth's views on dignity. Whereas the Kantian idea of dignity arises from free will and agency and implies a negative obligation,[145] Gewirth's views on dignity emphasize both the negative obligation of not harming a person's freedom and agency and the positive obligation, by individuals and the state, to help other humans in achieving and maintaining not only freedom but also "well-being."[146]

Violations of human dignity are found to consist of several types by scholars and judges. Human dignity can be violated by humiliation, which many judicial decisions identified as injuries to a person's self-esteem and self-worth.[147] It can be violated by degradation: practices that degrade the value of human beings in the eyes of modern society include slavery or putting pris-

142. *E.g.*, Stephen Riley & Gerhard Bos, *Human Dignity*, INTERNATIONAL ENCYCLOPEDIA OF PHILOSOPHY: A PEER-REVIEWED ACADEMIC RESOURCE, https://www.iep.utm.edu/hum-dign/ (last visited Jan. 2020).

143. Universal Declaration of Human Rgts., art. 1.

144. Int'l Covenant on Civil and Pol. Rgts. 1966, preamble.

145. PHILLIP ANTHONY O'HARA, ENCYCLOPEDIA OF POLITICAL ECONOMY 471 (1999).

146. *E.g.*, Mark D. White, Dignity, *in* HANDBOOK OF ECONOMICS AND ETHICS 85 (Jan Peil ed., 2009), originally from ALAN GEWIRTH, THE COMMUNITY OF RIGHTS (1996). For another twentieth-century philosopher, Mortimer Adler, human dignity indicates that human beings are "equally distinct from other species such as animals and as such are entitled to equal rights and treatments." MORTIMER ADLER, SIX GREAT IDEAS 165–66 (1997).

147. *E.g.*, PAULUS KAUFMANN, et al. (eds.), HUMILIATION, DEGRADATION, DEHUMANIZATION: HUMAN DIGNITY VIOLATED (2011); Doron Shultziner & Itai Rabinovici, *Human Dignity, Self-Worth and Humiliation: A Comparative Legal–Psychological Approach*, 18 PYCHOL., PUB. POL'Y, & L. 105 (2012).

oners in inhumane living conditions.[148] It can also be violated through dehumanization, which involves stripping a person or a group of their human characteristics: this happens frequently in genocides and other forms of state-sanctioned violence, where the victims are compared by state agents to insects.[149] Degradation and dehumanization (which historically led to mass imprisonment and murder of the dehumanized groups) harm the victim's free will and agency, while humiliation pertains to a more subjective dimension of well-being.

The last section mentioned that hate speech is defined broadly in some jurisdictions to include not only expressions that incite violence against certain groups but also those that harm the dignity of members of the groups. Given the fundamental importance of free speech and the subjective and indefinite nature of dignity, this definition of hate speech may be unnecessarily broad. Even though there is no requisite positive obligation, this standard can be challenging to meet considering that many constructive criticisms can harm an individual's, or a group of people's, self-worth. Examples include statements made by world-renowned modern Chinese author Lu Xun and Nobel Peace Prize winner Liu Xiao-bo.[150] In addition, if universities adopt an overly broad definition of dignity, then not only violating people's self-worth but also not actively promoting well-being in a university setting will be frowned upon. As a result, the range of conduct deemed violations of university policies can expand indefinitely. This subsection addresses whether and what policies and measures should be implemented to address microaggressions—which may be considered to violate dignity—in a university setting.

Many examples of microaggressions can be said to violate human dignity if self-worth and well-being are a core part of it. Although recipients of microaggressions often belong to historically oppressed or marginalized groups, and for that reason may feel various degrees of vulnerability, they should be encouraged to (re)claim their agency, a crucial part of their dignity according to Kant, by exercising their freedom of expression to resist words or acts, be they inten-

148. PAULUS KAUFMANN, et al. (eds.), HUMILIATION, DEGRADATION, DEHUMANIZATION: HUMAN DIGNITY VIOLATED (2011).

149. PAULUS KAUFMANN, et al. (eds.), HUMILIATION, DEGRADATION, DEHUMANIZATION: HUMAN DIGNITY VIOLATED (2011).

150. Lu is well-known for his biting criticisms of people in China as a group. Liu was likewise critical of the Chinese government and Chinese culture. He once said that China needed 300 years of Western colonialism to become an advanced and modern city like Hong Kong (James Palmer, *The Chinese Think Liu Xiaobo Was Asking for It*, FOREIGN POLICY, July 11, 2017, foreignpolicy.com/2017/07/11/the-chinese-think-liu-xiaobo-was-asking-for-it/). Judging from the devotion of these figures to their motherland, these statements were likely made out of love and concern, not hatred.

tional or not, that undermine their dignity. For example, when asked where they are "originally from," Asians can politely reply that people of many races and ethnicities are born in this country every day and they are just as native as the white majority. People of color or of foreign origins who feel slighted by remarks attributing their successes to their skin color or "diversity" factors can respond half-jokingly, "You know, I am smart actually, and people are more than their races/ethnicities." Women (or people of other genders) told to smile can react by "apologizing" that a loved one has a serious illness or that a family member just passed away—especially if the command comes from a stranger or someone who likely would not be able to fact-check their "excuse"—and enjoy seeing those who would direct their behavior recoil in embarrassment. Alternatively, recipients of "smile requests" can remain quiet and ignore these remarks and requests: refusing to speak when answers are expected is a strong exercise of agency, let alone of freedom of speech. If microaggressions unfortunately rise to the level of harassment, which is prohibited by law, they can, and must, be reported.

Over the past decade, diversity and sensitivity training programs have been set up on many university campuses in white-majority countries to help resolve the issue of microaggression.[151] This involves setting up diversity offices, hiring staff members focused on diversity issues ("diversity officers"), and offering mandatory sensitivity training sessions and workshops to employees.[152] At some universities, students are also required to attend classes on diversity and microaggression, and sometimes on more ideologically driven topics such as "white privilege."[153]

These well-intentioned training programs, by informing participants about potential biases and behaviors that may offend others, may help reduce conflicts and contribute to more respectful learning environments. Despite the possible educational values of such programs (as well as rules and policies), they may discourage offended people from exercising their agency and free-

151. *E.g.*, Association of American College & Universities, *Campuses Combatting Microaggressions*, AAC & U News (Dec. 2016), https://www.aacu.org/aacu-news/newsletter/2016/december/perspectives (last visited Jan. 20, 2020); *also Report of the Advisory Group on Equity, Diversity and Inclusion*, Concordia University (Sep. 30, 2019), http://www.concordia.ca/content/dam/concordia/offices/provost/docs/Report-Advisory-Group-Equity-Diversity-Inclusion.pdf (last visited Jan. 20, 2020).

152. Association of American College & Universities, *Campuses Combatting Microaggressions*, AAC & U News (Dec. 2016), https://www.aacu.org/aacu-news/newsletter/2016/december/perspectives (last visited Jan. 20, 2020).

153. *See, e.g.*, Association of American College & Universities, *Campuses Combatting Microaggressions*, AAC & U News (Dec. 2016), https://www.aacu.org/aacu-news/newsletter/2016/december/perspectives (last visited Jan. 20, 2020).

dom of expression to inform offenders, help mediate the conflicts, and cure the harm done to them.[154] Further, participants mandated to enroll and learn about their biases may suffer from wounded dignity if they do not in fact harbor any such biases, do not believe that they are biased, or always make substantial efforts to refrain from offensive conduct despite harboring some biases. After all, people with enough propriety, civility, or common sense would not likely, for instance, openly attribute the successes of their peers or students to their skin color, insinuate that foreign students got into law schools because of (imagined) waived requirements, imply that people of East Asian descent do not embrace democratic values, or order women (or anyone) to smile. People voluntarily and willingly enrolled in such programs may benefit from them without feeling harmed, but they may be able to benefit as much through thoughtful and civil everyday interactions with individuals.

Indeed, diversity officers implementing and running the sensitivity programs can let their own experiences, biases, and ideologies get in the way of offering a real education to enrollees. For example, some of these people may be deeply influenced by ideologies and so tend to perceive the complex, evolving—and diverse—world and humans through simplistic lenses. In the worst scenarios, they may become so ideologically driven and so fixated on racial categories that they fail to look past skin color and gender, and therefore make unfounded or shaky assumptions about people of different groups and how they act or want to be treated. In short, they may forget that all humans are individuals who are immensely diverse in terms of attributes and sensibilities and need to be respected and treated as such. Ironically, these diversity officers may end up becoming offenders and committing outrageous forms of microaggression to diverse individuals: for example, by presuming that a white person from an underprivileged or average background is more privileged than a mega-rich black person from Beverly Hills (such as the privileged offspring of Hollywood celebrities who like to lecture on how ordinary people should live), that a fair-skinned East Asian immigrant is more privileged than a brown-skinned person (a presumption which, sadly, many left-leaning types do make), or that people of East Asian descent are from China or, more outrageously still, by inferring that these East Asians love the Chinese government—which would rightly make recipients of such a microaggression feel insulted and violated!

The university might be a much better place if everybody is civil and sensi-

154. *See, e.g.*, the above paragraph; *E.g.*, Greg Lukianoff & Jonathan Haidt, *The Coddling of the American Mind*, ATLANTIC (Sep. 2015), https://www.theatlantic.com/magazine/archive/2015/09/the-coddling-of-the-american-mind/399356/

tive to other people's feelings. In fact, many people offer a clichéd, but perhaps sincere, answer, "world peace," when asked about their New Year's wishes. Thus, it may be tempting to think that real racists and sexists (and other "-ists") who cannot keep their thoughts to themselves and are prone to committing most of the "microassaults" should undergo mandatory reeducation and have their minds and behaviors reformed. These mandatory training programs may indeed be able to instill propriety, decency, and common sense in them. One must not forget, though, that freedom of thought, as well as freedom of speech, are both natural and fundamental rights. The costs—and beauty—of freedom are unpredictability, some level of chaos, and healthy conflicts.[155] Instead of relying on these programs, the cons of which may outweigh the pros, universities may as well set these people free, and allow them to learn their hard lessons from people with whom they interact, who should not—and must not—hesitate to call them out for their disrespectful behaviors before they escalate into full-blown harassment and discrimination.

• • •

Attempting to create a better world by outlawing what are deemed politically incorrect expressions can do more harm than good. Mandatory diversity workshops aimed to combat microaggressions may violate individuals' free will and freedom of thought while doing little to educate the university population about true diversity in an ever evolving, complex society. As this chapter has noted, lectures, debates, and discussions were canceled by universities not because they constituted harassment, discrimination, or hate speech, but due to threats of violence by those who took offense at what they personally considered "hate speech," or simply "hate," which has no legal basis. The foregoing discussion has raised questions about the place of feelings and the meanings of violence and safety in universities. The related concepts of "deplatforming," "trigger warning," and "safe space" deserve in-depth discussion and will be the focus of the next chapter.

155. For instance, people of East Asian descent whom some ill-informed Westerners presume to be from China can offer them a lecture on the fact that they are not from China or do not identify with China or, better still, on the atrocities of its government, whenever these naïve (or hypocritical) Westerners seek to appease them by praising the "peacefulness" of this country or by saying how they enjoyed this country as tourists.

CHAPTER SIX

Deplatforming, Trigger Warning, Safe Space

Can deplatforming provocative speakers be justified in the name of campus safety by the "pure in heart" who claim to act with their best intentions? In recent years, speakers with no track record of harassment or hate speech have been frequently deplatformed in universities. This chapter will debunk numerous popular arguments in favor of deplatforming without taking the absolutist position that it should never happen. It will also address the proper role of academics, who are often wrongly perceived to possess the authority or expertise to determine the relevance of topics in the university setting. Arguments that point to more pragmatic harms of giving a platform to speakers and their offensive opinions (e.g., harms to institutional reputation or in financial terms) will then be challenged. Because groups are made of individuals, group rights to peace and harmony generally do not trump individuals' right to respectfully express lawful opinions and to access those opinions in a civil atmosphere.

Certainly, patients of post-traumatic stress disorder need to seek professional treatment. The prevalence of "trigger warnings" in universities indicates that the meaning of "trigger" has deviated from its normal usage in the contexts of medicine and psychology: the word has become synonymous with "provoke." Despite its negative connotations, provocative ideas and methods have pedagogical value. Unfortunately, thought-provoking opinions and ideas, which serve to advance knowledge, democratic governance, and personal development, are often mistaken as personal attacks. The even more unfortunate reality is that personal attacks on those who dare to challenge orthodoxies and dogmas, quite ironically, are often excused—or even justified—on fake moral grounds and for virtue-signaling purposes. These recent developments in Western democracies bear a resemblance to some common phenomena in authoritarian countries that is both uncanny and alarming.

Finally, this chapter will explain why safe spaces in universities, which are currently as prevalent as trigger warnings, should be limited in scope. Attempts to make the entire university "safe" threaten free speech. Such attempts are justified by an overly broad, expanding concept of violence, which is part of a troubling, yet common, phenomenon called "concept creep." A safe space that shuts out "violent" messages—as perceived by the oversensitive, intellectually lazy/dishonest, and indoctrinated—may justify the use of preemptive violence against perceived threats to the "safety" in that space. It also ill-prepares young people for the real world, unless the real world itself becomes a safe space.

I. Deplatforming

"Deplatforming," sometimes also known as "no-platforming," is the practice of preventing individuals, groups, or organizations holding views or opinions regarded as unacceptable, dangerous, or offensive from accessing venues or platforms to express those views or opinions.[1] In the United States, the banning of speakers on university campuses originated in the suppressive McCarthy era through the strict policy of the University of California, Berkeley, formalized in 1951, which limited who could speak on its campus.[2] Among the people whom it was used to stop were socialist Max Shachtman and nine out of ten prospective speakers invited to an Anthropology Department forum, all members of organizations on the Attorney General's list of "subversive organizations."[3] While this ban, which targeted mainly—though not exclusively—communists, was lifted in 1963 in the midst of the liberalization of American campuses, "no platform" policies aimed to ban "racists" and "fascists" were not unheard of in

1. *See, e.g.*, *No-platform*, Cambridge Dictionary, https://dictionary.cambridge.org/dictionary/english/no-platform (last visited Feb. 6, 2020); *No-platform*, MacMillan Dictionary, https://www.macmillandictionary.com/dictionary/british/no-platform (last visited Feb. 6, 2020); *No-platform*, Lexico, https://www.lexico.com/definition/no-platform (last visited Feb. 6, 2020).
2. Jo Freeman, *A Short History of the University of California Speaker Ban* (2000), Jo Freeman (blog), https://www.jofreeman.com/sixtiesprotest/speakerban.htm (last visited Feb. 6, 2020); *Appendix D: The Removal of the Communist Speaker Ban*, Free Speech Movement Archives, http://www.fsm-a.org/stacks/AP_files/APCommSpkrBan.html (last visited Feb. 6, 2020).
3. Jo Freeman, *A Short History of the University of California Speaker Ban* (2000), Jo Freeman, https://www.jofreeman.com/sixtiesprotest/speakerban.htm (last visited Feb. 6, 2020).

other Western countries.[4] The first two decades of the twenty-first century have seen an alarming trend of disinvitations of controversial speakers invited to speak at numerous Western universities.[5] Some speakers have been banned from campuses altogether.[6]

In addition to disinviting speakers or banning them from university campuses, deplatforming practices include attempts to silence them through harassment, doxxing, and complaints or petitions to third parties.[7] In extreme cases, protesters have attempted to get professors holding views they found offensive fired from their jobs and banned from their workplaces.[8] Such actions have been justified on the grounds that these offenders produced "hate speech" and "dangerous" ideas and that their expressions and actions harmed their colleagues and students.[9]

Deplatforming speakers in universities both precipitated and reflects a larger trend in society. Law professor Glenn Reynolds, for example, dubbed 2018 the "Year of Deplatforming," during which several media giants suspended accounts of selected users on account of their political views.[10] The last chapter

---

4. For example, the British National Union of Students established its "No Platform" policy in 1973. Lindsey German, *No Platform: Free Speech for All?* SOCIALIST WORKER REVIEW 86 (Apr. 1986).
5. *See, e.g.*, John Fund, *In* No Safe Spaces, *an Odd Couple Teams Up to Fight Free-Speech Bans*, NAT'L REV. (Nov. 3, 2019), https://www.nationalreview.com/2019/11/documentary-no-safe-spaces-adam-carolla-dennis-prager-fight-free-speech-bans/; *Disinvitation Database*, FOUNDATION FOR INDIVIDUAL RIGHTS IN EDUCATION, https://www.thefire.org/research/disinvitation-database/#home/?view_2_per_page=1000&view_2_page=1 (last visited Feb. 6, 2020).
6. *E.g.*, Kasia Kovacs, *Inflammatory and Turned Away*, INSIDE HIGHER EDUC. (Oct. 21, 2016), https://www.insidehighered.com/news/2016/10/21/several-universities-cancel-appearances-conservative-writer-milo-yiannopoulos
7. *E.g.*, Conor Friedersdorf, *Camille Paglia Can't Say That*, ATLANTIC (May 1, 2019), https://www.theatlantic.com/ideas/archive/2019/05/camille-paglia-uarts-left-deplatform/587125/; Aidan Currie, *Hundreds Sign Open Letter to U of T Admin Calling for Jordan Peterson's Termination*, THE VARSITY (Nov. 29, 2017), https://thevarsity.ca/2017/11/29/hundreds-sign-open-letter-to-u-of-t-admin-calling-for-jordan-petersons-termination/ (last visited Feb. 6, 2010).
8. *E.g.*, Conor Friedersdorf, *Camille Paglia Can't Say That*, ATLANTIC (May 1, 2019), https://www.theatlantic.com/ideas/archive/2019/05/camille-paglia-uarts-left-deplatform/587125/; Aidan Currie, *Hundreds Sign Open Letter to U of T Admin Calling for Jordan Peterson's Termination*, THE VARSITY (Nov. 29, 2017), https://thevarsity.ca/2017/11/29/hundreds-sign-open-letter-to-u-of-t-admin-calling-for-jordan-petersons-termination/ (last visited Feb. 6, 2010).
9. *E.g.*, Conor Friedersdorf, *Camille Paglia Can't Say That*, ATLANTIC (May 1, 2019), https://www.theatlantic.com/ideas/archive/2019/05/camille-paglia-uarts-left-deplatform/587125/; Aidan Currie, *Hundreds Sign Open Letter to U of T Admin Calling for Jordan Peterson's Termination*, THE VARSITY (Nov. 29, 2017), https://thevarsity.ca/2017/11/29/hundreds-sign-open-letter-to-u-of-t-admin-calling-for-jordan-petersons-termination/ (last visited Feb. 6, 2010).
10. Reynolds cited Alex Jones, Gavin McInnes, and Dennis Prager as prominent 2018 victims of deplatforming, and noted that "[e]xtremists and controversialists on the left have been relatively safe from deplatforming." Glenn Reynolds, *When Digital Platforms Become Censors*, WALL ST. J. (Aug. 18, 2018), https://www.wsj.com/articles/when-digital-platforms-become-censors-1534514122; attempts to end offenders' careers through public backlash against their "problematic" views is also

has explained that academic discussions on contentious topics generally do not constitute harassment, discrimination, or hate speech. Yet views and opinions by controversial speakers are readily considered harmful or offensive, even though they by no means fall within these categories. Deplatforming has become common in the university setting as a result, which can impede the pursuit of knowledge, democratic governance, and self-development by depriving the right to expression by speakers and to access information by audiences. As the following section argues, the most common arguments against platforming such speakers—for example, that freedom of speech does not entitle one to a platform and that platforming hate would enable bad arguments to defeat good ones through rhetoric—are shaky at best.

A. Entitlement to a Platform, Platforming "Hate," and Bad Arguments Triumphing over Good Ones

Among the most common arguments in support of deplatforming offensive speakers is that freedom of speech entitles these speakers to speak freely, but the same freedom does not entitle them to a platform to communicate their opinions to an audience.[11] Indeed, free expression is a basic right, while access to public platforms is a special right or privilege.[12] The fact that no one is obliged to provide a platform to controversial speakers makes disinviting such speakers or banning them from public forums to prevent the spread of their harmful ideas seem both legally and morally justified.[13]

Yet no speaker—controversial or not—is entitled to a platform, if to be "entitled" means to have a legal right or moral claim to something. That certain people strongly deserve to be invited to speak on certain topics or at certain events does not mean that they are entitled to those platforms. J. K. Rowling, for example, is no more entitled to share at a children's literature

---

part of the "cancel culture" that has been on the rise. *E.g.*, Aja Romano, *Why We Can't Stop Fighting about Cancel Culture*, N.Y. Times (Dec. 30, 2019), https://www.vox.com/culture/2019/12/30/20879720/what-is-cancel-culture-explained-history-debate

11. *E.g.*, James Mazarakis, *Free Speech Doesn't Mean That Alex Jones Is Entitled to a Platform*, Daily Collegian (Sep. 9, 2018), https://dailycollegian.com/2018/09/free-speech-doesnt-mean-that-alex-jones-deserves-a-platform/ (last visited Feb. 8, 2020); Niamh McIntre & Anna Burn, *Free Speech Is a Right but a Platform Is Not*, Left Foot Forward (Nov. 25, 2014), https://leftfootforward.org/2014/11/free-speech-is-a-right-but-a-platform-is-not/ (last visited Feb. 8, 2020).
12. *E.g.*, Jenny Teichman, *Freedom of Speech and Public Platform*, 11 J. Applied Phil. 99 (1994).
13. *See, e.g.*, Niamh McIntre & Anna Burn, *Free Speech Is a Right but a Platform Is Not*, Left Foot Forward (Nov. 25, 2014), https://leftfootforward.org/2014/11/free-speech-is-a-right-but-a-platform-is-not/ (last visited Feb. 8, 2020).

forum on how to write best-selling children's fiction than Stephen King is to lecture at a horror fiction workshop on how to craft a great horror story. Bill Gates likewise is not entitled to share his success story at the commencement ceremony of his alma mater. Whereas these accomplished people may strongly deserve these platforms, none of them can be said to have any legal right or moral claim to any platform.

Entitlement to a platform does happen. Once invited to speak, whether at a commencement ceremony or an academic forum, speakers do become entitled to their platforms. Hence, disinviting them would mean breaching their agreements with the organizers and causing disservice to different parties. Once deplatforming has become a common practice, disinviting speakers, no matter how qualified and deserving, may then be excused or justified on different grounds. Rowling may get disinvited after massive protests targeting her criticism of mainstream transgender politics.[14] King may be deplatformed for not being an ardent supporter of "diversity" and for his expressed opinion that that only "merit," not "diversity," matters when nominating for the Academy Awards.[15] Gates may get shut down for his alleged associations with the Chinese government, no matter how tenuous that may be.[16] Rather than disinviting speakers and depriving audiences of the promised opportunities, time and energy might be better spent in making the events as productive and enriching as possible.[17] The same logic extends to banning speakers from universities who have not yet been invited—resources would be better spent on respecting agreements and enriching events when they happen rather than shutting them out.

Apparently, ideas and opinions not falling within harassment, discrimination, or hate speech categories may still be "hateful" and have harmful influences on society, and providing a platform to them facilitates such influences.[18]

---

14. *See, e.g.*, Liam Stack, *J. K. Rowling Criticized after Tweeting Support for Anti-Transgender Researcher*, N.Y. Times (Dec. 19, 2019), https://www.nytimes.com/2019/12/19/world/europe/jk-rowling-maya-forstater-transgender.html
15. *See, e.g.*, Kelly McCarthy, *Thousands of Twitter Replies Challenge Stephen King's Tweet on Diversity in Art*, ABC News (Jan. 16, 2020), https://abcnews.go.com/Entertainment/thousands-twitter-replies-challenge-stephen-kings-tweet-diversity/story?id=68326302 (last visited Feb. 12, 2020).
16. *See, e.g.*, Tyler O'Neil, *Gates Foundation Helped "Raise China's Voice of Governance" in Africa, Emails Show*, Fox News (Aug. 29, 2021), https://www.foxbusiness.com/technology/gates-foundation-helped-raise-chinas-voice-of-governance-in-africa-newly-released-emails-show (last visited Apr. 3, 2022).
17. Amy Lai, *On Campus, Unpopular Views Also Deserve a Platform*, Globe & Mail (May 27, 2019), https://www.theglobeandmail.com/opinion/article-on-campus-unpopular-views-also-deserve-a-platform/
18. *See, e.g.*, Jason Koebler, *Deplatforming Works*, Vice (Aug. 10, 2018), https://www.vice.com/en_us/article/bjbp9d/do-social-media-bans-work (last visited Feb. 2020, 2019).

Providing a platform to people and their expression, however, is not equivalent to endorsing such people or expression: it only endorses the belief that the platformed topics, like all, or almost all, topics in a democratic society, are up for debate.[19] Banning speakers from expressing controversial statements would not make their opinions and ideas disappear; quite the opposite, it may provide free publicity for these forbidden opinions and ideas and make them seem enticing.[20] There is some evidence indicating that deplatforming helps to discourage bad ideas at least in cases where the speakers do not wield any power to begin with as it strips them of coordinated means to help spread their ideas.[21] Yet deplatforming would also leave these speakers unchallenged and isolate individuals embracing similar beliefs.[22] This may even lead to the creation of alternative subcultures that reinforce those beliefs and facilitate the radicalization of their followers.[23] The argument that it is more harmful to society to have many people exposed to "hateful" content than to have a much smaller number of radicalized believers is unpersuasive[24]—it presumes that the audiences are passive recipients of "hateful" messages and cannot use their reasoning faculties to determine the merits of this expression and to contribute to the topics through meaningful interactions with speakers. This is an unfounded presumption especially in the context of an academic setting.

Alternatively, it may be argued that suppressing potentially harmful content can generate a more positive outcome than radicalizing believers upset by the suppression of that content: such policies can help the people become educated

19. *E.g.*, Amy Lai, *On Campus, Unpopular Views Also Deserve a Platform*, Globe & Mail (May 27, 2019), https://www.theglobeandmail.com/opinion/article-on-campus-unpopular-views-also-deserve-a-platform/

20. Nathan Cofnas, *Deplatforming Won't Work*, Quillette (Jul. 8, 2019), https://quillette.com/2019/07/08/deplatforming-wont-work/. This is known as the "Streisand effect." *E.g.*, T.C., *What Is the Streisand Effect?* Economist (Apr. 15, 2013), https://www.economist.com/the-economist-explains/2013/04/15/what-is-the-streisand-effect; Mario Cacciottolo, *When Censorship Backfires: The Streisand Effect*, BBC (Jun. 15, 2012), https://www.bbc.com/news/uk-18458567 (last visited Feb. 12, 2020).

21. *E.g.*, Jason Koebler, *Deplatforming Works*, Vice (Aug. 10, 2018), https://www.vice.com/en_us/article/bjbp9d/do-social-media-bans-work (last visited Feb. 2020, 2019).

22. *E.g.*, Nathan Cofnas, *Deplatforming Won't Work*, Quillette (Jul. 8, 2019), https://quillette.com/2019/07/08/deplatforming-wont-work/; *see, e.g., also* Denise Balkissoon, *After Christchurch: Turning Off Hatemongers' Mics*, Globe & Mail (Mar. 18, 2019), https://www.theglobeandmail.com/opinion/article-after-christchurch-turning-off-hatemongers-mics/

23. *E.g.*, Nathan Cofnas, *Deplatforming Won't Work*, Quillette (Jul. 8, 2019), https://quillette.com/2019/07/08/deplatforming-wont-work/; Denise Balkissoon, *After Christchurch: Turning Off Hatemongers' Mics*, Globe & Mail (Mar. 18, 2019), https://www.theglobeandmail.com/opinion/article-after-christchurch-turning-off-hatemongers-mics/

24. *See, e.g.*, Jason Koebler, *Deplatforming Works*, Vice (Aug. 10, 2018), https://www.vice.com/en_us/article/bjbp9d/do-social-media-bans-work (last visited Feb. 2020, 2019); *citing* Joan Donovan, the research lead of platform accountability of Data and Society, a US-based nonprofit advancing public understanding of the social implications of data-centric technologies and automation.

as to what is bad for society and become better, more informed individuals. However, there is no reason why lectures or debates that may not contain illegal expressions should be preemptively suppressed. Even if they do happen to contain certain harmful expressions that violate codes of civility as laid down by university authorities, educating people about civility can and should take place when those expressions have been made and the full extent of their hatefulness and incivility has been exposed.

There are people who do not buy the marketplace of ideas argument due to their belief that ill-informed opinions may defeat good ones when people use rhetoric to dress up bad arguments that appeal to emotions rather than to logic, especially where the audiences may not be sophisticated enough to judge arguments solely on logical principles.[25] Yet deplatforming speakers to help prevent the bad from triumphing over the good is to concede defeat in the face of ill-informed opinions. Rather than shying away from confronting harmful expressions or ill-informed opinions dressed in clever rhetoric, people should learn to disarm rhetoricians by identifying the fallacies in their bad arguments. They should also see rhetoric as a powerful weapon, seek to perfect their own rhetorical ability, and present their well-reasoned arguments in the most persuasive manner to win over their audiences.

Others challenge the marketplace of ideas argument by referring to the ways in which university institutions function to uphold a social order that benefits the historically privileged.[26] They point out that universities are one of the key places in which intergenerational wealth and privilege is passed down, to the exclusion of poor and underprivileged groups. The application of a free-market logic to the university therefore re-creates and perpetuates the status quo and continues the vicious cycle.[27] While this argument alludes to certain facts that must be acknowledged, the problem arising out of historical and social circumstances cannot be corrected by deplatforming otherwise lawful opinions delivered in a civil manner that are deemed to have come from or that

---

25. *See, e.g.*, George A. Kennedy, Classical Rhetoric and Its Christian and Secular Tradition: From Ancient to Modern Times 53–92 (2d. 1999). In ancient Greece, both Plato and Aristotle condemned "Sophists" for disregarding the truth and for using rhetorical tricks to persuade their audiences.
26. Caitlin Setnicar, *How Heterodox Academy Creates a Safe Space for Bad Ideas*, Demos J. (Jan. 31, 2020), https://demosjournal.com/article/how-heterodox-academy-creates-a-safe-space-for-bad-ideas/
27. *See* Caitlin Setnicar, *How Heterodox Academy Creates a Safe Space for Bad Ideas*, Demos J. (Jan. 31, 2020), https://demosjournal.com/article/how-heterodox-academy-creates-a-safe-space-for-bad-ideas/

benefit the historically privileged, or both. There is no guarantee that a simplistic solution as such may not "overcorrect" the situation by leading to new privileged and oppressed classes.

It may seem reasonable to deplatform controversial speakers invited to occasions where those who attend might not have the opportunity to ask questions or request clarification. Typical examples include opening and convocation ceremonies, which students often attend with parents and relatives. In such cases, if speakers include factual mistakes or misleading statements in their speeches,[28] attendees who are not well informed would walk away with the misinformation and half-truths. However, there is no way to ensure that an invited speaker would not make any mistakes prior to an event. Hence, it would be better to trust inviting parties to make good-faith efforts to select competent and suitable speakers than to deplatform invited speakers for fear that they may fail to live up to expectations. In recent years, universities have apologized to the public for what they found to be blunders made by convocation speakers.[29] Addressing mistakes made by speakers, especially those pertaining to ideologically charged topics, may require tremendous moral courage considering the potential backlash from overzealous supporters who might view any such measure as an attack on their beliefs. Nonetheless, if their speakers are found to have misled their audiences, universities can and should pluck up their moral

---

28. For example, Maracle Lee, an Indigenous woman who spoke at the convocation ceremony of the University of Waterloo in June 2019, told the audience that Indigenous people in Canada do not get "a single dollar" of Canadian tax money and that the Indigenous women were not allowed to go to college until 1968. Spring 2019 Convocation: Faculty of Arts (June 12, YOUTUBE, Jun. 21, 2019), https://www.youtube.com/watch?v=P1qQrAKHayQ&t=1678s (last visited Mar. 5, 2020). Lee thus seemed to indicate that the federal taxes paid by Canadians have gone elsewhere. In addition, the first Indigenous woman graduated from the University of Saskatchewan in 1915. Thomas Piller, *First Aboriginal Woman Graduated from U of S a Century Ago*, GLOBE & MAIL (May 28, 2015), https://globalnews.ca/news/2021769/first-aboriginal-woman-graduated-from-u-of-s-a-century-ago/. Lee was likely referring to the fact that federal program support for Aboriginal postsecondary education was nonexistent in the 1950s. It was not until 1968 that federal policy was passed introducing the Post-Secondary Student Support Program, which provided financial assistance for Indigenous students pursuing postsecondary studies. The Aboriginal Institutes Consortium, *A Struggle for the Education of Aboriginal Students, Control of Indigenous Knowledge, and Recognition of Aboriginal Institutions*, CANADIAN RACE RELATIONS FOUNDATION (2005).
29. *E.g.*, Martin Allen, *Western Speaker Apologizes for Sexist Convocation Remarks*, WESTERN GAZETTE (Jun. 18, 2019), https://westerngazette.ca/news/western-speaker-apologize-for-sexist-convocation-remarks/article_3d1dfc00-9181-11e9-a60e-a3ad93e66247.html; Martin Allen, *Western Apologizes after Convocation Comment about Female Students*, WESTERN GAZETTE (Oct. 30, 2019), https://westerngazette.ca/news/western-apologizes-after-convocation-comment-about-female-students/article_62f112fa-dcaa-11e8-a8cd-bf096531586c.html; Mike Brest, *NYU President Apologizes after Graduation Speaker Praises BDS Movement during Speech*, DAILY CALLER (May 23, 2019), https://dailycaller.com/2019/05/23/new-york-university-president-apologize-boycott-israel/

courage to issue apologies addressing the mistakes, half-truths, and concerns raised by them in a timely, fair, and respectful manner.

Some members of academic communities, seasoned academics included, believe that illegal measures (for example, pulling fire alarms) to disrupt talks by speakers with "harmful" opinions are preferable to giving them a platform to spread their ideas.[30] Hence, these members not only betray their intellectual laziness by admitting defeat in the face of what they consider dangerous expressions; they also condone the morally reprehensible position that diverting resources from real emergencies would be acceptable to shut down what may be valuable educational opportunities.[31] A seemingly clever but nonetheless fallacious argument would be to justify similar disruptive behavior or violent disinvitation attempts by alluding to the American civil rights movement and the necessity for disruptive protests to bring about social progress. This is a false equivalence that is nothing short of regressive. It ignores the changing historical circumstances of contemporary Western societies—in the case of America, its social progress since the 1960s—which do not justify such levels of disruption in cases where controversial figures are merely invited to speak on campus. Without a doubt, this egregious argument also dismisses the likelihood or possibility of potentially meaningful dialogue that would be suppressed.

B. "Irrelevant" and "Settled" Topics

Some critics do not espouse the marketplace of ideas argument for different reasons. Rather than functioning as a marketplace of ideas, some argue, university teaching should be guided by a curriculum that is determined by academic processes, and the contents of the curriculum should contain the ideas and thinking of appointed academics mandated to teach.[32] After all, taxpayers are paying for universities that educate people with a curriculum determined and reviewed by these academics, not "a facility for peddlers of religion" and other academically irrelevant or settled topics.[33]

---

30. Amy Lai, *On Campus, Unpopular Views Also Deserve a Platform*, Globe & Mail (May 27, 2019), https://www.theglobeandmail.com/opinion/article-on-campus-unpopular-views-also-deserve-a-platform/
31. Amy Lai, *On Campus, Unpopular Views Also Deserve a Platform*, Globe & Mail (May 27, 2019), https://www.theglobeandmail.com/opinion/article-on-campus-unpopular-views-also-deserve-a-platform/
32. *See, e.g.*, Amy Lai, *On Campus, Unpopular Views Also Deserve a Platform*, Globe & Mail (May 27, 2019), https://www.theglobeandmail.com/opinion/article-on-campus-unpopular-views-also-deserve-a-platform/, see the comment section [archived].
33. *See* Amy Lai, *On Campus, Unpopular Views Also Deserve a Platform*, Globe & Mail (May 27, 2019),

While universities are more than just marketplaces of ideas, the concept of a marketplace of ideas is far more relevant in the university than the above critics are willing to acknowledge. Appointed academics can be biased. In fact, liberal-leaning academics have been found to outnumber their conservative counterparts at universities in the U.S., the United Kingdom, and Canada, a fact that may have led to liberal biases in their teaching and research.[34] (Self-)censorship of conservative views on campuses in these countries are likely a result of such biases.[35] While the design of the curricula falls within the rights and duties of academics, they have neither the authority nor the expertise to define the scope of topics that are relevant enough to be discussed in a university setting, lest topics unpopular among academics of certain political leanings are shut down and limited perspectives keep getting reinforced, which would turn universities into nothing more than echo chambers of orthodoxies.[36] The possibility that liberal-leaning voices coming from or representing historically oppressed groups have been more frequently marginalized in universities, as some claim, does not invalidate the marketplace of ideas argument, as all voices—not only voices that have been historically suppressed—need to be heard in a real marketplace.[37] As chapter 2 has explained, the right to free speech is broader in scope than academic freedom, and chapter 3 has further illuminated that free speech in universities is itself a precondition for academic freedom. Hence, the proper duty of academics, regardless of their own politics,

---

https://www.theglobeandmail.com/opinion/article-on-campus-unpopular-views-also-deserve-a-platform/, see the comment section [archived].

34. A study conducted by professors from Brooklyn College and George Mason University found that liberal professors and researchers outnumber conservatives nearly twelve to one in the U.S. A study by the National Association of Scholars found that almost 40 percent of the top-ranked American liberal arts colleges have no professors who are registered Republicans. *E.g.*, Lauren Cooley, *Liberalism Is Rampant on Campus and Ruining Academia*, WASH. EXAMINER (Sep. 8, 2018), https://www.washingtonexaminer.com/red-alert-politics/liberalism-is-rampant-on-campus-and-ruining-academia. A study conducted by the Adam Smith Institute found that 80 percent of British university lecturers are liberal-leaning. Camilla Turner, *Eight in Ten British University Lecturers Are 'Left-wing,' Survey Finds*, THE TELEGRAPH (Mar. 2, 2017, 12:01 AM), https://www.telegraph.co.uk/education/2017/03/02/eight-ten-british-university-lecturers-left-wing-survey-finds/. Canadian academics were also found to fall on the liberal end of the political spectrum. M. Reza Nakhaie & Robert J. Brym, *The Ideological Orientations of Canadian University Professors*, 41 CAN. J. HIGHER EDUC. 18 (2011).

35. *See, e.g.*, Lauren Cooley, *Liberalism Is Rampant on Campus and Ruining Academia*, WASH. EXAMINER (Sep. 8, 2018), https://www.washingtonexaminer.com/red-alert-politics/liberalism-is-rampant-on-campus-and-ruining-academia

36. *See, e.g.*, Lauren Cooley, *Liberalism Is Rampant on Campus and Ruining Academia*, WASH. EXAMINER (Sep. 8, 2018), https://www.washingtonexaminer.com/red-alert-politics/liberalism-is-rampant-on-campus-and-ruining-academia

37. *See* Caitlin Setnicar, *How Heterodox Academy Creates a Safe Space for Bad Ideas*, DEMOS J. (Jan. 31, 2020), https://demosjournal.com/article/how-heterodox-academy-creates-a-safe-space-for-bad-ideas/

is not to prescribe/limit topics or perspectives on campuses but rather to draw upon their training to guide discussions.

Certainly, not all topics can be included in the curriculum, and the exclusion of certain topics may reflect limited time and resources rather than potential ideological biases. Regardless, academics can and should do a favor to their communities by not attempting to shut down topics that may not fall within their expertise or curriculum or are not in line with their own beliefs or that they personally deem irrelevant. After all, university learning arguably goes beyond the classroom curriculum, and members benefit from learning from areas that fall outside their own disciplines. Can one truly argue in good faith that topics such as what role multiculturalism should play in national policies and how Western countries should deal with hostile foreign nations with abysmal human rights records are irrelevant in university settings and to society more generally?

Still, some critics contend that a marketplace of ideas, even if it applies to the university setting, should only provide room for topics that are alive; for topics that have been settled, giving a platform to outdated and invalid ideas can revive and legitimize them and harm society.[38] Those who embrace this argument often cite examples involving established historical and scientific facts that have little room for disagreement, for example, how platforming flat-earth believers would be a waste of resources.[39] A convincing case cannot be made using this logic to shut down speakers on many—perhaps most—contested topics.[40]

Academics and university administrators who get to decide what topics are settled and therefore not up for further debate may undermine foundational democratic values by promoting simplistic ideologically driven narratives, if not outright dictating peoples' thoughts, in universities and society at large. Chapter 4 has explained why taking views or theories as established facts or holy doctrines that must not be challenged is risky and even authoritarian, citing as examples the merits of multiculturalism embraced by many Western nations and the narrative promoted by the Chinese government that Hong Kong is historically an inalienable part of China's territory and rightfully

38. *See, e.g.*, WitchofAeaea, Comment on Reddit re: *Opinion: On Campus, Unpopular Views Also Deserve a Platform* (May 2019) [archived], https://www.reddit.com/r/CanadaPolitics/comments/bv73ph/opinion_on_campus_unpopular_views_also_deserve_a/ (last visited Feb. 18, 2020).

39. *See, e.g.*, WitchofAeaea, Comment on Reddit re: *Opinion: On Campus, Unpopular Views Also Deserve a Platform* (May 2019) [archived], https://www.reddit.com/r/CanadaPolitics/comments/bv73ph/opinion_on_campus_unpopular_views_also_deserve_a/ (last visited Feb. 18, 2020).

40. *See, e.g.*, WitchofAeaea, Comment on Reddit re: *Opinion: On Campus, Unpopular Views Also Deserve a Platform* (May 2019) [archived], https://www.reddit.com/r/CanadaPolitics/comments/bv73ph/opinion_on_campus_unpopular_views_also_deserve_a/ (last visited Feb. 18, 2020).

belongs to China. Topics that may be considered "settled" also include the impacts of colonialism. Colonialism is generally considered to be evil and exploitative to the colonized.[41] However, deeming this a fully settled topic may lead to the shutting down of speakers from former colonies that benefited tremendously from colonial powers or came into existence because of colonialism. These people, who both detest oppression and exploitation and refuse to obsess over past injustices, may offer valuable insights into how far the decolonization movement should go and how current settler colonies should govern indigenous populations. Another "settled" topic concerns foreign policy objectives. Cooperation with foreign nations, even hostile ones whose values are incompatible with those of the civilized world, is commonly deemed to be of utmost importance in an era of globalization.[42] A failure or unwillingness to consider alternatives to this cliché may justify deplatforming people who have been brutalized by regimes that harbor little ethics or integrity, and who may make a convincing case of how cutting ties with those regimes will be hugely beneficial to the world order.

C. Nonintellectual Considerations: Donations, Security Risks, Group vs. Individual

Some arguments in favor of deplatforming rely not so much on the speakers' rights to free speech, or the merits and relevance of their expressions, as on several nonintellectual considerations. One such consideration is financial. The many stakeholders in university education include not only students and staff but also donors, who may find the views of controversial speakers so repulsive that they stop giving donations to universities.[43] Platforming such speakers

41. *See, e.g.*, Massimo Renzo, *Why Colonialism Is Wrong*, 72 Current Leg. Problems 347 (2019); Nathan J. Robinson, *A Quick Reminder of Why Colonialism Was Bad*, Current Affairs (Sep. 14, 2017), https://www.currentaffairs.org/2017/09/a-quick-reminder-of-why-colonialism-was-bad; Lea Epi, *What's Wrong with Colonialism*, 41 Phil. & Pub. Affairs 158 (2013).
42. *See, e.g.*, Vitor Gaspar, Sean Hagan & Maurice Obstfeld, *We Can't Abandon Global Cooperation, but It Needs an Update*, World Econ. Forum (Sep. 10, 2018), https://www.weforum.org/agenda/2018/09/steering-the-world-toward-more-cooperation-not-less/ (last visited Feb. 19, 2020); Australian Government, *Chapter Six: Global Cooperation*, 2017 Foreign Policy White Paper, https://www.fpwhitepaper.gov.au/foreign-policy-white-paper/chapter-six-global-cooperation (last visited Feb. 19, 2010).
43. *See, e.g.*, Robert B. Farrell, *Leadership Response to Campus Free Speech Incidents*, PhD diss., Univ. Penn. (2019); Emmett MacFarlane, *The Fear of Offending Is Sapping Universities of Common Sense*, Globe & Mail (Jan. 10, 2014), https://www.theglobeandmail.com/opinion/the-fear-of-offending-is-sapping-universities-of-common-sense/article16277915/

may also turn away potential donors who may not want their names associated with the offensive speakers.[44]

The belief that inviting controversial speakers may cause donors to withhold donations or turn away potential ones from donating is not without support.[45] However, donors may be equally likely to stop giving money to places that they believe no longer promote freedom of inquiry.[46] In fact, some critics contend that appealing to donors or alumni would be a good strategy to pressure universities into protecting free speech and discouraging deplatforming practices.[47] The key is to demonstrate to donors how inviting certain speakers would contribute to open inquiry. If there are donors who threaten to withhold future donations to universities merely for hosting speakers whose views they do not agree with, then perhaps universities, rather than pandering to these donors, can do better without them. To make up for the losses, administrators should diligently seek out donors whose beliefs align with the mission of a university: promoting knowledge through open inquiry.

Another nonintellectual justification for deplatforming is campus safety. Deplatforming speakers is only sensible, some believe, if their presence on campus would raise security concerns.[48] Indeed, stories abound of controver-

---

44. *See* Emmett MacFarlane, *The Fear of Offending Is Sapping Universities of Common Sense*, Globe & Mail (Jan. 10, 2014), https://www.theglobeandmail.com/opinion/the-fear-of-offending-is-sapping-universities-of-common-sense/article16277915/

45. *See, e.g.*, Joseph Bottum, *God and Obama at Notre Dame*, CBS News (May 11, 2009), https://www.cbsnews.com/news/god-and-obama-at-notre-dame/ (last visited Feb. 21, 2020). In 2009, a group of donors pressured Notre Dame University to disinvite President Barack Obama to speak at its commencement due to his support for abortion by pledging to withhold $8.2 million in future donations from the school.

46. *See, e.g.*, Wendy Stueck, *UBC Bows to Backlash by Re-inviting John Furlong to Give Speech*, Globe & Mail (Jan. 9, 2017), https://www.theglobeandmail.com/news/british-columbia/john-furlong-to-speak-again-at-ubc-fundraiser/article33549614/. In 2017, the University of British Columbia reinstated former Vancouver Olympic CEO John Furlong as keynote speaker for a fundraising breakfast in February after facing a backlash from donors and alumni.

47. *E.g.*, Noah Carl, *Threats to Free Speech at University, and How to Deal with Them—Part 2*, Areo Mag. (Dec. 17, 2019), https://areomagazine.com/2019/12/17/threats-to-free-speech-at-university-and-how-to-deal-with-them-part-2/ (last visited Feb. 21, 2010); *see, e.g.*, Tom Troy, *Notre Dame Alumnae Take to Social Media after Speaker Disinvited from May Crowning*, The Blade (May 3, 2013), https://www.toledoblade.com/Education/2013/05/03/Notre-Dame-alums-take-to-social-media-after-speaker-disinvited-from-May-Crowning.html?fb_comment_id=362837727150329_1785615 (last visited Feb. 21, 2010).

48. *See, e.g.*, Sean Boynton, *UBC Threatened with Legal Action over Free Speech Concerns after Cancelling Event*, Global News (Jan. 4, 2020), https://globalnews.ca/news/6367366/ubc-free-speech-andy-ngo/ (last visited Feb. 24, 2020); Megan Schellong, *Here's How Much Security Costs When an Incendiary Speaker Comes to Campus*, USA Today (Sep. 13, 2017), https://www.usatoday.com/story/college/2017/09/13/heres-how-much-security-costs-when-an-incendiary-speaker-comes-to-campus/37434939/

sial speakers receiving death threats or threats of violent protests after their visits were publicized, or drawing mobs of protesters at their events.[49] As campus police may not be well equipped to provide the level of safety for the events to go forward and the exorbitant costs of heightened security measures would fall on universities, platforming controversial speakers may not be worth the price.[50]

Disinviting speakers who do not cause violence for fear that they may trigger violent protesters is a bad policy both morally and practically. Peaceful protests should be tolerated, accommodated, and even encouraged as they may offer valuable input on contentious issues. Violent actions targeting individuals who merely exercise their freedom of expression are both illegal and morally unjustifiable. Like expressions that incite violence and thus fall within the legal definitions of hate speech or harassment, these actions should be prohibited. Thus, universities, rather than turning a blind eye to or coddling protesters who may try to justify or excuse their violence on moral grounds, should institute no-tolerance policies for violent actions and subject the lawbreakers to strict discipline. Implementing strict policies may deter violence and encourage peaceful means of protest, thus making potential high security costs of inviting speakers less of a concern. To give in to these violent protesters, on the other hand, would very likely empower them and encourage more violence by sending a signal to the communities that disruptive, violent methods to suppress free speech are both legitimate and effective.

It has been pointed out that Western cultures are not homogenous: some cultures value group rights more than others do.[51] In such cultures, individuals' rights to free speech need to be weighed against group rights to peace and harmony; it is reasonable to deplatform expressions that promote hate and racism against certain groups.[52] This chapter does not argue that deplatforming should

49. *See, e.g.*, Sudhin Thanawala, *Multiple Arrests at Ben Shapiro Berkeley Protests*, USA Today (Sep. 15, 2017), https://www.usatoday.com/story/news/nation/2017/09/15/ben-shapiro-berkeley-protest-arrests/669071001/

50. *See, e.g.*, Megan Schellong, *Here's How Much Security Costs When an Incendiary Speaker Comes to Campus*, USA Today (Sep. 13, 2017), https://www.usatoday.com/story/college/2017/09/13/heres-how-much-security-costs-when-an-incendiary-speaker-comes-to-campus/37434939/; Sudhin Thanawala, *Multiple Arrests at Ben Shapiro Berkeley Protests*, USA Today (Sep. 15, 2017), https://www.usatoday.com/story/news/nation/2017/09/15/ben-shapiro-berkeley-protest-arrests/669071001/

51. *See* Amy Lai, *On Campus, Unpopular Views Also Deserve a Platform*, Globe & Mail (May 27, 2019), https://www.theglobeandmail.com/opinion/article-on-campus-unpopular-views-also-deserve-a-platform/, see the comment section [archived].

52. Amy Lai, *On Campus, Unpopular Views Also Deserve a Platform*, Globe & Mail (May 27, 2019),

never happen: it argues that it is generally a bad policy. In addition, concepts like "hate" and "racism" can be challenging to define and can be expanded indefinitely to shut down discussion on such important topics as immigration and multiculturalism. As a hypothetical example, intellectually honest critiques of multiculturalism cannot be said to be racist or hateful by any measure if they are substantiated by evidence that a vast majority of immigrants from a certain country tend to hold values or act in ways that undermine the democratic governance of the host country, whether or not such actions are instigated by the government of their country of origin—such criticisms target the conduct of immigrants rather than their skin color and are motivated by grave concerns rather than by any hateful sentiment. The danger of expanding such concepts as harm and hate will be discussed further in section III. At this juncture it is important to note that groups are made of individuals. When individuals' rights to expression and to access opinions and ideas in a civil atmosphere are violated, the groups to which they belong would suffer.

II. Trigger Warning

Not all controversial speakers get deplatformed. As a result, they become a source of triggers on campus. This section begins by introducing two common triggers in the university setting. The first type consists of contentious topics and content, including those that cannot be avoided in classroom learning. The second type refers to personal attacks, which take the form of insults and public shaming targeting specific persons.

Imagine two colleagues: A and B. Colleague A, always civil and professional, embraces freedom of inquiry. Deeply convinced that the university should not be dominated by orthodoxies, colleague A therefore invites speakers to challenge mainstream ideologies. Colleague B, always harping on the importance of love, kindness, and tolerance, believes that most issues are long settled according to these principles. Hence, B incessantly shuts down opinions challenging his/her worldview and beliefs, often by attacking and shaming colleague A and urging other colleagues to do the same, in such an open manner that people from outside academia also witness it all (reasonable

https://www.theglobeandmail.com/opinion/article-on-campus-unpopular-views-also-deserve-a-platform/, see the comment section [archived].

members of society can only sympathize, sigh, and shake their heads at such "love"-induced hysteria, but hesitate to show their support for A, fearing that they may also get attacked).

Reasonable people who have little or no experience with academia would be tempted to believe that any member who endeavors to advance knowledge through open inquiry should be far more valued and respected in a university setting than those who attack and gang up on dissenters. Yet on today's campus, outspoken yet civil members may be more likely recognized as "troublemakers" or "bullies" than hysterical peace-lovers whose vitriolic attacks may be readily dismissed or excused on the ground that they could only have been motivated by a firm devotion to the truth and by love and kindness to people who might get offended by "bigotry." In the end, those who value open inquiry are ostracized by the "love brigade." Contentious topics and content that are unavoidable in the classroom are considered potentially traumatizing, to the extent that "trigger warnings" are deemed necessary to forewarn students about their disturbing nature and to reduce the emotional harm that they would cause.

A trigger warning is a statement made at the beginning of a work cautioning that its content may be distressing, or "triggering," to some people.[53] It is believed that such warnings, which originated in feminist websites discussing sexual violence, can provide temporary relief to trauma victims, especially those suffering from post-traumatic stress disorder (PTSD).[54] Richard McNally, a professor of psychology at Harvard University, expresses skepticism about its efficacy, noting that systematic exposure to triggers is the most effective means of overcoming PTSD, while their avoidance to prevent emotional discomfort might reinforce it.[55] In addition, a study he conducted with his team indicates that a trigger warning at the beginning of a work may also harm the audience who did not initially experience trauma-induced stress, by increasing their anxiety over potentially disturbing content in the work, as well as by reducing their perception of their own and other people's psychological resilience to

---

53. *E.g.*, *Trigger Warning*, Merriam-Webster Dictionary, https://www.merriam-webster.com/dictionary/trigger%20warning (last visited Mar. 9, 2020); *Trigger Warning*, Cambridge Dictionary, https://dictionary.cambridge.org/dictionary/english/trigger-warning (last visited Mar. 9, 2020).
54. *E.g.*, Colleen Flaherty, *Death Knell for Trigger Warnings*, Inside Higher Educ. (Mar. 21, 2019), https://www.insidehighered.com/news/2019/03/21/new-study-says-trigger-warnings-are-useless-does-mean-they-should-be-abandoned; Ouchlets, *Trigger Warnings: What Do They Do?* Ouch Blog, BBC (Feb. 25, 2014), https://www.bbc.com/news/blogs-ouch-26295437 (last visited Mar. 9, 2020).
55. Richard McNally, *If You Need a Trigger Warning, You Need PTSD Treatment*, N.Y. Times (Sep. 13, 2016), https://www.nytimes.com/roomfordebate/2016/09/13/do-trigger-warnings-work/if-you-need-a-trigger-warning-you-need-ptsd-treatment

traumas that the content might cause.[56] A low belief in such resilience in turn becomes a risk factor for developing PTSD in the future.[57]

In many Western universities, professors are now required to issue trigger warnings to alert students of potentially disturbing or upsetting content in their classes and allow them to skip classes that could make them feel too uncomfortable. The American Association of University Professors issued a report critical of trigger warnings in the university context, stating that "[t]he presumption that students need to be protected rather than challenged in a classroom is at once infantilizing and anti-intellectual."[58] Some disagree and contend that trigger warnings form part of a "sound pedagogy," one that acknowledges students' wide-ranging backgrounds and experiences and that prepares them for an important but at times painful journey of learning.[59]

A. Do Trigger Warnings Harm Freedom of Speech and Inquiry?

The efficacy of trigger warnings for people with PTSD is a topic that is best left to scientists. Whether they may harm free speech, however, is subject to open debate. It has been argued that trigger warnings aim not to encourage students to avoid important and potentially disturbing course contents, but to psychologically prepare them for these contents; only in extreme circumstances, when the contents are found to be too disturbing, would alternative modes of learning be provided.[60] Hence, trigger warnings cost almost nothing: they take little time or energy to administer and would not harm freedom of speech.

Numerous academics believe that trigger warnings hinder free speech. Jonathan Haidt and Greg Lukianoff, for example, agree that they may not be harmful per se, but may become part of a broader trend of coddling students rather

56. Benjamin Bellet, Payton J. Jones, & Richard J. McNally, *Trigger Warning: Empirical Evidence Ahead*, 61 Behavior Therapy & Experimental Psychiatry 134 (2018).
57. Benjamin Bellet, Payton J. Jones, & Richard J. McNally, *Trigger Warning: Empirical Evidence Ahead*, 61 Behavior Therapy & Experimental Psychiatry 134 (2018).
58. *On Trigger Warnings*, American Association of University Professors (Aug. 2014), https://www.aaup.org/report/trigger-warnings (last visited Mar. 9, 2020).
59. *E.g.*, Angus Johnston, *Why I'll Add a Trigger Warning*, Inside Higher Educ. (May 29, 2014), https://www.insidehighered.com/views/2014/05/29/essay-why-professor-adding-trigger-warning-his-syllabus
60. *E.g.*, Elanor A. Lockhart, *Why Trigger Warnings Are Beneficial, Perhaps Even Necessary*, 50(2) First Amend. Stud. 59 (2016); see *also* Angus Johnston, *Why I'll Add a Trigger Warning*, Inside Higher Educ. (May 29, 2014), https://www.insidehighered.com/views/2014/05/29/essay-why-professor-adding-trigger-warning-his-syllabus

than engaging them in difficult conversations.[61] Students can use warnings as an excuse to not prepare for sensitive materials and to avoid presenters or speakers whom they do not like.[62] This may play into the hands of those who desire to advance their agendas to restrict academic freedom on university campuses.[63] Even if there is no such agenda, trigger warnings may also make students feel uneasy about course contents and discourage them from engaging topics that they otherwise would feel comfortable to discuss. Some have proposed a one-time-only warning, for example, at the opening ceremony, forewarning students about the difficult or emotionally challenging topics that they may encounter over the course of their studies.[64]

This one-off warning may not achieve its intended effect, however, as it may be easily forgotten or dismissed as just another cliché at what is to some students a boring event. If given in class, warnings should perhaps be cut down: rather than issuing a warning every time before potentially triggering material is introduced, a one-off warning can be given at the beginning of the first class. Warnings can also be included on the first pages of syllabi.

---

61. Jonathan Haidt & Greg Lukianoff, The Coddling of the American Mind: How Good Intentions and Bad Ideas Are Setting up a Generation for Failure (2018); Jim Ver Steeg, *Free Speech and Trigger Warnings*, Rochester University News Center (Apr. 25, 2019), https://www.rochester.edu/newscenter/free-speech-and-trigger-warnings-377272/ (last visited Mar. 9, 2020); Scott O. Lilienfeld, Stephen J. Ceci & Wendy M. Williams, *The One-Time Only Trigger Warning*, Inside Higher Educ. (Oct. 18, 2018), https://www.insidehighered.com/views/2018/10/18/way-handle-trigger-warnings-develop-one-time-only-one-opinion
62. *E.g.*, Scott O. Lilienfeld, Stephen J. Ceci & Wendy M. Williams, *The One-Time Only Trigger Warning*, Inside Higher Educ. (Oct. 18, 2018), https://www.insidehighered.com/views/2018/10/18/way-handle-trigger-warnings-develop-one-time-only-one-opinion
63. *See* Scott O. Lilienfeld, Stephen J. Ceci & Wendy M. Williams, *The One-Time Only Trigger Warning*, Inside Higher Educ. (Oct. 18, 2018), https://www.insidehighered.com/views/2018/10/18/way-handle-trigger-warnings-develop-one-time-only-one-opinion
64. One such example would go like this: "Over the course of the next four years you will be encountering a number of topics that you may find emotionally challenging, even difficult. If some of this stuff makes you feel uncomfortable, that's perfectly normal, and we encourage you to talk to us and your friends about it. But bear in mind that a liberal arts education is designed to confront you with things that challenge and at times even threaten your worldviews. So if you feel intellectually or emotionally disturbed by what you learn in class, don't assume that you should be concerned. It may only mean that you are engaging with novel perspectives, which is what college is all about." Scott O. Lilienfeld, Stephen J. Ceci & Wendy M. Williams, *The One-Time Only Trigger Warning*, Inside Higher Educ. (Oct. 18, 2018), https://www.insidehighered.com/views/2018/10/18/way-handle-trigger-warnings-develop-one-time-only-one-opinion

B. Since When Has "Provocative" Become a Bad Word? The Value of Provocation in Pedagogy

According to psychologists, the avoidance of triggers is not a treatment, but a symptom of PTSD. Severe emotional reactions to course materials or the content of speech do not generally indicate that students or attendees should be forewarned that those materials could be triggering, or that potentially triggering materials should be removed from the syllabi or omitted from speech.[65] Rather, they are signals that the emotionally affected need to seek professional help to overcome PTSD.[66]

At the same time, the fact that many people consider "trigger warnings" even necessary for academic communities more generally indicates that the meaning of "trigger/triggering" has gone well beyond the contexts of psychology and medicine and become synonymous with "provoke/provocative." Although expressions that are thought to "provoke" are often frowned upon and people who make "provocative" comments are easily branded "troublemakers," "provoke" and "provocative" can be positive or negative. "Provocative" can mean causing a strong, usually negative, reaction such as anger or offense.[67] It can also mean causing a strong reaction with the intention to make one think more carefully about something.[68] In the latter case, "provocative" expressions are "thought-provoking"—interesting and with the ability to motivate people to ponder deeply about the issues at hand—which can only be positive, especially in universities.[69]

The value of provocation in pedagogy is recognized by at least some aca-

65. *E.g.*, Richard McNally, *If You Need a Trigger Warning, You Need PTSD Treatment*, N.Y. Times (Sep. 13, 2016), https://www.nytimes.com/roomfordebate/2016/09/13/do-trigger-warnings-work/if-you-need-a-trigger-warning-you-need-ptsd-treatment; Jonathan Haidt & Greg Lukianoff, The Coddling of the American Mind: How Good Intentions and Bad Ideas Are Setting up a Generation for Failure (2018).

66. *E.g.*, Richard McNally, *If You Need a Trigger Warning, You Need PTSD Treatment*, N.Y. Times (Sep. 13, 2016), https://www.nytimes.com/roomfordebate/2016/09/13/do-trigger-warnings-work/if-you-need-a-trigger-warning-you-need-ptsd-treatment; Jonathan Haidt & Greg Lukianoff, The Coddling of the American Mind: How Good Intentions and Bad Ideas Are Setting up a Generation for Failure (2018).

67. *E.g.*, *Provoke*, Cambridge Dictionary, https://dictionary.cambridge.org/dictionary/english/provoke (last visited Mar. 3, 2020); *Provocative*, Cambridge Dictionary, https://dictionary.cambridge.org/dictionary/english/provocative (last visited Mar. 3, 2020).

68. *E.g.*, *Provoke*, Cambridge Dictionary, https://dictionary.cambridge.org/dictionary/english/provoke (last visited Mar. 3, 2020); *Provocative*, Cambridge Dictionary, https://dictionary.cambridge.org/dictionary/english/provocative (last visited Mar. 3, 2020).

69. *Thought-provoking*, Cambridge Dictionary, https://dictionary.cambridge.org/dictionary/english/thought-provoking (last visited Mar. 4, 2020).

demics in disciplines as varied as psychology and literature.[70] A provocative pedagogical approach to teaching helps students to develop their critical thinking skills by introducing different perspectives, challenging and pushing back their preconceptions, enabling them to work through contradictions, correcting them on facts when necessary, and guiding them to form their own opinions.[71] In such subjects as philosophy and ethics, a provocative method of teaching helps broaden students' horizons with regard to issues about human nature, reality, and science.[72] Playing the devil's advocate is an excellent way to introduce provocative perspectives and help improve critical thinking capacity.

C. What Is Being "Triggered"? Provoking the Brain vs. Attacking the Person

Expressions provoke or trigger in different ways. As this section began with personal attacks, to this type of trigger it now returns. Expressions that provoke the brain must be distinguished from those that attack the person. Although personal attacks may not escalate to bullying or harassment, they can be disruptive enough to impede the goals that free speech is meant to accomplish. Provocative ideas and opinions, unlike personal attacks, need not offend individuals unless they choose to be offended, in which case offended individuals, not the holders of those ideas and opinions, are to blame.

Attacking people's physical attributes, such as weight, is harmful to the attacked and creates a toxic atmosphere unfavorable to learning and research. Personal attacks of this nature may be inappropriate even when they are levied against people working in jobs for which a healthy weight or body size is a requirement. However, a lecture addressing the correlation between weight and productivity—even one presenting evidence of the negative impact of obesity on companies and society[73]—provokes the brain and cannot be con-

---

70. *See, e.g.*, Aimee Morrison, *A Pedagogy of Provocation*, Hook & Eye (Jan. 27, 2016), https://hookandeye.ca/category/teaching/ (last visited Mar. 4, 2020); Jon Mills, *An Unorthodox Pedagogy: Fostering Empathy Through Provocation*, *in* A Pedagogy of Becoming 123–24 (Jon Mills, ed. 2002).

71. *E.g.*, Aimee Morrison, *A Pedagogy of Provocation*, Hook & Eye (Jan. 27, 2016), https://hookandeye.ca/category/teaching/ (last visited Mar. 4, 2020).

72. *E.g.*, Aimee Morrison, *A Pedagogy of Provocation*, Hook & Eye (Jan. 27, 2016), https://hookandeye.ca/category/teaching/ (last visited Mar. 4, 2020).

73. This is not a pure hypothesis invented by the author and is backed by scientific research. *See, e.g.*, Ian Kudel, Joanna C. Huang & Rahul Ganguly, *Impact of Obesity on Work Productivity in Different US Occupations*, 60 J. Occup. Envir. Med. 6 (2018); Andrea Goettler, Anna Grosse & Diana Sonntag,

sidered an attack on overweight people. First, the statement that overweight people on average tend to be less productive than their healthy-weight counterparts is very general, meaning that the overweight among the audience may very well be exceptions. Second, even assuming that the statement applies to all, the overweight can compensate with other attributes, such as diligence and conscientiousness, so that they end up being as productive as people of healthy weight. Third, being overweight, for many people, is a behavioral choice, such as a result of eating habits or not doing enough to lose weight, and in such cases people can work hard to reach and maintain a healthy weight and boost their efficiency.

Addressing the correlation between weight and productivity therefore provides food for thought, motivates people to stay healthy, and increases societal productivity. Stating that there may be a correlation between weight and productivity is a far cry from attacking overweight or obese colleagues by insulting and intimidating them (for example, by calling a colleague "fat ass") or by insinuating that they do not belong where they are due to their body size (for example, by sarcastically inquiring how they obtained their jobs). Unless the topic is weaponized for personal attacks, a reasonable person should not take offense at it.

It is not always easy to draw the line between opinions and ideas that provoke the brain and those that attack the person, and potentially controversial topics no doubt must be contextualized with care. Contrary to popular belief, provocative critiques of race-based affirmative action in American higher educational institutions (and their counterparts in other Western countries) need not attack minority candidates who benefit from it. Under this policy, for instance, "underrepresented racial minorities" receive a boost in their law school applications by virtue of their race and thus generally gain admission with (substantially) lower LSAT scores and GPAs than those who are not underrepresented minority candidates.[74] The policy can be criticized from a socioeconomic framework, which posits that class, not race, is the chief determinant of academic success, and admission committees therefore should look past applicants' race and give more weight to their socioeconomic status.[75] It

---

Productivity Loss Due to Overweight and Obesity: A Systematic Review of Indirect Costs, 7 BMJ Open e014632, https://doi.org/10.1136/bmjopen-2016-014632

74. *See, e.g.*, *Do Underrepresented Minority (URM) Applicants Have a Law School Admissions Advantage?* Powerscore (Mar. 17, 2017), https://blog.powerscore.com/lsat/do-underrepresented-minority-urm-applicants-have-a-law-school-admissions-advantage/ (last visited Mar. 1, 2020).

75. *See, e.g.*, Richard Kahlenberg, *Affirmative Action Should Be Based on Class, Not Race*, Economist

can also be criticized from a race framework for privileging certain races over others: while African Americans have suffered a history of oppression, many Asians (and whites) have very humble backgrounds and committees should not dismiss their "lived experiences" by assuming that they are more privileged—to do so would "erase" their existence (words and terms that left-leaning scholars, according to whom Asian Americans often rank lower on the oppression hierarchy, use to give voice to oppressed groups or to advance their rights).[76] The policy can be further attacked from a diversity framework for privileging race over other forms of diversity: there is no good reason why checking the "black" box in the race category should give such a big boost to the application while most other forms of diversity, such as overcoming hardships, unique experiences, and knowledge of widely spoken foreign languages, should only count as soft factors in a country like America and Canada, where most applicants are monolingual.

Impersonal criticisms that target admission policies by identifying their inadequacies are often thought-provoking and can motivate reforms. Targeting racial minorities' academic performance in the schools that implement these policies, on the other hand, would only make the students feel attacked and belittled—and unnecessarily so. It does not contribute much to the arguments against affirmative action, as various factors can influence one's performance, and even lackluster or subpar academic performances may not prevent graduates from becoming competent lawyers.

Provocative critiques of multiculturalism and open-borders policies likewise are not personal attacks on racial and ethnic minorities. Those skeptical of these policies can argue, without dismissing the benefits that cultural diversity brings to a country, that immigrants of non-Western cultural origins must embrace the democratic values of the countries to which they willingly immigrate; to that end, they can preserve their own cultural values only if these values do not contradict the fundamental values of host countries. Critics may also show evidence that many immigrants from certain authoritarian countries

---

(Sep. 4, 2018), https://www.economist.com/open-future/2018/09/04/affirmative-action-should-be-based-on-class-not-race; Richard Kahlenberg & Halley Potter, *Class-Based Affirmative Action Works*, N.Y. Times (Apr. 27, 2014), https://www.nytimes.com/roomfordebate/2014/04/27/should-affirmative-action-be-based-on-income/class-based-affirmative-action-works

76. *See, e.g.*, Anemona Hartocollis, *The Affirmative Action Battle at Harvard Is Not Over*, N.Y. Times (Feb. 18, 2020), https://www.nytimes.com/2020/02/18/us/affirmative-action-harvard.html; Jay Caspian Kang, *Where Does Affirmative Action Leave Asian-Americans?* N.Y. Times (Aug. 28, 2019), https://www.nytimes.com/2019/08/28/magazine/affirmative-action-asian-american-harvard.html

have been undermining the democratic values of host countries, for example, by exporting authoritarianism and violently suppressing peaceful criticisms of their former governments in their host countries.[77] Hence, applicants from these authoritarian countries should be more carefully vetted than those from other countries. A reasonable person harboring doubts regarding these culture- and behavior-based criticisms should at least agree that they are not personal attacks on immigrants of racial and ethnic minority groups. Perhaps those jumping on discussions about cultures and behaviors and quickly labeling them as "racist" or "personal attacks" that need to be shut down should take a long, hard look at themselves, to find out what made them take criticisms so personally or find everything they do not agree with "racist."

On the contrary, race-based critiques of multiculturalism and open-borders policies would make racial minorities feel attacked personally—and rightly so. Whereas people of different cultures can learn from and influence one another, and nonwhite immigrants in white-majority countries can acculturate through time and effort, race is inborn and cannot be changed. Examples of race-based critiques include the argument that the white race is inherently superior, nonwhite minorities cannot integrate into white-majority societies even if they work hard to do so, and Western civilization, based upon "white cultures," would decline and collapse as white people seek to accommodate these inferior nonwhite "invaders."[78] This argument has been taken further to suggest that racial minorities are different species than the dominant race.[79] Critiques as such also do not contain substance, unless there is substantial evidence indicating that race has any definite bearing on culture and behavior (if this is true, how can one account for the observable fact that the overwhelming majority of East Asian immigrants from some countries tend to follow rules and embrace Western democratic values, while immigrants of the same race coming from

---

77. *See, e.g.*, Jeremy Luedi, *Beijing-Linked Student Groups Threaten Academic Freedom in Canada*, True N. Far E. (Jan. 19, 2020), https://truenorthfareast.com/news/china-influence-canada-universities-cssa (last visited Mar. 1, 2020); Emma Goldberg, *Hong Kong Protests Spread to US Colleges, and a Rift Grows*, N.Y. Times (Oct. 26, 2019), https://www.nytimes.com/2019/10/26/us/hong-kong-protests-colleges.html; Danien Cave, *Chinese Nationalists Bring Threat of Violence to Australian Universities*, N.Y. Times (Jul. 30, 2019), https://www.nytimes.com/2019/07/30/world/australia/hong-kong-china-queensland-protests.html

78. Ricardo Duchesne made this argument in his book *Canada in Decay: Mass Immigration, Diversity, and the Ethnocide of Euro-Canadians* (2018).

79. Some of Duchesne's followers on Twitter took his argument further and suggested that nonwhite minorities are different species than the white race through bizarre and insulting analogues, for example, by saying that putting mice in the oven would not turn them into cookies. *See* https://twitter.com/duchesnericardo?lang=en (last visited Mar. 1, 2020).

some other countries tend not to?). Even toning down the argument, such as by emphasizing that racial superiority is a general statement that does not apply to all individuals, might not make it less likely to be interpreted as a personal attack by members of "inferior" races. Perhaps those who are fixated on race and cannot spend a day without justifying why one race (be it white, East Asian, Hispanic, or black) is superior to others, just like those labeling civil and thought-provoking discussions as "racist" attacks, should also take a long, hard look at themselves to find out the reasons behind their obsession with race and their failure to see past people's skin color.

Unfortunately, thought-provoking opinions and ideas, which serve to advance knowledge, democratic governance, and personal development, and which are presented in a civil manner, are often mistaken for personal attacks, which accomplish little other than hurt feelings (and, perhaps, satisfy attackers' desires to harm and cause havoc). Interestingly, the conflation of these two can be easily found under authoritarian/dictatorial regimes, which aim to indoctrinate their subjects with ideologies emphasizing devotion and obedience to the state. As a result, it is not uncommon for people who spent their formative years in places such as China, where they were cut off from ideologies contradicting those promoted by their state, to overreact to the slightest criticism of their governments, which they regard as personal attacks against themselves—an overreaction uncommon in developing countries that value free speech (such as India).[80] On Western campuses, overreactions to novel ideas and opinions can be and are often used to justify shutting down lectures and discussions deemed so provocative and triggering that even trigger warnings would not serve their purpose.

Quite ironically, though, people who resort to personal attacks, such as by ridiculing, belittling, or publicly shaming colleagues for daring to think and speak differently and for challenging their worldviews, may have their actions excused or justified on the grounds that they are motivated by the noblest of intentions. When this happens, the campus turns into a twisted universe, or a place of contradictions—one that tolerates and normalizes personal attacks but discourages or shuts down "unsafe" viewpoints and ideas. Just as dissenting

---

80. *E.g.*, John Pomphret, *Is China's Government Ever Going to Grow Up?*, Wash. Post. (Oct. 9, 2019), https://www.washingtonpost.com/opinions/2019/10/09/is-chinas-government-ever-going-grow-up/; Chaguan, *China's Thin-Skinned Online Nationalists Want to Be Both Loved and Feared by the West*, Economist (Aug. 22, 2019), https://www.economist.com/china/2019/08/22/chinas-thin-skinned-online-nationalists-want-to-be-both-loved-and-feared-by-the-west

opinions and ideas often get mistaken for personal attacks in authoritarian/dictatorial countries, this phenomenon characterizes everyday lives in such countries (for example, Stalin's Russia and the People's Republic of China) where people, who are not allowed to criticize state authorities, indulge in vindictive impulses to attack, persecute, and spread rumors about neighbors, friends, and colleagues. Motivated by their ideologies and a toxic sense of justice derived from embracing such beliefs, or by state-sponsored reward systems, or both, they even spy on one another, identify people who dare to challenge orthodoxies or their very own dogmas, and turn these "offenders" over to the authorities to get them fired or jailed.[81] When similar things happen in Western universities, "offenders" whose views did not initially get deplatformed may ultimately get "canceled" as their jobs, social statuses, and platforms to speak are stripped from them by the authorities.[82]

III. Safe Space

Advocates of trigger warnings claim that those warnings prepare students for challenging course content and allow those finding the content too stress-inducing to skip classes and access the material through alternative modes of learning. Providing a haven for students where they feel safe from disturbing messages may deprive them of the opportunity to engage in important discussions for which there are no easy substitutes. Arguably, students are free, autonomous individuals entitled to remove themselves from situations causing them discomfort. Yet the decision to prioritize emotional well-being over learning may not be as personal and inconsequential as it seems. The "safe space" concept has far-reaching implications for free speech and democratic governance and needs to be critically examined.

The term "safe space" refers broadly to places created by educational institutions, student bodies, or professors for individuals, notably those in minority

81. *E.g.*, Emily Feng & Amy Cheng, *Chinese Universities Are Enshrining Communist Party Control in Their Charters*, NPR (Jan. 20, 2020), https://www.npr.org/2020/01/20/796377204/chinese-universities-are-enshrining-communist-party-control-in-their-charters (last visited Feb. 26, 2020); Javier C. Hernández, *Professors, Beware: In China, Student Spies Might Be Watching*, N.Y. Times (Nov. 1, 2019), https://www.nytimes.com/2019/11/01/world/asia/china-student-informers.html; Sebastian Shakespeare, *Traitors in the Family: Stalin's Informers*, Daily Mail (Sep. 22, 2009, 1:00 PM), https://www.dailymail.co.uk/columnists/article-483230/Traitors-family-Stalins-informers.html

82. *See, e.g.*, Delilah Alvarado, *Cancel Culture Is Toxic*, Univ. Star (Dec. 2, 2019), https://universitystar.com/33233/opinions/cancel-culture-is-toxic/ (last visited Feb. 26, 2020).

groups, to share their experiences in an environment that is free from violence, harassment, hate speech, discrimination, or even criticism.[83] Like trigger warning, this concept has feminist origins. It was invented during the feminist movement of the 1960s to empower women to carve out "women only" places where they can speak and act freely.[84] In the late 1980s, gay and lesbian communities borrowed the concept to advocate for universal acceptance of sexual/gender minorities and set up workplaces free from homophobia.[85] Since then, the concept has entered the common lexicon, to refer to welcoming spaces, especially those provided by youth groups, where members feel respected and free from discrimination, harassment, and intimidation.[86]

Over the past decade, safe space initiatives have become prevalent in Western universities. While universities commonly define a safe space as a place inclusive of all people, many such initiatives are geared toward serving sexual and gender minority communities, due to high levels of reported violence against these groups.[87] Heeding the call of Muslim scholars and educators, some universities more recently have set up safe spaces for Muslim students to

---

83. *E.g.*, Katherine Ho, *Tackling the Term: What Is a Safe Space?* HARV. POL. REV. (Jan. 30, 2017), http://harvardpolitics.com/harvard/what-is-a-safe-space/; Katy Waldman, *What Science Can Tell Us about Trigger Warnings*, SLATE (Sep. 5, 2016), http://www.slate.com/articles/double_x/cover_story/2016/09/what_science_can_tell_us_about_trigger_warnings.html; Teddy Amenabar, *The New Vocabulary of Protest*, WASH. POST (May 19, 2016), https://www.washingtonpost.com/sf/style/wp/2016/05/19/2016/05/19/what-college-students-mean-when-they-ask-for-safe-spaces-and-trigger-warnings/
84. *E.g.*, MOIRA R KENNEY, MAPPING GAY L.A.: THE INTERSECTION OF PLACE AND POLITICS 24 (2001); Malcolm Harris, *What's a Safe Space? A Look at the Phrase's 50-Year History*, SPLINTER NEWS (Nov. 11, 2015), https://splinternews.com/what-s-a-safe-space-a-look-at-the-phrases-50-year-hi-1793852786 (last visited Mar. 11, 2020).
85. NICOLE C. RAEBURN, CHANGING CORPORATE AMERICA FROM INSIDE OUT: LESBIAN AND GAY WORKPLACE RIGHTS 209 (2004).
86. *See, e.g.*, *Creating Safe Space for GLBTQ Youth: A Toolkit*, GIRL'S BEST FRIEND FOUNDATION AND ADVOCATES FOR YOUTH (2005), https://advocatesforyouth.org/wp-content/uploads/storage//advfy/documents/safespace.pdf (last visited Mar. 12, 2020); *Saskatchewan's Advocate for Children and Youth Is a Safe Space*, SASKATCHEWAN'S ADVOCATE FOR CHILDREN AND YOUTH, https://www.saskadvocate.ca/children-youth-first/saskatchewan's-advocate-children-and-youth-safe-space (last visited Mar. 12, 2020).
87. *See, e.g.*, The Sexual and Gender Diversity website at the University of Alberta reads: "The University of Alberta strives to build a diverse, inclusive community for all students, staff, and faculty by celebrating differences and encouraging a sense of belonging for all. We support sexual and gender minorities across our campuses through policies, programs, services, and events." *Sexual and Gender Diversity*, UNIVERSITY OF ALBERTA, https://www.ualberta.ca/sexual-gender-diversity (last visited Mar. 14, 2020); the Safe Spaces for LGBTQ+ Students website of the Northern Alberta Institute of Technology reads: "At NAIT, everyone deserves to feel safe. Safe Spaces is an initiative to mark safe and inclusive spaces for students who are lesbian, gay, bisexual, transgender, two-spirited, queer and questioning (LGBTQ)." *Safe Spaces for LGBTQ+ Students*, NAIT, https://student.nait.ca/student-services/safe-campus/safe-spaces-for-lgbtq-students (last visited Mar. 14, 2020).

conduct their religious practices.[88] More universities have been urged to follow the lead to combat Islamophobia.[89]

A. Different "Safe Spaces"

The right to association is derived from the right to freedom of expression. Arguably, the idea of safe space has a special appeal to minority groups and vulnerable members of society who look to their peers for healing and empowerment.[90] However, hosting group gatherings for the sake of friendship and support is not unique among those considered marginalized and vulnerable. For example, like-minded individuals form special interest groups that are exclusive of people not sharing the same interests or embracing similar worldviews. To the extent that group members seek empowerment at their gatherings, and even shut out whoever does not share their views or whom they perceive to harm their group dynamics, communities not generally regarded as marginalized and vulnerable also crave their "safe spaces."

Yet the designation of some spaces as "safe" indicates that spaces outside them are "unsafe" or less "safe" and that they too should be made "safe" or "safer," even though harassment and hate speech laws and, in many university settings, policies prohibiting insults are already in place.[91] The concept would make sense only if "safe" means freedom from offensive opinions and criticisms, not merely prohibited conduct like hate speech and insults. Advocates for safe spaces emphasize that these spaces aim not to shut down free speech, but to allow people to discuss opinions and ideas comfortably and respectfully. Related laws and policies nonetheless are already aimed at making the univer-

---

88. *E.g.*, Na'ilah Suad Nasir & Jasiyah Al-Amin, *Creating Identity-Safe Spaces on College Campuses for Muslim Students*, 38(2) CHANGE: THE MAG. OF HIGHER LEARNING 22 (2000); Lara Korte, *What It's Like to Be Muslim at KU*, UNIV. DAILY KANSAN (Oct. 6, 2015), http://www.kansan.com/news/what-it-s-like-to-be-muslim-at-ku/article_3d694bb6-6c77-11e5-a1fc-bb5bb741c56f.html

89. *E.g.*, Oset Barbu, *How Can Colleges Help Muslim Students Feel Safer?* VICE (Nov. 8, 2017), https://www.vice.com/en_us/article/d7ey7x/how-can-colleges-help-muslim-students-feel-safer

90. In the words of Chris Waugh, safe spaces "represent an often clumsy—but still vital—attempt to create counterpublics for marginalised groups. These counterpublics serve two purposes; firstly, they provide spaces for groups to recuperate, reconvene, and create new strategies and vocabularies for resistance. Secondly, the presence of these counterpublics makes visible collective and individual traumas which disrupt neoliberal narratives of self-resilience." Chris Waugh, "In Defence of Safe Spaces: Subaltern Counterpublics and Vulnerable Politics in the Neoliberal University," *in* MADDIE BREEZE, YVETTE TAYLOR & CRISTINA COSTA (eds.), TIME AND SPACE IN THE NEOLIBERAL UNIVERSITY: FUTURES AND FRACTURES IN HIGHER EDUCATION (2019).

91. Judith Shulevitz, *In College and Hiding from Scary Ideas*, N.Y. TIMES (Mar. 21, 2015), https://www.nytimes.com/2015/03/22/opinion/sunday/judith-shulevitz-hiding-from-scary-ideas.html

sity a safe enough environment conducive to civil dialogues. Expanding safe spaces—those that do not tolerate contrarian and potentially offensive opinions—infantilize students by shielding them from emotional harm caused by offensive ideas.[92] They also create echo chambers by shielding inhabitants from views challenging their own and thereby reinforcing their own biases.[93] Student clubs legitimately function as safe spaces for their members by promoting certain viewpoints and ideologies while excluding others. It does not follow that organizations serving the entire university community, such as student newspapers, dormitories, or universities themselves, should also be turned into "safe" havens where only limited opinions and perspectives are permitted, and anything falling out of line becomes "unsafe" and needs to be shut out.

But then, it may be suggested that a space that is free from harassment and hate speech does not necessarily feel safe. This leads to the question of whether people have a right not to be continually exposed to expressions that they find offensive and revolting but do not constitute harassment, hate speech, or even personal attacks and insults. Indeed, forced exposure to offensive expressions is not unlike being trapped in a small living space with people who are not remotely violent or intimidating, but whom one finds repulsive personally. If individuals should and can, in some circumstances, be excused from sharing a space with repulsive but objectively nonviolent and nonintimidating people, should they also be excused from continued exposure to unwanted speech?

B. Applying the Captive Audience Doctrine to "Safe Spaces"

The captive audience doctrine protects people from unwanted speech in certain places and circumstances. First laid down by the United States Supreme Court, it has been borrowed by scholars in the study of university safe spaces. The U.S. Supreme Court, applying this doctrine, held that individuals in their homes,[94]

92. *E.g.*, Jonathan Haidt & Greg Lukianoff, The Coddling of the American Mind: How Good Intentions and Bad Ideas Are Setting up a Generation for Failure (2018); Judith Shulevitz, *In College and Hiding from Scary Ideas*, N.Y. Times (Mar. 21, 2015), https://www.nytimes.com/2015/03/22/opinion/sunday/judith-shulevitz-hiding-from-scary-ideas.html

93. *E.g.*, Frank Furedi, *Campuses Are Breaking Apart into "Safe Spaces,"* L.A. Times (Jan. 5, 2017), http://www.latimes.com/opinion/op-ed/la-oe-furedi-safe-space-20170105-story.html; Candice Russell, *Safe Spaces and Echo Chambers, How Progressive Movements Stagnate Themselves*, Huffington Post (Apr. 13, 2015), https://www.huffpost.com/entry/safe-spaces-and-echo-cham_b_7043548 (last visited Mar. 12, 2020).

94. Rowan v. Post Office Dept., 397 U.S. 728 (1970).

passengers in a public vehicle,[95] and even inhabitants in a neighborhood[96] were captive audiences as they were unable to avoid objectionable, though legal, speech in their homes, vehicles, and neighborhoods. Because they had a right not to be continually exposed to messages that they found offensive, the banning or removal of the messages was constitutional.[97] To a certain extent, the doctrine applies to university settings. Arguably, people studying and working at universities are captive audiences.[98] Whereas people on an internet forum or in a public space can disengage or walk away to avoid unwanted speech, including from racist attacks and insults, members in universities cannot leave their work and educational environments just as easily.[99] Thus, rules governing the right to speak in classrooms and public areas in universities ought to be stricter than those for public forums and places.[100] Many universities sensibly implemented policies, including those prohibiting personal attacks and insults, to promote civil work and study environments.

Yet the captive audience doctrine should not apply uncritically to universities. Universities should be safe to the extent that personal attacks are discouraged or forbidden in classrooms. They should not be safe spaces where no contentious topics or contrarian views are allowed. The difference between personal attacks and provocative opinions partly justifies this difference. A toxic environment where personal attacks are tolerated or where avoiding those attacks might be difficult is not conducive to learning. Placing the burden of fighting or avoiding personal attacks on victims would also be unfair. On the other hand, people who dislike an invited speaker or a professor for their opinions may simply choose not to attend the talk or enroll in the course.

Indeed, a university consists of numerous spaces: some spaces can be "safe"; others should—or must—not be. Newspapers or bulletins published by clubs, like the clubs themselves, can function as safe spaces: they represent the club members' views, cater mainly to club members, and need not tolerate dissenting opinions. Student-run newspapers that serve university populations, like universities, should not be safe spaces: people who dislike certain topics can simply skip

95. Lehman v. City of Shaker Heights, 418 U.S. 298 (1974).
96. Young v. American MiniTheatres, 427 U.S. 50 (1976).
97. Rowan, 397 U.S. 728; Lehman, 418 U.S. 298; Young, 427 U.S. 50.
98. Richard Moon, *Understanding the Right to Freedom of Expression and Its Place on Campus*, Academic Matters (2018), https://academicmatters.ca/assets/AcademicMatters_Fall2018.pdf
99. *See, e.g.*, Richard Moon, *Understanding the Right to Freedom of Expression and Its Place on Campus*, Academic Matters (2018), https://academicmatters.ca/assets/AcademicMatters_Fall2018.pdf
100. Richard Moon, *Understanding the Right to Freedom of Expression and Its Place on Campus*, Academic Matters (2018), https://academicmatters.ca/assets/AcademicMatters_Fall2018.pdf

them after glancing at the headlines. Dormitories are both homes and places of learning. Residents are captive audiences in their own units. Thus, placing pamphlets with potentially offensive messages under their doors would be intrusive. Residents are not captive audiences in other parts of the dormitories. Hosting talks or discussions on contentious issues in the common rooms would not be intrusive, as residents are not obliged to attend them. Residents' social media accounts may serve as safe spaces for their owners, but not for visitors. Owners can post anything that is legal, and others who feel uncomfortable with messages can and should disengage. Hence, monitoring public postings on residents' social media accounts for contentious topics that may offend some people, and requesting them to be taken down, are intrusive measures. Administrators who do so overreach their authority and are utterly unqualified for their positions.

C. Concept Creep, Troubling Examples, and Free Speech Implications

Attempts to turn the entire university—all its difference spaces and not only student clubs and special interest groups set up for mutual support and comfort—into one big safe space may be rationalized on the grounds that some opinions cause emotional harm and that language can be violent. Language, especially in cases of hate speech and incitement of violence, can indeed be quite violent. The rationale that language is often violent nonetheless can lead to an overly broad concept of violence—for example, one encompassing constructive opinions that are respectfully delivered but that happen to offend or "trigger" some people—which stifles free speech and frustrates the pursuit of knowledge, democratic governance, and individual development.

The expanding concept of violence is a manifestation of a phenomenon called "concept creep" observed by psychologist Nick Haslam. Haslam argues that concepts referring to negative aspects of human experience and behavior, such as abuse, bullying, trauma, mental disorder, addiction, and prejudice, have extended their meanings so that they now encompass a much broader range of phenomena than before.[101] These concepts have crept outward—horizontally—to capture qualitatively new phenomena, and downward—vertically—to capture quantitatively less extreme phenomena.[102] Although the expansion of

---

101. Nick Haslam, *Concept Creep: Psychology's Expanding Concepts of Harm and Pathology*, 27 Psychological Inquiry: An Int'l J. for the Advancement of Psychological Theory 1 (2016).
102. Nick Haslam, *Concept Creep: Psychology's Expanding Concepts of Harm and Pathology*, 27 Psychological Inquiry: An Int'l J. for the Advancement of Psychological Theory 1 (2016).

meanings is often well motivated, it encourages the pathologization of everyday experiences, oversensitivity to emotional harm, and victimhood in those who suffer these experiences.[103] Haidt and Lukianoff borrow the concept creep idea to coin the term "safetyism," which they use to characterize a "culture [on American campus] that allows the concept of 'safety' to creep so far that it equates emotional discomfort with physical danger."[104]

Ironically, for people who have experienced real oppression, such as freedom-loving (definitely not all) Hong Kong people, a "safe space" would be one that is free from teargas, bullets, surveillance, and arbitrary detention. For many Western people who have never set foot outside their democratic home countries, or suffered any punch, a "safe space" is one that is free from any opinions that trigger them or make them feel uncomfortable. Yet unlike bullets, tear gas, and punches, which are almost invariably destructive, words seldom lead to physical harm. Although real life may resemble literature, they are not the same: whereas characters' every word and gesture in a fictional work can carry symbolic significance and a character can be made to disappear from the text, it would be risky to read too much into expressions in real life to find meanings and implications that are not there. Real people cannot be obliterated or snuffed out by mere words (except perhaps under certain authoritarian regimes such as North Korea and China where people are readily "suicided" or "disappeared" at state orders).[105] In democracies, real people, should they feel endangered by words, can fight back with words. They need to learn from freedom-loving Hongkongers who may feel uneasy should members of the Chinese government get invited to lecture on their campuses. Any feeling of unease or insecurity would be fleeting, as it likely won't take much time or effort to expose the hollowness of their narratives and the depravity of their government. Whereas a well-intentioned moral agenda might account for expanding concepts of harm, such as violence and danger, this phenomenon may have been motivated or complemented by intellectual dishonesty or laziness, mental biases, indoctrination, or even a lack of moral courage. To add to the examples given by the foregoing scholars, the following discussion explains how some other concepts

103. Nick Haslam, *Concept Creep: Psychology's Expanding Concepts of Harm and Pathology*, 27 Psychological Inquiry: An Int'l J. for the Advancement of Psychological Theory 1 (2016).

104. Jonathan Haidt & Greg Lukianoff, The Coddling of the American Mind: How Good Intentions and Bad Ideas Are Setting up a Generation for Failure 29 (2018).

105. "Suicide" and "disappear" are both used in the passive voice to indicate that some people were killed by the government that created the appearance that these victims took their own lives or disappeared of their own accord.

have expanded likely due to a combination of these factors. Unfortunately, these examples of the conceptual slippery slope fallacy can be—and often are—used to curtail free speech.

Concepts like "racism," "white supremacist," and "alt-right" have expanded—horizontally to encompass qualitatively new phenomena—to such an extent that their original and proper meanings may have been lost. Racism refers to the belief that people's traits and capabilities are determined by their race, and that members of certain (typically the believers' own) races are inherently superior to other races.[106] A white supremacist is a person who believes that the white race is inherently superior to other races and so should have dominance over them.[107] The "alt-right" (abbreviation for "alternative-right") is a right-wing, U.S.-based, primarily online, political movement that rejects mainstream conservative politics and instead embraces extremist policies centered on white nationalism.[108]

On today's campus, one may be accused of being a racist, white supremacist, or an alt-right follower without showing any of these beliefs. While the expansion of such concepts was partly fueled by a zealous and well-intentioned agenda to protect minorities, they are often weaponized to shut down discussions. Stating that the Chinese government was to blame for the spread of COVID-19 in early 2020 is an honest assessment and indicates no racism on the part of the speaker.[109] It is egregious to use "alt-right" to smear outspoken people daring to say that immigrants who oppose free speech and embrace authoritarianism should not have settled in democratic countries. Whether President Donald Trump is a white supremacist is beyond the scope of this chapter. Assuming that he is, it is a bold leap of logic to call people white supremacists for showing gratitude for some of his actions,[110] unless not being a white supremacist means disapprov-

106. *E.g.*, *Racism*, CAMBRIDGE DICTIONARY, https://dictionary.cambridge.org/dictionary/english/racism (last visited Mar. 19, 2020); *Racism*, MERRIAM-WEBSTER DICTIONARY, https://www.merriam-webster.com/dictionary/racism (last visited Mar. 19, 2020).

107. *E.g.*, *White Supremacist*, MERRIAM-WEBSTER DICTIONARY, https://www.merriam-webster.com/dictionary/white%20supremacist (last visited Mar. 19, 2020).

108. *E.g.*, *Alt-right*, MERRIAM-WEBSTER DICTIONARY, https://www.merriam-webster.com/dictionary/alt-right (last visited Mar. 19, 2020); *Alt-right*, CAMBRIDGE DICTIONARY, https://dictionary.cambridge.org/dictionary/english/alt-right (last visited Mar. 19, 2020).

109. *See, e.g.*, Josh Rogin, *Don't Blame China for the Coronavirus—Blame the Chinese Communist Party*, WASH. POST (Mar. 19, 2020); Shadi Hamid, *China Is Avoiding Blame by Trolling the World*, ATLANTIC (Mar. 19, 2020), https://www.theatlantic.com/ideas/archive/2020/03/china-trolling-world-and-avoiding-blame/608332/

110. *E.g.*, Hillary Leung, *Trump Signs Legislation to Protect Human Rights in Hong Kong amid Ongoing Protests*, TIME (Nov. 28, 2019), https://time.com/5741043/trump-human-rights-protest-act-hong-kong/. One example is Hongkongers showing gratitude to Trump after he signed a law that sanctions China-backed human rights abusers in Hong Kong.

ing of all his actions. How about professors who are (closeted) Trump supporters and who gave bonus points to or wrote the strongest letters of recommendation for black students whom they judged on their own merits and appreciated for their diligence and civility? In the current campus climate, if they made their preference known, they likely would still be deemed white supremacist, regardless of their reason(s) for voting for Trump. They may be branded as benevolent white supremacists who are willing to show mercy to minority students due to their innate superiority, or white supremacists who make exceptions for their favorites. On rare occasions, they might be considered misguided fools who were utterly incapable of making the right choice and became white supremacists unwittingly.

Aside from the often-mentioned concepts of harm, many other concepts have expanded their meanings. One such example is "virtue-signaling." To "virtue-signal" is defined as an attempt to garner approval and appear morally superior by expressing socially acceptable opinions, especially on social media, not unlike the two evil daughters expressing their love for their father in an obsequious manner in Shakespeare's *King Lear*.[111] Most typical examples include expressions of moral outrage in contemporary debates on such issues as sexual assault, immigration, and police brutality.[112] More often used against left-leaning people than against their right-wing counterparts, this concept may have sprung out of a moral agenda to identify hypocrites who do harm by not walking the talk and by making people who care more about substance than appearance look inferior. However, mindlessly accusing others of virtue-signaling can discourage those with strong convictions from expressing their beliefs and motivating others to join their good causes.

Still, one may be able to tell virtue-signalers with feigned righteousness from people with genuine, passionate convictions by checking for the consistency between their actions and words and among their expressed opinions. One would suspect that academics on job search committees who harp on "diversity" are virtue-signalers, like King Lear's two daughters, if they obsess over race/gender/sexual identities but turn down candidates in visible minority groups upon discovering that they are independent thinkers who do not sub-

---

111. *E.g.*, *Virtue-Signalling*, CAMBRIDGE DICTIONARY, https://dictionary.cambridge.org/dictionary/english/virtue-signalling (last visited Mar. 17, 2020); David Shariatmadari, *"Virtue-Signalling"–the Put-down That Has Passed Its Sell-by Date*, GUARDIAN (Jan. 20, 2016), https://www.theguardian.com/commentisfree/2016/jan/20/virtue-signalling-putdown-passed-sell-by-date

112. Jillian Jordan & David Rand, *Are You "Virtue Signalling"?* N.Y. TIMES (Mar. 30, 2019), https://www.nytimes.com/2019/03/30/opinion/sunday/virtue-signaling.html

scribe to their dogmas. Virtue-signalers might also be detected among those social justice advocates and academics who, like Hollywood celebrities, decry the injustices and human rights violations under Trump's presidency to garner approval among their "woke" base, but even when consulted, avoid saying a word against the Chinese government for instigating worse human rights abuses in Tibet, Xinjiang, and Hong Kong that are well publicized in the news. "That would be racism," they tend to throw out this overused concept creep to excuse their silence. "Don't add fuel to fire—we are in the midst of the pandemic." In reality, the price of incurring the wrath of wealthy Chinese compatriots both in their countries and worldwide and of violating codes of diversity and tolerance would be too high for these people. The sad thing is that the concept-creep-cum-excuse is often given with such sincerity and earnestness that it can be difficult to tell whether cowardice, intellectual dishonesty/laziness, or indoctrination has been the real cause. Certainly, no person should be compelled to take a public stance. In any case, however, one is reminded of how banal evil can be, and wonder whether the hottest places in hell in Dante's *Inferno* would be hot enough for these people.

The meaning of "dog whistle" has likewise extended such that people engaging in meaningful discussions and making good-faith and well-reasoned arguments can become suspects in harmful agendas through "dog whistling." The term refers to coded language that has one meaning for the general public and an additional layer of meaning understood only by targeted subgroups of people.[113] While certain coded language can contain discriminatory messages,[114] attempts to attach meanings to facially neutral language, like finding ulterior motives behind innocent acts, curtail free speech. In extreme left-wing politics, "liberty" and "free speech" are sometimes considered code words for bigotry and discrimination.[115] Ironically, liberty and free speech, both fundamental values in many Western nations, do not conflict with, but complement, equality. Hence, "liberty" and "free speech" are no more code words for racism and

113. *Dog Whistles*, Merriam-Webster Dictionary, https://www.merriam-webster.com/words-at-play/dog-whistle-political-meaning (last visited Mar. 18, 2020).

114. *See, e.g.*, Ian Haney López, Dog Whistle Politics (2014).

115. *E.g.*, Penny Starr, *Civil Rights Commission: "Religious Liberty," "Religious Freedom" Code Words for Intolerance, Homophobia, and 'Christian Supremacy,'* CNS News (Sep. 9, 2016, 11:05 AM), https://www.cnsnews.com/news/article/penny-starr/civil-rights-commission-religious-liberty-religious-freedom-code-words; *see also, e.g.*, John Semley, *Are University Campuses Where Free Speech Goes to Die?* Walrus (May 22, 2019), https://thewalrus.ca/are-university-campuses-where-free-speech-goes-to-die/

other forms of discrimination than "antiracism" is a code word for antiwhite.[116] Even George Orwell's *Nineteen Eighty-Four* can possibly be seen as a dog whistle by extremists who seek to impose utopian worldviews on society, because it challenges their worldviews by illuminating the importance of free speech and how a utopia easily turns into a dystopia.[117] For extremists wary of people who call this novel their all-time favorite and embrace its critique of authoritarianism, their distrust says little or nothing about the merits of this masterpiece or the morality of Orwell's fans. Rather, it reveals much about their own extreme politics, warped worldviews, and prejudices. Orwell's fans, like the author of this book, who feel wronged and misunderstood in this cultural climate should be slightly comforted by the thought that Orwell, who would be rolling over in his grave should he know that his name and masterpiece are getting smeared, has suffered the most injustice at the hands of these extremists.

A safe space where expressions are vetted for their "violent" messages, "racism," or "dog whistles" may also justify the use of preemptive violence to fend off perceived threats to its "safety." This already happens in dictatorships and authoritarian countries like China where many people live in gigantic safe bubbles created by state media, educational institutions, and the police that quash dissent.[118] The impacts have turned out to be lasting. Unsurprisingly, those failing to venture out of these bubbles, even after settling in democratic nations, react violently to ideas and opinions threatening to jeopardize their "safety."[119]

Turning the university campus into one big safe space ill-prepares students for the real world, which is not a safe space where adults can find refuge from ideas that make them uncomfortable but are necessary for a healthy, function-

---

116. *E.g.*, *Anti-Racist Is a Code for Anti-White*, ADL, https://www.adl.org/education/references/hate-symbols/anti-racist-is-a-code-for-anti-white (last visited Mar. 19, 2020).

117. *See, e.g.*, Brendan O'Neill, *Orwell's* Nineteen Eighty-Four *Describes the Authoritarian Left Better Than It Does Trump*, REASON (Feb. 10, 2017), https://reason.com/2017/02/10/orwells-1984-a-better-reflection-of-the/. An increasing number of commentators have noticed an affiliation between the world described in Orwell's novel and authoritarian politics advocated by extremists.

118. *E.g.*, John Pomphret, *Is China's Government Ever Going to Grow Up?*, WASH. POST. (Oct. 9, 2019), https://www.washingtonpost.com/opinions/2019/10/09/is-chinas-government-ever-going-grow-up/; Chaguan, *China's Thin-Skinned Online Nationalists Want to Be Both Loved and Feared by the West*, ECONOMIST (Aug. 22, 2019), https://www.economist.com/china/2019/08/22/chinas-thin-skinned-online-nationalists-want-to-be-both-loved-and-feared-by-the-west

119. *See, e.g.*, Jeremy Luedi, *Beijing-Linked Student Groups Threaten Academic Freedom in Canada*, TRUE N. FAR E. (Jan. 19, 2020), https://truenorthfareast.com/news/china-influence-canada-universities-cssa (last visited Mar. 1, 2020); Emma Goldberg, *Hong Kong Protests Spread to US Colleges, and a Rift Grows*, N.Y. TIMES (Oct. 26, 2019), https://www.nytimes.com/2019/10/26/us/hong-kong-protests-colleges.html

ing society. People stressing that there are safe spaces outside of campus, such as places where they seek support and advocate for social change, cannot justify turning the entire campus into a safe space.[120] On the other hand, those argue against providing for a safe space by forewarning about the horrors of the real world and thus making the worst violence look inevitable are speaking in hyperbole. Such threats are not warranted: as long as harassment, assaults, and discrimination laws are in place to prohibit real forms of violence, the real world need not be plagued by them.[121]

All in all, nurturing students in a "safe" environment would well prepare them for the real world only if the real world itself became a safe space. Authoritarian countries, where the media are controlled by the government, dissent is suppressed, and dissenters are jailed, "suicided," or "disappeared," are gigantic safe spaces for those have surrendered their freedoms and individualities and allowed the state to dictate their thoughts and actions. Democratic countries and their educational institutions must be cautioned against heading down this path, which would signal the demise of Western civilization—and civilization more generally. Many people in North Korea and China, convinced from their dates of birth that their countries are the best, do live in a perpetual state of bliss and harmony. It would be a misfortunate for people in the West to crave this kind of safety and harmony, which can be achieved only at the expense of their fundamental democratic values and the sanctity of the individual.

• • •

"Deplatforming" lawful but provocative speakers, even by the "pure in heart," is generally not desirable or justifiable, despite seemingly strong and well-intended arguments to the contrary. The deplatforming of speakers and "triggering" opinions and messages, often accompanied by personal attacks on speakers and inviting parties, is both ludicrous and hypocritical especially if it is done for the sake of showcasing one's passion for social justice causes—or virtuousness. People, regardless of their political leanings, are entitled to form safe spaces. Turning the entire university and all of its different units

---

120. *See, e.g.*, Kyeland Jackson, *Letter to the Editor: Safe Spaces in the "Real World,"* LOUISVILLE CARDINAL (Feb. 12, 2017), https://www.louisvillecardinal.com/2017/02/letter-editor-safe-spaces-real-world/ (last visited Mar. 22, 2020).

121. *See, e.g.*, Sarah Jeffe, *There Are No Safe Spaces*, NEW REPUBLIC (Nov. 24, 2017), https://newrepublic.com/article/145970/no-safe-spaces

into one giant "safe space" where expressions are vetted to ensure they contain no trigger or "violence" justifies the use of preemptive violence against perceived threats to that "safety," let alone ill prepares young people for the real world. Part III of this book will turn to numerous case studies in three jurisdictions to explain why and how academic speech has been threatened or protected on university campuses, and how universities can and should provide better learning environments.

Part Three

If liberty means anything at all, it means the right to tell people what they do not want to hear.

—George Orwell

Evil knows of the Good, but Good does not know of Evil.

—Franz Kafka

If harsh criticism disappears completely, mild criticism would become harsh. If mild criticism is not allowed, silence would be considered ill-intended. If silence is no longer allowed, complimenting not hard enough would be a crime. If only one voice is allowed, then that only voice tells a lie.

—Anonymous

CHAPTER SEVEN

The United Kingdom

Human Rights Act, a New Bill, and the Uncertain Future of Campus Speech

In the United Kingdom, freedom of expressiosn is protected by the Human Rights Act 1998 (HRA), which incorporates substantive provisions of the European Convention on Human Rights into its domestic law. British courts are also required by the HRA to consider the European Court of Human Rights' decisions with regard to free speech, which will continue to retain some influence on their decisions after Brexit. Notwithstanding existing laws protecting free expression and academic freedom in British universities, and despite constant denials by left-leaning scholars and critics, self-censorship and suppression of free expression on campuses are concerning. From 2018 through 2019, the Equality and Human Rights Commission prepared guidance affirming individuals' right to free expression and higher education providers' responsibility to promote civil debates on university campuses. Following the Conservative Party's 2019 manifesto pledge to "strengthen free speech and academic freedom in universities," an education bill was put forward in early 2020, both to give life to the pledge and to ensure that universities and their students' unions comply with existing law and policy.

This chapter will examine the "cancel culture" at many British universities that has evolved over the past decade and the uncertain future of academic free speech. It looks at numerous attempts to deplatform speakers, who were accused of "bigotry" for challenging mainstream ideologies dominating universities, either by banning them from campuses or by petitioning universities to sanction them or terminate their academic positions. Even free speech guarantees at universities and a new education law might fail to protect the freedom of speech of academics who were fired for expressing or publishing "wrong" opinions. Sadly, some universities seem to apply double standards in policing free speech, by deeming certain groups to be more entitled to free speech and more deserving of protection than other groups from any harm caused by free expression. Admittedly, universities walk a tightrope as they seek to facilitate respectful communication while prohibiting conduct reasonably considered intimidating and abusive, both on and off social media platforms.

Lastly, this chapter will turn to the Chinese government's growing threat to free speech in British academia and argue that British universities must ditch their passivity, complacency, and at times complicity to put a stop to the continual erosion of their autonomy. It suggests that to avert this trend, lawsuits should be brought against universities that suppress free expression to appease China and its agents. Admittedly, this hostile foreign power has applied financial and political pressure and not infrequently resorted to violence to make British universities conform to its agenda. The activities of the Confucius Institutes particularly have been enabled by complacent university managers. Closing these institutes will not violate any party's freedoms but will protect the freedom to criticize this rogue state, support those it has persecuted and oppressed, and learn Chinese culture and language untainted by party ideologies. One must watch out for signs of infiltration and remember that even if "every man has his price,"[1] the sanctity of academia and democracy is priceless.

I. *Freedom of Speech in British Universities*

Freedom of expression in the United Kingdom is protected by the Human Rights Act 1998, which incorporates substantive provisions of the European Convention on Human Rights (European Convention) into domestic law.[2] What might come as a surprise is that English law has traditionally taken little notice of freedom of speech.[3] While the Magna Carta recognizes the basic lib-

1. *See* ROBERT BOLT, A MAN FOR ALL SEASONS, Act 1 (a statement by character Richard Rich, who serves as a foil to Thomas More) (1954, 1957).
2. *See* Human Rights Act, 1998, c. 42.
3. Eric Barendt, *Freedom of Expression in the United Kingdom under the Human Rights Act 1998*, 84 IND.

erties of "freemen of the realm" and the state's obligation to protect them, it has been of little practical importance throughout the history of England and the U.K.[4] Even the Bill of Rights 1689 benefited members of Parliament and not ordinary citizens.[5] Before passage of the HRA, freedom of speech therefore existed in the form of a limited and residual liberty.[6] British citizens were free to express an opinion only if the expression was not forbidden by legislation or the common law.[7]

Nonetheless, even before passage of the HRA, British judges had been willing to address free speech claims for many years. By relying on societal traditions to check abuses of governmental powers to restrict the "fundamental human right" to freedom of speech,[8] the judges articulated a common law right to this freedom.[9] The increasing liberalization of the freedom of speech tradition was particularly apparent during the passage of the HRA in Parliament and the period between the law's enactment and coming into effect in October 2000.[10]

The HRA marked a shift in the treatment and perception of freedom of expression from a residual freedom without much textual guarantee to a positive right expressly recognized by law.[11] Article 10 § 1 is identical to Article 10 of the European Convention and provides that "[e]veryone has the right to free-

---

L.J. 851, 851 (2009); Douglas W. Vick, *The Human Rights Act and the British Constitution*, 37 TEX. INT'L L.J. 329, 330 (2002).

4. Douglas W. Vick, *The Human Rights Act and the British Constitution*, 37 TEX. INT'L L.J. 329, 337 (2002).
5. Douglas W. Vick, *The Human Rights Act and the British Constitution*, 37 TEX. INT'L L.J. 329, 337 (2002).
6. Douglas W. Vick, *The Human Rights Act and the British Constitution*, 37 TEX. INT'L L.J. 329, 330, 341 (2002).
7. Eric Barendt, *Freedom of Expression in the United Kingdom under the Human Rights Act 1998*, 84 IND. L.J. 851, 852–53 (2009).
8. RONALD J. KROTOSZYNSKI, JR., THE FIRST AMENDMENT IN CROSS-CULTURAL PERSPECTIVE: A COMPARATIVE LEGAL ANALYSIS OF THE FREEDOM OF SPEECH 187, 197 (2006). *Brind* demonstrates that the absence of a written provision protecting free expression did not bar consideration of speech interests as either a "right" or a decisional "principle," citing R v. Secretary of State for the Home Department ex p Brind (1991) 1 A.C. 696 (E.W.C.A. Civ.).
9. Eric Barendt, *Freedom of Expression in the United Kingdom under the Human Rights Act 1998*, 84 IND. L.J. 851, 852–53 (2009). The classic example is Lord Reid in *Brutus v. Cozens*, which argued that the word "insulting" in the public order legislation should not be construed to penalize the use of offensive language during an antiapartheid demonstration at Wimbledon. [1972] UKHL 6, [1973] A.C. 854 (H.L.) (appeal taken from Eng.).
10. Eric Barendt, *Freedom of Expression in the United Kingdom under the Human Rights Act 1998*, 84 IND. L.J. 851, 853–54 (2009).
11. Eric Barendt, *Freedom of Expression in the United Kingdom under the Human Rights Act 1998*, 84 IND. L.J. 851, 851 (2009); Douglas W. Vick, *The Human Rights Act and the British Constitution*, 37 TEX. INT'L L.J. 329, 330 (2002).

dom of expression," including "freedom to hold opinions and to receive and impart information and ideas without interference by public authority and regardless of frontiers."[12] Article 10 § 2 directly limits its scope, stating that "the exercise of these freedoms, since it carries with it duties and responsibilities, may be subject to such formalities, conditions, restrictions or penalties as are prescribed by law and are necessary in a democratic society."[13]

Since then, British courts have confidently asserted the fundamental nature of the right to freedom of expression and demanded careful scrutiny of any restriction on this right.[14] In *R. v. Shayler*, the first important free speech case after the HRA came into force, Lord Bingham stated that this right, which had been recognized in common law for some time, was now "underpinned by statute."[15] More recently, in the *Laporte* case, he contrasted the common law's approach to freedom of expression, which was "hesitant and negative," with the "constitutional shift" represented by Articles 10 and 11 of the HRA, whereby freedoms of expression and association became "fundamental rights" and "[a]ny prior restraint on their exercise must be scrutinised with particular care."[16]

The HRA limits freedom of expression "in the interests of national security, territorial integrity or public safety, for the prevention of disorder or crime, for the protection of health or morals, for the protection of the reputation or rights of others, for preventing the disclosure of information received in confidence, or for maintaining the authority and impartiality of the judiciary."[17] Indeed, laws had been enacted throughout the history of England and the U.K. to prohibit expression falling into the above categories. One example is defamation law.[18] English law had for a long time put the burden of proving the truth of allegedly defamatory statements on defendants without recognizing any gen-

12. European Convention for the Protection of Human Rights and Fundamental Freedoms, art. 10 § 1 (Nov. 4, 1950).
13. European Convention for the Protection of Human Rights and Fundamental Freedoms, art. 10 § 2.
14. Eric Barendt, *Freedom of Expression in the United Kingdom under the Human Rights Act 1998*, 84 Ind. L.J. 851, 854–55 (2009).
15. Eric Barendt, *Freedom of Expression in the United Kingdom under the Human Rights Act 1998*, 84 Ind. L.J. 851, 854 (2009); citing R. v. Shayler [2002] UKHL 11, [2003] 1 A.C. 247, paras. 21–22 (appeal taken from Eng.).
16. Eric Barendt, *Freedom of Expression in the United Kingdom under the Human Rights Act 1998*, 84 Ind. L.J. 851, 854 (2009); citing R (on the application of Laporte) v. Chief Constable of Gloucestershire Constabulary [2006] UKHL 55, [2007] 2 A.C. 105, paras. 34, 85 (appeal taken from Eng.).
17. HRA, 1998, c. 42, art. 10 § 2.
18. Common law action for defamation was established in sixteenth-century England. Reputation was protected by the law—meaningfully albeit narrowly—from the twelfth to the sixteenth century in local and ecclesiastical courts. Lawrence McNamara, Reputation and Defamation 68–79 (2007).

eral privilege for the press or for any people to defame even the most well-known public figures.[19] The Defamation Act 2013 introduced new statutory defenses of truth, honest opinion, and "publication on a matter of public interest."[20] Harassment and bullying are prohibited under both civil and criminal laws. The Protection from Harassment Act 1997 prohibits pervasive conduct that one knows or ought to know would put the other person "in fear of violence."[21] The Equality Act 2010 further prohibits discrimination, which can take verbal forms, on the grounds of age, disability, gender reassignment, race, religion or belief, sex, and sexual orientation.[22]

Hate speech laws are relatively recent in the U.K. With the influx of immigrants in the twentieth century, the Race Relations Acts were passed to maintain a tolerant multicultural society.[23] Later, the Public Order Act 1986 made it an offense, among other things, to use "threatening, abusive or insulting" words, behavior, or written material, with the intent to "stir up racial hatred," or in circumstances where racial hatred is "likely to be stirred up."[24] The Racial and Religious Hatred Act 2006, passed after numerous terrorist attacks, extends the proscription of incitement to hatred to protect "group[s] of persons defined by reference to religious belief or lack of a religious belief."[25] The Criminal Justice and Immigration Act 2008, which amended part 3A of the Public Order Act, now makes it an offense to incite hatred on the grounds of sexual orientation through the use of words, behavior, or written material, public performances, broadcasting programs, or possession of inflammatory materials that are "threatening" rather than merely abusive or insulting.[26]

The HRA and its speech restrictions apply to British universities. In addition to the HRA's adoption of parts of the European Convention, British courts are also required by the HRA to consider the decisions of the European Court

---

19. *See, e.g.*, Campbell v. Spottiswoode [1863] 3 B. & S. 769, 777 (Q.B.); Blackshaw v. Lord [1984] 1 Q.B. 42 (E.W.C.A.).
20. Clive Coleman, *Defamation Act 2013 Aims to Improve Libel Laws*, BBC NEWS (Dec. 31, 2013), http://www.bbc.com/news/uk-25551640 (last visited Oct. 10, 2017).
21. Protection from Harassment Act 1997, c. 40, s. 4; *e.g.*, Majrowski v. Guys & St Thomas' NHS Trust [2006] UKHL 24.
22. Equality Act 2010, c. 15, pt. 2, ch. 2; *e.g.*, Mr. R Craggs v. BMS Elec. Serv. Ltd.: 2503350/2018; Pnaiser v. NHS Eng. & Another [2016] IRLR 170.
23. Race Relations Act 1965, c. 73; Race Relations Act 1968, c. 71.
24. Public Order Act, 1986, c. 4, s. 18(1).
25. Racial and Religious Hatred Act, 2006, c. 1, s. 29(A).
26. Criminal Justice and Immigration Act, 2008, c. 4, s. 74; *see Sexual Orientation: CPS Guidance on Stirring Up Hatred on the Grounds of Sexual Orientation*, CROWN PROSECUTION SERVICE (Mar. 17, 2010).

of Human Rights (ECHR) with regard to free speech, defamation, hate speech, bullying/harassment, and discrimination, without being bound by them.[27] While the U.K. withdrew from the European Union in 2020 and its European Union (Withdrawal Agreement) Act 2020 also affirms the sovereignty of the British Parliament,[28] the U.K. remains a member of the European Council and a signatory to the European Convention. Hence, the ECHR's decisions, though never binding on British courts, will continue to impact their decisions.[29] In addition, when the U.K. was still a member of the EU, the European Court of Justice's (CJEU) free speech decisions, which applied relevant sections of the EU Charter of Fundamental Rights (the Charter), were binding on British courts.[30] Because the CJEU no longer has general jurisdiction over the U.K. in relation to any acts that take place on or after January 1, 2021 except regarding concepts of EU law, it is less clear whether the CJEU's decisions will continue to exert any influence on British courts.[31] Generally, therefore, people on university campuses enjoy freedom of speech except where their expression would constitute harassment/bullying, discrimination, or hate speech under relevant British laws and, to a lesser extent, the European Convention.

Compared to Canada and especially the United States, there has been surprisingly little litigation involving free speech and academic freedom in the U.K.[32] The few known cases involve alleged harassment on campus. In one example, a white student pled guilty to racial harassment in court for making racist chants.[33] Another example involved a mixed-race student who was found

---

27. *See* HRA, s. 2; *E.g.*, in *Incal v. Turkey*, app. no. 41/1997/82 (Eur. Ct. H.R. 1998) and *Zana v. Turkey*, app. no. 18954/91 (Eur. Ct. H.R. 1997), the ECHR acknowledged the right to reputation in defamation cases, but prioritized freedom of expression over the preservation of reputation where matters of public concern are involved. It also examined the contextual factors in assessing whether expressions would or had incite(d) hatred and whether their censorship would violate the speakers' right to freedom of expression. In *Buturuga v. Romania*, app. No. 56867/15 (Eur. Ct. H.R. 2020), it recognized cyberbullying as a form of violence.
28. European Union (Withdrawal Agreement) Act 2020, c. 1.
29. *E.g.*, Supreme Court, *The Supreme Court and Europe*, http://www.supremecourt.uk/about/the-supreme-court-and-europe.html (last visited Dec. 27, 2020).
30. *See* Charter of Fundamental Rights of the European Union, arts. 11–13.
31. Under the European Union (Withdrawal) Act 2018, courts and tribunals are not bound by any new decisions made by the CJEU after the end of 2018, although they can "have regard to" such decisions "so far as it is relevant to any matter before the court or tribunal."
32. Terrence Karran & Lucy Mallinson, *Academic Freedom in the U.K.: Legal and Normative Protection in a Comparative Context*, UNIVERSITY AND COLLEGE UNION (May 7, 2017), http://www.ucu.org.uk/media/8614/Academic-Freedom-in-the-UK-Legal-and-Normative-Protection-in-a-Comparative-Context-Report-for-UCU-Terence-Karran-and-Lucy-Mallinson-May-17/pdf/ucu_academicfreedomstudy_report_may17.pdf (last visited Dec. 27, 2020).
33. *Student Who Chants "We Hate Blacks" Admits Racial Charge*, BBC (May 24, 2018), http://www.bbc.com/news/uk-england-nottinghamshire-44238308 (last visited Dec. 27, 2020).

not guilty for making racially motivated insults targeting white people on the grounds that it was not motivated by hostility and was a response to their anti-black chanting.[34] Although there is no lack of cases in which academics were suspended or even fired for their expressed opinions or research, they typically did not end up in court.[35]

While some have attributed the lack of free speech litigation to several factors, including the likelihood that many disputes were resolved through settlements, the suggestion that British universities have shown much respect for their members' freedom of expression and academic freedom, hence greatly reducing the circumstances for disputes, is not a likely reason in light of the number of documented disputes.[36] Regardless, considering the lack of judicial precedents on campus free speech in the U.K., relevant decisions by the ECHR may provide some guidance on how British courts might rule on disputes of this nature in the future.

The ECHR has upheld the fundamental right to free speech protected under Article 10 of the European Convention, a right that by logic extends to people speaking on university campuses. It has also affirmed the importance of academic freedom and established freedom of expression as a precondition to academic freedom by resolving numerous academic freedom cases.[37] In *Sorguç v. Turkey* (2009), it cited the Parliamentary Assembly of the Council of Europe's 2006 declaration for the protection of academic freedom in accordance with the *Magna Charta Universitatum*, to point out that academic freedom "comprises the academics' freedom to express freely their opinions about the institution or system in which they work and freedom to distribute knowledge and truth without restriction."[38] In *Erdoğan v. Turkey* (2014), the ECHR stated that freedom of expression, freedom to conduct research, and freedom to dissemi-

34. Jon Sharman, *Mixed-Race Student Who shouted "We Hate Whites" Cleared as Court Rules She Was "Not Motivated by Hostility,"* THE INDEPENDENT (Jul. 19, 2018), http://independent.co.uk/news/lauren-leigh-nottingham-trent-racist-chanting-we-hate-blacks-whites-a8453656.html

35. *E.g.*, David Gunkel, *A Clear and Present Danger*, TIMES HIGHER EDUC. (Feb. 26, 2010), http://gunkelweb.com/articles/THE2_gunkel.pdf

36. Terrence Karran & Lucy Mallinson, *Academic Freedom in the U.K.: Legal and Normative Protection in a Comparative Context*, UNIVERSITY AND COLLEGE UNION (May 7, 2017), http://www.ucu.org.uk/media/8614/Academic-Freedom-in-the-UK-Legal-and-Normative-Protection-in-a-Comparative-Context-Report-for-UCU-Terence-Karran-and-Lucy-Mallinson-May-17/pdf/ucu_academicfreedomstudy_report_may17.pdf (last visited Dec. 27, 2020); citing E. BARENDT, ACADEMIC FREEDOM AND THE LAW: A COMPARATIVE STUDY 74 (2010).

37. Kula v. Turkey, appl. no. 20233/06, paras. 29–30 (2018); Erdoğan v. Turkey, appl. nos. 346/04 and 39779/04, paras. 27–37 (2014); Sorguç v. Turkey, appl. no. 17089/03, paras. 3, 22, 27–29, 39–40 (2009).

38. *Sorguç*, para. 35.

nate information "are not limited to scientific or academic research, but also cover opinions and views, even when the views are unpopular."[39] Most recently, in *Kula v. Turkey* (2018), it reiterated that "freedom of expression and of action, freedom to disseminate information and freedom to 'conduct research and distribute knowledge and truth without restriction'" are necessary conditions for academic freedom.[40] Any interference having a chilling effect on this freedom would constitute a violation of Article 10 of the European Convention unless it is "'prescribed by law,' pursues one or more legitimate aims for the purposes of Article 10 § 2 and can be regarded as 'necessary in a democratic society.'"[41] These decisions by the ECHR will continue to impact British courts.[42]

In recent years, self-censorship and suppression of free expression on British university campuses have raised concerns in the British government and among some politicians and educators. From 2018 through 2019, the Equality and Human Rights Commission,[43] in consultation with numerous governmental units and nonprofit organizations, prepared a document affirming individuals' right to free expression and higher education providers' responsibility to promote balanced and respectful debates in university settings.[44] Citing Section 43 of the Education (No. 2) Act 1986, the document emphasizes the legal duty of universities to take "reasonably practicable" steps to ensure freedom of speech within the law for their members, students, employees, and visiting speakers, and to advise them to tolerate peaceful protests.[45] One must note that the Education Reform Act 1988 already established academic freedom as a legal

39. *Erdoğan*, para. 3.
40. *Kula*, para. 38.
41. *Kula*, para. 41–43.
42. In 2020, the CJEU affirmed that freedom of speech is a precondition for academic freedom, holding that academic freedom has "an individual dimension in so far as it is associated with freedom of expression and, specifically in the field of research, the freedoms of communication, of research and of dissemination of results thus obtained" as well as "an institutional and organisational dimension reflected in the autonomy of those institutions." Commission v. Hungary, c-66/18 (2020). However, the CJEU's decisions have diminished force now that the U.K. is not part of the EU.
43. It is an independent commission established by the Equality Act 2006 and funded by the Government Equalities Office.
44. Equality and Human Rights Commission, *Freedom of Expression: A Guide for Higher Education Providers and Students' Unions in England and Wales*, EQUALITY AND HUMAN RIGHTS COMMISSION, https://www.equalityhumanrights.com/sites/default/files/freedom-of-expression-guide-for-higher-education-providers-and-students-unions-england-and-wales.pdf (last visited Dec. 28, 2020).
45. Equality and Human Rights Commission, *Freedom of Expression: A Guide for Higher Education Providers and Students' Unions in England and Wales*, EQUALITY AND HUMAN RIGHTS COMMISSION, https://www.equalityhumanrights.com/sites/default/files/freedom-of-expression-guide-for-higher-education-providers-and-students-unions-england-and-wales.pdf (last visited Dec. 28, 2020), at 6–12.

right for university staff "to question and test received wisdom and to put forward new ideas and controversial or unpopular opinions without placing themselves in jeopardy of losing their jobs or the privileges they may have."[46] Without referencing this law in particular, the 2018/19 document affirms the responsibility of educational providers to ensure that this freedom would not be inhibited by internal policies or students or protesters.[47]

Following the Conservative Party's 2019 manifesto pledge to "strengthen free speech and academic freedom in universities," the Department for Education began preparing an eleven-clause education bill in early 2020 to give life to the pledge and to ensure that universities and their students' unions comply with the existing law and policy.[48] In 2020, at the height of the COVID-19 pandemic, it further issued guidance requiring proof from universities suffering financial hardships or facing bankruptcy due to the pandemic that they were fully complying with their legal duties to secure freedom of speech as a condition of receiving emergency loans from the British government.[49] Unsurprisingly, many working or studying in academia responded to the government's actions by denying that there is a free speech crisis on university campuses.[50] Some even consider the crisis a "myth" invented and weaponized by the extreme right to introduce dangerous expression into universities and to demonize students who oppose and are threatened by this kind of speech.[51]

---

46. Equality and Human Rights Commission, *Freedom of Expression: A Guide for Higher Education Providers and Students' Unions in England and Wales*, EQUALITY AND HUMAN RIGHTS COMMISSION, https://www.equalityhumanrights.com/sites/default/files/freedom-of-expression-guide-for-higher-education-providers-and-students-unions-england-and-wales.pdf (last visited Dec. 28, 2020), at 13–14; citing the Education (No 2) Act 1986, c. 61, s. 43.
47. Equality and Human Rights Commission, *Freedom of Expression: A Guide for Higher Education Providers and Students' Unions in England and Wales*, EQUALITY AND HUMAN RIGHTS COMMISSION, https://www.equalityhumanrights.com/sites/default/files/freedom-of-expression-guide-for-higher-education-providers-and-students-unions-england-and-wales.pdf (last visited Dec. 28, 2020), at 15; citing Education Reform Act 1988, c. 40, s. 202(2).
48. Paul Waugh, *Ministers Preparing New Law to "Protect Freedom of Speech" at Universities*, HUFFINGTON POST (Mar. 7, 2020), http://www.huffingtonpost.co.uk/entry/gavin-williamson-new-law-freedom-of-speech-university-oxford_uk_5e63fa78c5b6670e72f90ef5 (last visited Dec. 28, 2020).
49. *E.g.*, Richard Adams, *English Universities Must Prove "Commitment" to Free Speech for Bailouts*, THE GUARDIAN (Jul. 16, 2020), http://www.theguardian.com/education/2020/jul/16/english-universities-must-prove-commitment-to-free-speech-for-bailouts
50. *E.g.*, John Morgan, *Most UK Students "Don't Think Free Speech under Threat" on Campus*, TIMES HIGHER EDUC. (Dec. 7, 2019), http://www.timeshighereducation.com/news/most-uk-students-dont-think-free-speech-under-threat-campus; Sean Coughlan, *Free Speech Pledge*, BBC (May 3, 2018,) http://www.bbc.com/news/education-43989236 (last visited Dec. 28, 2020).
51. *E.g.*, Evan Smith, *The University "Free Speech Crisis" Has Been a Rightwing Myth for 50 Years*, THE GUARDIAN (Feb. 22, 2020), http://www.theguardian.com/commentisfree/2020/feb/22/university-fr

The free speech and academic freedom bill, if passed, would put more pressure on universities and student organizations as well as make people more aware of their rights and freedoms. Thus, universities and students' unions may implement more productive measures in promoting free speech and exercise more restraint in monitoring the speech of their members and guests. At the same time, free speech disputes, which previously would have ended in settlements, may more likely escalate into lawsuits from those who believe that their rights have been violated and need vindication from courts. The following section will examine numerous case studies over the past decade by drawing exclusively upon open-access resources. It will address whether the disputes were properly dealt with and the implications of a new stringent law for similar disputes.

II. *Case Studies*

The pushback against calls to protect academic free speech on British university campuses is not difficult to understand. One may attribute it in part to a lack of consensus on whether free speech is threatened in universities. Formal studies on this matter, which adopt different methods of examining campus speech and censorship, have led to contradictory conclusions. For example, a 2015 nationwide study by *Spiked* magazine shows that more than 80 percent of British universities have restricted or actively censored free expression on their campuses through their policies or actions that go beyond the requirements of the law.[52] A 2020 study by a British think tank examined a randomly collected sample of more than 800 working and retired professors and lecturers in British universities to discover the reality that left-leaning academics outnumbered their conservative counterparts by almost 4 to 1. A sizeable proportion of the latter group revealed a reluctance to express their own views or challenge the views of their left-wing colleagues.[53] The state of campus free speech revealed in

---

ee-speech-crisis-censorship-enoch-powell; Neesrin Malik, *There Is a Crisis on Campus—but It's about Racism, Not Free Speech*, The Guardian (Oct. 13, 2019), http://www.theguardian.com/commentisfree/2019/oct/13/universities-crisis-racism-not-political-correctness

52. Louise Tickle, *Free Speech? Not at Four in Five Universities*, The Guardian (Feb. 2, 2015), http://www.theguardian.com/education/2015/feb/02/free-speech-universities-spiked-ban-sombreros, citing Tom Slater, *Free Speech University Rankings: Exposing the Staggering Scale of Censorship on Campus*, Spiked (Feb. 3, 2015), http://www.spiked-online.com/2015/02/03/free-speech-university-rankings-exposing-the-staggering-scale-of-censorship-on-campus/ (last visited Jan. 10, 2021).

53. Remi Adekoya, Eric Kaufmann & Tom Simpson, *Academic Freedom in the UK: Protecting Viewpoint*

these studies does not align with the perceptions of their students or even academics and administrators. In a 2019 study by King's College London, which is based in part on a survey of 2,153 students enrolled in British higher educational institutions, most student interviewees believe that freedom of speech is threatened in the wider society but much less so at their own universities.[54]

Despite ample evidence indicating a free speech crisis on at least some campuses, and the fact that conservative speakers have been much more frequently suppressed than liberals—and with far more vicious attacks[55]—some consider the free speech crisis a myth concocted by the far right to advance their harmful agendas. One commentator, noting that Britain's right-wing politicians and media in the 1960s already criticized liberal students for mindlessly suppressing their opponents, contends that the crisis has almost always been a "rightwing myth," which has now coincided with the rise of the "global far right."[56] This occludes the fact that during the free speech movement on campuses in the 1960s, those were liberal academics and students who fought to get heard on university campuses, which were then dominated and ruled by conservatives. It would, perhaps, be no less erroneous to say that the current crisis was a myth invented by the conservatives than to say that the one back then was concocted by the liberals.

What and whose speech is suppressed or marginalized thus depends in part on who is in power. To say that conservative speech is more threatened in universities than liberal speech, as evidence shows, is not to insinuate that liberal academics or students are any less tolerant than their conservative counterparts: it simply alludes to the reality that there are far more left-leaning mem-

Diversity, Policy Exchange (Aug. 2020), http://policyexchange.org.uk/publication/academic-freedom-in-the-uk-2/ (last visited Jan. 10, 2020).

54. Jonathan Grant & Kirstie Hewlett, *Student Experience of Freedom of Expression in UK Universities*, Policy Institute, King's College London, http://www.kcl.ac.uk/policy-institute/assets/student-experience-freedom-of-expression.pdf (last visited Jan. 10, 2020).

55. Evan Smith, *The University "Free Speech Crisis" Has Been a Rightwing Myth for 50 Years*, The Guardian (Feb. 22, 2020), http://www.theguardian.com/commentisfree/2020/feb/22/university-free-speech-crisis-censorship-enoch-powell; William Davies, *The Free Speech Panic: How the Right Concocted a Crisis*, The Guardian (Jul. 26, 2018), http://www.theguardian.com/news/2018/jul/26/the-free-speech-panic-censorship-how-the-right-concocted-a-crisis

56. The "ban list" shows that deplatforming attempts from 2005 to 2020 were overwhelmingly initiated by left-wing groups targeting conservative-leaning speakers (for example, those openly critical of progressive immigration policies and transgender rights), while there were almost no attempts to deplatform liberal speakers. Among the rare exceptions was progressive lecturer Rosa Freedman of the University of Reading. Jewish speakers were targeted by both the far left and the extreme right. *See* Academics for Academic Freedom, *The Banned List*, http://www.afaf.org.uk/the-banned-list/ (last visited Jan. 10, 2020).

bers than those holding moderate and right-leaning perspectives and the majority overpower the minority.[57] The rest of this chapter, while examining representative examples where speakers—many of whom are conservative—were attacked for their views, should not be seen as a defense of conservativism or a vindication of conservative opinions. It seeks rather to study whether the regulatory measures were justified. Ultimately, it argues for the equal application of the free speech principle to all expression regardless of the politics to facilitate respectful debates and the pursuit of knowledge.

Example 1

In 2020, world-renowned British children's author J. K. Rowling offended many transgender people and trans activists by her blog post on sex, gender, and transgender rights. Despite her support for trans women, Rowling expressed concern that the rise of trans activism would erase the concept of sex defining the lives of many women, and that allowing "any man who believes or feels he's a woman" and who is granted a gender certificate without any need for surgery or hormone therapy into women's bathrooms and changing rooms may jeopardize the safety of the latter.[58] While her outspokenness on the issue earned her respect from some people, it drew harsh criticisms from others who called her opinions "ill-informed," "hurtful," and ultimately "transphobic."[59] It is challenging how she can share her "lived experience" as a survivor of domestic abuse and sexual assault who harbors genuine concerns for women's welfare, as Rowling called it, without offending transgender people whose feelings and opinions are no doubt as legitimate as the former's and who deem that the former's expressions "deny their identity/existence."[60]

57. Remi Adekoya, Eric Kaufmann & Tom Simpson, *Academic Freedom in the UK: Protecting Viewpoint Diversity*, POLICY EXCHANGE (Aug. 2020), http://policyexchange.org.uk/publication/academic-freedom-in-the-uk-2/ (last visited Jan. 10, 2020).
58. J. K. Rowling, *J.K. Rowling Writes about Her Reasons for Speaking Out on Sex and Gender Issues*, J. K. ROWLING (OFFICIAL WEBSITE) (Jun. 10, 2020), http://www.jkrowling.com/opinions/j-k-rowling-writes-about-her-reasons-for-speaking-out-on-sex-and-gender-issues/ (last visited Feb. 19, 2021).
59. *E.g.*, A.J. Sass, *I'm a Nonbinary Writer of Youth Literature. J. K. Rowling's Comments on Gender Identity Reinforced My Commitment to Better Representation*, TIME (Jun. 19, 2020), http://time.com/5855633/jk-rowling-gender-identity/; *J. K. Rowling Says She Survives Sexual Abuse and Domestic Violence*, DEUTSCHE WELLE (Jun. 11, 2020), http://www.dw.com/en/jk-rowling-says-she-survived-sexual-abuse-and-domestic-violence/a-53770327; Amber Jamieson, *J. K. Rowling Followed Up Her Anti-Trans Tweets with a Full Anti-Trans Essay*, BUZZ FEED NEWS (Jun. 10, 2020), http://www.buzzfeednews.com/article/amberjamieson/jk-rowling-antitrans-statement (last visited Feb. 19, 2021).
60. *E.g.*, Nardine Saad, *J. K. Rowling Backed a Woman Who Made Transphobic Remarks. Now She's Facing the Backlash*, L.A. TIMES (Dec. 19, 2019), http://www.latimes.com/entertainment-arts/books/story/2019-12-19/jk-rowling-transphobic-tweet

Rowling very likely would meet with protests or be deplatformed if she were invited to speak at any British university regardless of her topic, due to her high profile and the amount of negative attention her essay has drawn. Over the past few years, many talks and seminars aimed at discussing mainstream transgender ideologies through critical lenses and given by speakers in different disciplines were canceled. In late 2019, Essex University canceled the lecture of Jo Phoenix, professor of criminology at the Open University, on transgender rights in prison, after uproar among trans activists threatening to shut it down.[61] Also in late 2019, Shereen Benjamin, senior lecturer in primary education at the University of Edinburgh, tried to organize a conference on diversity in schools by bringing together gender-critical speakers who believe that there are social causes for the rise in referral rates of children to gender identity clinics, with speakers from trans rights organisations who attribute the rise to an increasing number of schoolchildren discovering their true identities at a younger age. Not only was Benjamin unable to persuade any trans rights organizations to participate in the event, but she also ended up canceling it when a colleague urged opponents to protest speakers "with a history of transphobia."[62] In early 2020, the Oxford International Women's Festival canceled Oxford historian Selina Todd's talk due to pressure from trans activists. Todd was also labeled "transphobic" for her view that "trans women should be allowed to call themselves trans women," but that in certain circumstances provisions that differentiate "on the basis of sex" are necessary.[63] Germaine Greer, who outright refused to accept men having undergone sex-change surgeries as women, was—quite surprisingly—among the rare critics of mainstream transgender ideologies who did not get deplatformed: her 2015 lecture at Cardiff University proceeded under high security despite vehement calls to cancel it.[64]

The rationale adopted by many trans activists to deplatform the above speakers is grounded in the conflation of expressions that may be "hurtful" and "offensive" with conduct that is illegal, such as harassment and discrimination,

---

61. Anna Fazackerley, *Sacked or Silenced: Academics Said They Are Blocked from Exploring Trans Issues*, THE GUARDIAN (Jan. 14, 2020, 7:15 AM), http://www.theguardian.com/education/2020/jan/14/sacked-silenced-academics-say-they-are-blocked-from-exploring-trans-issues
62. Anna Fazackerley, *Sacked or Silenced: Academics Said They Are Blocked from Exploring Trans Issues*, THE GUARDIAN (Jan. 14, 2020), http://www.theguardian.com/education/2020/jan/14/sacked-silenced-academics-say-they-are-blocked-from-exploring-trans-issues
63. *Oxford University Professor Condemned Exclusion from Event*, BBC (Mar. 4, 2020), http://www.bbc.com/news/uk-england-oxfordshire-51737206 (last visited Feb. 19, 2021).
64. Steven Morris, *Germaine Greer Gives University Lecture Despite Campaign to Silence Her*, THE GUARDIAN (Nov. 18, 2015), http://www.theguardian.com/books/2015/nov/18/transgender-activists-protest-germaine-greer-lecture-cardiff-university

as well as overly broad definitions of "harm" and "transphobic" to include anything that challenges mainstream gender ideologies and causes emotional discomfort.[65] The overbroad definitions are examples of concept creep that dilute the original meanings of concepts and encourage those who might have been thoughtful participants in academic discussions to shun opinions challenging their perspectives.[66] Canceling events at Essex, Oxford, and Edinburgh, which do appear to be valuable opportunities for thoughtful engagement on these topics, might even radicalize people from both ends of the thought spectrum. The calls to deplatform Greer were more understandable: while she enjoyed freedom of speech and thought, her flat-out denial in public that trans women are women made her action suspect under the Equality Act 2010.[67] Nevertheless, one-off academic events, if properly moderated, might not sufficiently lead to discriminatory campus environments even if they feature speakers expressing discriminatory views. Efforts should be channeled into finding experienced moderators and well-informed opponents, not shutting down controversial speakers. Are there respected experts in the field who can bring opposing views to the table? Will there be sufficient time for meaningful engagement? Among all colleagues, who might best serve as the moderator of these difficult conversations? As transphobic as Greer's views appeared to be, events like the one at Cardiff might have enabled her opponents to challenge her views and the public to better understand transgender issues. Even in the absence of any consensus, these events should lead to less—not more—transphobia.[68] Assuming that many of these feminists argued in good faith and their views were grounded in lived experiences, shouldn't they deserve respect as much as the trans women do?

---

65. *See, e.g.*, Anna Fazackerley, *Sacked or Silenced: Academics Said They Are Blocked from Exploring Trans Issues*, THE GUARDIAN (Jan. 14, 2020), http://www.theguardian.com/education/2020/jan/14/sacked-silenced-academics-say-they-are-blocked-from-exploring-trans-issues; Marc Horn, *"Stalinist" Open University Removed Trans Comment*, THE TIMES (Dec. 7, 2020), http://www.thetimes.co.uk/article/stalinist-open-university-removed-trans-comment-dkss0683w

66. *See* chapter 6.

67. *See* Equality Act 2010, c. 15, s. 7(1): "A person has the protected characteristic of gender reassignment if the person is proposing to undergo, is undergoing or has undergone a process (or part of a process) for the purpose of reassigning the person's sex by changing physiological or other attributes of sex."

68. *See, e.g.*, Zoe Williams, *Silencing Germaine Greer Will Let Prejudice against Trans People Flourish*, THE GUARDIAN (Oct. 25, 2015), http://www.theguardian.com/commentisfree/2015/oct/25/germaine-greer-prejudice-trans-people

Example 2

If the lived experiences of all people are all valid and none should get erased or overlooked, it would be utterly discriminatory to say that some are more deserving to be expressed and listened to than others. In late May 2020, the killing of George Floyd in Minneapolis triggered major antiracism protests in many American cities. In the following months, the Black Lives Matter (BLM) movement in the U.S., reinvigorated by this tragedy, spread to other parts of the Western world. In the U.K., this led in part to a shift in the public's attitude toward British colonialism. The governing body of Oxford's Oriel College, for example, voted to remove the statue of Cecil Rhodes on its campus in June 2020.[69] An essay in the *London Review of Books* lauded this move and urged more antiracist movements in British higher education.[70]

Arguably, Canterbury Christ Church University rightly removed its history professor from his visiting position for his recent racist statement, "So many damn blacks in Africa," to avoid fostering a discriminatory environment.[71] Yet lawful expressions critical of the BLM concept or movement sometimes also got suppressed and their speakers risked punishment. At the height of the BLM movement in Britain, people saying "All Lives Matter," regardless of their intent, were harshly criticized by some BLM supporters for what they considered to be ignorance, dismissiveness of hardships suffered by black people, or downright racism. A scholar in black slavery, for instance, pointed out that black people in Western nations experienced "unique suffering" and suffered wrongs that these societies have yet to address.[72] The phrase "all lives matter," he argued, acts to "diminish and suppress the voice of black people challenging the status quo" and so could only have been made on "bad faith."[73] Throughout Britain and

---

69. Aamna Mohdin, Richard Adams & Ben Quinn, *Oxford College Backs Removal of Cecil Rhodes Statue*, THE GUARDIAN (Jun. 17, 2020), http://www.theguardian.com/education/2020/jun/17/end-of-the-rhodes-cecil-oxford-college-ditches-controversial-statue
70. Natalya in-Kariuki, *After Rhodes Falls*, LONDON REV. BK. (Jun. 29, 2020), http://www.lrb.co.uk/blog/2020/june/after-rhodes-falls
71. Tom Embury-Dennis, *David Starkey Apologises for Racist Claim Slavery Was Not Genocide Because There Are "So Many Damn Blacks" in UK and Africa*, THE INDEPENDENT (Jul. 6, 2020), http://www.independent.co.uk/news/uk/home-news/david-starkey-racist-slavery-genocide-apology-darren-grimes-black-lives-matter-a9603826.html
72. Katie O'Malley, *History of Slavery Professor Explains the Mistake in Saying "All Lives Matter,"* ELLE MAG. (Jun. 10, 2020), http://www.elle.com/uk/life-and-culture/culture/a32800835/all-lives-matter-fake-equality/ (last visited Feb. 20, 2021).
73. Katie O'Malley, *History of Slavery Professor Explains the Mistake in Saying "All Lives Matter,"* ELLE

elsewhere, many BLM supporters tended to share this sentiment. For example, some black students at the University of Sussex criticized the university's public statement acknowledging the BLM as a BAME (Blacks, Asians, and Minority Ethnic) issue and not as a movement about the unique problems faced by black students.[74] A lecturer at Plymouth University was put under investigation by the university authority for tweeting "all lives matter," among other things, on his Twitter page. The university soon dropped the investigation and reaffirmed its members' right to challenge prevailing orthodoxies.[75]

Insinuating that people are racist or acting in bad faith merely for disagreeing with the "Black Lives Matter" concept or movement unfairly suppresses constructive criticisms, especially from people in other racial groups.[76] It dismisses sincere concerns that this phrase creates a hierarchy of oppression, in which black people suffer more and thereby deserve more sympathy and support than other races. In addition, it is presumptuous to believe that only black experiences are unique and those of other races are not. For example, there are Asian immigrants who survived traumas before moving to Western nations and continued to struggle in their new homes, and whose sufferings may simply be as "heavy and palpable" as those of black people.[77] Faulting these people for saying "Asian lives matter," as some BLM activists do, would be to invalidate the "lived experiences" of Asians. Yet acknowledging that "Asian lives (or lives of any ethnicity who have suffered) matter" would ultimately lead to the conclusion that "all lives matter." Notwithstanding that "all lives matter" has been used by white supremacists to advance their racist agendas, many people saying

---

MAG. (Jun. 10, 2020), http://www.elle.com/uk/life-and-culture/culture/a32800835/all-lives-matter-fake-equality/ (last visited Feb. 20, 2021).

74. Georgia Mooney, *Sussex under Fire for Posting BAME Support Post Instead of Black Lives Matter*, THE TAB (Jun. 4, 2020), http://thetab.com/uk/sussex/2020/06/04/sussex-under-fire-for-posting-bame-support-post-instead-of-black-lives-matter-41939 (last visited Feb. 20, 2021).

75. Artillery Row, *Physicist Could Be Fired over "All Lives Matter" Tweet*, THE CRITIC (Jun. 26, 2020), http://thecritic.co.uk/physicist-could-be-fired-over-all-lives-matter-tweet/ (last visited Feb. 20, 2021).

76. The slavery scholar, in his attempt to argue that "all lives matter" is cruel and hurtful, made two improper analogies by equating it to saying "everyone's parents die" to a colleague grieving over his father's death and a man saying "I love everyone" to his wife. It would indeed be cruel to say "everyone's parents die" to a colleague who has recently lost his father, just as it would be insensitive for a married man, whose duty is to love his wife, to say he loves everyone. From a societal point of view, all lives are indeed created equal and should be treated as such, and death is indeed the final destiny for all. Laws and policies should be informed by broad societal perspectives and not by personal feelings. Katie O'Malley, *History of Slavery Professor Explains the Mistake in Saying "All Lives Matter,"* ELLE MAG. (Jun. 10, 2020), http://www.elle.com/uk/life-and-culture/culture/a32800835/all-lives-matter-fake-equality/ (last visited Feb. 20, 2021).

77. *See* Katie O'Malley, *History of Slavery Professor Explains the Mistake in Saying "All Lives Matter,"* ELLE MAG. (Jun. 10, 2020), http://www.elle.com/uk/life-and-culture/culture/a32800835/all-lives-matter-fake-equality/ (last visited Feb. 20, 2021).

"all lives matter" may agree that black lives matter but want to stress that ultimately all lives are equal and matter just as much. Although Plymouth University affirmed its members' right to free speech, the incident is a chilling indication of how criticism of prevailing orthodoxies might have been suppressed at other universities and not reported in the news. That some academics may have to bet their hopes on the new free speech bill to safeguard lawful expressions like "all lives matter" is unfortunate.

Even more sadly, in some circles, "all lives matter" is considered racist, but "white lives do not matter" is not. In response to a banner flown over a Premier League football stadium that read "White lives matter Burnley," Priyamvada Gopal, an English professor of Indian descent at Cambridge University and a fellow of Churchill College, publicly tweeted, "I'll say it again. White Lives Don't Matter. As white lives," "Abolish whiteness," and "Yes, all lives matter. White lives as white do not." on her Twitter page.[78] Outraged readers launched an online petition to Cambridge, requesting that the university and its college "immediately discontinue their relationship with Ms. Gopal in the best interest of all students and the community at large" on the grounds of her "racist and hateful" statements.[79] Hateful messages targeting Gopal appeared on the petition site, including one calling her "disgusting inside and out," and another telling her: "If you don't like white people, pack up your sh*t and go home. Problem solved." One was even mildly threatening: "On another note, kill yourself. Else someone might show you which lives really Matter :)."[80] Calling these messages "harassment," Gopal urged people to report them to the website owner. Cambridge publicly denounced her attackers' actions: "The University defends the right of its academics to express their own lawful opinions which others might find controversial and deplores in the strongest terms abuse and personal attacks. These attacks are totally unacceptable and must cease."[81] Gopal later claimed that her tweets were meant to oppose "the concept of whiteness—

78. Sophie Huskisson, *Cambridge Condemns Abuse against Academics, After Petition to Fire Dr Gopal Launched*, VARSITY (Jun. 24, 2020), http://varsity.co.uk/news/19539 (last visited Feb. 20, 2021).
79. Sophie Huskisson, *Cambridge Condemns Abuse against Academics, After Petition to Fire Dr Gopal Launched*, VARSITY (Jun. 24, 2020), http://varsity.co.uk/news/19539 (last visited Feb. 20, 2021); citing http://twitter.com/priyamvadagopal/status/1275321778961866752?lang=en (last visited Feb. 20, 2021). Some of these tweets were soon deleted, although they were once available at http://webcache.googleusercontent.com/search?q=cache:Wt2AboR2xrAJ:https://twitter.com/priyamvadagopal/status/1275329037888602112+&cd=2&hl=en&ct=clnk&gl=de (last visited Feb. 20, 2021).
80. Sophie Huskisson, *Cambridge Condemns Abuse against Academics, After Petition to Fire Dr Gopal Launched*, VARSITY (Jun. 24, 2020), http://varsity.co.uk/news/19539 (last visited Feb. 20, 2021). (The petition site itself was soon removed.)
81. Sophie Huskisson, *Cambridge Condemns Abuse against Academics, After Petition to Fire Dr Gopal Launched*, VARSITY (Jun. 24, 2020), http://varsity.co.uk/news/19539 (last visited Feb. 20, 2021).

the societal structure that presumes the superiority of white people" rather than to attack white people.[82]

Because Gopal's tweets were misleading, Cambridge was wrong to put the entire blame on her attackers. While people well versed in critical race theories may have been able to connect "White Lives Don't Matter. As white lives" and "Abolish whiteness" with what she claimed to be an attack on the "concept of whiteness" as a "societal structure," the general audience likely took her tweets literally and interpreted them as attacks on the white race, hence racism by its very own definition. Gopal should have foreseen the confusion and outrage they caused and not withheld their proper contexts. Without those contexts, remarks on her tweets were only understandable. The request that she kill herself, which sounded abusive and threatening, could reasonably be taken as hyperbole motivated by disgust and disapproval. The other two hateful remarks were similarly disgust-ridden retaliation to what were reasonably perceived as attacks on white people as a group. None of these contained hate speech or harassment under British law. Neither did the petition to have her fired, which was a peaceful call for action despite the radical nature of the action itself. While Cambridge was right in upholding free speech and the right to express controversial opinions and discouraging personal attacks and abusive remarks, it should have also reflected on the causes of the attacks and advised Gopal to provide timely and proper contexts to her tweets. That the author of the tweets was a member of a racial minority group did not absolve her of personal responsibility or place her above constructive criticism. Most unfortunately, as the following example will show, Cambridge has not applied the same free speech standard to all its free speech controversies.

Example 3

While lawsuits involving academic speech violations have been extremely rare in the U.K., one such lawsuit could have been brought against Cambridge. In May 2019, Cambridge dismissed young sociologist Noah Carl from his position as Jackman Newton Trust Research Fellow at St Edmund's College. Not long after Carl's appointment in December 2018, more than 500 academics and 800 students signed an open letter calling his research on race and intelligence "eth-

82. Sophie Huskisson, *Cambridge Condemns Abuse against Academics, After Petition to Fire Dr Gopal Launched*, VARSITY (Jun. 24, 2020), http://varsity.co.uk/news/19539 (last visited Feb. 20, 2021).

ically suspect and methodologically flawed" and urging the university to terminate his employment.[83] This open letter prompted a petition, signed by 650 academics, defending him on the grounds of free speech and academic freedom.[84] The internal investigation team of St. Edmund's College concluded that Carl's work "demonstrated poor scholarship, promoted extreme right-wing views and incited racial and religious hatred," that he "had collaborated with a number of individuals who were known to hold extremist views," and that continuing his affiliation as a fellow would risk allowing the college to be used to "promote views that could incite racial or religious hatred and bring the college into disrepute."[85] The college also apologized "unreservedly for the hurt and offence" felt by its members due to the appointment.[86] No irregularities, however, were found in the recruitment process.[87] By September 2019, Carl crowdfunded over 100,000 British pounds to support his legal action against Cambridge, both to restore his own reputation and to protect the rights of other scholars persecuted for challenging prevailing orthodoxies.[88]

Given that no irregularities were found in Carl's recruitment and his appointment was merit-based, it is worth looking into his research to determine whether the termination of his fellowship was justified. Indeed, Carl seems to be a highly accomplished researcher, as shown by his numerous pub-

---

83. No to Racist Pseudoscience, *Open Letter: No to Racist Pseudoscience in Cambridge* (Dec. 18, 2018), http://medium.com/@racescienceopenletter/open-letter-no-to-racist-pseudoscience-at-cambridge-472e1a7c6dca (last visited Feb. 21, 2021).

84. Claire Lehmann, *Cambridge Capitulates to the Mob and Fires a Young Scholar*, QUILLETTE (May 2, 2019), http://quillette.com/2019/05/02/cambridge-capitulates-to-the-mob-and-fires-a-young-scholar/

85. St. Edmund's College, Cambridge, *Statement from the Master Regarding the Outcome of the Investigations into Complaints about the Appointment of Research Fellow*, ST. EDMUND'S COLLEGE, UNIVERSITY OF CAMBRIDGE (Apr. 30, 2019), http://www.st-edmunds.cam.ac.uk/sites/www.st-edmunds.cam.ac.uk/files/Statement%20by%20Master%20for%20website_outcome%20FINAL30%20April%202019.pdf (last visited Feb. 21, 2021).

86. St. Edmund's College, Cambridge, *Statement from the Master Regarding the Outcome of the Investigations into Complaints about the Appointment of Research Fellow*, ST. EDMUND'S COLLEGE, UNIVERSITY OF CAMBRIDGE (Apr. 30, 2019), http://www.st-edmunds.cam.ac.uk/sites/www.st-edmunds.cam.ac.uk/files/Statement%20by%20Master%20for%20website_outcome%20FINAL30%20April%202019.pdf (last visited Feb. 21, 2021).

87. St. Edmund's College, Cambridge, *Statement from the Master Regarding the Outcome of the Investigations into Complaints about the Appointment of Research Fellow*, ST. EDMUND'S COLLEGE, UNIVERSITY OF CAMBRIDGE (Apr. 30, 2019), http://www.st-edmunds.cam.ac.uk/sites/www.st-edmunds.cam.ac.uk/files/Statement%20by%20Master%20for%20website_outcome%20FINAL30%20April%202019.pdf (last visited Feb. 21, 2021).

88. Stephanie Stacey, *Dismissed Research Fellow Noah Carl Raises over $100,000 to Fund Legal Action against Eddie's*, VARSITY (Sep. 24, 2019), http://www.varsity.co.uk/news/17849 (last visited Feb. 21, 2021).

lications in reputable mainstream academic journals.[89] What caused great concern were his articles in *Open Quantitative Sociology & Political Science*, considered a "pseudoscience factory-farm" and for whom he also served as a reviewer, and *Mankind Quarterly*, labeled a "white supremacist journal."[90] Among his five publications in the former journal, which Cambridge likely considered to promote ethnic and religious hatred, one found that the public's opposition to immigrants of different nationalities in the U.K. correlates strongly with immigrant arrest rates, thereby concluding that the public's beliefs about the likelihood of arrests among different immigrant groups may be reasonably accurate.[91] Two found that larger Muslim populations in Western countries correlate strongly with a higher number of Islamist terrorist attacks in those countries.[92] His only publication in the latter journal tested Federico R. León's and Mayra Antonelli-Ponti's theory that regions of countries subject to higher levels of UV radiation tend to have lower average IQs and found that it does not apply to the U.K.[93] Carl also spoke twice at the London Conference on Intelligence and collaborated with fourteen other attendees on a letter defending this conference against what they considered mischaracterization by the media.[94] His prolific research on two difficult subjects, namely, whether immigration has led to higher crime and intelligence studies, triggered protests about his appointment. As his article in *Evolutionary Psychological Science* argues, the societal costs of discussing certain topics have not proven to inevitably outweigh its benefits, and stifling debate around taboo topics can do active harm and is not ethical.[95]

89. See his list of publications on http://scholar.google.com/citations?user=CUywRJoAAAAJ&hl=th, many of which are mainstream academic journals including *Intelligence, Personality and Individual Differences, Learning and Individual Differences, Frontiers in Psychology, Frontiers in Human Neuroscience, Journal of Experimental Psychology: General, Evolutionary Psychological Science, Twins Research and Human Genetics, Cortex*, and *Evolutionary Behavioral Sciences* (last visited Feb. 22, 2021).
90. Ben van der Merwe, *No, Objecting to Cambridge's Appointment of a Eugenicist Is Not about Free Speech*, NEW STATESMAN (Dec. 20, 2018), http://www.newstatesman.com/politics/education/2018/12/no-objecting-cambridge-s-appointment-eugenicist-not-about-free-speech; AARON GRESSON, JOE L. KINCHELOE & SHIRLEY R. STEINBERG, MEASURED LIES: THE BELL CURVE EXPLAINED 39 (1997).
91. Noah Carl, *Net Opposition to Immigrants of Different Nationalities Correlates Strongly with Their Arrest Rates in the UK*, OPEN QUANTITATIVE SOC. & POL. SCI. (Nov. 10, 2016).
92. Noah Carl, *A Global Analysis of Islamist Terrorism*, OPEN QUANTITATIVE SOC. & POL. SCI. (2017); Noah Carl, *An Analysis of Islamist Terrorism across Western Countries*, OPEN QUANTITATIVE SOC. & POL. SCI. (2016).
93. Noah Carl, *The Relationship between Solar Radiation and IQ in the United Kingdom*, MANKIND Q. 58.4 (2018).
94. Carl's open response to the accusations, which he coauthored with fourteen other participants, was published in *Intelligence* journal. *See* Noah Carl & others, *Communicating Intelligence Research: Media Misrepresentation, the Gould Effect, and Unexpected Forces*, 70 INTELLIGENCE 84 (2018).
95. Noah Carl, *How Stifling Debate Around Race, Genes and IQ Can Do Harm*, 4 EVOLUTIONARY PSYCHOL. SCI. 399 (2018).

It is challenging to determine whether the social costs of his research outweigh its benefits. As another of his studies shows, academia is dominated by left-wing views:[96] writing about what left-wing academics consider taboo topics finally cost him his job.

Absent substantial proof that Carl conducted his research in bad faith and with the intention to promote racism and Islamophobia, St. Edmund's College should have given him the benefit of the doubt, rather than punishing him and violating his right to academic free speech. While stating as a ground of dismissal that Carl "had put a body of work into the public domain that did not comply with established criteria for research ethics and integrity," it did not specify whether his research methods or the topics, or both, were at issue.[97] If the former were the problem, the university should have considered his junior status, helped him to identify the flaws in his methods, and advised him to submit his work to mainstream academic outlets with vigorous peer review processes. On the other hand, if the university had taken issue with his research topics or results, or both, it essentially implied that people must steer clear of these topics, or else make statements that contradict Carl's findings and lend support to orthodox—in this case liberal—ideologies. Certainly, academic free speech is subject to hate speech and discrimination laws. Carl's findings and conclusions nonetheless cannot be fairly described as racist or Islamophobic. His belief in the reasonable accuracy of the public's beliefs about the likelihood of arrests among different immigrant groups is a far cry from stating that racist stereotypes are rational or justified.[98] Likewise, saying that larger Muslim populations in Western countries correlate strongly with higher number of Islamist terrorist attacks in those countries does not promote religious hatred, not only because Muslims are a highly diverse group but also because numerous factors other than religion could contribute, and likely have contributed, to this correlation. Above all, he claimed to have never produced original research in the field of intelligence studies or stated that genetics account for group differences

96. Noah Carl, *The Political Attitudes of British Academics*, Open Quantitative Soc. & Pol. Sci. (Jan. 16, 2018).

97. St. Edmund's College, Cambridge, *Statement from the Master Regarding the Outcome of the Investigations into Complaints about the Appointment of Research Fellow*, St. Edmund's College, University of Cambridge (Apr. 30, 2019), http://www.st-edmunds.cam.ac.uk/sites/www.st-edmunds.cam.ac.uk/files/Statement%20by%20Master%20for%20website_outcome%20FINAL30%20April%202019.pdf (last visited Feb. 21, 2021).

98. *See* Noah Carl, *Net Opposition to Immigrants of Different Nationalities Correlates Strongly with Their Arrest Rates in the UK*, Open Quantitative Soc. & Pol. Sci. (Nov. 10, 2016); *see also* Noah Carl, *Noah Carl Controversy: Q & A*, Noteworthy: The Journal Blog (May 7, 2019), http://blog.usejournal.com/noah-carl-controversy-faq-ad967834b12d (last visited Feb. 21, 2021).

in IQ—a claim that is attested to by his research and interviews.[99] Any attempt by extremists to misuse his research for their own agendas would not have been his fault.

Undoubtedly, Carl should have steered clear of taboo topics and focused on "safe" research studies whose results would not challenge orthodoxies, if keeping his job had been his top priority. As controversial as his works may be, it would nonetheless be unfair to equate the termination of his appointment with a Canadian university's dismissal of its professor for publishing a racist book: his studies might be prone to being exploited by the extreme right, while the Canadian professor's book argues that white people are superior to all other races and immigrants of minority backgrounds are destroying Canada (see chapter 9). In March 2021, Carl announced his settlement with Cambridge on undisclosed terms.[100] Should Carl have taken the university to court, the British judge, depending on his background, might have lacked the expertise to evaluate his publications and perceive the nuances in his arguments. If so, he would have lost—even if the free speech bill becomes law. Nonetheless, even if Carl was handsomely compensated, the settlement was hardly a victory for him or for academia, considering that he should never have been dismissed from his position, nor should his reputation ever have been tainted in the first place.

Carl's dismissal was by no means the only case in which Cambridge stripped scholars of their platforms. In March 2019, it rescinded its offer of a two-month fellowship to Jordan Peterson, a professor of psychology at the University of Toronto (a full account of his work, media appearances, and public engagement is given in chapter 9).[101] When Peterson applied for a fellowship at its Faculty of Divinity and was initially granted an offer, he was already famous as a best-selling author and public intellectual who openly protested the "gender-neutral pronoun bill" recently passed in Canada.[102] Other than saying that his fellowship was rescinded "after a further review," Cambridge's spokesperson refused to provide a clear explanation. It nevertheless emphasized that "[Cambridge] is an inclusive environment," that all its staff and visitors are expected to uphold the principles of inclusiveness, and that there is "no place" for anyone who can-

---

99. *See* http://scholar.google.co.uk/citations?user=CUywRJoAAAAJ&hl=en (last visited Feb. 21, 2021).
100. *See* his Twitter post on Mar. 23, 2021, https://twitter.com/NoahCarl90/status/1374279144251535361 (last visited Jun. 23, 2021).
101. Sarah Marsh, *Cambridge University Rescinds Jordan Peterson Invitation*, THE GUARDIAN (Mar. 20, 2019), http://www.theguardian.com/education/2019/mar/20/cambridge-university-rescinds-jordan-peterson-invitation
102. *See* chapter 9.

not.[103] Cambridge Vice-Chancellor Stephen Toope soon issued a statement revealing that the divinity faculty disinvited Peterson after it discovered a photograph of him posing with his arm around a man wearing a T-shirt that bore the slogan, "I'm a proud Islamophobe," and determined that Peterson went against the divinity faculty's goal to promote interfaith understanding.[104] Its students' union expressed relief at this decision, deeming the fellowship offer "a political act to associate the University with an academic's work" and judging Peterson's work and views as "not representative of the student body" but rather standing "in opposition to the principles of the University."[105] On January 21, 2021, Cambridge clarified that the decision to rescind the fellowship was not a result of any backlash from its members and students, but made by the Research Committee of its Faculty of Divinity "prior to and independently of the receipt of any external comment on the matter by other university staff or students."[106]

Whether Peterson's views and works violated the principle of inclusiveness is up for debate.[107] Assuming Peterson's guilt (Islamophobia) by his association with a man who appeared to be an Islamophobe, when that association was based on nothing more than his appearance with the man in a photograph, was logically fallacious. As well, considering that he likely took countless pictures of people with whom he may not even be acquainted and whose T-shirt slogans he may not have paid attention to, the decision to disinvite him was irrational and reflected poorly on the divinity faculty. Cambridge's late disclaimer also smacks of desperation. Because its earlier admission that its decision was motivated by Peterson's failure to uphold the principle of inclusiveness coincided with his opponents' complaints, both in content and timing, the disclaimer raises reasonable suspicion about the role that members external to the divinity faculty played in the decision and the university's attempt to cover up its

103. Sarah Marsh, *Cambridge University Rescinds Jordan Peterson Invitation*, The Guardian (Mar. 20, 2019), http://www.theguardian.com/education/2019/mar/20/cambridge-university-rescinds-jordan-peterson-invitation
104. Stephen J. Toope, *Rescindment of Visiting Fellowship: Statement from Vice-Chancellor Professor Stephen J Toope*, Cambridge University (Mar. 25, 2019), http://www.cam.ac.uk/news/rescindment-of-visiting-fellowship-statement-from-vice-chancellor-professor-stephen-j-toope (last visited Feb. 25, 2021).
105. Sarah Marsh, *Cambridge University Rescinds Jordan Peterson Invitation*, The Guardian (Mar. 20, 2019), http://www.theguardian.com/education/2019/mar/20/cambridge-university-rescinds-jordan-peterson-invitation
106. Sarah Marsh, *Cambridge University Rescinds Jordan Peterson Invitation*, The Guardian (Mar. 20, 2019), http://www.theguardian.com/education/2019/mar/20/cambridge-university-rescinds-jordan-peterson-invitation
107. *See* chapter 9 for a brief introduction to his views on Canada's pronoun bill and mandatory diversity training programs run by his employer and other Canadian universities.

appeasement of his opponents. The students' union's belief that the works and views of invited scholars—not only employed academics—need to be "representative of the student body" and to reflect the values of the university imposes unnecessary restrictions on free speech and academic freedom. It may be excusable for young and idealistic students to hold such authoritarian views, but it's inexcusable and utterly presumptuous for seasoned academics to demand that invited scholars or employed academics toe their party line.[108] That a world-renowned university might have pandered to such authoritarians is deeply concerning.

If Cambridge wants to turn itself into a gigantic safe space where no one would feel hurt and offended and to eliminate the presence of people who might have collaborated with "extremists," it must lead by example to avoid accusations of double-standards and hypocrisy. It must take reasonable steps to avoid offending all Muslims and other minority groups. At the very least, it must stop taking funding from Chinese state-owned companies and terminate all collaborations with entities that are affiliated in any way with the Chinese government—isn't there enough documented evidence of its genocide of Muslim Uyghurs in western China and gross human rights violations elsewhere? It must also expel rabidly nationalistic students from China who regularly and habitually assault people challenging their beliefs. Failing to do any of these indicates its belief that some extremists deserve to be excused and even welcomed, while ethnic minority groups oppressed by China deserve less or no protection from hurtful words and bodily harm. As important as international collaboration and student diversity are to a world-class institution, they do not justify pandering to a hostile foreign government or convenient dismissals of its atrocious acts.

Interestingly, though, Cambridge implemented a new free speech policy before its statement concerning the fellowship revocation—a policy that hopefully will help redeem its reputation and align its position with the government's free speech pledge. In December 2020, the university governing body voted by a large majority to reaffirm the importance of free speech on its campus amid concerns about censorship and persecution in a rising climate of fear.[109] It overturned proposals to require staff, students, and visiting speakers

108. *See, e.g.*, Cambridge Professor Priyamvada Gopal's Twitter posts on Mar. 22, 2019, which stated that Peterson should not be given a fellowship or any loose affiliation with Cambridge, http://twitter.com/priyamvadagopal/status/1109179439164862467?lang=en (last visited Feb. 25, 2021).

109. Ben Quinn, *Cambridge University Rejects Proposal It Be "Respectful" of Views*, THE GUARDIAN (Dec.

to remain "respectful" of the views and "identities" of others, on the ground that this requirement would block controversial ideas and debates.[110] The revised guidelines instead require its "staff, students and visitors to be tolerant of the differing opinions of others," to ensure protection of the right to express "controversial or unpopular opinions within the law, without fear of intolerance or discrimination."[111] To that end, those invited to speak at the university "must not be stopped from doing so" as long as their conduct remains within the law.[112] Hence, the university "will not unreasonably either refuse to allow events to be held on its premises or impose special or unreasonable or onerous conditions upon the running of those events."[113] It "may only restrict speaker events given a reasonable belief that such events are likely to involve speech that violates the law, that falsely defames a specific individual, that constitutes a genuine threat or harassment, that unjustifiably invades substantial privacy or confidentiality interests, or that is otherwise directly incompatible with the functioning of the University."[114]

It was fortunate that Cambridge's governing body voted down the initial proposals. Respect is earned rather than taken for granted. Compelling people to respect people, views, or ideas is at least as authoritarian as compelling them to make prescribed expressions. Cambridge's new policy requiring tolerance of different opinions allows its members to act "respectfully" to people embracing opinions that they do not agree with without harboring actual respect for them

---

9, 2020), http://www.theguardian.com/world/2020/dec/09/cambridge-university-rejects-proposal-it-be-respectful-of-all-views; Sean Coughlan, *Cambridge University Votes to Safeguard Free Speech*, BBC (Dec. 9, 2020), http://www.bbc.com/news/education-55246793 (last visited Feb. 25, 2021); citing Cambridge University, *University Statement on Freedom of Speech*, UNIVERSITY OF CAMBRIDGE, http://www.governanceandcompliance.admin.cam.ac.uk/governance-and-strategy/university-statement-freedom-speech (last visited Feb. 25, 2021).

110. Ben Quinn, *Cambridge University Rejects Proposal It Be "Respectful" of Views*, THE GUARDIAN (Dec. 9, 2020), http://www.theguardian.com/world/2020/dec/09/cambridge-university-rejects-proposal-it-be-respectful-of-all-views; Sean Coughlan, *Cambridge University Votes to Safeguard Free Speech*, BBC (Dec. 9, 2020), http://www.bbc.com/news/education-55246793 (last visited Feb. 25, 2021).

111. Cambridge University, *University Statement on Freedom of Speech*, UNIVERSITY OF CAMBRIDGE, http://www.governanceandcompliance.admin.cam.ac.uk/governance-and-strategy/university-statement-freedom-speech (last visited Feb. 25, 2021).

112. Cambridge University, *University Statement on Freedom of Speech*, UNIVERSITY OF CAMBRIDGE, http://www.governanceandcompliance.admin.cam.ac.uk/governance-and-strategy/university-statement-freedom-speech (last visited Feb. 25, 2021).

113. Cambridge University, *University Statement on Freedom of Speech*, UNIVERSITY OF CAMBRIDGE, http://www.governanceandcompliance.admin.cam.ac.uk/governance-and-strategy/university-statement-freedom-speech (last visited Feb. 25, 2021).

114. Cambridge University, *University Statement on Freedom of Speech*, UNIVERSITY OF CAMBRIDGE, http://www.governanceandcompliance.admin.cam.ac.uk/governance-and-strategy/university-statement-freedom-speech (last visited Feb. 25, 2021).

or their opinions. After all, being respectful and showing real respect—what the original proposal was intended to foster—are not always the same. One can harbor zero respect for people and yet remain respectful—or civil to be more precise—to them or in their presence.

Unsurprisingly, Cambridge's new policy was not welcomed by all its members. Two Cambridge academics, in an op-ed that is rife with contradictions and ironies, fervently argue that it will do more harm than good, rehashing the clichéd argument that universities should carry out their duty to filter out "flawed thinking" and ideas "historically rejected in both academic debate and popular deliberation," so that free speech does not to become "a Trojan horse" for "retrograde ideas" and "discriminatory, hateful or discredited viewpoints that explicitly target racial and sexual minorities."[115] However, given that universities are places, as they claim, where "ideas and opinions are constantly evaluated for their adequacy and credibility," it is counterproductive to hastily and conclusively label as "flawed thinking" opinions and ideas diverging from one's own or mainstream ideologies. The authors are especially critical of the new policy's removal of university members' right to "justifiably" deplatform those "whose work is found to have been fraudulent, plagiarised, defamatory, threatening or, indeed, incompatible with an institution committed to an equal and inclusive environment."[116] This criticism nonetheless cannot get any flimsier: "threatening" is subjective and vague, unless it means physical threats, which, together with fraudulent, plagiarized, and defamatory expressions, are already prohibited by laws and university policies, and therefore do not need to be deplatformed.[117] Their claim that "the new ban [on deplatforming] essentially amounts to the compulsory platforming of discredited or discriminatory views" is logically flawed, and erroneously equates banning suppression of expression with actively affirming that expression.[118] Ironically enough, they urge the university to remain "alert to the damage being wrought by vested

115. Priyamvada Gopal & Gavan Titley, *The Free Speech Row at Cambridge Will Restrict, Not Expand, Free Speech*, THE GUARDIAN (Dec. 18, 2020), http://www.theguardian.com/commentisfree/2020/dec/18/free-speech-row-cambridge-restrict-expression-minorities-freedom-thought

116. Priyamvada Gopal & Gavan Titley, *The Free Speech Row at Cambridge Will Restrict, Not Expand, Free Speech*, THE GUARDIAN (Dec. 18, 2020), http://www.theguardian.com/commentisfree/2020/dec/18/free-speech-row-cambridge-restrict-expression-minorities-freedom-thought

117. Priyamvada Gopal & Gavan Titley, *The Free Speech Row at Cambridge Will Restrict, Not Expand, Free Speech*, THE GUARDIAN (Dec. 18, 2020), http://www.theguardian.com/commentisfree/2020/dec/18/free-speech-row-cambridge-restrict-expression-minorities-freedom-thought

118. Priyamvada Gopal & Gavan Titley, *The Free Speech Row at Cambridge Will Restrict, Not Expand Free Speech*, THE GUARDIAN (Dec. 18, 2020), http://www.theguardian.com/commentisfree/2020/dec/18/free-speech-row-cambridge-restrict-expression-minorities-freedom-thought

interests who seek to engineer specific ideological outcomes."[119] They are seemingly unaware that there is no better way to facilitate certain ideological outcomes by deplatforming, in various ways, views that do not align with one's politics or opinions because they are deemed "threatening" according to vague, ill-defined standards.[120] All is not lost—the op-ed is right on one issue: ideological engineering is something to which Cambridge must stay alert and against which it must keep fighting to live up to its fine reputation.

Cambridge's announcement of its new policy was followed by urgent calls for Peterson to be reinvited to its campus. As the author predicted, the university authorities did not go so far as to withdraw its poor decision. Nonetheless, Peterson was reinvited, this time by a senior faculty member of the Faculty of Divinity, to Cambridge for two weeks in November 2021 to participate in research seminars on the relationship between the philosophy of religion and the psychology of religion, the challenges of interpreting sacred texts, and the place of religion in society.[121] This roughly coincided with the announcement by Cambridge's vice-chancellor—who publicized the reason for terminating Peterson's earlier fellowship—of his retirement from his role in 2022, which cut his seven-year tenure two years short.[122]

Example 4

Given the popularity of Twitter use among academics, the instances of free speech disputes originating from Twitter posts, which are often short and sometimes lacking in context, will likely rise. On October 26, 2020, Tarek Younis, a Muslim lecturer at Middlesex University, responded to King's College London (KCL) professor Peter Neumann's Twitter post attributing the "gradual implosion of French society" to terrorism, and suggested that the

---

119. Priyamvada Gopal & Gavan Titley, *The Free Speech Row at Cambridge Will Restrict, Not Expand, Free Speech*, The Guardian (Dec. 18, 2020), http://www.theguardian.com/commentisfree/2020/dec/18/free-speech-row-cambridge-restrict-expression-minorities-freedom-thought

120. Ironically enough, the authors find that the International Holocaust Remembrance Alliance's definition of "antisemitism" overbroad and Cambridge's wholesale adoption of this definition is problematic and threatens free expression. It seems that they are concerned about the suppression of free expression only if their own expression risks being suppressed. Arguably, a policy allowing all expressions that are not harassment, hate speech, discrimination, or otherwise illegal can avoid any potential inconsistency resulting from the authors' very own ideological biases.

121. Bethan Moss, *Controversial Professor Jordan Peterson to Return to Cambridge after Being Disinvited in 2019*, Varsity (Oct. 1, 2021), http://www.varsity.co.uk/news/22119 (last visited Jun. 17, 2022).

122. Georgia Goble, *A Farewell from Toope: The Vice-Chancellor's Tenure So Far*, Varsity (Oct. 1, 2021), http://www.varsity.co.uk/news/22113 (last visited Jun. 17, 2022).

actions of the French state may also have caused the divisions.[123] Neumann responded: "Nothing justifies killing innocent people. I hope we can at least agree on that. Or do we not?" Younis did not respond except to post on Twitter the following day explaining his disappointment in Neumann's response and calling it an example of Islamophobia.[124] Within a few days, immediately after the terrorist attack in Nice (France), Neumann again took to Twitter to openly ask Younis in a series of messages why he was silent on the attack and whether he would stand with France's view on freedom of expression, this time tagging Younis's employer in these open messages. He demanded answers even when others presented evidence that Younis had already expressed dismay over the killings.[125]

Younis called Neumann's response not "'simply' abuse," but "a pretty open and callous threat" to his employment at Middlesex University.[126] In an open letter to KCL, a group of academics, researchers, and activists accused Neumann of "ethically and morally objectionable" conduct, "clear and unequivocal display of Islamophobia," and abuse of his power to "intimidate and harass a junior scholar at another university."[127] The letter considered racist and Islamophobic Neumann's expectation that a Muslim scholar should first agree that "nothing justifies the killing of innocents" and then answer questions on the Nice attacks.[128] That a renowned counterterrorism professor would only address his questions to Muslim scholars suggested that he was indicating that their religious beliefs were connected to the political points they made.[129] What

---

123. Lily Hardcastle, *KCL Professor Peter Neumann Is under Investigation after Claims of Islamophobia and Bullying*, The Tab (Dec. 3, 2020), http://thetab.com/uk/kings/2020/12/03/kcl-professor-peter-neumann-is-under-investigation-after-claims-of-islamophobia-and-bullying-30844 (last visited Feb. 25, 2021); Samuel Teale Chadwick, *Professor Being Investigated for Alleged Islamophobia on Twitter*, Roar News (Nov. 7, 2020), http://roarnews.co.uk/2020/professor-being-investigated-for-alleged-islamophobia-on-twitter/ (last visited Feb. 25, 2021).
124. Lily Hardcastle, *KCL Professor Peter Neumann Is under Investigation after Claims of Islamophobia and Bullying*, The Tab (Dec. 3, 2020), http://thetab.com/uk/kings/2020/12/03/kcl-professor-peter-neumann-is-under-investigation-after-claims-of-islamophobia-and-bullying-30844 (last visited Feb. 25, 2021).
125. Lily Hardcastle, *KCL Professor Peter Neumann Is under Investigation after Claims of Islamophobia and Bullying*, The Tab (Dec. 3, 2020), http://thetab.com/uk/kings/2020/12/03/kcl-professor-peter-neumann-is-under-investigation-after-claims-of-islamophobia-and-bullying-30844 (last visited Feb. 25, 2021).
126. *Open Letter to King's College London*, http://docs.google.com/forms/d/e/1FAIpQLSf9dW3qrXAgu3NhK8wdTG4Q6y-p86pfyLHi24IWawhLbzoo_Q/viewform (last visited Feb. 25, 2021).
127. *Open Letter to King's College London*, http://docs.google.com/forms/d/e/1FAIpQLSf9dW3qrXAgu3NhK8wdTG4Q6y-p86pfyLHi24IWawhLbzoo_Q/viewform (last visited Feb. 25, 2021).
128. *Open Letter to King's College London*, http://docs.google.com/forms/d/e/1FAIpQLSf9dW3qrXAgu3NhK8wdTG4Q6y-p86pfyLHi24IWawhLbzoo_Q/viewform (last visited Feb. 25, 2021).
129. *Open Letter to King's College London*, http://docs.google.com/forms/d/e/1FAIpQLSf9dW3qrXAgu3NhK8wdTG4Q6y-p86pfyLHi24IWawhLbzoo_Q/viewform (last visited Feb. 25, 2021).

was even more alarming, the letter argued, was Neumann's attempts to provoke conflicts between a Muslim academic who writes about terrorism and his employer.[130] Hence, Neumann's apology for his "tone" in questioning Younis attended neither to his racist and Islamophobic questioning nor to the fear of employment consequences that it caused, let alone to the potential harm and discrimination to which it subjected all his students and colleagues.[131]

To be fair, Neumann's question about the killing of innocent people cannot reasonably be construed as a display of Islamophobia. Moral people would agree that killing innocents is unjustifiable. Moreover, as condescending as its tone seems to be, the question might have been rhetorical—one motivated by his zealousness about counterterrorism and his hatred of terrorist violence. His messages pressuring Younis for opinions on the Nice attack and France's view on freedom of expression were not inherently intimidating as long as they did not contain threats, because Younis easily could have ignored or blocked them outright. Arguably, even his "tone" may not be the issue, given how difficult it would be to fully determine one's tone on Twitter. What crossed the line and made his messages bullyish and threatening, regardless of his intent, was his tagging Younis's employer in those messages. In doing so, he undermined Younis's freedom of speech by pressuring him to reveal his stance on the topic despite his right to remain silent. By bringing his employer into the conflict, Neumann even indicated that Younis's refusal to speak up or agree with the French government made him an apologist for Islamist terrorism and unqualified for his position at Middlesex. To supplement this analysis with an analogy: imagine a scenario in which Hong Kong pro-democracy protesters were assaulted by rabid Chinese nationalists and the attack was found to be instigated by the Chinse consulate. It would be improper for an angered Hong Kong professor to pressure a colleague of Chinese descent to give opinions on Twitter by tagging his employer, so long as the Chinese colleague is not personally responsible for the attacks. If, however, the professor is affiliated with or a member of the Chinese consulate, the professor should be held answerable for the attack. (Ironically, though, the university likely would find the Hong Kong professor's conduct, motivated by nothing but justice and concerns for national sovereignty and academic integrity, to be unacceptable, given the level of corruption and pandering to the Chinese government it would take for an educa-

130. *Open Letter to King's College London*, http://docs.google.com/forms/d/e/1FAIpQLSf9dW3qrXAgu3NhK8wdTG4Q6y-p86pfyLHi24IWawhLbzoo_Q/viewform (last visited Feb. 25, 2021).
131. *Open Letter to King's College London*, http://docs.google.com/forms/d/e/1FAIpQLSf9dW3qrXAgu3NhK8wdTG4Q6y-p86pfyLHi24IWawhLbzoo_Q/viewform (last visited Feb. 25, 2021).

tional institution in a democratic nation to offer an appointment to someone from the Chinese consulate [see example 7 of this chapter]). In this case, KCL should coach Neumann about proper online etiquette and advise him to apologize to Tarek, meanwhile emphasizing its commitment to free speech and civil dialogue.

Example 5

Among cases showing universities' attempts to police their members' expressions, one of the most atrocious and intriguing happened at the University of Warwick. In early 2014, Thomas Docherty, professor of English and comparative literature, was suspended by the university onde the charge of insubordination, after accusations by Catherine Bates, who was then the department head, that he "undermined" her authority and showed "disrespect" to job candidates for a position at the department.[132] While Warwick refused to discuss in detail the grounds for the suspension, news reports indicated that he disagreed with Bates over colleague submissions to the Research Excellence Framework and had a "heated discussion" over whether to create a new position in the department.[133] Among the things he allegedly did that his accusers deemed to indicate "disrespect" to job candidates included "inappropriate sighing," "making ironic comments," and "projecting negative body language" to them.[134] It should be noted that Docherty had been a prominent critic of British higher education leadership and policy, namely the bureaucratization and marketization of its higher education and the declining role of the faculty in university governance. Besides writing for the British media,[135] he authored *For the University: Democ-*

---

132. *E.g.*, Bill Gardner, *Professor Suspended from Top University for Giving Off Negative Vibes*, TELEGRAPH (Oct. 24, 2021), http://www.telegraph.co.uk/education/11187063/Professor-suspended-from-top-university-for-giving-off-negative-vibes.html; Duncan Gibbons, *Coventry Professor Cleared after Accusations*, COVENTRY TELEGRAPH (Oct. 23, 2014), http://www.coventrytelegraph.net/news/coventry-professor-cleared-after-accusations-7982229; David Matthews, *Thomas Docherty to Face Insubordination Charge in Tribunal*, TIMES HIGHER EDUC. (Jul. 24, 2014), http://www.timeshighereducation.com/news/thomas-docherty-to-face-insubordination-charge-in-tribunal/2014711.article

133. David Matthews, *Thomas Docherty to Face Insubordination Charge in Tribunal*, TIMES HIGHER EDUC. (Jul. 24, 2014), http://www.timeshighereducation.com/news/thomas-docherty-to-face-insubordination-charge-in-tribunal/2014711.article

134. Bill Gardner, *Professor Suspended from Top University for Giving Off Negative Vibes*, TELEGRAPH (Oct. 24, 2021), http://www.telegraph.co.uk/education/11187063/Professor-suspended-from-top-university-for-giving-off-negative-vibes.html; Duncan Gibbons, *Coventry Professor Cleared after Accusations*, COVENTRY TELEGRAPH (Oct. 23, 2014), http://www.coventrytelegraph.net/news/coventry-professor-cleared-after-accusations-7982229

135. Bill Gardner, *Professor Suspended from Top University for Giving Off Negative Vibes*, TELEGRAPH

racy and the Future of the Institution, recognized as a book that "helps to make more people aware of the contradictory and short-sighted way that universities are now discussed and managed in Britain."[136] Warwick declared that "the disciplinary allegations in no way relate to the content of the individual's academic views or their views on HE [higher education] policy."[137]

When Docherty was finally cleared of wrongdoing at a formal tribunal run by Warwick in October 2014, he had been suspended for nearly nine months. During this period, he was prohibited from visiting its campus, contacting his colleagues and students, writing references for his students without permission, returning work to students, and providing guidance on their doctoral dissertations.[138] He was banned even from contacting students to cancel meetings after this suspension.[139] Unsurprisingly, he was also forbidden to attend in person a conference at which he was scheduled to speak.[140]

Warwick was wise to declare Docherty's suspension unrelated to his outspoken and well-received criticism of British higher education leadership and policy, whether or not his books and op-eds did anger Warwick's administra-

---

(Oct. 24, 2021), http://www.telegraph.co.uk/education/11187063/Professor-suspended-from-top-university-for-giving-off-negative-vibes.html; Duncan Gibbons, *Coventry Professor Cleared after Accusations*, COVENTRY TELEGRAPH (Oct. 23, 2014), http://www.coventrytelegraph.net/news/coventry-professor-cleared-after-accusations-7982229

136. John Mogan, *Warwick Suspends Prominent Critic of Higher Education Policy*, TIMES HIGHER EDUC. (Mar. 11, 2014), http://www.timeshighereducation.com/cn/news/warwick-suspends-prominent-critic-of-higher-education-policy/2012013.article

137. Bill Gardner, *Professor Suspended from Top University for Giving Off Negative Vibes*, TELEGRAPH (Oct. 24, 2021), http://www.telegraph.co.uk/education/11187063/Professor-suspended-from-top-university-for-giving-off-negative-vibes.html; Duncan Gibbons, *Coventry Professor Cleared after Accusations*, COVENTRY TELEGRAPH (Oct. 23, 2014), http://www.coventrytelegraph.net/news/coventry-professor-cleared-after-accusations-7982229

138. Bill Gardner, *Professor Suspended from Top University for Giving Off Negative Vibes*, TELEGRAPH (Oct. 24, 2021, 7:57 PM), http://www.telegraph.co.uk/education/11187063/Professor-suspended-from-top-university-for-giving-off-negative-vibes.html; Duncan Gibbons, *Coventry Professor Cleared after Accusations*, COVENTRY TELEGRAPH (Oct. 23, 2014), http://www.coventrytelegraph.net/news/coventry-professor-cleared-after-accusations-7982229

139. Ann Yip, *Suspended Professor Prevented from Attending Conference on Campus*, THE BOAR (Jun. 23, 2014), http://theboar.org/2014/06/suspended-professor-prevented-attending-conference-campus/ (last visited Jan. 26, 2021).

140. Docherty was scheduled to speak at a conference about the "authoritarian" nature of universities, organized by the Warwick branch of the University and College Union and scheduled to take place at the Warwick Arts Centre in June 2014. Coincidentally, and quite ironically, the conference was devoted to the republication of E. P. Thompson's *Warwick University Ltd.*, which discusses the legal battles waged by Warwick in 1970 to prevent the publication of evidence that it was spying on its own staff and students and curbing academic freedom on behalf of business interests. The university initially denied Doherty the opportunity to participate in any form but later allowed him to have his contribution read aloud on his behalf. Ann Yip, *Suspended Professor Prevented from Attending Conference on Campus*, THE BOAR (Jun. 23, 2014), http://theboar.org/2014/06/suspended-professor-prevented-attending-conference-campus/ (last visited Jan. 26, 2021).

tion to the extent that they contributed in part to his suspension. Punishing members of academia for criticizing the governance of universities, which is a worthy topic that can contribute to the betterment of their workplaces, would have been the most blatant form of violation of free speech and academic freedom. Punishing Docherty for his earnest and well-informed opinions, more specifically, would have served as a deeply ironic indicator of the declining role of the faculty in university governance, whose dissent—even expressed in good faith—is met with suppression and punishment.

Warwick's suspension of Docherty, nonetheless, could not be justified even on the stated grounds that he "undermined" the authority of the department head and showed "disrespect" for job candidates. Having disagreements and "heated debates" with colleagues is not only normal in work settings and can be vital to the betterment of the institutions, but it stems from the fundamental right to freedom of thought and expression. Reports did not indicate that Docherty violated British law or university policies, or even behaved unprofessionally in expressing his disagreements or in debating with the department head. Assuming that Docherty did commit what were deemed disrespectful acts and should have treated job candidates with more tact and respect, penalizing professors for "making ironic comments," "inappropriate sighing," and "projecting negative body language" could easily lead universities down a slippery slope, as the definitions of all three—the latter two being nonverbal forms of communication—are highly subjective and contextual and drawing lines between acceptable and unacceptable conduct would be both challenging and futile. One might be inclined to compare Warwick's treatment of Docherty to Macalester College's termination of its professor's employment for her allegedly atrocious conduct, as detailed in chapter 8. It would, however, be erroneous to equate the two or even to consider them similar: the magnitude of the harm caused by Docherty's lack of tact to job candidates, who were not his colleagues at Warwick and could have walked away from the interviews, could not compare to that caused by the allegedly abusive conduct of Macalester's teacher to her students, whom she had a contractual duty to treat with respect and professionalism, with whom she interacted regularly, and whose speech was chilled due to the hostile classroom atmosphere fostered by her sheer unprofessionalism.

Arguably, the tribunal's verdict could not mitigate the damage that his wrongful suspension had inflicted on his and possibly his colleagues' and students' careers, as his correspondence with them was put on hold during the nine months. Although Docherty was vindicated in the end, the whole incident might have had a chilling effect on free speech at Warwick, as at least some of its members likely had felt more inhibited in expressing their opinions during the period of suspension and even beyond. Unsurprisingly, both Docherty's suspension and vindication were followed by calls to investigate and reform the university's policies and procedures to ensure that its members would not be penalized for expressing their opinions and that future charges are dealt with speedily.[141] One can only hope that this case, as well as others, would persuade the public that the free speech crisis may not be a myth invented by the far right, or even a problem overstated by free speech advocates. Hopefully, the education bill, if passed, would put pressure on universities to be more circumspect in asserting control over the expression of their members.

Example 6

In recent years, the Chinese Communist Party (CCP) has posed a growing threat to free speech in British universities. Measures taken to eliminate or even to resist this threat are long overdue. Yet university officials have been surprisingly tolerant of this hostile foreign force, which stifles free expression and chips away at the very core of British academia and democratic governance. Their political and financial considerations, namely their attempts to foster good will between the nations and their reliance on Chinese money in the form of tuition and research funding, are but lame excuses. The passivity, complacency, and at times complicity of these universities betray a shameful lack of moral courage and integrity in the people who run them and have already undermined free speech in British academia and the nation's democratic governance.

In 2008, the London Metropolitan University honored the Dalai Lama, the world-renowned Tibetan spiritual leader, for his promotion of world peace by awarding him an honorary doctorate degree.[142] This was a courageous act as it

---

141. *E.g.*, Duncan Gibbons, *Coventry Professor Cleared after Accusations*, Coventry Telegraph (Oct. 23, 2014), http://www.coventrytelegraph.net/news/coventry-professor-cleared-after-accusations-7982229; Howard Hotson, *The Man Who Sighed Too Much*, Council for the Defense of British Universities (Oct. 29, 2014), http://cdbu.org.uk/the-man-who-sighed-too-much/ (last visited Jan. 30, 2021).

142. *E.g.*, Polly Curtis, *University Apologizes to China for Dalai Lama's Degree*, The Guardian (Jul. 9, 2008), http://www.theguardian.com/education/2008/jul/09/highereducation.uk1; Anthea Lipsett, *Dalai Lama Receives PhD from London Metropolitan*, The Guardian (May 20, 2008, 1:1 PM), http://www.theguardian.com/education/2008/may/20/highereducation.uk1

stood in direct opposition to the CCP, which saw the Dalai Lama as a secessionist and traitor to China. Yet the university failed all its employees and students who embraced freedom of expression and academic freedom. When the Chinese embassy expressed anger at its actions and Chinese internet groups suggested a boycott of the university, the university's vice-chancellor visited the embassy to apologize—not for honoring the Dalai Lama but for causing them "unhappiness" by its decision.[143] This was a shameful act that should never have been undertaken, even as a token of diplomacy. Apologies from a British university, supposed to be making its decisions independently from foreign regimes, would be readily taken as a sign of weaknesses by the CCP, which it would exploit in its continued attempt to pressure British universities to conform to its ideologies and to dominate the United Kingdom.

Indeed, mounting evidence suggests that the CCP has already taken advantage of the weaknesses of British universities and some of their academics. Aside from putting financial and political pressure on universities, the CCP has bribed their researchers to censor their speech as part of its attempt to expand its dominance. British university professors have reported being asked by the Chinese embassy and consulates to tone down lectures and avoid controversial topics related to China, such as the "3Ts" (Tibet, the Tiananmen Square Massacre, and Taiwan), in exchange for visas to China to conduct fieldwork.[144] One British university professor disclosed that his failing to speak positively about China led to his visa being revoked.[145] It would be fair to surmise that some researchers have chosen to trade their fundamental right to free speech in exchange for visas, fieldwork opportunities, and resources. One cannot wonder whether quality—or real—research could have been produced with compromised academic integrity.

Not infrequently has the CCP as well as its supporters combined political and financial pressure with verbal and physical assaults to exert dominance on British universities. In 2019, when large-scale pro-democracy protests broke

143. Polly Curtis, *University Apologizes to China for Dalai Lama's Degree*, THE GUARDIAN (Jul. 9, 2008), http://www.theguardian.com/education/2008/jul/09/highereducation.uk1

144. Shanti Das, *Beijing Leans on UK Dons to Praise Communist Party and Avoid the Three Ts—Tibet, Tiananmen and Taiwan*, THE TIMES (Jun. 23, 2019), http://www.thetimes.co.uk/article/beijing-leans-on-uk-dons-to-praise-communist-party-and-avoid-the-three-ts-tibet-tiananmen-and-taiwan-mdt3vjnb6

145. Shanti Das, *Beijing Leans on UK Dons to Praise Communist Party and Avoid the Three Ts—Tibet, Tiananmen and Taiwan*, THE TIMES (Jun. 23, 2019), http://www.thetimes.co.uk/article/beijing-leans-on-uk-dons-to-praise-communist-party-and-avoid-the-three-ts-tibet-tiananmen-and-taiwan-mdt3vjnb6

out in Hong Kong, Hong Kong students who peacefully expressed their solidarity on numerous British university campuses were assaulted, often physically, by supporters of the CCP. At Cambridge University, a Hong Kong student received death threats from his fellow students from China for organizing the protests.[146] On Aston University's campus, Hong Kong student protesters reported being followed around by older Chinese men filming them with a camera, and one student claimed to have been grabbed by a Chinese man who tried to remove the mask he wore to hide his identity.[147] In general, however, British universities have disgracefully refused to defend Hong Kong students' right to peacefully protest, such as by issuing a public statement to denounce the assaults, let alone seriously investigating these matters and penalizing those committing them. Some universities even facilitated their suppression of democracy protests. At Warwick University, security staff removed a popular protest image of a pig put up by Hong Kong students after Chinese students played the race card and filed an out-of-context racism complaint about it.[148] At York University, Hong Kong students were asked by security staff to remove protest materials that Chinese students found "offensive," but which contained no hate speech or discriminatory message.[149]

In the face of financial and political pressures and physical violence from the CCP and its supporters, taking a strong stance against its interference with academic free speech and penalizing bullyish conduct are not enough. Ideally, lawsuits should be filed against the university authorities who bow to pressure from the CCP and its cronies, to enable British courts to set precedents under current laws or the new free speech bill that may become law. Less radical actions would include de-ratifying and banning clubs such as the Chinese Students and Scholars Association, which are well funded by the CCP and essentially serve as its foreign arms that facilitate the suppression of democracy pro-

---

146. Ben Quinn, *Hong Kong Protesters in U.K. Say They Face Pro-Beijing Intimidation*, The Guardian (Oct. 18, 2019), http://www.theguardian.com/uk-news/2019/oct/18/hong-kong-protesters-uk-pro-beijing-intimidation

147. Laura Mannering, *Hong Kong Students in UK Call for Actions over Pro-China Threats and Harassment*, HK Free P. (Nov. 26, 2019), http://hongkongfp.com/2019/11/26/hong-kong-students-uk-call-action-pro-china-threats-harassment/ (last visited Jan. 25, 2021).

148. Rosemary Bennett, *Hong Kong Students Told to Remove Protest Display at University at York*, The Times (Oct. 26, 2019), http;//www.thetimes.co.uk/article/hong-kong-students-told-to-remove-protest-display-at-university-of-york-q0t5rfqgs

149. Rachel Stretton, *University of Warwick Criticized as Protest Image Removed from Lennon Wall in Racism Row*, Coventry Telegraph (Nov. 13, 2019), http://www.coventrytelegraph.net/news/coventry-news/university-warwick-criticised-protest-image-17217906

tests on Britain soil.[150] This wise and resolute step, pioneered by a Canadian university, has yet to be taken by any British university. Yet these associations are by no means the only ones that must be eliminated. As the next example shows, the CCP's infiltration of British academia has become so deep that British universities have become breeding grounds for its agents and lackeys.

Example 7

The Confucius Institutes (CIs) on British university campuses have become a subject of great controversy. British politicians were made aware that these Chinese state agencies, which purport to promote Chinese culture by offering Chinese language and cultural programs, are arguably a tool for the Chinese government to spread its propaganda in the Western world, to suppress criticism of China on Western university campuses, and possibly to conduct industrial and military espionage and spy on members of academic communities. Because of the very nature of CIs, the threats they pose to freedom of speech and academic freedom, and their attacks on the democratic governance of the nation, they must be closed. Indeed, they should never have been allowed to operate in the first place.

CIs are public educational partnerships between colleges and universities in China and those in other countries, named after ancient Chinese philosopher Confucius (551–479 BC) and with the stated goal to promote Chinese language and culture, facilitate cultural exchanges, and provide information about contemporary China. Officials from China have compared them to language and culture promotion organizations, such as Britain's British Council, France's Alliance Français, and Germany's Goethe-Institut.[151] Since the first CI was set up in late 2004 in Seoul, South Korea, hundreds have opened in various countries around the world, including Japan, the U.K., the U.S., and Canada.[152] Han-

150. *See, e.g.*, Ben Quinn, *Hong Kong Protesters in U.K. Say They Face Pro-Beijing Intimidation*, THE GUARDIAN (Oct. 18, 2019), http://www.theguardian.com/uk-news/2019/oct/18/hong-kong-protesters-uk-pro-beijing-intimidation; Charls Parton, *China-UK Relations: Where to Draw the Border between Influence and Interference?*, ROYAL UNITED SERVICES INSTITUTE FOR DEFENCE AND SECURITY STUDIES (Feb. 2019), http://static.rusi.org/20190220_chinese_interference_parton_web.pdf (last visited Jan. 26, 2021).

151. *E.g.*, Jessica Shepherd, *"Not a Propaganda Tool,"* THE GUARDIAN (Nov. 6, 2007), http://www.theguardian.com/education/2007/nov/06/highereducation.internationaleducationnews; *see also* Justin Norrie, *Confucius Says School's in, but Don't Mention Democracy*, SYDNEY MORNING HERALD (Feb. 20, 2011), http://www.smh.com.au/education/confucius-says-schools-in-but-dont-mention-democracy-20110219-1b09x.html

152. *E.g.*, Pratik Jakhar, *Confucius Institutes: The Growth of China's Controversial Cultural Branch*, BBC (Sep. 6, 2019), www.bbc.com/news/world-asia-china-49511231

ban (the Office of Chinese Language Council International, an affiliate of the Chinese Ministry of Education), which is partially responsible for their funding and arrangements, claims to take a hands-off approach towards their management.[153] Hence, individual universities, which shoulder the rest of the funding, are said to be primarily responsible for their management, with Chinese partner universities providing many instructional materials and teachers to CI-hosting universities.[154]

There has been much disagreement over the degree of autonomy that host universities have enjoyed in running their CIs. Faculty members of some host universities reported making all decisions regarding the topics and guest speakers for events at their institutes. Some were even able to host conferences and programs critical of the CCP.[155] At other host universities, however, faculty members were pressured to avoid contentious topics like human rights abuses in China. Even more outrageous forms of interference include the removal of literature about Taiwan on a professor's door by a CI's Chinse director and the attempted removal of information about Taiwanese institutions from an international conference brochure by another CI's chief executive who also served as Hanban's representative.[156]

Since 2010, many universities in different countries have wisely terminated their contracts with their CIs. In June 2014, the American Association of University Professors issued a statement urging American universities to terminate their collaboration with the CI unless these universities have unilateral control of the academic affairs, that the teachers in CIs enjoy the same academic freedom enjoyed by other faculty members, and that the agreements between universities and CIs are available to the community.[157] Numerous universities

153. *A Message from Confucius: New Ways of Projecting Soft Power*, Bridgeman Art Library (Oct. 24, 2009), http://www.economist.com/special-report/2009/10/24/a-message-from-confucius (last visited Jan. 25, 2021).
154. *Introduction to the Confucius Institutes*, Aug. 29, 2009 [archived from the original on Jul. 7, 2011], http://www.web.archive.org/web/20110707081524/http://college.chinese.cn/en/article/2009-08/29/content_22308.htm (last visited Jan. 25, 2021).
155. *Agreements Establishing Confucius Institutes at U.S. Universities Are Similar, but Institute Operations Vary*, U.S. Government Accountability Office (Feb. 2019), http://www.gao.gov/assets/700/696910.pdf (last visited Jan. 25, 2021).
156. *E.g.*, *Agreements Establishing Confucius Institutes at U.S. Universities Are Similar, but Institute Operations Vary*, U.S. Government Accountability Office (Feb. 2019), http://www.gao.gov/assets/700/696910.pdf (last visited Jan. 25, 2021); *Beijing's Propaganda Lessons: Confucius Institute Officials Are Agents of Chinese Censorship*, Wall St. J. (Aug. 7, 2014), http://www.wsj.com/articles/beijings-propaganda-lessons-1407430440
157. *Our Partnerships with Foreign Governments: The Case of Confucius Institutes*, American Association of University Professors (Jun. 2014), http://www.aaup.org/report/confucius-institutes (last visited Jan. 26, 2021).

heeded the call, before the U.S. Department of State, under the Trump presidency, aptly and courageously designated the Confucius Institute U.S. Center as a "foreign mission" of the Chinese government in August 2020.[158] In January 2014, the Canadian Association of University Teachers urged Canadian universities and colleges to cease ties with the CI.[159] This precipitated the closures of numerous CIs in the country in the years that followed.[160] While Joe Biden, upon becoming the U.S. president, withdrew the policy requiring universities and K-12 schools certified to host foreign exchange programs to disclose contracts and partnerships with or financial transactions from Confucius Institutes or Confucius Classrooms—a withdrawal that was a gross injustice to the U.S. and its long-standing democratic traditions—no Canadian government has never mustered up enough moral courage to call a spade a spade, let alone denounce these foreign state agencies.[161]

On the contrary, CIs seem to be increasing their influence in Australian and New Zealand universities, the disastrous consequences of which have regularly made shocking headlines. Sadly, evidence from the past few years indicates that some universities might have been complicit in or even actively enabled foreign interference and their erosion of academic independence. The University of Queensland, for instance, has allowed its CI to cofund several classes. One such class, "Understanding China," was designed by an economics lecturer who had received a fellowship from the Chinese government and contains course materials that can fairly be considered Communist Party propaganda.[162] The CI's director even nominated China's consul-general in Brisbane to serve as an

---

158. Kate O'Keeffe, *U.S. to Classify Beijing-Backed Confucius Institute as Foreign Mission*, WALL ST. J. (Aug. 13, 2020), http://www.wsj.com/articles/u-s-to-classify-beijing-backed-confucius-institute-u-s-center-as-foreign-mission-11597336675 (last visited Jan. 26, 2021).

159. *Canadian Campuses Urged to End Ties with Confucius Institutes*, CANADIAN ASSOCIATION OF UNIVERSITY TEACHERS (Jan. 2014), http://bulletin-archives.caut.ca/bulletin/articles/2014/01/canadian-campuses-urged-to-end-ties-with-confucius-institutes.html (last visited Jan. 26, 2021).

160. *E.g.*, Omid Ghoreishi, *Canadian Province Closing China's Confucius Institute*, EPOCH TIMES (Feb. 22, 2019), http://www.theepochtimes.com/canadian-province-to-shut-down-chinas-confucius-institute_2811723.html (last visited Jan. 26, 2021); James Bradshaw & Colin Freeze, *McMaster Closing Confucius Institute over Hiring Issues*, GLOBE & MAIL (Feb. 7, 2013), http://www.theglobeandmail.com/news/national/education/mcmaster-closing-confucius-institute-over-hiring-issues/article8372894/

161. Mary Ellen Cagnassola, *Fact Check: Did Biden Revoke a Trump Ban on Chinese Communist Propaganda in Schools?*, NEWSWEEK (Feb. 9, 2021), http://www.newsweek.com/fact-check-did-biden-revoke-trump-ban-chinese-communist-propaganda-schools-1568043

162. One example is labeling the activities of the Uyghur minority in China "terrorist" and linking Hong Kong democracy protests to "terrorism," which by logic justify their brutal suppression by the CCP. Fergus Hunter, *UQ Course on "Understanding China" Established with Chinese Government Funding*, SIDNEY MORNING HERALD (Oct. 13, 2019), http://smh.com.au/politics/federal/uq-course-on-understanding-china-established-with-chinese-government-funding-20191011-p52zun.html

adjunct professor, who later praised Chinese students for attacking anti-Beijing protesters on the university campus.[163] An undergraduate student who rightly protested against the institute and the university's vice-chancellor for enabling massive interference by the CCP, as well as against the CCP for its human rights abuses, was suspended by the university for "misconduct," a fiasco that ended in his lawsuit against the university and its administrators.[164] In 2020, the CI's director at the University of Auckland filed a formal complaint against a China specialist at the University of Canterbury for coauthoring an extensively researched article and parliamentary submission raising concerns about the ties between New Zealand academics and universities in China engaged in defense research, suggesting that Kiwi-developed technology could end up being used by the Chinese military.[165] Fortunately, Canterbury dismissed the complaint upon finding that the scholar's work met all obligations stated in the university policy and the Education Act 1989.[166]

At present, there are almost thirty CIs in the U.K., more than in any other European country.[167] A 2020 parliamentary report indicates that the CCP has tried to use CIs to shape the agendas of host universities and limit academic activities on British university campuses. One example happened at the University of Nottingham, where academics were pressured to cancel events relating to Tibet and Taiwan after complaints from Chinese CI officials.[168] Another example showed Chinese CI officials confiscating academic conference papers

---

163. Ben Doherty, *Queensland Student Sues Chinese Consul General, Alleging He Incites Death Threats*, THE GUARDIAN (Oct. 23, 2019), http://www.theguardian.com/world/2019/oct/23/queensland-student-sues-chinese-consul-general-alleging-he-incited-death-threats

164. Its vice-chancellor, Professor Peter Høj, was a senior consultant to Beijing's global Confucius Institute headquarters and a member of its governing council. Aaron Patrick, *University of Queensland Student Seeks $3.5m Damages*, AUST. FIN. REV. (Jun. 11, 2020), http://www.afr.com/policy/health-and-education/university-of-queensland-student-seeks-3-5m-damages-20200611-p551l5; John Ross, *Queensland Chancellor to Revisit "Concerning" Suspension*, TIMES HIGHER EDUC. (Jun. 2, 2020), http://www.timeshighereducation.com/news/queensland-chancellor-revisit-concerning-suspension

165. Jamie Smyth, *New Zealand University Dismisses Complaints against China Expert*, FIN. TIMES (Dec. 11, 2020), http://www.ft.com/content/2b4f5f99-8c3c-477d-b7f1-447966e5cce5

166. Jamie Smyth, *New Zealand University Dismisses Complaints against China Expert*, FIN. TIMES (Dec. 11, 2020), http://www.ft.com/content/2b4f5f99-8c3c-477d-b7f1-447966e5cce5

167. As of 2019, there are twenty-nine Confucius Institutes in the U.K. Liexu Cai, *A Comparative Study of the Confucius Institute in the United Kingdom and the British Council in China*, 18 CITIZENSHIP, SOC. & ECON. EDUC. (2019), http://www.journals.sagepub.com/doi/full/10.1177/2047173419845531

168. *A Cautious Embrace: Defending Democracy in an Age of Autocracies: 2. Autocracies' Influence in Academia*, para. 10, BRITISH PARLIAMENT (2019), http://publications.parliament.uk/pa/cm201919/cmselect/cmfaff/109/10905.htm#footnote-049 (last visited Jan. 26, 2021); citing *Security Services Fear the March on Universities of Beijing's Spies*, THE TIMES (Oct. 27, 2012).

that mentioned Taiwan.[169] In addition, an investigation conducted by a major British newspaper reveals that the CI at the University of Leeds, branded as the "Business Confucius Institute," provides free Chinese culture and language courses for British government officials and business executives who plan to visit China, and its dismissal of any conflict of interest entailed by this arrangement betrayed its attempt to foster political influence in the U.K.[170] In light of what happened in the U.K. and other countries, neither ensuring that the curriculum taught in CIs is "balanced, independent, holistic, and comprehensive" nor reviewing all current related agreements[171] would be a sufficient condition for them to continue their existence in British universities. Both strategies naively and vastly underestimate the CCP's aggression in seeking dominance over the free world. Closing them all is the only solution.

It might be argued that not all cultural events hosted by CIs have been problematic: some likely have been beneficial. Yet the benefits of some events neither outweigh the potential harm of others nor justify the operation of Chinese state agencies in British universities, not least democratic Britain. Back in 2010, still clueless about the history and nature of CIs, the author of this book accepted an invitation to a large-scale writers' event organized by a CI in Scotland.[172] To be fair, the author cannot recall criticisms of the Chinese government, whether coming from guest speakers or attendees, being censored at that event, which celebrated writers in English, invited not only Chinese but also Scottish and Indian writers among its numerous guests, and catered to both university and high school students. Notwithstanding the benefits of cultural conversations and new friendships at events like this one, they did not preclude the possibility that conversations on taboo subjects may be hushed or pro-CCP propaganda may be presented as objective accounts of China at other CI-organized events. Invitees may be tempted by the free flights, accommodations, and meals generously offered by CIs to form favor-

---

169. *A Cautious Embrace: Defending Democracy in an Age of Autocracies: 2. Autocracies' Influence in Academia*, para. 8, British Parliament (2019), http://publications.parliament.uk/pa/cm201919/cmselect/cmfaff/109/10905.htm#footnote-049 (last visited Jan. 26, 2021).

170. Billy Kenber, *"China Is Using UK Universities to Lobby Officials,"* The Times (Aug. 24, 2019), http://www.thetimes.co.uk/article/china-is-using-uk-universities-to-lobby-officials-rbxv5vcbn

171. *Fiona Chairs Report on "China's Confucius Institutes,"* Fiona Bruce Website (Apr. 10, 2019), http://www.fionabruce.org.uk/news/fiona-chairs-report-chinas-confucius-institutes (last visited Jan. 26, 2021); citing the Conservative Party's Human Rights Commission, *Confucius Institutes Report* (Feb. 2019).

172. The said conference was titled China Inside-Out and was held Mar. 11–13, 2010 at the Confucius Institute for Scotland.

able impressions of them and China, dismiss their problematic agenda, or even help spread CCP propaganda. Even assuming that every single event has been beneficial and noncensorial, the very presence of such state agencies on university campuses still poses a threat too big to be dismissed. Nothing might prevent these state agencies from interfering with free speech or academic freedom on other occasions, one example being to facilitate spying on dissidents, or, more generally, to put members of academic communities in reasonable fear of persecution and threats to personal safety.[173]

Criticisms of CIs by no means equate to criticisms of traditional Chinese culture and language or vilification of international students and immigrants from China. They aim to bring awareness to the fact that these government branches are not at all necessary for the promotion of Chinese culture and language. Just as Alliance Français and the Goethe-Institut are not the only places where French and German learners go, there is no lack of opportunities both on- and off-campus to learn Chinese. Where such opportunities may be absent, universities can invest in their own Chinese-language programs and businesses and organizations staffing native or proficient Chinese speakers with no ties to the CCP can be set up for such purposes. Indeed, the argument that state agencies are necessary to promote language or culture is flimsy at best. If state agencies were necessary, how could people from different backgrounds in Taiwan and British Hong Kong have become proficient Chinese speakers, some even acquiring profound knowledge of traditional and contemporary Chinese literatures? Given how traditional Chinese culture and the Chinese language itself have been unfairly appropriated and corrupted by the one-party state to advance its agendas and buttress its regime,[174] one can fairly surmise that learning the Chinese language, culture, and literature at organizations or businesses

173. *See, e.g.*, Mark McLaughlin, *Cut Ties with "Suppressive" China, Leading Academic Tells Edinburgh University*, THE TIMES (Nov. 17, 2020), http://www.thetimes.co.uk/article/cut-ties-with-suppressive-china-leading-academic-tells-edinburgh-university-crjw290h0; David Leask, *Hong Kong Security Law: Students Demand Closure of Confucius Institutes*, THE TIMES (Jul. 17, 2020), http://www.thetimes.co.uk/article/hong-kong-security-law-students-demand-closure-of-confucius-institutes-n6fk5k07z

174. An example of the CCP's corruption of the Chinese language is its adoption of the simplified writing system in the 1950s to replace the traditional writing system that has existed for thousands of years, in its attempt to improve the literacy rate of the population. Many of the simplified characters leave out essential parts in the traditional characters that convey the words' meanings in pictographical forms (for example, the simplified character for "love" lacks the Chinese word for "heart" that is found in its traditional counterpart). Naming the state institute after a well-known ancient Chinese philosopher whose teaching may bear little or no relation to many of its activities, not least its whitewashing and omission of historical events, is an instance of the CCP's appropriation of ancient traditions to advance its agendas.

unaffiliated with the CCP would be more beneficial and relaxing, and the knowledge acquired—relatively untainted by toxic one-party ideologies—much less biased and far more authentic.

In 2020, the Chinese government transferred the management of CIs from Hanban to a nonprofit organizations formed by twenty-seven universities and other Chinese organizations, and rebranded the CIs as "centres for language education and cooperation," in an attempt to lessen the suspicion they have drawn over the last few years.[175] Yet, "what's in a name?" To parody Shakespeare's famous line,[176] that which we call a pile of dung by any other name shalt smell as foul. Closing CIs will not violate freedom of speech or the academic freedom of its members, people interested in Chinese language and culture, or even Chinese immigrants and students, some of whom, despite their enjoyment of liberties on British soil otherwise denied to them in China, uncritically embrace the CCP. On the contrary, eliminating these propaganda machines—which have been bred by a stealthy rogue state and complacent British universities—will protect the freedom to criticize the CCP, support those it has persecuted and oppressed, and learn Chinese culture and language untainted by party ideologies.

• • •

Watching out for signs of infiltration by the CCP as well as other hostile governments, nipping its toxic influence in the bud, and disallowing it and its agents to exploit Western liberal concepts like diversity and tolerance to advance its illiberal agendas are important steps in safeguarding British academia. This should form part of the much-needed campaign to protect free speech in universities, which, despite constant denials by many critics, has been under severe attack in the United Kingdom. Amid the uncertain future of academic speech in the U.K., one must remember that even if every person has a price, the sanctity of academia and democracy is priceless and must not be traded for money, superficial friendships, or twisted ideas of peace and harmony.

---

175. Zachary Ethans, *China's Confucius Institutes Attempt to Rebrand Following Backlash*, Nat'l Rev. (Jul. 8, 2020, 12:35 PM), http://www.nationalreview.com/news/chinas-confucius-institutes-attempt-to-rebrand-following-backlash/

176. William Shakespeare, Romeo and Juliet, 2.1: 85–86.

CHAPTER EIGHT

The United States

First Amendment, Speech Codes, and Promising but "Not Quite There Yet" Results

The Supreme Court of the United States has affirmed the fundamental importance of free speech to American universities. Whereas the First Amendment applies only to public universities, courts have relied on a contract theory to determine that private universities must also live up to promises of free inquiry made to students. Over the years, courts have found speech codes at some public universities to be unconstitutional for being overly broad or vague, or both. In addition, speech policies at private universities are not completely immune from constitutional challenges.

Despite the legal mechanisms for protecting free speech at both public and private universities, cases abound where attempts to deplatform or disinvite speakers succeeded. To make matters worse, some universities terminated or considered terminating the employment of professors who challenged dominant ideologies. Others denied support to members harassed or threatened for expressing constructive criticisms of those ideologies. Fortunately, some universities have managed to safeguard their members' freedoms while seeking to prevent conduct that would amount to discrimination, unprofessionalism, and abuses of power.

Recent years have seen numerous cases where not only students, but also university employees from China attempted to control the discourse on China in American universities and thereby undermine free speech and academic freedom on campuses. There were instances where Western liberal concepts of free speech, racial equality, and diversity were exploited to suppress expression challenging the official narrative of the Chinese government or to camouflage unprofessionalism and misconduct, or both. Various examples, including that of the disgraced professor at Macalester College, show that American universities have fared better in resisting these authoritarian intrusions and upholding their fundamental values compared to their Canadian and British counterparts. While their principled actions should be lauded, they need to muster more courage in "draining the swamp." Even if "every man has his price,"[1] and tuition money of students and other funding from hostile foreign nations help support American universities, these universities must set their prices high enough and must keep fighting off hostile forces that seek to jeopardize their very existence as institutions that are dedicated to free inquiry and free speech.

I. The First Amendment, Contract Theory, and (Un)Constitutional "Speech Codes"

In the United States, the right to free speech is protected by the First Amendment of the Constitution, which states that "Congress shall make no law . . . abridging the freedom of speech, or of the press."[2] The Founding Fathers, or revolutionary leaders of the period when its political institutions were created, agreed that free speech was a fundamental freedom stemming from the inalienable rights to "Life, Liberty and the Pursuit of Happiness" in the Declaration of Independence.[3] James Madison, one of the founders who later became the fourth president of the U.S., asserted that the right to free speech was one of the "natural rights" in his introduction of the Bill of Rights to the first Congress.[4] These rights, which may not be alienated by the state, are distinguished from government-created civil rights.[5] Free speech, which was never confined to speech about political matters, served as a means to other freedoms in founding documents.[6]

---

1. *See* Robert Bolt, A Man for All Seasons, act 1 (a statement by character Richard Rich, who serves as a foil to Thomas More) (1954, 1957)
2. U.S. Const. amend. I.
3. Thomas West defines this period as roughly between 1765 and 1820. Thomas West, *Free Speech in the American Founding and in Modern Liberalism*, 21 Soc. Phil. & Pol'y 310, 314–15 (2004).
4. Thomas West, *Free Speech in the American Founding and in Modern Liberalism*, 21 Soc. Phil. & Pol'y 310, 320 (2004).
5. Thomas West, *Free Speech in the American Founding and in Modern Liberalism*, 21 Soc. Phil. & Pol'y 310, 321 (2004).
6. For example, the Mass Declaration of Rights, 1780, art. 41 states: "The liberty of the press is essential

The nationalization of free speech took much longer. The ratification of the Bill of Rights, which took place in 1791, was soon followed by major national free speech controversies surrounding the 1798 Sedition Act, antislavery speech, and antiwar speech during the Civil War.[7] These became crucial to the drafting of the Fourteenth Amendment, ratified in 1868, which provides that persons born in the nation are American citizens and that "no state shall . . . abridge the privileges or immunities of citizens of the United States; nor shall any state deprive any person of life, liberty, or property without due process of law."[8] The Supreme Court in *Barron v. Baltimore* (1833) had previously held that the Bill of Rights applied only to the federal government, and that states were free to enforce statutes restricting its enumerated rights.[9] In *Gitlow v. New York* (1925), the Court relied upon the due process clause of the Fourteenth Amendment to determine that almost every provision of the Bill of Rights applies to both the federal and the state governments.[10] Hence, the Fourteenth Amendment, or the "second" Bill of Rights, requires states to respect the freedoms of speech, press, religion, and assembly articulated in the First Amendment.[11]

The Supreme Court of the mid- to late-twentieth century adopted an expansive stance toward the First Amendment under Chief Justice Earl Warren, by treating free speech as a presumptively protected constitutional value during this period.[12] The later courts, though not as strongly committed to free speech, have adhered to the general rule that the government cannot regulate the content of speech unless specific exceptions apply. In *Cohen v. California* (1971), Justice John Marshall Harlan emphasized that the constitutional right of free expression is a "powerful medicine" that operates to protect a marketplace of ideas.[13] In *Police Department of Chicago v. Mosley* (1972), Justice Thurgood Marshall explained that "the government has no power to restrict expression

---

to the security of freedom in a state: it ought not, therefore, to be restrained in this commonwealth." The New Hampshire Declaration of Rights, 1783, art. 22 states: "the liberty of the press is essential to the security of freedom in a state; it ought, therefore, to be inviolably preserved." Thomas West, *Free Speech in the American Founding and in Modern Liberalism*, 21 Soc. Phil. & Pol'y 310, 321–22 (2004).

7. Michael K. Curtis, Free Speech, The People's Darling Privilege: Struggles for Freedom of Expression in American History 3 (2000).
8. Michael K. Curtis, Free Speech, The People's Darling Privilege: Struggles for Freedom of Expression in American History 3 (2000).
9. Michael K. Curtis, Free Speech, The People's Darling Privilege: Struggles for Freedom of Expression in American History 10 (2000).
10. Gitlow v. N.Y., 268 U.S. 652 (1925).
11. Gitlow v. N.Y., 268 U.S. 652 (1925).
12. Bernard Schwartz, The Warren Court: A Retrospective 72, 76 & 79 (1996).
13. Cohen v. Cal., 403 U.S. 15, 24 (1971); citing Whitney v. Cal., 274 U.S. 357, 375–77 (1927).

because of its message, its ideas, its subject matter, or its content" under the First Amendment.[14] His opinion continued:

> To permit the continued building of our politics and culture, and to assure self-fulfillment for each individual, our people are guaranteed the right to express any thought, free from government censorship. The essence of this forbidden censorship is content control. Any restriction on expressive activity because of its content would completely undercut the "profound national commitment to the principle that debate on public issues should be uninhibited, robust, and wide-open.[15]

Therefore, a law that inhibits freedom of speech must have an important and compelling interest to do so and must be narrowly tailored to serve that interest.[16]

The limits of free speech were not explicitly stated in the federal Constitution or in any of the early state constitutions, although the idea that free speech is not equivalent to licentious speech was implicit in the concept of freedom.[17] Later, its limits were made explicit. One major kind of injurious speech recognized by the Founders was "personal libel."[18] Over the years, free speech has nonetheless become a presumptively protected value: the government cannot regulate its content unless specific exceptions apply, and the meaning of defamation, like other exceptions, has been narrowly circumscribed by the courts. At the height of the civil rights movement in the 1960s, the Supreme Court radically changed its common law definition that privileged the rights of plaintiffs,[19] by holding that public officials cannot recover for defamation unless they can show that defendants acted with "actual malice," defined as "knowledge that the information was false" or as harboring "reckless disregard of whether it was false or not."[20] The same

14. Police Dept. of Chi. v. Mosley, 408 U.S. 92, 95 (1972).
15. Police Dept. of Chi. v. Mosley, 408 U.S. at 95–96 (1972).
16. Most cases dealing with content-based restrictions were decided in favor of the defendants instead of the government. One "rare" exception was *Burson v. Freeman*, which involved a Tennessee state law prohibiting election campaigning within 100 feet of a building housing a polling place. Justice Harry Blackmun wrote that the case, which involved a "content-based restriction on political speech," required strict scrutiny and the 100-feet limit was "narrowly tailored" to serve the "compelling interest" in preserving the secrecy of the ballot. 504 U.S. 191, 206, 211 (1992).
17. Thomas West, *Free Speech in the American Founding and in Modern Liberalism*, 21 SOC. PHIL. & POL'Y 310, 325 (2004).
18. Thomas West, *Free Speech in the American Founding and in Modern Liberalism*, 21 SOC. PHIL. & POL'Y 310, 325 (2004).
19. Russell L. Weaver & David F. Partlett, *Defamation, Free Speech, and Democratic Governance*, 50 N.Y. L. SCH. L. REV. 57, 65–66 (2006).
20. N.Y. Times Co. v. Sullivan, 376 U.S. 254, 280 (1964).

standard was soon extended to cover "public figures,"[21] while the standard for private individuals is understandably lower.[22]

While hate speech, or inflammatory speech targeting people for such attributes as race, religion, or gender, is prohibited in many Western countries, there is no hate speech law in the U.S. Hence, racist and bigoted expressions are lawful. In addition, the Supreme Court ruled in *Brandenburg v. Ohio* (1969) that "[t]he constitutional guarantees of free speech and free press do not permit a state to forbid or proscribe advocacy of the use of force, or of law violation except where such advocacy is directed to inciting imminent lawless action and is likely to incite or produce such action."[23] The *Brandenburg* standard has been used to protect all kinds of political expressions, including those that impliedly endorse violence.[24] Although the First Amendment does not protect "fighting words," this exception is an extremely limited one applying only to intimidating speech directed at a specific individual in a face-to-face confrontation that would likely provoke a violent reaction.[25] While purely offensive or inflammatory speech not inciting or likely to incite "imminently lawless action" is not proscribable, expressions constituting harassment or creating pervasively hostile and discriminatory work or educational environments are prohibited by the federal Civil Rights Act as well as by state human rights and criminal laws.[26]

The above restrictions no doubt apply to American higher institutions, of which free speech is a fundamental value. Throughout the past decades, the U.S. Supreme Court has reiterated time and again the importance of free speech in American education. Justice Robert Jackson opined in 1943 that the role of

---

21. Curtis Publishing Co. v. Butts, 388 U.S. 130 (1967).
22. In *Gertz v. Robert Welch, Inc.*, the Supreme Court held that actual malice is not necessary for defamation of a private person if negligence is present. 418 U.S. 323 (1974).
23. Brandenburg v. Ohio, 395 U.S. 444, 447 (1969).
24. For example, in *Brandenburg*, the court held that a Ku Klux Klan leader could not be jailed for stating "that there might have to be some revengeance [*sic*] taken" for the "continued suppression of the white, Caucasian race." In *NAACP v. Clairborne Hardware*, the court held that a civil right activist could not be held liable for the statement, "If we catch any of you going in any of them racist stores, we're going to break your damn neck." In *Hess v. Indiana*, the court held that an antiwar protestor could not be arrested for telling protestors, "We'll take the fucking street later."
25. In *Chaplinsky v. New Hampshire*, the Supreme Court defined fighting words as words that "by their very utterance, inflict injury or tend to incite an immediate breach of the peace. It has been well observed that such utterances are no essential part of any exposition of ideas, and are of such slight social value as a step to truth that any benefit that may be derived from them is clearly outweighed by the social interest in order and morality." 315 U.S. 568 (1942). In *Texas v. Johnson*, the Supreme Court redefined the scope of the fighting words doctrine to mean words that are "a direct personal insult or an invitation to exchange fisticuffs." The burning of a United States flag, which was considered symbolic speech, did not constitute fighting words. 491 U.S. 397 (1989).
26. *See* Civil Rights Act 1964, Title VII & IX; *e.g.*, N.Y. Penal L. § 240.30 & 31; N.Y. Human Rgts. L. § 296.

schools in inculcating constitutional values, in "educating the young for citizenship is reason for scrupulous protection of Constitutional freedoms of the individual, if we are not to strangle the free mind at its source and teach youth to discount important principles of our government as mere platitudes."[27] While Justice Jackson was referring to grade school students, elsewhere the Court has held that free speech should enjoy as much protection in universities as in society and that free speech on university campuses is necessary for the preservation of democracy. In 1957, Chief Justice Earl Warren emphasized that "[t]eachers and students must always remain free to inquire, to study and to evaluate, to gain new maturity and understanding," so that the American civilization would not "stagnate and die."[28] In 1967, he reiterated that America "is deeply committed to safeguarding academic freedom, which is of transcendent value to all of us and not merely to the teachers concerned."[29] In 1972, Chief Justice Warren Burger opined that "the vigilant protection of constitutional freedoms is nowhere more vital than in the community of American schools."[30]

While the Court affirmed the fundamental value of free speech to the academy more generally, the First Amendment applies only to public universities, which are considered actors of the state. In *Keyishian v. Board of Regents* (1967), the Court declared unconstitutional New York statutes and administrative rules designed to prevent employment of professors in state educational institutions and to dismiss them if they were found guilty of "treasonable or seditious" acts.[31] Their vagueness, the Court opined, undermined the professors' academic freedom, "a special concern of the First Amendment, which does not tolerate laws that cast a pall of orthodoxy over the classroom."[32] In *Healy v. James* (1972), the Supreme Court determined that First Amendment protections should apply with the same force at public universities as in the community at large, and overturned a state college president's decision to deny official status to a left-wing student group.[33] In *Widmar v. Vincent* (1981), the same Court reaffirmed the applicability of the First Amendment to public universities by overturning a state university's decision that its facilities could not be used by student groups for purposes of religious worship or religious teaching,

27. W. Vir. State Bd. of Educ. v. Barnette, 319 U.S. 624 (1943).
28. Sweezy v. New Hampshire, 354 U.S. 234, 250 (1957).
29. Keyishian v. Bd. of Regents, State Univ. of N.Y., 385 U.S. 589 (1967).
30. Healy v. James, 408 U.S. 169, 180 (1972).
31. *Keyishian*, 385 U.S. 589.
32. *Keyishian*, 385 U.S. 589.
33. *Healy*, 408 U.S. at 180.

on the grounds that the state was not assumed to be in support of all messages communicated in their facilities.[34]

Private universities are not legally obligated to uphold First Amendment rights. In fact, these universities enjoy a First Amendment right of assembly to determine their own terms of matriculation.[35] However, private universities generally advertise themselves as bastions of free speech and inquiry.[36] Courts have held in numerous cases that private institutions must live up to promises of free inquiry made to students, whether in handbooks, regulations, or the speeches of presidents, based upon a "contract theory" and in accordance with the parties' reasonable expectations.[37] Certainly, some courts have ruled that the contractual relationship cannot be based on isolated provisions in student brochures.[38] Nevertheless, courts have tended to hold universities accountable for the promises they make to students and using the "contract theory" to enforce students' free speech rights at private universities.[39] Private universities may also declare openly and consistently that they prioritize certain values over free speech, and students are considered to have given their informed consent to the contracts in choosing to enroll in those universities.[40]

However, regulating speech is not unique to private universities. Public universities may also enact regulations that restrict, prohibit, and punish a substantial amount of what would be protected speech under the First Amendment. One example of such "speech codes" is harassment and discrimination policies.[41] Over the years, courts have found in many cases such speech codes, though often well intentioned, to be unconstitutional because they were too vague and insuffi-

---

34. Widmar v. Vincent, 454 U.S. 263 (1981).
35. *State of the Law: Speech Codes*, The Fire, https://www.thefire.org/legal/state-of-the-law-speech-codes/ (last visited Aug. 15, 2020).
36. *State of the Law: Speech Codes*, The Fire, https://www.thefire.org/legal/state-of-the-law-speech-codes/ (last visited Aug. 15, 2020).
37. *E.g.*, Havlik v. Johnson & Wales Univ., 509 F.3d 25, 34 (1st Cir. 2007); Ross v. Creighton Univ., 957 F.2d 410, 416 (7th Cir. 1992).
38. *E.g.*, Pacella v. Tufts Univ. School of Dental Med., 66 F. Supp. 2d 234 (D. Mass. 1999); Romeo v. Seton Hall Univ., 378 N.J. Super. 384, 395 (App. Div. 2005).
39. *See, e.g.*, Kelly Sarabyn, *Free Speech at Private Universities*, 39 J. L. & Educ. 145 (2010), which argues that the contract theory provides the best legal mechanism for holding universities accountable for such violations.
40. For example, Brigham Young University states that students are not guaranteed robust free speech rights on its campus. One of its policies says the following about free expression: "[T]he exercise of individual and institutional academic freedom must be a matter of reasonable limitations. In general, at BYU a limitation is reasonable when the faculty behavior or expression seriously and adversely affects the university mission or the Church."
41. *See State of the Law: Speech Codes*, The Fire, https://www.thefire.org/legal/state-of-the-law-speech-codes/ (last visited Aug. 15, 2020).

ciently specified what speech was banned.[42] In other cases, courts have found them to be overly broad and easily prohibited constitutionally protected speech, and so could not be reconciled with the First Amendment.[43] In some cases, courts have found them unconstitutional on both grounds.[44]

Although the First Amendment normally applies only to public universities, speech policies at private universities are not immune from challenges of constitutionality. This was what happened in *Corry v. Leland Stanford Junior University*, where the California state court found the speech code at Stanford University unconstitutional, by relying on California's "Leonard Law," which provides students attending private institutions in California with the same amount of speech rights as those attending public institutions.[45] Stanford's policy on "harassment by personal vilification" prohibited speech "intended to insult or stigmatize an individual . . . on the basis of their sex, race, color, handicap, religion, sexual orientation, or national and ethnic origin."[46] In response to the university's argument that its policy targeted only fighting words, the court held that even if limited to fighting words, it violated the First Amendment's requirement of content neutrality by not prohibiting all fighting words but only those based on the enumerated categories. It also found the policy, which prohibited more than just fighting words, unconstitutionally overbroad.[47]

In March 2019, President Donald Trump signed an executive order protecting freedom of speech on college campuses, in his attempt to take "historic action to defend American students and American values that have been under siege."[48] It requires colleges to follow the First Amendment on public campuses or their own contractual commitments to protect the free speech of students and professors on private campuses. While the right to free speech is given more protection in American universities than in their Canadian and British counterparts, this fundamental freedom is still under attack on various fronts. Hardly a month has gone by without a new incident involving campus free

42. *E.g.*, *Keyishian*, 385 U.S. 589.
43. *E.g.*, Roberts v. Haragan, 346 F. Supp. 2d 853 (N.D. Tex. 2004); UWM Post v. Bd. of Regents of the Univ. of Wisconsin, 774 F. Supp. 1163 (E.D. Wis. 1991); Doe v. Univ. of Michigan, 721 F. Supp. 852 (E.D. Mich. 1989).
44. *E.g.*, DeJohn v. Temple Univ., 537 F.3d 301, 319 (3d Cir. 2008); Booher v. Bd. of Regents, 1998 U.S. Dist. LEXIS 11404 (E.D. Ky. Jul. 21, 1998).
45. Corry v. Leland Stanford Junior Univ., No. 740309 (Cal. Super. Ct. Feb. 27, 1995) (slip op.).
46. Corry v. Leland Stanford Junior Univ., No. 740309 (Cal. Super. Ct. Feb. 27, 1995) (slip op.).
47. Corry v. Leland Stanford Junior Univ., No. 740309 (Cal. Super. Ct. Feb. 27, 1995) (slip op.).
48. Susan Svrluga, *Trump Signs Executive Order on Free Speech on College Campuses*, WASH. POST (Mar. 21, 2019), https://www.washingtonpost.com/education/2019/03/21/trump-expected-sign-executive-order-free-speech/

speech getting featured in the news. This chapter will examine a selection of these numerous cases in the U.S., including both widely discussed and lesser-known ones, with reference to concepts discussed in part II of this book. The author does not know any of the people involved and the following study draws exclusively upon open-access resources such as news reports and postings on social media platforms.

II. Case Studies

Certainly, speakers across the political spectrum have faced censorship in American universities. One study argues that both left-leaning and conservative scholars, speakers, and students have self-censored, or otherwise have had their right to free speech threatened.[49] Princeton professor Keeanga-Yamahtta Taylor, on receiving death threats and threats of physical violence for criticizing President Donald Trump, canceled her commencement speech at the University of California, San Diego.[50] The president of Sonoma State University apologized openly for allowing a black student to read a poem critical of police violence and President Trump at the commencement.[51] Dana Cloud, a racial left-wing professor at Syracuse University, was criticized for labeling protesters in the "March Against Sharia" (Islamic law) rally "fascists" on Twitter and for calling upon "Syracuse people" to "come down to the federal building to finish them off."[52]

---

49. Sanford J. Ungar, *Campus Speech Protests Don't Only Target Conservatives, and When They Do, It's Often the Same Few Conservatives, Georgetown Free Speech Tracker Find*, MEDIUM (Mar. 26, 2018), https://medium.com/informed-and-engaged/campus-speech-protests-dont-only-target-conservatives-though-they-frequently-target-the-same-few-bda3105ad347

50. Sanford J. Ungar, *Campus Speech Protests Don't Only Target Conservatives, and When They Do, It's Often the Same Few Conservatives, Georgetown Free Speech Tracker Find*, MEDIUM (Mar. 26, 2018), https://medium.com/informed-and-engaged/campus-speech-protests-dont-only-target-conservatives-though-they-frequently-target-the-same-few-bda3105ad347

51. Sanford J. Ungar, *Campus Speech Protests Don't Only Target Conservatives, and When They Do, It's Often the Same Few Conservatives, Georgetown Free Speech Tracker Find*, MEDIUM (Mar. 26, 2018), https://medium.com/informed-and-engaged/campus-speech-protests-dont-only-target-conservatives-though-they-frequently-target-the-same-few-bda3105ad347

52. Sanford J. Ungar, *Campus Speech Protests Don't Only Target Conservatives, and When They Do, It's Often the Same Few Conservatives, Georgetown Free Speech Tracker Find*, MEDIUM (Mar. 26, 2018), https://medium.com/informed-and-engaged/campus-speech-protests-dont-only-target-conservatives-though-they-frequently-target-the-same-few-bda3105ad347; Julie McMahon, *Syracuse University Chancellor Defends Prof after Tweet Sets off Right-Wing Backlash*, SYRACUSE UNIV. NEWS (Jun. 26, 2017), https://www.syracuse.com/su-news/2017/06/syracuse_university_chancellor_defends_prof_after_tweet_sets_off_right-wing_back.html

Yet these examples indicate that left-wing academics and students have had their speech shut down or received criticisms for reasons quite different than those of their conservative counterparts. Taylor was not in fact disinvited by university authorities who likely did not object to her ideologies: she canceled her own talk due to death threats from anonymous email-senders who might not be affiliated with any university.[53] The president of Sonoma State University apologized for the student's poem not for its anti-Trump message, of which no criticism was aired, but for the expletives that reportedly offended some parents attending the ceremony.[54] To be fair, to the extent that the Syracuse professor's call to "finish [. . .] off" her opponents could rightly be interpreted as a call for violence, the criticisms were completely reasonable and justified regardless of the politics of the critics and therefore need not be ideologically motivated.[55]

Quite the contrary, the deplatforming of conservative speakers and attempts to censor conservative expressions of academics /or students, or both, were almost always ideologically motivated.[56] In some cases, the common accusations—that the speech of these speakers incited violence against minority groups—did appear to be reasonable; in most others, however, they turned out to be completely groundless. In addition, while American universities used to enjoy some success in resisting the Chinese Communist Party's long-arm censorship on American campuses, the passing of the national security law in Hong Kong, which facilitated China's authoritarian claws across the free world, has unfortunately posed an unprecedented threat to free speech on American campuses.

Example 1

The past few years have seen a rise in attempts to deplatform controversial speakers on American university campuses.[57] A successful example occurred at Mid-

53. Paige Cornwell, *Princeton Professor Cancels Seattle Talk after Fox News Segment, Death Threats*, SEATTLE TIMES (Jun. 1, 2017), https://www.seattletimes.com/seattle-news/princeton-professor-cancels-seattle-talk-after-fox-news-segment-death-threats/
54. Scott Jaschik, *Anger over Poem and Apology at Sonoma State*, INSIDE HIGHER EDUC. (Jun. 9, 2017), https://www.insidehighered.com/quicktakes/2017/06/09/anger-over-poem-and-apology-sonoma-state
55. *See* Julie McMahon, *Syracuse University Chancellor Defends Prof after Tweet Sets off Right-Wing Backlash*, SYRACUSE UNIV. NEWS (Jun. 26, 2017), https://www.syracuse.com/su-news/2017/06/syracuse_university_chancellor_defends_prof_after_tweet_sets_off_right-wing_back.html
56. *E.g.*, Maleeha Syed, *Middlebury College Cancels Talk with Conservative Speaker for Safety Purposes*, BURLINGTON FREE PRESS (Apr. 17, 2019), https://www.burlingtonfreepress.com/story/news/local/2019/04/17/campus-free-speech-middlebury-college-charles-murray-european-parliament-ryszard-legutko/3494450002/
57. An excellent example not studied in this chapter is Ben Shapiro. *E.g.*, Amanda Casanova, *Grand Canyon University Disinvites Ben Shapiro from Speaking at Their Campus*, CHRISTIAN HEADLINES

dlebury College, a private institution. In March 2017, a conservative student group invited controversial scholar Charles Murray, author of *The Bell Curve* and *Coming Apart*, to campus.[58] The former work, which argues that intelligence is partly genetic, that there may be genetic differences among races, and that such differences account for much of the class stratification in America, led to accusations of racism.[59] The latter work, which was supposed to be the topic of the talk, explains income inequality in America through a perceived gap in virtue, and was denounced by some critics for what they considered class biases.[60] An open letter signed by 450 Middlebury alumni argued that free speech did not entitle Murray to a platform for his "offensive views."[61] To ensure that his views would be challenged, the student group also invited left-learning professor Allison Stanger to engage Murray in a public conversation following his talk.

Murray was not disinvited. However, on the day of the talk, students refused to heed the call for engagement. As Murray approached the podium, they turned their backs and began chanting: "Hey, hey ho ho, Charles Murray has got to go," "Your message is hatred, we cannot tolerate it," "Charles Murray go away, Middlebury says no way," and "Shut it down."[62] A university representative came on stage to announce that if the students did not relent, Murray and Stanger would continue their conversation at a secret location, which would then be broadcast. Stanger then asked the students, "Can you just listen for one minute," adding that she "spent a lot of time preparing hard questions," but many answered "no."[63] Murray and Stanger found themselves surrounded by protesters, some of whom were wearing masks, and one grabbed Stanger's hair and twisted her neck as she tried to shield Murray from them. They finally escaped by entering a waiting car, as the protesters "pounded on it, rocked it

---

(Feb. 5, 2019), https://www.christianheadlines.com/blog/grand-canyon-university-disinvites-ben-shapiro-from-speaking-at-their-campus.html (last visited Nov. 13, 2020); Susan Svriuga, *Berkeley Free-Speech Fights Flared Up Again over Ben Shapiro*, WASH. POST (Jul. 20, 2017), https://www.washingtonpost.com/news/grade-point/wp/2017/07/19/berkeley-free-speech-fight-flares-up-again-over-ben-shapiro/

58. *E.g.*, Peter Beinart, *A Violent Attack on Free Speech at Middlebury*, ATLANTIC (Mar. 6, 2017), https://www.theatlantic.com/politics/archive/2017/03/middlebury-free-speech-violence/518667/

59. *E.g.*, Stephen Metcalf, *Moral Courage: Is Defending* The Bell Curve *an Example of Intellectual Honesty?*, SLATE (Oct. 17, 2005), https://slate.com/culture/2005/10/the-bell-curve-revisited.html; JOSEPH L. GRAVES, THE EMPEROR'S NEW CLOTHES 8 (2001).

60. *E.g.*, Joan Walsh, *The Stunning Dishonesty of Charles Murray*, SALON (Mar. 18, 2014), https://www.salon.com/2014/03/18/paul_krugman_demolishes_charles_murrays_stunning_racist_dishonesty/

61. Peter Beinart, *A Violent Attack on Free Speech at Middlebury*, ATLANTIC (Mar. 6, 2017), https://www.theatlantic.com/politics/archive/2017/03/middlebury-free-speech-violence/518667/

62. Peter Beinart, *A Violent Attack on Free Speech at Middlebury*, ATLANTIC (Mar. 6, 2017), https://www.theatlantic.com/politics/archive/2017/03/middlebury-free-speech-violence/518667/

63. Peter Beinart, *A Violent Attack on Free Speech at Middlebury*, ATLANTIC (Mar. 6, 2017), https://www.theatlantic.com/politics/archive/2017/03/middlebury-free-speech-violence/518667/

back and forth, and jumped onto the hood."[64] One even took a large traffic sign to prevent them from leaving.[65]

The deplatforming of Murray, whose invitation to speak at Middlebury had been approved by the university authorities and who therefore was entitled to speak there, was wrong. Despite the apparent biases in his books as well as their racist or classist implications, or both, there is no evidence that he aimed to or would have incited violence, and any racist or discriminatory messages at the talk likely would have been questioned by Stanger. While there was no indication that his speech would have contained any illegal content or that the dialogue it would have initiated would have been disrespectful and unconducive to learning, what the protesters did went squarely against the foundational values of the university, violated its policies, and American laws. One may be tempted to compare the deplatforming of Murray with the suspension of a Canadian professor that I discuss in chapter 9, and query why the Canadian professor, who published race-based criticism of immigration, might have been fairly stripped of the position, but Murray should not have been deplatformed. Allowing a racist platform to someone whom many consider to be a racist, nonetheless, is nowhere close to allowing a racist to stay in a long-term or permanent position: the racist can be challenged at the talk so that people can be persuaded that his views are unsubstantiated or take away whatever they consider valuable, or both. On the contrary, the racist professor, after being exposed for his racist ideas, may well continue to exploit university resources to promote racism and engage in research that offers little or no benefit to a multicultural society—resources that can and should be allocated to more deserving researchers.

While Middlebury was reported to have punished the protesters who injured Stanger and violently disrupted Murray's talk,[66] this incident unfortunately failed to strengthen its resolve to uphold free speech in the face of possible violent disruption. In 2019, it canceled a lecture by Ryszard Legutko, a Polish professor and member of the European Parliament, citing "safety" con-

---

64. Peter Beinart, *A Violent Attack on Free Speech at Middlebury*, ATLANTIC (Mar. 6, 2017), https://www.theatlantic.com/politics/archive/2017/03/middlebury-free-speech-violence/518667/

65. Peter Beinart, *A Violent Attack on Free Speech at Middlebury*, ATLANTIC (Mar. 6, 2017), https://www.theatlantic.com/politics/archive/2017/03/middlebury-free-speech-violence/518667/

66. *E.g.*, Scott Jaschik, *Another Speaker Unable to Appear at Middlebury*, INSIDE HIGHER EDUC. (Apr. 18, 2019), https://www.insidehighered.com/news/2019/04/18/middlebury-calls-lecture-conservative-polish-leader-amid-threats-protests

cerns of students, faculty, staff, and community members.[67] Legutko was a controversial figure embraced by supporters for his stance against dictatorship in communist Poland, but detested by many for his "far-right" views and what they deemed his "homophobic, racist, xenophobic, misogynistic discourse."[68] As the open letter criticizing his invitation explained, bringing such a speaker to campus amounted to "shutting out large swaths of the Middlebury community, all of whom are engaged, critical and rigorous thinkers whose energies would be better spent not combating degrading and dehumanizing rhetoric."[69]

Evidence, however, indicates that Legutko's ideas and position have been grossly misunderstood. For instance, his opinion that people should be proud of their conduct, something they can choose, rather than their gay identity, something they were born with ("Be proud of what you do, not of being a homosexual."),[70] is most often cited as an example of his homophobic opinions. This comment merely indicates that one's gay identity should not be a source of pride on its own, and therefore does not denigrate gay people by virtue of their sexual orientation and contains nothing remotely homophobic. The complainants' refusal to even debate Legutko's ideas at a one-time event, which they concluded to be "degrading and dehumanizing" and not worth spending their time and energies on, indicated that they might not be as "engaged, critical and rigorous" as they purported to be. By canceling the lecture, even in anticipation of possible violent disruption, Middlebury encouraged their intellectual laziness and ideological intolerance and was complicit in undermining its free speech principles.

Example 2

One of the most discussed recent free speech cases happened at Evergreen State College, a public institution. In March 2017, Bret Weinstein, a professor of biol-

67. Peter Beinart, *A Violent Attack on Free Speech at Middlebury*, Atlantic (Mar. 6, 2017), https://www.theatlantic.com/politics/archive/2017/03/middlebury-free-speech-violence/518667/
68. Peter Beinart, *A Violent Attack on Free Speech at Middlebury*, Atlantic (Mar. 6, 2017), https://www.theatlantic.com/politics/archive/2017/03/middlebury-free-speech-violence/518667/
69. Peter Beinart, *A Violent Attack on Free Speech at Middlebury*, Atlantic (Mar. 6, 2017), https://www.theatlantic.com/politics/archive/2017/03/middlebury-free-speech-violence/518667/
70. Riley Board, *College Braces for Right-Wing Speaker Accused of Homophobia*, Middlebury Campus (April 16, 2019), https://www.middleburycampus.com/article/2019/04/college-braces-for-right-wing-speaker-accused-of-homophobia. For some background on Legutko's views, see Rajeev Syal, Gay Rights Critic Fights to Lead David Cameron's Allies in Europe, The Guardian (Feb. 17, 2011), https://www.theguardian.com/world/2011/feb/17/conservatives-eu-poland-allies-ryszard-legutko

ogy, expressed his objection to a change in the college's decades-old tradition of observing a "Day of Absence." According to the tradition, students and faculty of color would voluntarily stay away from campus to highlight their contributions to the college.[71] The change encouraged white participants to voluntarily stay off campus to attend a program on race issues while the on-campus program would be designated for people of color.[72] In his email, Weinstein noted "a huge difference between a group or coalition deciding to voluntarily absent themselves from a shared space in order to highlight their vital and underappreciated roles . . . and a group or coalition encouraging another group to go away."[73] In May, student protests alleging racism, intolerance, and threats broke out on Evergreen's campus. According to Weinstein, he was subjected to verbal and physical harassment from protesters during a serious clash on campus, who demanded that he be fired simply for expressing dissent.[74] Protesters' version of the event, however, told of Weinstein's alliances with right-wing media to demonize protesters as dangerous speech-hating totalitarians, to mislead the public into thinking that the protests were triggered by his email while they were in fact caused by other race-related incidents, and to weaponize free speech for suppressing race-related protests and activism.[75]

Weinstein and his wife and fellow biologist Heather Heying brought a tort claim against Evergreen, alleging that it failed to "protect its employees from repeated provocative and corrosive verbal and written hostility based on race, as well as threats of physical violence" and seeking $3.8 million in damages.[76] In September 2017, they finally reached a settlement, in which Weinstein and Heying resigned and were awarded $250,000 each.[77] After his resignation, Weinstein

---

71. *E.g.*, Nick Roll, *Evergreen Professor Receives $500,000 in Settlement*, Inside Higher Educ. (Sep. 18, 2017), https://www.insidehighered.com/quicktakes/2017/09/18/evergreen-professor-receives-500000-settlement
72. *E.g.*, Nick Roll, *Evergreen Professor Receives $500,000 in Settlement*, Inside Higher Educ. (Sep. 18, 2017), https://www.insidehighered.com/quicktakes/2017/09/18/evergreen-professor-receives-500000-settlement
73. *E.g.*, Nick Roll, *Evergreen Professor Receives $500,000 in Settlement*, Inside Higher Educ. (Sep. 18, 2017), https://www.insidehighered.com/quicktakes/2017/09/18/evergreen-professor-receives-500000-settlement
74. *E.g.*, Anemona Hartocollis, *A Campus Argument Goes Viral, Now the College Is under Siege*, N.Y. Times (Jun. 16, 2017), https://www.nytimes.com/2017/06/16/us/evergreen-state-protests.html
75. *E.g.*, Noah Berlatsky, *How Right-Wing Media Has Tried to Stifle Student Speech at Evergreen State College*, Pac. Standard (Jul. 10, 2018), https://psmag.com/education/the-real-free-speech-story-at-evergreen-college
76. Nick Roll, *Evergreen Professor Receives $500,000 in Settlement*, Inside Higher Educ. (Sep. 18, 2017), https://www.insidehighered.com/quicktakes/2017/09/18/evergreen-professor-receives-500000-settlement
77. Abby Spegman, *Evergreen Settles with Weinstein, Professor at the Center of Campus Protests*, The Olympian (Sep. 16, 2017), https://www.theolympian.com/news/local/article173710596.html

took a high profile by appearing on the podcasts of what are known as "conservative" media personalities as well as in *No Safe Spaces*, a film addressing free speech on campuses that documents the Evergreen incident.[78] For the 2019–21 academic years, he and his wife were visiting fellows at Princeton University's James Madison Society.[79] On the other hand, Evergreen, with its reputation tarnished, has suffered substantial drops in student enrollment since this incident.[80]

Both Weinstein and the protesters might have been guilty of suppressing free speech at Evergreen. Given that it was a public institution, Weinstein was no doubt within his First Amendment right to object to the change to Evergreen's tradition and to stay on campus to make his statement of objection. While some considered him a "white supremacist" for even objecting and staying on campus, nothing in his email constituted racial discrimination or provoked violence against racial minorities. The protesters were equally entitled to criticize his objection. If Weinstein had been harassed by the protesters without himself committing any violence, the university apparently failed to fulfill its obligation to protect him at the site of conflict to ensure that he could fully exercise his right to free speech. Regarding Weinstein's alleged alliance with right-wing media, it was highly possible that such media had expressed more interest in his story than their left-wing counterparts. If, however, the student protesters' version is to be trusted and Weinstein indeed had misled the public with regard to the facts surrounding the incident, then he would also have been guilty of stoking the flames of extreme right-wing activists who tried to silence the student protesters. In such a case, he should have apologized to those being harmed and denounced the violence inflicted on them. If he had not intentionally misled the public or committed any violence before getting harassed, and he and his wife had resigned under pressure from the university, then Evergreen undermined its foundational values not only once but twice—by caving in to the demands of those he offended.

Like Weinstein, Samuel Abrams, politics professor at Sarah Lawrence College, was attacked and harassed for voicing his objection to progressive initiatives on his campus. The incident originated in his op-ed in the *New York Times*,

78. Spencer Irvine, *"No Safe Spaces" Documentary Warns of Dangers Facing First Amendment Rights in America*, Accuracy in Academia (Nov. 25, 2019), https://www.academia.org/no-safe-spaces-documentary-warns-of-dangers-facing-first-amendment-rights-in-america/

79. *Current Visiting Fellows*, James Madison Program, https://jmp.princeton.edu/about/people/visiting (last visited Nov. 15, 2020); *The James Madison Program Announces 2019–20 Fellows*, Princeton Univ. (Apr. 12, 2019), https://jmp.princeton.edu/announcements/james-madison-program-announces-2019-20-fellows

80. Lilah Burke, *A New Path for Evergreen*, Inside Higher Educ. (Jan. 10, 2020), https://www.insidehighered.com/news/2020/01/10/evergreen-addresses-enrollment-decline-academic-changes

which expressed his concerns about the college's sponsorship of what he considered a "politically lopsided" conference touching on "progressive topics" like "liberation spaces on campus," Black Lives Matter, and justice for women and other minority groups.[81] What was equally disconcerting, according to his op-ed, was that "many overtly progressive events" organized by its Office of Student Affairs, including those about "Microaggressions" and "Understanding White Privilege," were not counterbalanced by events offering a "meaningful ideological alternative."[82] Soon after its publication, Abrams found his office door vandalized. A student group called "Diaspora Coalition" demanded that his position at the college be put up to tenure review by a panel of that group and at least three faculty members of color; that the college issue a statement "condemning the harm that Abrams has caused to the college community, specifically queer, black and female students, whilst apologizing for its refusal to protect marginalized students wounded by his op-ed and the ignorant dialogue that followed"; and that Abrams issue a public apology to the "broader [college] community and cease to target black people, queer people and women."[83] Sarah Lawrence's president, while addressing "the inappropriateness of demands" related to Abrams's tenure, accused Abrams of "attacking" members of the Sarah Lawrence "community"[84] and, according to Abrams, even advised him privately to seek new employment elsewhere.[85]

Publicly expressed opinions overwhelmingly supported Abrams's op-ed, which respectfully identifies ideological imbalances at his college and promotes freedom of thought and critical thinking.[86] One critic rightly and fairly pointed out that "publishing truthful information about ideological imbalances threatens no one's 'safety.' Questioning the priorities of progressive administrators endangers no one's 'wellbeing.' Colleges should not 'protect'

81. Samuel Abrams, *Think Professors Are Liberal? Try School Administrators*, N.Y. TIMES (Oct. 16, 2018).
82. Samuel Abrams, *Think Professors Are Liberal? Try School Administrators*, N.Y. TIMES (Oct. 16, 2018).
83. Colleen Flaherty, *When Students Want to Review a Tenured Professor*, INSIDE HIGHER EDUC. (Mar. 13, 2019), http://www.insidehighered.com/news/2019/03/13/students-sarah-lawrence-want-review-tenure-conservative-professor-who-criticized
84. Colleen Flaherty, *When Students Want to Review a Tenured Professor*, INSIDE HIGHER EDUC. (Mar. 13, 2019), http://www.insidehighered.com/news/2019/03/13/students-sarah-lawrence-want-review-tenure-conservative-professor-who-criticized
85. Robby Soave, *Sarah Lawrence Professor's Office Door Vandalized after He Criticized Leftist Bias*, REASON (Nov. 2, 2018), http://www.reason.com/2018/11/02/sarah-lawrence-professor-samuel-abrams/
86. *E.g.*, David French, *A Professor Spoke the Truth, He Still Pays the Price*, NAT'L REV. (Mar. 12, 2019), http://www.nationalreview.com/2019/03/professor-samuel-abrams-spoke-the-truth-he-still-pays-the-price/; I. K., *Student Activists Demand the Punishment of a Dissenting Professor*, ECONOMIST (Apr. 4, 2019), http://www.economist.com/democracy-in-america/2019/04/04/student-activists-demand-the-punishment-of-a-dissenting-professor

anyone from *New York Times* essays."[87] In fact, even direct criticisms of the progressive concepts, which the op-ed does not do, would not in themselves constitute racism or biases of any kind. Abrams was likely correct about his judgment of the degree of ideological tolerance at his workplace (which perhaps also explained the overreaction): twenty-five professors at the college signed a petition declaring their solidarity with the student activism.[88] One can only wonder whether these professors also endorsed their request to have his tenure reviewed by students, and to what extent the president, who failed her role with her accusations and employment advice, was responsible for promoting such intellectual laziness and ideological intolerance even among the college's academics. Fortunately, though, Abrams stood his ground, and unlike Weinstein, did not resign under pressure.[89]

Example 3

Over the past few years, Harvard College caught media attention through its drastic actions that some believe manifest a lack of regard for free speech. In 2017, the university rescinded admissions offers to at least ten prospective students upon finding out that they traded sexually explicit memes and messages targeting minority groups in a Facebook group chat.[90] In 2019, it revoked its admission offer to prospective student Kyle Kashuv over some racist statements he had made on social media two years previously, includ-

87. David French, *A Professor Spoke the Truth, He Still Pays the Price*, NAT'L REV. (Mar. 12, 2019), http://www.nationalreview.com/2019/03/professor-samuel-abrams-spoke-the-truth-he-still-pays-the-price/; I. K., *Student Activists Demand the Punishment of a Dissenting Professor*, ECONOMIST (Apr. 4, 2019), http://www.economist.com/democracy-in-america/2019/04/04/student-activists-demand-the-punishment-of-a-dissenting-professor
88. David French, *A Professor Spoke the Truth, He Still Pays the Price*, NAT'L REV. (Mar. 12, 2019, 2:08 PM), http://www.nationalreview.com/2019/03/professor-samuel-abrams-spoke-the-truth-he-still-pays-the-price/; I. K., *Student Activists Demand the Punishment of a Dissenting Professor*, ECONOMIST (Apr. 4, 2019), http://www.economist.com/democracy-in-america/2019/04/04/student-activists-demand-the-punishment-of-a-dissenting-professor
89. *E.g.*, Robby Soave, *Sarah Lawrence Professor's Office Door Vandalized after He Criticized Leftist Bias*, REASON (Nov. 2, 2018), http://www.reason.com/2018/11/02/sarah-lawrence-professor-samuel-abrams/. In 2019, Abrams was given the Open Inquiry Courage Award by the Heterodox Academy, an American nonprofit aimed at promoting diversity of thought in academia, for his uprightness and moral courage. HaX Executive Team, *Meet the 2019 Open Inquiry Award Winners*, HETERODOX ACADEMY (May 2019).
90. Hannah Natanson, *Harvard Rescinds Acceptances for at Least Ten Students for Obscene Memes*, THE CRIMSON (Jun. 5, 2017), https://www.thecrimson.com/article/2017/6/5/2021-offers-rescinded-memes/

ing his multiple uses of the "N-word."[91] Kashuv confessed that he was embarrassed by his comments and has since matured: "We were 16-year-olds making idiotic comments, using callous and inflammatory language in an effort to be as extreme and shocking as possible. . . . I want to be clear that the comments I made are not indicative of who I am or who I've become in the years since."[92] William R. Fitzsimmons, dean of admissions and financial aid, wrote that he appreciated Kashuv's "candor and expressions of regret" for his past comments, but also said that Harvard "takes seriously" the "qualities of maturity" and of "character" of those it admits.[93]

By revoking Kashuv's and the others' offers, not only did Harvard do what its policies on admission, free speech, and discrimination entitled it to do, but it also acted rightly in seeking to build an environment free from racial aggression and possibly discrimination in various forms. Kashuv pleaded with Harvard to reconsider its decision on the grounds that Harvard's faculty has included "slave owners, segregationists, bigots and anti-Semites."[94] Unlike Kashuv's speech, which is racist by today's standards, their conduct nonetheless was not problematic by the standards of their bygone eras, or they would not likely have become faculty members. Many also defended Kashuv on free speech grounds, given that his expressions are not illegal. One even called Harvard's decision a "major victory for the online mobs of cancel culture."[95] Yet Harvard was right in its attempt to "cancel" racial aggression and reduce chances of discrimination on its own campus. Faced with an outstanding applicant pool, it was seeking to eliminate from its incoming class people who had used racist slurs and whose similar conduct may persist and offer their places to those who had not exhibited such conduct and therefore can be fairly presumed to be less likely to violate school policies on discrimination. By rescinding offers to people who showed no sign of personal responsibility, it did not shut down

---

91. Kashuv boasted that "im really good at typing nigger ok like practice uhhhhhh makes perfect." Arwa Mahdawi, *Kyle Kashuv May Not Be Attending Harvard, but He's Learning a Valuable Lesson*, THE GUARDIAN (Jun. 19, 2019, 7:00 AM), https://www.theguardian.com/commentisfree/2019/jun/19/kyle-kashuv-parkland-survivor-harvard-rightwing-response
92. Arwa Mahdawi, *Kyle Kashuv May Not Be Attending Harvard, but He's Learning a Valuable Lesson*, THE GUARDIAN (Jun. 19, 2019, 7:00 AM), https://www.theguardian.com/commentisfree/2019/jun/19/kyle-kashuv-parkland-survivor-harvard-rightwing-response
93. Adam Harris, *Harvard's Drastic Decision*, ATLANTIC (Jun. 17, 2019), https://www.theatlantic.com/education/archive/2019/06/harvard-rescinds-admissions-offer-kyle-kashuv-racist-remarks/591847/
94. Adam Harris, *Harvard's Drastic Decision*, ATLANTIC (Jun. 17, 2019), https://www.theatlantic.com/education/archive/2019/06/harvard-rescinds-admissions-offer-kyle-kashuv-racist-remarks/591847/
95. Adam Harris, *Harvard's Drastic Decision*, ATLANTIC (Jun. 17, 2019), https://www.theatlantic.com/education/archive/2019/06/harvard-rescinds-admissions-offer-kyle-kashuv-racist-remarks/591847/

expression that may or may not contribute to academic dialogues and, therefore, by no means violated its own free speech policy.

Also in 2019, Harvard refused to renew law professor Ronald Sullivan's deanship at Winthrop House, an undergraduate dormitory, after student activists complained that his decision to defend Harvey Weinstein against his sexual assault allegations made the campus an "unsafe place" for women.[96] In an op-ed for the *New York Times*, Sullivan, a lawyer acclaimed for his defense of unfairly incarcerated people, criticized the students for letting their feelings override reason, and the administration for bowing to their demands rather than helping them to distinguish between "unchecked emotions" and those backed by "thoughtful reasoning."[97] It is beyond dispute that defending a sexual assault suspect is a form of speech: it is expressing, through action, that the suspect deserves competent representation. Depending on Sullivan's personal beliefs, it may also be a statement of skepticism toward the "Me Too" movement inspired by this lawsuit.[98] Making such statements, through words or actions, was not against Harvard's policies on free speech and discrimination. Sullivan was right about many American universities' tendency to give in to student activists driven by their emotions and ideologies, and Harvard's decision became part of this worrying trend. At the same time, it may be argued that the student dormitory, which serves as a home for students, enjoys a special status: while not a "safe space" like each of its individual units where the student occupant is entitled to be free from uncomfortable ideas (see chapter 6), it is a more intimate space than the university classroom, where no ideas are too uncomfortable or even dangerous. Quite understandably, some female students, especially those who had been victims of sexual assault, did not prefer someone defending Weinstein to preside over this space. Hence, it might also be understandable for Harvard to allow feelings to play a more important role than they otherwise should have in its decision to

---

96. *E.g.*, Robby Soave, *Fired Harvard Dean Ronald Sullivan: "Unchecked Emotion Has Replaced Thoughtful Reasoning on Campus,"* REASON (Jun. 25, 2019), https://reason.com/2019/06/25/harvard-ronald-sullivan-university-students/; Kate Taylor, *Harvard's First Black Faculty Let Go amid Uproar over Harvey Weinstein's Defense*, N.Y. TIMES (May 11, 2019), https://www.nytimes.com/2019/05/11/us/ronald-sullivan-harvard.html
97. Ronald Sullivan, *Why Harvard Was Wrong to Make Me Step Down*, N.Y. TIMES (Jun. 24, 2019), https://www.nytimes.com/2019/06/24/opinion/harvard-ronald-sullivan.html
98. Criticisms of the "Me Too" movement include whether and to what extent accusers should be believed before evidence is presented and punished without due process confirming their wrongdoing. *E.g.*, Bret Stephens, *When Me Too Goes Too Far*, N.Y. TIMES (Dec. 20, 2017), https://www.nytimes.com/2017/12/20/opinion/metoo-damon-too-far.html

not renew Sullivan's deanship, while overlooking the ramifications that this decision would have for free speech and academic freedom.

Despite Harvard's controversial decision to revoke admission offers to students making racist remarks and even more controversial decision to remove Sullivan from his deanship, Steven Pinker, a famous linguist and social psychologist at the same university whose recent tweets and other expressions led to accusations of racism and racial insensitivity, was fortunately left unscathed. In the wake of the tragic killing of George Floyd in May 2020 and the historic Black Lives Matter protests that followed, more than 550 academics signed a letter seeking to remove Pinker from the list of "distinguished fellows" of the Linguistics Society of America.[99] The letter focused on his activity on Twitter, especially his tweets in relation to the tragedy. One set of tweets were "Data: Police don't shoot blacks disproportionately," "Problem: Not race, but too many police shootings," and "Don't abolish the police," made with reference to the work of a black social scientist. The letter alleged that Pinker "co-opted" the work to downplay racism.[100] It also accused Pinker of using the dog whistle "urban crime/violence" in two other tweets that, as it argued, "signaled covert and, crucially, deniable support of views that essentialize Black people as lesser-than, and, often, as criminals."[101]

Nonetheless, in the first example, Pinker did not merely share the common sentiment that the killing of Floyd should not be the reason to defund the police. Clearly, he also wanted to point out that all racial groups interacting with the police frequently risked becoming victims of police violence due to poorly trained officers, armed suspects, or overreaction, which tended to escalate the conflicts.[102] In addition, "urban crime" can simply refer to crime in big cities, and most likely does.[103] Calling what seems a straightforward reference a "dog whistle" is a stretch and an example of how a concept denoting negative experiences has been expanded to include a transparent and direct reference and thereby weaponized to shut own dissent. Pinker was fully entitled to share

99. Connor Friedersdorf, *The Chilling Effect of an Attack on a Scholar*, ATLANTIC (Jul. 20, 2020), https://www.theatlantic.com/ideas/archive/2020/07/steven-pinker-will-be-just-fine/614323/
100. Connor Friedersdorf, *The Chilling Effect of an Attack on a Scholar*, ATLANTIC (Jul. 20, 2020), https://www.theatlantic.com/ideas/archive/2020/07/steven-pinker-will-be-just-fine/614323/
101. Connor Friedersdorf, *The Chilling Effect of an Attack on a Scholar*, ATLANTIC (Jul. 20, 2020), https://www.theatlantic.com/ideas/archive/2020/07/steven-pinker-will-be-just-fine/614323/
102. Connor Friedersdorf, *The Chilling Effect of an Attack on a Scholar*, ATLANTIC (Jul. 20, 2020), https://www.theatlantic.com/ideas/archive/2020/07/steven-pinker-will-be-just-fine/614323/
103. *See* Connor Friedersdorf, *The Chilling Effect of an Attack on a Scholar*, ATLANTIC (Jul. 20, 2020), https://www.theatlantic.com/ideas/archive/2020/07/steven-pinker-will-be-just-fine/614323/

his views through these tweets, which do not seem to be made in bad faith, and which a thoughtful, contextualized reading has not shown to be racist—or even insensitive by any measure, especially in the second case. The Linguistics Society of America's executive committee aptly declined the request to remove him, stating: "It is not the mission of the society to control the opinions of its members, nor their expression."[104] Should his tweets have met with any form of penalty by Harvard—which would have been highly unlikely due to their very nature—he would have been able to make a strong case against the university.

Example 4

At some universities, the terminations of faculty employment and suspension of students escalated into lawsuits—or almost did. A lawsuit likely would have occurred at the University of California, Los Angles (UCLA) if accounting professor Gordon Klein had not been reinstated. In June 2020, Klein was placed on involuntary leave after turning down a student's email request that he exercise "compassion and leniency with black students" and give a low-stakes final exam for the class, especially black students, in light of the protests for racial justice over Floyd's death.[105] Klein thanked the student, who identified as a white ally for the black students, for his suggestion, but asked, "Do you know the names of the classmates that are black? How can I identify them since we've been having online classes only?"[106] He continued, "Are there any students that may be of mixed parentage, such as half black-half Asian? What do you suggest I do with respect to them? A full concession or just half? Also, do you have any idea if any students are from Minneapolis? I assume that they probably are especially devastated as well. I am thinking that a white student from there might be possibly even more devastated by this, especially because some might think that they're racist even if they are not."[107] Referring to Martin Luther King's famous saying that people should not be evaluated based on the color of their skin, he asked whether the stu-

104. *See* Connor Friedersdorf, *The Chilling Effect of an Attack on a Scholar*, ATLANTIC (Jul. 20, 2020), https://www.theatlantic.com/ideas/archive/2020/07/steven-pinker-will-be-just-fine/614323/

105. *E.g.*, Natalie O'Neill, *UCLA Suspends Professor for Refusing Leniency for Black Students*, N.Y. POST, https://nypost.com/2020/06/10/ucla-suspends-professor-for-refusing-leniency-for-black-students/

106. Natalie O'Neill, *UCLA Suspends Professor for Refusing Leniency for Black Students*, N.Y. POST, https://nypost.com/2020/06/10/ucla-suspends-professor-for-refusing-leniency-for-black-students/

107. Natalie O'Neill, *UCLA Suspends Professor for Refusing Leniency for Black Students*, N.Y. POST, https://nypost.com/2020/06/10/ucla-suspends-professor-for-refusing-leniency-for-black-students/

dent thought his request ran afoul of his admonition.[108] The reply offended the student, who petitioned to have his professorship terminated for "his extremely insensitive, dismissive, and woefully racist response to his students' request for empathy and compassion during a time of civil unrest."[109] After an investigation into his alleged racist conduct, the university reinstated Klein, emphasizing that "regardless of how many people demand his firing, UCLA cannot justify using that anger to erode Gordon's rights."[110]

Despite Klein's reinstatement, UCLA's initial response was depressing. A reasonable observer cannot help asking: if the students' grades suffered because of Floyd's death and subsequent protests, wouldn't the low grades testify to their involvement in or willingness to sacrifice for a good cause, or both, and shouldn't they become a source of pride rather than a cause for regret—or at least a trade-off that the students should have been willing to make? Klein was not at all racist in stating the importance of treating students equally. On the other hand, he would have been racist if he had offered preferential treatment to black students, as it would have indicated his perception that black students are academically, mentally, and emotionally weaker than students of other races, many of whom also participated in protests or were devastated by Floyd's death. He might have avoided the racism charges if he had rephrased his message and conveyed it in the form of plain statements rather than (rhetorical) questions, such as by pointing out that students of all races likely had been affected by the protests and it was important not to make assumptions about their needs on racial grounds. Nevertheless, whether his message, devoid of racism, indeed sounded insensitive, rude, and dismissive depended at least in part on how it was spoken: given that the message was delivered entirely through email, and one cannot read the speaker's facial expression, it could not be fairly considered so. The quick inference of insensitivity and dismissiveness arguably said more about the recipient's vulnerability than about the speaker's attitude. If UCLA had not reinstated Klein and he had filed suit against it, the court would likely have ruled in his favor on First Amendment grounds.

Fordham's mishandling of false allegations about an Asian student, unfor-

---

108. Natalie O'Neill, *UCLA Suspends Professor for Refusing Leniency for Black Students*, N.Y. Post, https://nypost.com/2020/06/10/ucla-suspends-professor-for-refusing-leniency-for-black-students/

109. Natalie O'Neill, *UCLA Suspends Professor for Refusing Leniency for Black Students*, N.Y. Post, https://nypost.com/2020/06/10/ucla-suspends-professor-for-refusing-leniency-for-black-students/

110. Colleen Flaherty, *Professor Who Questioned Student's Request Reinstated*, Inside Higher Educ. (Sep. 16, 2020), https://www.insidehighered.com/quicktakes/2020/09/16/professor-who-questioned-students-request-reinstated

tunately, led to a lawsuit. The controversy arose out of Austin Tong's two Instagram posts in the wake of the Floyd incident in June 2020. One post, captioned "Y'all a bunch of hypocrites," showed a photo of a retired St. Louis police captain who was fatally shot by looters during the protests.[111] On June 4, 2020, the thirty-first anniversary of the Tiananmen Square Massacre in Beijing, he made a second post, captioned "Don't tread on me. #198964," which showed a photo of himself bearing a rifle.[112] After a formal inquiry and hearing concerning these "threatening" posts, Fordham's assistant vice president and dean of students put Tong on disciplinary probation on the grounds that he violated university regulations relating to bias or hate crimes, or both, as well as threats and intimidation, and threatened to expel him should he violate the probation.[113] Tong refused to attend bias training or write a letter of apology as ordered. He filed suit against the university, claiming that his posts were free expression protected under school policy and the U.S. Constitution.[114]

While it might have been understandable for the assistant vice president and dean of students, without knowing the full context of Tong's posts, to find them threatening, Tong's explanation about their political messages at the formal hearing should have convinced even the faintest of heart that they did not intend to threaten anyone or cause bias against minority groups. If anything, his posts, as his careful deliberation revealed, aimed to promote equality and peace. The first post identified the hypocrisy of some Black Lives Movement supporters who focused only on the damage committed by the police and not those committed by violent protesters (such as the killing of the African American police captain featured in Tong's post). The second post denounced the tyrannical Chinese government that instigated the Tiananmen Square Massacre while suggesting that the right to bear arms would enable civilians to combat state violence.[115] Fordham should have advised him on choosing methods

---

111. *E.g.*, Prescilla DeGregory & Doree Lewak, *Fordham Student Says School Wrongfully Penalized Him for Social Media Posts*, N.Y. Post (Jul. 23, 2020), https://nypost.com/2020/07/23/fordham-student-wrongfully-penalized-for-social-media-posts-suit/
112. Prescilla DeGregory & Doree Lewak, *Fordham Student Says School Wrongfully Penalized Him for Social Media Posts*, N.Y. Post (Jul. 23, 2020), https://nypost.com/2020/07/23/fordham-student-wrongfully-penalized-for-social-media-posts-suit/
113. Prescilla DeGregory & Doree Lewak, *Fordham Student Says School Wrongfully Penalized Him for Social Media Posts*, N.Y. Post (Jul. 23, 2020), https://nypost.com/2020/07/23/fordham-student-wrongfully-penalized-for-social-media-posts-suit/
114. Prescilla DeGregory & Doree Lewak, *Fordham Student Says School Wrongfully Penalized Him for Social Media Posts*, N.Y. Post (Jul. 23, 2020), https://nypost.com/2020/07/23/fordham-student-wrongfully-penalized-for-social-media-posts-suit/
115. *See* Prescilla DeGregory & Doree Lewak, *Fordham Student Says School Wrongfully Penalized Him for*

to express his views that would be less likely to make some of his more sensitive complainants feel unsafe. The unreasonable—even ludicrous—decision to sanction Tong will end up tarnishing Fordham's reputation. Although Fordham is a private institution, the court should have relied on the contractual theory and that it applied to Tong and order the university to annul its sanctions.[116] That the lawsuit was finally dismissed indicates that the court, rather unfortunately, prioritized the unjustified feelings of the complainants over Tong's right to free expression.[117]

Another lawsuit against a university and its staff was filed by the Alliance Defending Freedom on behalf of Nathaniel Hiers, who taught in the Mathematics Department of the University of North Texas, until his spring contract was rescinded by his department chair in November 2019. Hiers, on noticing some fliers on microaggression in the department lounge, wrote "Don't leave garbage lying around" in jest on a chalkboard, with arrows pointing down to the fliers.[118] According to the fliers, certain sayings are microaggressions that "propagate the 'myth of meritocracy' and promote 'color blindness,'" including "I believe the most qualified person should get the job" and "America is the land of opportunity."[119] The department chairman allegedly informed Hiers that his "actions and response are not compatible with the values of this department," and ordered him to apologize, to undergo additional diversity training on top of the mandatory training that he was already scheduled to attend and to retract his criticism of the fliers.[120] After Hiers declined and was fired, he sued the chairman and other involved personnel of the university, alleging that the University of North Texas had engaged in content- and viewpoint-based discrimination, attempted to compel speech from him, and retaliated against him by rescinding his contract without notice.

The chair clearly mishandled Hiers's case. While Hiers rejected the concept

---

Social Media Posts, N.Y. POST (Jul. 23, 2020), https://nypost.com/2020/07/23/fordham-student-wrongfully-penalized-for-social-media-posts-suit/

116. *See, e.g.*, Havlik, 509 F.3d at 34; Ross, 957 F.2d at 416.

117. Tong v. Fordham Univ., N.Y. Slip Op. 33299 (N.Y. Manhattan Sup. Ct. 2020).

118. Connor Ellington, *Public University Fired Professor for Calling Microaggressions Handout Garbage Lawsuit*, COLLEGE FIX (Apr. 17, 2020), https://www.thecollegefix.com/public-university-fired-professor-for-calling-microaggressions-handout-garbage-lawsuit/ (last visited Oct. 9, 2020).

119. Connor Ellington, *Public University Fired Professor for Calling Microaggressions Handout Garbage Lawsuit*, COLLEGE FIX (Apr. 17, 2020), https://www.thecollegefix.com/public-university-fired-professor-for-calling-microaggressions-handout-garbage-lawsuit/ (last visited Oct. 9, 2020).

120. Connor Ellington, *Public University Fired Professor for Calling Microaggressions Handout Garbage Lawsuit*, COLLEGE FIX (Apr. 17, 2020), https://www.thecollegefix.com/public-university-fired-professor-for-calling-microaggressions-handout-garbage-lawsuit/ (last visited Oct. 9, 2020).

of microaggression, offering the reason that it "actually hurts diversity and tolerance,"[121] there is no evidence that he was ever guilty of racism or hate speech, or even committed microaggression. The chairman should have asked him to be more civil in expressing his dissent, which is well reasoned, or perhaps encouraged him to apologize for his perceived lack of civility. Yet he seemed to target the substance of Hiers's speech and therefore indicated that even expressing dissent with the utmost civility would be incompatible with the department's values and that compatibility means conformity. While Hiers was an adjunct professor whose continual employment by the department might not have been taken for granted, the chairman made it clear that his decision to rescind the contract was based on Hiers's speech in the lounge and his subsequent refusal to undergo more diversity training and retract his criticism. Because the University of North Texas is a public institution, I predicted that it would likely hold that the university and the chair violated Hiers's constitutional right to free speech.[122] Indeed, while the court rejected, among others, Hiers's breach of contract claim, it rightly ruled that university officials may have violated Hiers's First Amendment right to express his opinion on a topic of public interest and to be free from compelled speech by allegedly asking him to apologize for his speech.[123]

As emphasized in the beginning of this section, left-leaning professors' right to free speech and academic freedom may also be threatened. Yet assuming that their actions are in fact legal and do not call for violence, their university employers would more likely and readily offer support to them than to their right-leaning counterparts. One example concerns a professor's offering of a first-year writing seminar titled "How to Overthrow the State?" at Washington and Lee University. Matt Gildner, the visiting professor of history, explained that the course aimed to place students "at the head of a popular revolutionary movement aiming to overthrow a sitting government and forge a better society," introduce them to the works of famous revolutionaries, and help them become more persuasive writers.[124] Despite its highly provocative title, the

---

121. *See* Connor Ellington, *Public University Fired Professor for Calling Microaggressions Handout Garbage Lawsuit*, College Fix (Apr. 17, 2020), https://www.thecollegefix.com/public-university-fired-professor-for-calling-microaggressions-handout-garbage-lawsuit/ (last visited Oct. 9, 2020).

122. *See, e.g.*, Widmar, 454 U.S. 263; Sweezy, 354 U.S. at 250.

123. Hiers v. Bd. of Regents of Univ. of N. Tex. Sys., Civ. No. 4:20-CV-321-SDJ (E.D. Tex. 2022).

124. Colleen Flaherty, *Washington and Lee Offers Full-Throated Defense of Targeted Professors*, Inside Higher Educ. (Sep. 29, 2020), https://www.insidehighered.com/news/2020/09/29/washington-and-lee-offers-full-throated-defense-targeted-professors

course was not about anarchy and did not advocate violence. Gildner nonetheless received hate voice mails and emails from "patriots," as did a black law professor from the law faculty who was not responsible for the course and who stood with him.[125] Gildner received prompt support from interim provost Elizabeth Goad Oliver who issued a statement with the deans of the university to "unequivocally" condemn the harassment of faculty members who exercised their academic freedom, and to point out that any physical threat due to the content of their teaching or scholarship or the expression of their ideas was a threat to "the very heart" of their "institutional character and mission as educators."[126] The dean of the law school issued his own statement of support for his colleague. The provost's and dean's actions were both proper and timely, given that the course design as well as participation in the course were both exercises of academic freedom and free speech more generally. If the same principles had been adhered to regardless of the political leanings of the professors, there would likely have been fewer disputes and lawsuits on American university campuses.

Example 5

In recent years, a big threat to free speech on American university campuses has been posed by the Chinese government, which has tried, often through coercive measures, to control the discourse on China and suppress views and opinions that it deems harmful to its national sovereignty and image. This threat has assumed an increasingly ominous presence since the passage of the National Security Law in Hong Kong on July 1, 2020. It enables the Chinese government to pursue offenders regardless of their citizenship and the places where they allegedly committed the offenses and, in theory, to put anyone in any part of the world on a fugitive list.[127] In response to the ultraterritorial

125. Hiers v. Bd. of Regents of Univ. of N. Tex. Sys., Civ. No. 4:20-CV-321-SDJ (E.D. Tex. 2022). Colleen Flaherty, *Washington and Lee Offers Full-Throated Defense of Targeted Professors*, Inside Higher Educ. (Sep. 29, 2020), https://www.insidehighered.com/news/2020/09/29/washington-and-lee-offers-full-throated-defense-targeted-professors

126. Hiers v. Bd. of Regents of Univ. of N. Tex. Sys., Civ. No. 4:20-CV-321-SDJ (E.D. Tex. 2022). Colleen Flaherty, *Washington and Lee Offers Full-Throated Defense of Targeted Professors*, Inside Higher Educ. (Sep. 29, 2020), https://www.insidehighered.com/news/2020/09/29/washington-and-lee-offers-full-throated-defense-targeted-professors

127. *E.g.*, Emily Feng, 5 *Takeaways from China's Hong Kong National Security Law*, NPR (Jul. 1, 2020), https://www.npr.org/2020/07/01/885900989/5-takeaways-from-chinas-hong-kong-national-security-law (last visited Aug. 23, 2020).

power claimed by the Chinese government, at least several prestigious American universities took immediate action to implement measures to shield students and faculty, regardless of their national origin, from prosecution by the Chinese authorities. Examples include attaching warning labels to class materials that criticize the Chinese government, allowing students in a Chinese politics class to put codes instead of names on their work, and not penalizing students who do not participate in the discussion of politically sensitive topics.[128]

The National Security Law's far-reaching impacts on campus free speech cannot be denied. The CCP cannot prosecute or jail its critics from all over the world, and Americans who criticize the CCP, instead of starting to obey this "law," can avoid traveling to China. Attaching warning labels to class materials can be viewed as a concession to an authoritarian regime that does not and should not have any place in American academia and might chill expression critical of the CCP—often intellectually honest ones—that can, should, and need to be made in academia without reservation. The aforementioned new participation policy is also not justified: while it may be inhumane to encourage students to discuss politically sensitive topics if participation in such discussions would put their personal safety at risk, policies should be implemented to enable the at-risk students from Hong Kong and China to participate and be assessed (for example, by allowing them to convey their views to their teachers, either in person or anonymously, who can then communicate their views to the class). Certainly, given that free speech is pivotal to self-development and autonomy, openly expressing one's opinions and ideas is integral to this important function. Nonetheless, considering the risks faced by these students, this may already be the best solution.

The looming threat of the Chinese government was not entirely unforeseeable—it was foreshadowed by seemingly minor incidents on American campuses over the past few years. American universities have sometimes reacted aptly and properly to what can now be considered preludes to the CCP's war on American academia. One example was the response of the University of California, San Diego (UCSD) to Chinese students' campaign to deplatform the Dalai Lama, the exiled Tibetan spiritual leader, with the help of the Chinese consulate in Los Angeles, after his invitation to speak at the university's 2017 commencement. The Chinese students accused the Dalai Lama of "separatism"

128. *E.g.*, Lucy Craymer, *China's National-Security Law Reaches into Harvard, Princeton Classrooms*, Wall St. J. (Aug. 19, 2020), https://www.wsj.com/articles/chinas-national-security-law-reaches-into-harvard-princeton-classrooms-11597829402?mod=itp_wsj&yptr=yahoo

and of spreading "provocative and extremely politically hostile discourse" and tainting China's international image, and UCSD of violating "respect, accommodation, equality and earnestness—the founding spirit of the university" and dampening "their passion for learning."[129] UCSD's chancellor, in an open letter, described the Dalai Lama as "a man of peace" who "promotes global responsibility and service to humanity."[130] He added that the university has always been "dedicated to the civil exchange of views" and "served as a forum for discussion and interaction on important public policy issues."[131] Hence, the commencement was "one of many events that provide an appropriate opportunity to present to graduates and their families a message of reflection and compassion."[132]

Protests and campaigns of this sort are typical from Chinese students who remain enslaved by Chinese state propaganda while living in Western democracies, to such an extent that they take criticisms of the Chinese government as personal attacks and exploit Western liberal concepts of equality and tolerance in their attempt to camouflage their own bigotry and suppress other people's rights to free speech and inquiry. UCSD's willingness to stand by its decision and its principles should be applauded. Its stance and message indicated that those who felt triggered by the Dalai Lama's speech had no one but themselves—and, impliedly, the state that indoctrinated them and turned them into bigots—to blame.

UCSD's response not only failed to quell the discontent of the protesters, but further revealed the extent of the power and influence of Chinese state propaganda. A Chinese student at an American high school bemoaned what he considered to be a lack of cultural sensitivity in UCSD's selection of the Dalai Lama, and urged the university to "look outside of American media to make an educated decision on whom to invite."[133] An "educated" decision—which aimed

129. *E.g.*, Elizabeth Redden, *Chinese Students vs. Dalai Lama*, Inside Higher Educ. (Feb. 16, 2017), https://www.insidehighered.com/news/2017/02/16/some-chinese-students-uc-san-diego-condemn-choice-dalai-lama-commencement-speaker

130. Elizabeth Redden, *Chinese Students vs. Dalai Lama*, Inside Higher Educ. (Feb. 16, 2017), https://www.insidehighered.com/news/2017/02/16/some-chinese-students-uc-san-diego-condemn-choice-dalai-lama-commencement-speaker

131. Elizabeth Redden, *Chinese Students vs. Dalai Lama*, Inside Higher Educ. (Feb. 16, 2017), https://www.insidehighered.com/news/2017/02/16/some-chinese-students-uc-san-diego-condemn-choice-dalai-lama-commencement-speaker

132. Elizabeth Redden, *Chinese Students vs. Dalai Lama*, Inside Higher Educ. (Feb. 16, 2017), https://www.insidehighered.com/news/2017/02/16/some-chinese-students-uc-san-diego-condemn-choice-dalai-lama-commencement-speaker

133. Haitong Du, *The Dalai Lama's Commencement Speech Is Problematic for UC San Diego*, Times of San Diego (Jun. 6, 2017), https://timesofsandiego.com/opinion/2017/06/06/opinion-the-dalai-lamas-commencement-speech-is-problematic-for-uc-san-diego/

to appease every attendant of the ceremony—might mean inviting someone who is uninspiring and bland. This advice also dismissed the possibility, or likelihood, that the American media had already provided a fair portrayal of the Dalai Lama, and suggested that the university should accept the falsehoods propagated by China's state media as truths in order to be "culturally sensitive." While an American education at such a young age had failed to liberate the mind of this student, who likely had spent his childhood in China, and to enable him to appreciate facts and opinions diverging from state propaganda, tremendous suffering under the brutal Chinese regime, followed by a long period of exile, proved to be much more enlightening—at least to some. An older writer from China, who served time in a Chinese prison for his political activism before emigrating to America, pointed out that the Dalai Lama was not a separatist as claimed by the Chinese students as he had long abandoned the idea of Tibetan independence and made clarifications about Tibetan history that contradicted the Chinese official narrative.[134] Since the spiritual leader had never expressed disrespect toward China or Chinese citizens, this writer argued, there could be no implied disrespect to the students at UCSD.[135] Indeed, even a more radical position—like calling for Tibetan independence—is no disrespect to students as individuals and such views should never be deplatformed. Regardless, those who most vehemently oppose the Dalai Lama would benefit the most from his speech, if only they are willing to open their minds to hard facts and opinions and views challenging their own.

Example 6

The threat that Chinese nationalism posed to free speech at American universities has become increasingly ominous since 2019, even before the massive pro-democracy protests against both the Chinese and Hong Kong governments broke out in Hong Kong, which garnered sympathy and support from many Western nations. In April, Emerson College student Francis Hui published an article in the student newspaper, entitled "I Am From Hong Kong, Not China," which began with "I am from a city owned by a country that I don't belong

134. Jianli Yang, *UCSD Chinese Should Welcome Dalai Lama, Not Parrot Party-Line*, Times of San Diego (Jun. 11, 2017), https://timesofsandiego.com/opinion/2017/06/11/ucsd-chinese-should-welcome-dalai-lama-not-parrot-party-line/
135. Jianli Yang, *UCSD Chinese Should Welcome Dalai Lama, Not Parrot Party-Line*, Times of San Diego (Jun. 11, 2017), https://timesofsandiego.com/opinion/2017/06/11/ucsd-chinese-should-welcome-dalai-lama-not-parrot-party-line/

to."[136] A group of three Chinese students left messages on Facebook stating that Hui's article was "factually wrong," while signaling "respect" for her freedom of speech and political views.[137] Hui clarified later that she was talking about her sense of her self-identity as a Hongkonger, which was deeply personal to her, without denying that Hong Kong was legally part of China. This, however, did not deter Chinese students from insulting and harassing her. One even left a death threat on her social media platform: "Anyone who offends our China will be executed, no matter how far they are."[138] While Emerson College reassured the public about its deep commitment to "fostering a respectful exchange of diverse viewpoints and perspectives," it reportedly did not take any form of disciplinary action against students who harassed Hui, including the one who issued the death threat.[139]

Sadly, Emerson College's refusal to discipline the Chinese students who harassed and threatened to kill a Hong Kong student for introducing her readers, both Chinese and American, to the distinct cultural differences between Hong Kong and China and "Hongkonger" as a newly evolved ethnic identity indicates that its commitment to foster free speech and respectful dialogue was no more than lip service. Given that conflating Hong Kong with China and mistaking a Hongkonger for a Chinese can feel like an affront to Hongkongers' dignity—something akin to microaggression, especially among those who feel strongly about their ethnicity and identity—Emerson College's inaction in the face of such brute attempts at undermining free discourse may well facilitate the rise of microaggression toward Hongkongers. Such hypocrisy, as the threats show, could be fatal. It also ironically mirrored the hypocrisy of those Chinese students who signaled "respect" for Hui's right to free speech, while trying to not only suppress her speech but also correct her thoughts and feelings by insisting that her article about personal sentiments, identity, and belonging was "factually wrong."

As the pro-democracy protests in Hong Kong were suppressed by government authorities, and Western nations, including the U.S., expressed support

136. *E.g.*, Zhaoyin Feng, *Hong Kong Protests: How Tensions Have Spread to US*, BBC (Jun. 23, 2019), https://www.bbc.com/news/world-us-canada-48721969 (last visited Aug. 30, 2020).

137. Zhaoyin Feng, *Hong Kong Protests: How Tensions Have Spread to US*, BBC (Jun. 23, 2019), https://www.bbc.com/news/world-us-canada-48721969

138. This sentence is taken from an ancient Chinese history book published more than 2,000 years ago. After being featured prominently in a Chinese nationalist action film in 2017, it has been frequently cited by Chinese netizens when they find China under attack.

139. Zhaoyin Feng, *Hong Kong Protests: How Tensions Have Spread to US*, BBC (Jun. 23, 2019), https://www.bbc.com/news/world-us-canada-48721969

for and solidarity with the protesters, Chinese students' coercive, at times violent, measures to protect their beloved motherland's image, "unity," and "sovereignty" escalated. For example, a University of Pennsylvania professor received angry emails from Chinese students who accused him of writing articles in support of the protests and being complicit in "threatening the unity and security of the China."[140] At a Hong Kong event held at Princeton University, a Chinese student flipped his middle finger at a panelist—not for directly criticizing the Chinese or Hong Kong governments, but for making a comment about police brutality against the protesters.[141] At the University of California at Davis, Chinese students urged the administrators to cancel a Hong Kong rally. They also attacked students collecting signatures in support of Hong Kong protesters by grabbing their pro-democracy flag, breaking the pole, and throwing it into the trash.[142] On many campuses, the "Lennon Walls," where people posted artwork and notes expressing solidarity with the protesters, as well as other displays informing the public about the protests, were vandalized or torn down.[143]

While universities acted properly by not canceling the Hong Kong–related rallies and events, they fell short of their duties by refusing to discipline the Chinese students for their misconduct according to their policies. Notwithstanding the saying that one cannot wake up someone who is pretending to be asleep, a good way to discourage such disruptive and violent conduct is to continue the promotion of respectful conversations on these sensitive but important topics while ensuring the safety of all participants.[144] The need for educational and respectful conversations is made more urgent by the parent-child analogy used by a Chinese student at Princeton, who proclaimed his sympathy for Hong Kong protesters, to describe the China–Hong Kong relationship.[145]

140. Jonathan Zimmerman, *My Chinese Students Don't Want You to Talk about Hong Kong. Clearly, We're Failing Them*, USA TODAY (Nov. 13, 2019), https://www.usatoday.com/story/opinion/voices/2019/11/13/chinese-international-students-college-education-hong-kong-column/2575189001/

141. Rory Truex, *Colleges Should All Stand Up to China*, ATLANTIC (Dec. 28, 2019), https://www.theatlantic.com/ideas/archive/2019/12/how-defend-campus-free-speech-china/604045/

142. Jonathan Zimmerman, *My Chinese Students Don't Want You to Talk about Hong Kong. Clearly, We're Failing Them*, USA TODAY (Nov. 13, 2019), https://www.usatoday.com/story/opinion/voices/2019/11/13/chinese-international-students-college-education-hong-kong-column/2575189001/

143. Emma Goldberg, *Hong Kong Protests Spread to U.S. Colleges, and a Rift Grows*, N.Y. TIMES (Oct. 26, 2019), https://www.nytimes.com/2019/10/26/us/hong-kong-protests-colleges.html

144. *See, e.g.*, Rory Truex, *Colleges Should All Stand Up to China*, ATLANTIC (Dec. 28, 2019), https://www.theatlantic.com/ideas/archive/2019/12/how-defend-campus-free-speech-china/604045/

145. Emma Goldberg, *Hong Kong Protests Spread to U.S. Colleges, and a Rift Grows*, N.Y. TIMES (Oct. 26, 2019), https://www.nytimes.com/2019/10/26/us/hong-kong-protests-colleges.html. "It's like the mainland is the conventional Asian parent who thinks everything must be controlled and dictated by

Underlying this analogy is the Chinese government's official narrative that Hong Kong is historically part of China and must remain so—a restrictive worldview leaving no room for other possibilities that better preserve Hong-kongers' basic liberties and help China maintain peaceful relations, such as Hong Kong becoming fully autonomous, or even independent from this authoritarian regime. That this analogy came from an avowedly sympathetic Chinese student at one of the nation's top universities testified to the extent of state indoctrination among young, liberal-minded Chinese.

American universities have, in some cases, done remarkably well in safe-guarding free speech on their campuses by fighting against illiberal acts by Americans. They have no excuse at all for surrendering to a hostile foreign government and nationalistic-fevered Chinese immigrants or students. The need to protect free speech has become even more urgent despite—and because of—the passage of the National Security Law in Hong Kong, which is a testimony to China's ambition to extend its authoritarian control beyond its borders. Any sign of indifference or complacency would play into the hands of the Chinese Communist Party, its agents, and supporters, who likely will continue to use death threats and other coercive methods to undermine free speech on American campuses.

Example 7

Undoubtedly, just as Western ideas of tolerance and equality were exploited by the protesters at UCSD, other liberal concepts, freedom of speech included, may also get abused by the manipulative. Terminating the employment of people who abuse their rights to free speech does not trample upon their free speech and academic freedom, but rather serves to advance these freedoms and preserve the sanctity of academia. This last section will look at two notable but hitherto unexamined cases, in which university employees who came from China apparently abused their freedom of expression to undermine the same freedoms of their colleagues and camouflage what appeared to be unprofessional and abusive conduct. In the first case, the person whose speech right was under attack acted properly by standing up for herself and not caving in to the abusive conduct of the Chinese librarian. In the second case, the university

the parent's rules," Mr. Zou said. "Hong Kong is like the rebellious punk kid who ran away from home. Now Hong Kong has matured and it's this nightmare scenario for a mature adult state to be forced to live with its parents."

acted rightly and honorably by terminating the employment of the Chinese professor who seemingly attempted to hide what appeared to be unprofessionalism and misconduct behind her allegations of racism.

The first case concerns Ye Xu, a librarian at the University of Wisconsin at Madison, who sued her university, alleging that its administrators discriminated against her because of her race and national origin.[146] A naturalized U.S. citizen originally from China, she forwarded to her supervisor a student's request that the Taiwan Nichinichi Shinpo database be listed under a "Specific Databases—Taiwan" heading, and explained that her decision to list the database under a "China" heading was based on the 1979 "Joint Communique of the United States of America and the People's Republic of China" and United Nations General Assembly Resolution 2758.[147] The supervisor decided to accept the student's request to list the database under the heading of "Specific Databases—Taiwan," as well as the China and Japan headings, in order to increase its accessibility for students. When technological limitations forced the supervisor to choose Taiwan only, Xu argued that the library was making a political gesture by disregarding the United Nations' "One China" policy and essentially recognizing Taiwan as its own country separate from China.[148]

The two parties offered different versions of the dispute that followed. In the supervisor's version, Xu "became very angry during the meeting, stood up when speaking, raised her voice, and interrupted" the supervisor as she tried to explain her decision-making process.[149] According to Xu, the supervisor shouted to her: "This is not a discussion! I already made the decision! You don't have to do it! I'll do it! I'll talk to the [Taiwanese] student!"[150] When Xu tried to leave the meeting, the supervisor ordered her to sit down and accused her of insubordination. However, the supervisor denied that she ever yelled at Xu, saying "You are unprofessional! You just serve your country!" as Xu claimed she did.[151] Although Xu later produced a letter from her physician stating that she

146. Ye Xu v. Bd. Regents of the Univ. Wis. Sys. No. 16-cv-510-jdp. (2018), https://www.leagle.com/decision/infdco20180123h95 (last visited Sep. 7, 2020).
147. Ye Xu v. Bd. Regents of the Univ. Wis. Sys. No. 16-cv-510-jdp. (2018), https://www.leagle.com/decision/infdco20180123h95 (last visited Sep. 7, 2020).
148. Ye Xu v. Bd. Regents of the Univ. Wis. Sys. No. 16-cv-510-jdp. (2018), https://www.leagle.com/decision/infdco20180123h95 (last visited Sep. 7, 2020).
149. Ye Xu v. Bd. Regents of the Univ. Wis. Sys. No. 16-cv-510-jdp. (2018), https://www.leagle.com/decision/infdco20180123h95 (last visited Sep. 7, 2020).
150. Ye Xu v. Bd. Regents of the Univ. Wis. Sys. No. 16-cv-510-jdp. (2018), https://www.leagle.com/decision/infdco20180123h95 (last visited Sep. 7, 2020).
151. Ye Xu v. Bd. Regents of the Univ. Wis. Sys. No. 16-cv-510-jdp. (2018), https://www.leagle.com/decision/infdco20180123h95 (last visited Sep. 7, 2020).

suffered from stress and high blood pressure due to the conflict, and requested a new supervisor or other accommodation, the university decided that there was not enough information to warrant a change. Despite a series of difficult meetings and correspondence that ensued, Xu continued working as a librarian and suffered no loss in pay, benefits, job duties, or education or travel opportunities.

Xu nonetheless filed a formal complaint with the United States Equal Opportunity Commission on March 11, 2016. After the commission issued her a right-to-sue letter in April 2016, she brought Title VII claims against the university for disparate treatment, retaliation, and a hostile work environment, contending that the workplace conflicts following the dispute about the library catalogue were a manifestation of discrimination against her because she was born in China.[152] The U.S. District Court, Western District of Wisconsin granted the university's motion for summary judgment, on the grounds that no reasonable jury could conclude on the evidence that library administrators discriminated against her or subjected her to a hostile work environment.[153]

The soundness of the court's ruling on this discrimination suit nonetheless is not the focus of this section. It is noteworthy that the decision to put the database under the "Taiwan" heading, though undertaken for convenience of access purposes, can be considered an exercise of First Amendment free speech rights (as would an expressed agreement with the UN's "One China policy" and China's official narrative). Any attempt by Xu to overrule her supervisor's decision—not least a decision by her superior in the workplace who had the final say on the matter—can be considered an attempt to suppress her fundamental rights. Should the state university have obliged the supervisor to follow Xu's advice, she could have taken the case to court, which accordingly would have held the university's action unconstitutional. Fortunately, the university did not do so. One cannot help but be amused by the zealous attempt to impose a "One China" nationalistic worldview on other people by an immigrant who voluntarily gave up her Chinese citizenship to become an American citizen, her anger when other people do not capitulate to this unreasonable imposition, and her use of race to camouflage such abusive conduct and lack of professionalism. It would have been insensitive for Xu's supervisor to accuse Xu of working not

152. Ye Xu v. Bd. Regents of the Univ. Wis. Sys. No. 16-cv-510-jdp. (2018), https://www.leagle.com/decision/infdco20180123h95 (last visited Sep. 7, 2020).
153. Ye Xu v. Bd. Regents of the Univ. Wis. Sys. No. 16-cv-510-jdp. (2018), https://www.leagle.com/decision/infdco20180123h95 (last visited Sep. 7, 2020).

for America but for her country of origin (and perhaps insinuating that she was a spy). At the same time, she had every reason to feel concerned about a naturalized American subordinate's attempt to undermine her judgment and overrule her decision on the grounds that it might offend the U.N.—a political organization—and ultimately China, a notorious authoritarian government.

The second case about university employees seemingly exploiting Western liberal ideologies of free speech and racial equality to camouflage what appeared to be unprofessionalism and potentially undermine other people's right to free expression involves a professor, also from China, at Macalester College in Minnesota. As Wang Ping, an English professor, began teaching a new poetry course in the spring semester of 2019, she reached out to members of a Macalester student group called Proud Indigenous People for Education, asking them to participate in a semester-long drum-making activity led by a Native American elder.[154] An Indigenous student responded that the inclusion of Indigenous cultural practices in the course was "highly inappropriate" and accused Wang of using racist language.[155] Agreeing to leave the problematic parts out of her syllabus, Wang showed parts of the email exchange to students in her poetry class, and expressed frustration that her syllabus had been shared with students outside of the class. The class atmosphere turned toxic enough that some students reached out to administration officials and other faculty with concerns about the classroom environment.[156]

As the investigation into the matter continued, further questions were raised about Wang's professional conduct, including her handling of student privacy issues, her actions and comments in relation to a faculty search for a new creative writing professor, and her alleged favoritism. She was accused of violating her students' privacy by forwarding emails from the Indigenous stu-

154. Margaret Moran & Abe Asher, *Professor Wang Ping to Depart Macalester at Year's End*, MacWeekly (Nov. 14, 2019), https://themacweekly.com/77048/news/professor-ping-wang-to-depart-macalester-at-years-end/ (last visited Sep. 10, 2020); Margaret Moran & Abe Asher, *Professor Wang Ping and Macalester Embroiled in Legal Battle*, MacWeekly (Sep. 13, 2019), https://themacweekly.com/76468/news/professor-wang-ping-and-macalester-embroiled-in-legal-battle-2/ (last visited Sep. 10, 2020).

155. Margaret Moran & Abe Asher, *Professor Wang Ping to Depart Macalester at Year's End*, MacWeekly (Nov. 14, 2019), https://themacweekly.com/77048/news/professor-ping-wang-to-depart-macalester-at-years-end/ (last visited Sep. 10, 2020); Margaret Moran & Abe Asher, *Professor Wang Ping and Macalester Embroiled in Legal Battle*, MacWeekly (Sep. 13, 2019), https://themacweekly.com/76468/news/professor-wang-ping-and-macalester-embroiled-in-legal-battle-2/ (last visited Sep. 10, 2020).

156. Margaret Moran & Abe Asher, *Professor Wang Ping to Depart Macalester at Year's End*, MacWeekly (Nov. 14, 2019), https://themacweekly.com/77048/news/professor-ping-wang-to-depart-macalester-at-years-end/ (last visited Sep. 10, 2020); Margaret Moran & Abe Asher, *Professor Wang Ping and Macalester Embroiled in Legal Battle*, MacWeekly (Sep. 13, 2019), https://themacweekly.com/76468/news/professor-wang-ping-and-macalester-embroiled-in-legal-battle-2/ (last visited Sep. 10, 2020).

dent group to her class and by uploading her course evaluations to an online petition with students' names attached.[157] Her disclosure of the details about the faculty search to the students and her admission that she voted for a candidate on the basis of race also led to accusations of racial discrimination by the administration.[158] Above all, she allegedly fostered a hostile classroom environment in her poetry class by stifling free discussion and by favoring certain students over others, depending on whether they had been loyal to her in her conflict with the administration.[159]

In late March, Wang went before Macalester's Faculty Personnel Committee, the body responsible for investigating faculty misconduct, which recommended that the university and Wang end their relationship. Although both parties wanted to resolve it through mediation during the summer and fall of 2019, they could not agree to the terms of negotiation. In June, Wang filed a discrimination charge with the Equal Employment Opportunity Commission, while the Minnesota chapter of the American Association of University Professors sent a letter of support to her in July, as well as a letter detailing its position on the matter to the university administration. In November 2019, Wang finally reached an agreement with Macalester, where she had been teaching for two decades, according to which her employment would terminate in fall 2020. Initially planning to teach until 2022, she therefore had to depart two years before her planned retirement date.

Based on the reports in Macalester's official newspaper, it is fair to say that

---

157. Wang managed to mobilize a group of zealous supporters to set up an online petition to defend her and urge Macalester College to renew her employment contract and respect her academic freedom, which they believed had been violated by the university. *See* https://www.change.org/p/macalester-trustee-chair-macalester-must-respect-academic-freedom-renew-dr-wang-s-contract-stop-discrimination?redirect=false (last visited Sep. 10, 2020).

158. According to one student, Wang said in her poetry class that she would refuse to consider a Native American candidate for the open position in the aftermath of the controversy over Native course content. Another student, however, denied that Wang had ever said it. When the rest of the search committee decided to hire a non–Native American candidate, Wang consented initially, but later recanted her consent and instead advocated for a Native candidate, emphasizing that she wanted to create a record of her support for a Native candidate to defend herself against the allegations of bias. Margaret Moran & Abe Asher, *Professor Wang Ping and Macalester Embroiled in Legal Battle*, MACWEEKLY (Sep. 13, 2019), https://themacweekly.com/76468/news/professor-wang-ping-and-macalester-embroiled-in-legal-battle-2/ (last visited Sep. 10, 2020).

159. For example, after Wang made public her conflict with the administration and allegedly intruded upon the privacy of her students, those in her poetry class expressed a reluctance to ask her questions in class or send her emails, fearing that she might either forward their emails to others or single them out in the classroom. One student felt that Wang's relationships with certain students were "tantamount to emotional manipulation." Margaret Moran & Abe Asher, *Professor Wang Ping and Macalester Embroiled in Legal Battle*, MACWEEKLY (Sep. 13, 2019), https://themacweekly.com/76468/news/professor-wang-ping-and-macalester-embroiled-in-legal-battle-2/ (last visited Sep. 10, 2020).

Wang's conduct apparently was unprofessional and outrageous enough to warrant the investigation and subsequent disciplinary action. Hence, whether or not the university administrators had secretly harbored biases against her because of her race or national origin did not truly matter.[160] If she could not find an Indigenous person to coteach her class or advise her on materials with which she was not familiar and was not qualified to teach, all she needed to do was to omit the materials from her syllabus, apologize profusely and sincerely to offended students, and let the initial dispute deescalate and fade out. Instead, her unprofessionalism, namely, getting her students involved in the conflict and disclosing confidential details of the job search to them, enabled what seemed a minor dispute to spiral out of control. While she probably would argue that it was within her rights to free speech and academic freedom to design her syllabus, by involving the students in her disputes with the Indigenous students and the university administration, she essentially undermined the very same freedoms of the students, who felt intimidated and reluctant to speak in her class. It is beyond the scope of this chapter to examine whether Wang had been discriminated against by the university administration previously. Her online petition site indicated that she, and her supporters, believed that the school used the misconduct claims and disciplinary action as a pretext for their continued discrimination against her on the grounds of sex, race, and national origin and their retaliation against her for standing up to discrimination in the past.[161] Assuming the truthfulness of Macalester's reports, however, one has good reason to suspect that her claims of discriminatory treatment by the university functioned more like a mask to hide her own misconduct and lack of professionalism.

---

160. Before this incident, Wang had repeatedly clashed with the university administration. In 2003, she claimed that the English Department has promoted underqualified white, male professors ahead of her, when she sought an early promotion to the rank of associate professor. In 2009, she made the same claim as she sought promotion to the rank of full professor. In 2011, after experiencing what she deemed retaliation from the college in the form of research funding cuts, she filed a discrimination charge with the Equal Employment Opportunity Commission, which, after completing its investigation in 2012, dismissed that charge. In response, Wang sued Macalester for lost earnings and emotional distress based on allegedly discriminatory practices on the grounds of sex, race, and national origin. The suit was resolved by mediation, and Wang resumed teaching at Macalester. Margaret Moran & Abe Asher, *Professor Wang Ping and Macalester Embroiled in Legal Battle*, MacWeekly (Sep. 13, 2019), https://themacweekly.com/76468/news/professor-wang-ping-and-macalester-embroiled-in-legal-battle-2/ (last visited Sep. 10, 2020).

161. *See* "Macalester Must Respect Academic Freedom, Renew Dr. Wang's Contract & Stop Discrimination!," petition on Change.org website, https://www.change.org/p/macalester-trustee-chair-macalester-must-respect-academic-freedom-r.enew-dr-wang-s-contract-stop-discrimination?redirect=false (last visited Sep. 10, 2020).

The author has no basis for judging whether Wang fostered a hostile classroom atmosphere and was even "emotionally manipulative," as the reports and some students claimed.[162] Yet on Wang's Facebook account, which she chose to make public and which still bears her title as (emeritus) professor at Macalester College, she showed how she was often prone to be driven by ideologies and emotions to the extent that she dismissed plain facts and evidence countering her beliefs and violated codes of decorum to those presenting those facts and evidence. One example was found in April 2020, when she called a netizen "an idiot" on Facebook for attempting to refute her argument that the Chinese government offered generous and timely assistance to Western nations plagued by COVID-19 by referring her to reliable news showing that China sold defective products to those nations.[163] Another example, also found in early April, found her accusing the same netizen of separating Hong Kong from China and of embracing colonialism, when all that netizen did was state that Cantonese has a written form and suggest that it is a language rather than a dialect—a view supported by major research and held by qualified linguists.[164] Elsewhere, she insinuated that Hong Kong pro-democracy activists, the majority of whom have engaged only in peaceful protests against an authoritarian government, had "organized riots."[165]

On Wang's Twitter account, also made public, she seemingly endorsed (by "liking") the opinions of China's infamous Foreign Ministry director and spokesperson Hua Chunying, including Hua's views that Hongkongers have enjoyed more prosperity and liberties as well as a better legal system after the handover of Hong Kong to China than during the British colonial period, and

162. *E.g.*, "Macalester Must Respect Academic Freedom, Renew Dr. Wang's Contract & Stop Discrimination!," petition on Change.org website, https://www.change.org/p/macalester-trustee-chair-macalester-must-respect-academic-freedom-renew-dr-wang-s-contract-stop-discrimination?redirect=false (last visited Sep. 10, 2020); Steven Johnson, *An Escalating Tenure Fight Catches Students in the Crossfire*, Chronicle of Higher Educ. (Aug. 7, 2019), https://www.chronicle.com/article/an-escalating-tenure-fight-catches-students-in-the-crossfire/

163. *See* https://ibb.co/4F7Fv1w, which shows a screenshot of Wang's Facebook post calling the netizen an "idiot" and requesting him/her to "get out": "Don't infect [*sic*: infest] my house!"

164. *See* https://ibb.co/0hgksvd, which shows a screenshot of another Facebook post of hers accusing the netizen of "separating HK from China" and spreading misinformation. Wang, who has never received formal training in linguistics, was dead wrong, as Cantonese and Mandarin are not mutually intelligible and their differences are far greater than those between, for instance, Spanish and Portuguese.

165. *See* https://ibb.co/42FFrWb, for the screenshot. Wang expressed disappointment that many people in Taiwan, Hong Kong, and Southeast Asian countries supported Donald Trump in the 2020 U.S. presidential election. Indeed, many pro-democracy activists believed that Trump, and not Joe Biden, would sanction China.

Hongkongers' resistance to the CCP and plea for help to Western nations when their rights were violated by Beijing was a plain betrayal of their "ancestry" and "motherland."[166] A Twitter post of hers further revealed her belief, founded upon her highly twisted logic, questionable data, and perhaps nationalistic fever, that Hong Kong would do better if it was governed by the principle of "One Country, One System," under which its governance would be subsumed under the CCP in both name and substance, than the "One Country, Two Systems" principle as agreed upon by both China and Britain in the 1984 Sino-British Joint Declaration, which grants a high degree of autonomy to the territory.[167] One must note, however, that Wang has never lived in Hong Kong, both before and after the 1997 handover, or received any formal training in linguistics or in law.

Undoubtedly, professors enjoy freedom of thought and are entitled to their opinions and judgments, no matter how warped or erroneous. Hence, Wang is entitled to embrace the views of the CCP's disreputable spokesperson, dismiss the expert opinion that Cantonese is a language, and condemn the Hong Kong pro-democracy movement (just as people are entitled to believe that a Hongkonger should surrender to—and perhaps cooperate with—a rapist who happens to be Chinese, that resisting rape is "riotous," and that seeking help from a Westerner betrays their so-called ancestry and reveals their colonialist mindset). Yet her support of the tyrannical government and its officials by no means justified or excused her uncivil behavior, as in calling people with whom she

---

166. *See* https://ibb.co/FY98bKG, for the screenshot showing Wang's twitter "likes" and tacit approval of the disreputable Hua Chunying's ill-informed twitter posts about Hong Kong.

167. *See* https://ibb.co/BCgNdmF, which contains a screenshot of her post: "There's freedom to live with die—100,000 deaths in USA in 3 months. There's freedom to live with dignity—like this 87-year-old man surviving corona virus, under the care of doctors and nurses in Wuhan. Which freedom does HK want? Please watch & think." The post betrays the nationalistic-fevered and ideologically driven mindset and simplistic worldview of its author, according to whom China enjoys an excellent medical system enabling its patients to live with dignity, whereas democratic governance in the U.S. only led to chaos and deaths during the pandemic. Hence, the post implies, Hong Kong would be better off if governed by the Chinese system than by a liberal system that grants them freedoms. The post blatantly ignores the third possibility: that people can make good use of, rather than abuse, their freedoms. In fact, one may attribute the low number of COVID-19 cases in Hong Kong, despite its high population density, not to any governmental policies, but to the fact that its people took safety precautions deferentially and generally did not trust the figures published by the CCP or the allegedly CCP-corrupted World Health Organization. Ironically, Wang chose to leave her beloved motherland for chaotic and deadly America, where she has been living for three decades. The gross inconsistencies between her and many of her compatriots' words and actions, as well as the fact that Wang had been allowed to sing the praises of the CCP in Western academia, enjoy benefits as an American resident, and file complaint after complaint about her American colleagues, are nothing short of baffling and reveal the tolerance of Americans and not the opposite.

did not agree "idiots," whether she is speaking in the capacity of a professor or as a fellow human being, especially when their opinions are based on facts, well-reasoned arguments, and expert opinions (this is no less uncivil and unjustifiable than attaching the "idiots" label to people who present facts, evidence, and expert testimonies showing that a virtue- and peace-touting neighbor is in fact a serial rapist, or who believe that human beings should resist serial rapists by seeking help from powerful allies). Her readiness to accuse people who consider Cantonese a language of separatism (a crime punishable by death in China) and of embracing colonialism similarly indicates that she is prone to be emotionally and ideologically driven at least when it comes to certain political topics. To be fair, Wang might have acted with civility to her students. However, similarly uncivil, emotionally and ideologically driven conduct, if exhibited in class, would chill free speech or dampen any motivation for respectful dialogue. Tendencies to allow emotions and ideologies to override reason may be excusable among passionate budding academics with no more than a few years of experience, but inexcusable for seasoned academics who have been teaching for decades and who take pride in and regularly showcase their accomplishments. Freedom of speech and respectful dialogue aside, one should ask whether experienced teachers who are intellectually dishonest enough to dismiss all facts and arguments countering their ideologies and beliefs, and who tout themselves as human rights advocates and express solidarity with the oppressed—except those oppressed by governments they embrace—truly deserve the "academic" or "intellectual" title.

Macalester College acted rightly and honorably in terminating Wang's employment. Sympathy for the disgraced professor is understandable, considering her cries of white supremacy and racial discrimination during the dispute and long after her departure.[168] It is also not at all surprising that university hiring committees, who might only form rather superficial impressions of job candidates at interviews, can make grave mistakes by hiring well-credentialed people who later violate codes of conduct and decorum. After all, many highly educated, self-proclaimed human rights advocates may leave overly positive impressions of virtuousness and uprightness even though their passion for human rights goes no further than pure virtue-signaling. One can only wonder why Wang, patriotic and nationalistic as she seems, chose to stay in the U.S. for three decades, where she decries the freedoms that it offers while continuing to

168. See, again, her Facebook platform and online petition.

embrace the authoritarian government of her beloved motherland. One also cannot help but notice the hypocrisy in her mockery of Hongkongers for fighting for the same freedoms that she has enjoyed for decades and suppression of the expressions of those who contradicted her views. She—and people like her—may believe that they play an important role in fighting white supremacy in America. Yet Macalester College—and academia more generally—likely has little to gain from academics like her who appear to be driven by their ideologies, beliefs, and emotions to the degree that they ignore plain facts, expert opinions, and alternative views, and who seemingly exploit liberal concepts of free speech and diversity to undermine other people's freedoms and cover up what seem, according to official reports, to be their own unprofessionalism and lack of decorum.

• • •

Safeguarding free speech in academia can, and should, go hand in hand with fostering an environment free of racism and discrimination. Open-access reports and evidence indicate that by terminating Wang's employment, Macalester did not undermine her free speech or academic freedom. It rather helped to safeguard the foundational values of the university and promote respectful classroom environments. This proper and courageous move played a small but important part in "draining the swamp" of academia. It should also inspire its peers to safeguard free speech and promote respectful dialogue and not allow the ideologies of diversity and equality to play into the hands of authoritarian people or governments—both in the U.S. and abroad—which would lead to the demise of the university as an institution that values free speech and academic freedom.

CHAPTER NINE

Canada

The (Ir)relevance of the Charter to Campus Speech

Freedom of expression is recognized as fundamental to Canadian democracy, protected by section 2(b) of the Canadian Charter of Rights and Freedoms, and subjected to laws on hate speech and harassment. Whether section 2(b) also applies in university settings, however, remains uncertain. For the most part, Canadian courts have affirmed the autonomy of postsecondary institutions, and overturned universities' decisions on free speech issues only when they found the decisions highly unreasonable or unfair. Due to courts' deference toward university administrations, universities have long implemented their own speech policies. Despite numerous campus free speech controversies, there has been no consensus on whether a free speech crisis even exists in Canadian universities.

This chapter will critically examine numerous attacks on free speech on Canadian university campuses. Certainly, even on liberal campuses, speakers with conservative or right-of-center views were not the only ones who have ignited criticism and sparked protests. Nonetheless, attempts to shut down speakers advancing liberal ideologies have been extremely rare. Any protests targeting speakers with left-of-center views have also been very peaceful, hence a far cry from the massive, disruptive, and not infrequently violent protests aimed to deplatform conservative speakers, as well as speakers who dared to challenge the left-wing ideologies upheld by Canada's Liberal government and dominating many universities. The latter, which happened across different campuses, will be the focus of this analysis.

The recent years have seen a surge in attempts to harass, threaten, and shut down critics of the Chinese government. The inaction and complacency of Canadian universities have played into the hands of nationalistic Chinese students, as well as the Chinese embassy that backed their criminal behavior, which habitually pulls the race card and appropriates Western liberal narratives of free speech, tolerance, and dignity to suppress meaningful discussions on China-related topics. If "every man has his price,"[1] university administrators and educators must strive to raise theirs. They must not surrender to the tyranny of a foreign government, or trade their long-standing missions, democratic values, and national sovereignty for money and a fake harmony that (seemingly) aligns with their multiculturalism and diversity initiatives.

I. *The Charter Right to Freedom of Expression and Its (Ir)relevance to Campus Free Speech*

Freedom of expression is recognized as fundamental to Canadian democracy.[2] Section 2(b) of the Canadian Charter of Rights and Freedoms (1982) ("the Charter"), which applies to both the federal and provincial governments, provides for the fundamental freedoms of "thought, belief, opinion and expression, including freedom of the press and other media of communication."[3] Other related freedoms in section 2 include "freedom of conscience and religion," "freedom of peaceful assembly," and "freedom of association."[4] These fundamental freedoms are subject "to such reasonable limits prescribed by law as can be demonstrably justified in a free and democratic society."[5] Parliament or a provincial legislature may also adopt legislation "notwithstanding" the protections of section 2 by making an express declaration that its action complies with section 1.[6]

---

1. *See* Robert Bolt, A Man for All Seasons, Act 1 (a statement by character Richard Rich, who serves as a foil to Thomas More) (1954, 1957).
2. Peter Greenawalt, *Free Speech in the United States and Canada*, 55 L. & Contemp. Probs. 1, 5 (1992).
3. Can. Charter of Rts. & Freedoms, s 2(b), Part I of Const. Act, 1982, Schedule B to the Can. Act 1982 (U.K.), 1982, c. 11.
4. Can. Charter of Rts. & Freedoms, s. 2(a)(c)(d).
5. Can. Charter of Rts. & Freedoms, s. 1. According to the two-prong approach established in *R. v. Oakes*, the state's objective must be of "pressing and substantial concern in a free and democratic society," and the impugned measure must meet a proportionality test. R v. Oakes [1986] 24 C.C.C. (3d) 321, 348 (S.C.C.).
6. Can. Charter of Rts. & Freedoms, s. 1, s. 33(1). Although s. 33 in theory authorizes direct legislative overrides of Charter rights, Parliament has never invoked this power, while provincial legislatures

The Canadian Constitution and free speech tradition originated from the English common law, which is not particularly sympathetic to free speech claimants.[7] Section 2(b) of the Charter therefore brought fundamental changes to Canada's constitutional landscape regarding freedom of expression.[8] The influences of natural law are apparent in both the Charter and the decisions of the Supreme Court of Canada (SCC). The preamble of the Charter states that "Canada is founded upon principles that recognize the supremacy of God and the rule of law."[9] The SCC has justified the protection of freedom of expression by calling it an essential component of democratic self-government, which aligns with Locke's and Rawls's writings described in chapter 4.[10] Its endorsement of "the pursuit of truth," "self-fulfillment and human flourishing" as important social values that justify the protection of freedom of expression[11] are also reminiscent of Locke and Kant. Further, it has described freedom of expression as "the matrix, the indispensable condition of nearly every other freedom."[12] Expressive activities constituting speech are "infinite in variety," including "the written or spoken word, the arts, and even physical gestures or acts"; "all expressions of the heart and mind, however unpopular, distasteful or contrary to the mainstream" are deserving of Charter protection.[13]

Hate speech has been prohibited in Canada in both the pre- and post-Charter eras. As chapter 5 has explained, some hate speech laws intend to protect public order, while others aim also to safeguard human dignity. Arguably, hate speech laws in Canada, as vague and broad as they may seem, aim to protect primarily the former. Its criminal law has prohibited hate speech for five decades.[14] At present, section 319(1) and (2) of the Criminal Code prohibits the

---

have been reluctant to override Charter rights. RONALD J. KROTOSZYNSKI, JR., THE FIRST AMENDMENT IN CROSS-CULTURAL PERSPECTIVE: A COMPARATIVE LEGAL ANALYSIS OF THE FREEDOM OF SPEECH 38 (2006).

7. Kent Roach & David Schneiderman, *Freedom of Expression in Canada*, 61 S. CT. L. REV. 429, 431–32 (2013).

8. Kent Roach & David Schneiderman, *Freedom of Expression in Canada*, 61 S. CT. L. REV. 429, 429 (2013).

9. Can. Charter of Rts. & Freedoms, Preamble.

10. In *Dolphin Delivery Ltd. v. R.W.D.S.U., Local 580*, Justice McIntyre, writing for the majority, held that "[r]epresentative democracy . . . which is in great part the product of free expression and discussion of varying ideas, depends upon its maintenance and protection." "The principle of freedom of speech and expression has been firmly accepted as a necessary feature of modern democracy." [1986] 33 D.L.R. (4th) 174, 176 (S.C.C.).

11. Irwin Toy Ltd. v. Quebec (Attorney General) [1989] 25 C.P.R. (3d) 417, 452 (S.C.C.).

12. R. v. Sharpe [2001] 150 C.C.C. (3d) 321, 342 (S.C.C.).

13. *Irwin Toy Ltd.*, 25 C.P.R. (3d) at 446.

14. Kent Roach & David Schneiderman, *Freedom of Expression in Canada*, 61 S. CT. L. REV. 429, 462 (2013).

communication of statements in public that "incites hatred against any identifiable group where such incitement is likely to lead to a breach of the peace," and that "wilfully promotes hatred against any identifiable group."[15] In addition, the Charter states that its provisions, including section 2(b), "shall be interpreted in a manner consistent with the preservation and enhancement of the multicultural heritage of Canadians."[16] The SCC ruled that the Charter's guarantee of freedom of expression does not extend to "the public and willful promotion of hatred against an identifiable group."[17] While repealing the section of the Canadian Human Rights Act prohibiting "hate messages," it reiterated support for prohibitions on hate speech in provincial human rights codes if it leads to discriminatory effects on minorities.[18] Nonetheless, the deliberate publication of statements that the speaker knows to be false and that might excite prejudices against minorities or offend their dignity is a protected form of expression under section 2(b): "[I]f there is any principle of the Constitution that more imperatively calls for attachment than any other it is the principle of free thought—not free for those who agree with us but freedom for the thought that we hate."[19]

Indeed, expressions alone can constitute discrimination under the federal Human Rights Act of Canada and provincial human rights laws, which prohibit discrimination in work, employment, and commercial settings on the basis of race, national or ethnic origin, color, religion, age, sex, sexual orientation, gender identity or expression, marital status, disability, and others.[20] Thus, Canadian courts and human rights tribunals have found that expressions such as race-based jokes and jokes targeting disabled people constituted discrimina-

15. Crim. Code, S.C. 1985, c C-46, s. 319 (1) & (2).
16. Can. Charter, s. 27.
17. R. v. Keegstra [1990] 61 C.C.C. (3d) 1, 3, 5 (S.C.C.).
18. In *Canada (Human Rights Commission) v. Taylor*, Justice Robert Dickson defined "hatred" for the purposes of human rights legislation to refer to "unusually strong and deep-felt emotions of detestation, calumny, and vilification" [1990] 75 D.L.R. (4th) 577, 601 (S.C.C.). He defended speech restriction in the Canadian Human Rights Act by emphasizing the discriminatory effects of hate speech on minorities. See page 609. In *Saskatchewan (Human Rights Commission) v. Whatcott*, Justice Marshall Rothstein reaffirmed each of the principal holdings of the Saskatchewan human rights tribunal and Justice Dickson's majority opinion in *Taylor*. The *Whatcott* decision found that the hate speech provision in the Saskatchewan Human Rights Code minimally impaired the impugned right to freedom of expression, but severed the words "ridicules, belittles or otherwise affronts the dignity of" from the Code on the grounds that they were not rationally connected to the objective of reducing systemic discrimination. [2013] 355 D.L.R. (4th) 383, 414–16 (S.C.C.).
19. *R. v. Zundel* [1992] 75 C.C.C. (3d) 449, 507 (S.C.C.); *see also* Whatcott, [2013] 355 D.L.R. (4th) at 414–16.
20. Can. Hum. Rts. Act, R.S.C., 1985, c. H-6, s. 3(1); *e.g.*, Sask. Hum. Rts. Code, 2018, c. S-24.2; Alta. Hum. Rts. Act, 2018, c. A-25.5.

tion, on the grounds that they created a poisoned environment and harmed the disabled.[21] Similarly, words alone may constitute criminal harassment under the Criminal Code if they cause recipients to fear for their safety or the safety of anyone known to them.[22] Expressions made in various settings may also amount to a discriminatory form of harassment under the Human Rights Act and provincial human rights laws if they are threatening, intimidating, or humiliating.[23] Hence, a court found that degrading and sexualized online commentaries targeted toward an individual constituted criminal harassment.[24] Racial and sexual insults in employment settings have been commonly found to constitute discriminatory harassment.[25]

Canadian laws prohibiting hate speech and different forms of harassment apply to universities in Canada. It remains unclear, however, whether section 2(b) of the Charter safeguarding freedom of expression also applies in the university setting so that university administrators are obligated to uphold this Charter right as well as other rights and freedoms in their decisions.[26] Section 32(1) of the Charter says that it applies to the "government of Canada" and the "government of each province."[27] Courts have debated what "government" means for the purposes of Charter application. The SCC in *McKinney v. University of Guelph* suggested that universities are not "government" by arguing that they are "legally autonomous" and "not organs of government even though their scope of action is limited either by regulation or because of their dependence on government funds."[28] The SCC apparently expanded the scope of "government" in *Eldridge v. British Columbia (Attorney General)* to include an entity that was "putting into place a government program or acting in a governmental capacity."[29] In *Doré v. Barreau du Québec* and *Loyola High School v. Quebec (Attorney General)*, the SCC further suggested that administrative actors

21. Chiswell v. Valdi Foods 1987 Inc. [1994] 25 C.H.R.R. D/400 (Ont. Bd. Inq.); Morgan Lowrie, *Comedian Mike Ward Loses Quebec Appeal over Penalty for Joke about Disabled Boy*, GLOBE & MAIL (Nov. 28, 2019), https://www.theglobeandmail.com/canada/article-comedian-mike-ward-loses-quebec-appeal-over-penalty-for-joke-about/
22. Crim. Code, S.C. 1985, c C-46, s. 264 (1) & (2).
23. Can. Hum. Rts. Act, R.S.C., 1985, c. H-6, s. 14.
24. R. v. Sim, 2017 ONCA 856.
25. *E.g.*, E.T. v. Dress Code Express Inc., 2017 HRTO 595; Baylis-Flannery v. DeWilde, 2003 HRTO 28.
26. *E.g.*, Rory Rogers & Jennifer Taylor, *Canada: An Update on Freedom of Expression & Charter Application to Universities*, MONDAQ (Mar. 1, 2018), https://www.mondaq.com/canada/Consumer-Protection/678606/An-Update-On-Freedom-Of-Expression-Charter-Application-To-Universities
27. Can. Charter, s. 32(1).
28. *McKinney v. University of Guelph*, 1990 CanLII 60 (SCC), [1990] 3 SCR 229, at para. 5.
29. Eldridge v. B.C. (Att'y Gen.) [1997] 3 S.C.R. 624, at para. 37.

making discretionary decisions pursuant to statutory authority—a definition that would include university administrators—have to determine whether their decisions could limit an individual's Charter rights; if so, discretionary decision-makers need to ensure these rights are "limited no more than necessary" given the applicable statutory objectives.[30]

In numerous cases, Canadian courts have affirmed the autonomy of post-secondary institutions in making decisions, and overturned universities' decisions on free speech issues only when they found the decisions highly unreasonable or unfair, regardless of whether the university is a "government" under section 32(1) of the Charter.[31] In one case involving students' derogatory Facebook comments about their professor, the provincial court held that the university was acting as an agent of the provincial government in providing accessible postsecondary education services to students; hence, its review board infringed on students' freedom of expression under section 2(b) of the Charter by holding that their actions constituted academic misconduct.[32] In another case concerning abusive conduct of students, however, the provincial court held that the Charter did not apply when the university was applying its disciplinary policy to students' actions that went beyond political discourse and created a hostile environment.[33] The same deference toward universities on free speech issues except where the decisions were unreasonable is also found in cases where students tried to use university properties for expressive purposes. In two cases, the provincial courts rejected claims by pro-life student groups that the universities breached their rights to freedom of expression by refusing them spaces for antiabortion protests and posters, on the grounds that universities were not government and extracurricular activities fell outside of "government programs."[34] In another case, the court held that a private university had the authority to approve or deny student clubs for funding based on whether their mandates and ideologies complied with the university's policies and the pro-

30. Loy. High Sch. v. QC (Attorney General) [2015] 1 S.C.R. 613, at para. 4.

31. *See* Rory Rogers & Jennifer Taylor, *Canada: An Update on Freedom of Expression & Charter Application to Universities*, Mondaq (Mar. 1, 2018), https://www.mondaq.com/canada/Consumer-Protection/678606/An-Update-On-Freedom-Of-Expression-Charter-Application-To-Universities

32. Pridgen v. Univ. of Calgary [2010] ABQB 644 (CanLII).

33. Telfer v. Univ. of W. Ont. [2012] ONSC 1287. In a case involving students' abusive conduct, an Ontario court similarly held that the Charter did not apply as the university's dismissal of a student for a violation of standards of academic conduct was an internal matter. AlGhaithy v. Ottawa Univ. [2012] 289 O.A.C. 382 (DC).

34. B.C. Civ. Liberties Ass'n v. Univ. of Vict. [2016] BCCA 162, at paras. 30, 40; Lobo v. Carleton Univ. [2012] ONCA 498, at paras. 3–4.

vincial human rights code.[35] On the contrary, when a university refused to hear the appeal of students found guilty of nonacademic misconduct for setting up a pro-life display on campus, the court applied the *Doré* framework to find that this decision was "unreasonable" as it failed to balance its safety objectives with Charter values by interfering "no more than is necessary" with the students' right to express differing views in a university.[36]

On January 6, 2020, the Court of Appeal of Alberta determined in *UAlberta Pro-Life v. Governors of the University of Alberta* that the "the University's regulation of freedom of expression by students on University grounds should be considered to be a form of governmental action" for the purposes of section 32 of the Charter.[37] The court identified the education of students, largely by means of free expression, as the "core purpose of the University dating from its beginnings and into the future," "a responsibility given by government for over a century under both statute and the Constitution Act, 1867," and "largely funded by government and private sector donors who likewise support and adhere to" this core purpose and responsibility.[38] This was the core purpose "even by the University's own view of its mandate and responsibility."[39] Besides, the infrastructure and land holdings granted to the university or sustained by its funding were designed to serve this purpose by permitting debate and sharing of ideas in a community space. The affirmation that the Charter was applicable to the exercise of freedom of expression by students on the grounds of the university reinforced the rule of law as well as "the core values of human rights and freedoms, democracy, federalism, constitutionalism, equality and respect for minority interests."[40] Finally, recognizing that the university is subject to section 32 of the Charter did not threaten its ability to "maintain its independence," "uphold its academic standards," or "manage its facilities and resources."[41] The Alberta Court of Appeal determined that the lower court's decision was fatally flawed by not considering whether the university's decision that UAlberta Pro-Life should bear the security costs minimally impaired the student group's Charter right to freedom of expression. Although the *UAlberta Pro-Life* decision is binding in Alberta, it may have an impact on how other provincial courts determine similar cases in the future.

35. Grant v. Ryerson Students' Union [2016] ONSC 5519.
36. Wilson v. Univ. of Calgary [2014] ABQB 190, at paras. 143–63.
37. UAlberta Pro-Life v. Governors of Univ. of Alta [2020] ABCA 1, at para. 148.
38. UAlberta Pro-Life v. Governors of Univ. of Alta [2020] ABCA 1, at para. 148.
39. UAlberta Pro-Life v. Governors of Univ. of Alta [2020] ABCA 1, at para. 148.
40. UAlberta Pro-Life v. Governors of Univ. of Alta [2020] ABCA 1, at para. 148.
41. UAlberta Pro-Life v. Governors of Univ. of Alta [2020] ABCA 1, at para. 148.

Due to the deference of Canadian courts to university administrations, universities have long implemented their own free speech policies. For example, the Governing Council of the University of Toronto passed the *Statement of Institutional Purpose* and *Statement on Freedom of Speech* in 1992, acknowledging that the rights to "examine, question, investigate, speculate upon, and comment on issues without reference to prescribed doctrine, as well as the right to criticize society at large" are the necessary precondition for "the pursuit of truth, the advancement of learning and the dissemination of knowledge."[42] They also affirm that "the principles of equity, diversity, and inclusion operate in concert with the rights of free expression to foster excellence."[43] Likewise, the University of British Columbia acknowledges the importance of promoting "the freest possible exchange of information, ideas, beliefs and opinions in diverse forms," including "controversial topics and unpopular points of view," to promote "excellence in learning, research and work in the university community."[44] Freedom of expression and free inquiry, both central to the university's mission, "cannot exist without an equally vigorous commitment to recognition of and respect for the freedoms of others, and concern for the well-being of every member of the university community."[45] McGill University recognizes the freedom of opinion, expression, and peaceful assembly enjoyed by students.[46] Christopher Manfredi, the provost and academic vice president, affirmed that the university's recognition of such freedoms "does not derogate from its overarching commitment to equity, diversity, and inclusion on our campus."[47] While all these policies and statements may look reasonable and encouraging, they are also vague—perhaps understandably so—especially with regard to how they balance free speech with commitments to equity, diversity,

---

42. Meric Gertler (president) & Cheryl Regehr (vice-president & provost), *Freedom of Speech at the University of Toronto*, University of Toronto (Mar. 8, 2018), https://memos.provost.utoronto.ca/freedom-of-speech-at-the-university-of-toronto-pdadc-68/ (last visited Apr. 16, 2020).
43. Meric Gertler (president) & Cheryl Regehr (vice-president & provost), *Freedom of Speech at the University of Toronto*, University of Toronto (Mar. 8, 2018), https://memos.provost.utoronto.ca/freedom-of-speech-at-the-university-of-toronto-pdadc-68/ (last visited Apr. 16, 2020).
44. University of British Columbia's Executive, *UBC Statement on Respectful Environment for Students, Faculty and Staff*, University of British Columbia (May 2014), http://www.hr.ubc.ca/respectful-environment/files/UBC-Statement-on-Respectful-Environment-2014.pdf (last visited Apr. 15, 2020).
45. University of British Columbia's Executive, *UBC Statement on Respectful Environment for Students, Faculty and Staff*, University of British Columbia (May 2014), http://www.hr.ubc.ca/respectful-environment/files/UBC-Statement-on-Respectful-Environment-2014.pdf (last visited Apr. 15, 2020).
46. McGill University's Office of the Dean of Students, *Student Rights and Responsibilities*, McGill University, https://www.mcgill.ca/students/srr/personalrights/opinion (last visited Apr. 16. 2020).
47. Adam Steiner, *Senate Discusses Free Speech and Naming Policies*, McGill Tribune (Nov. 26, 2019), http://www.mcgilltribune.com/news/senate-discusses-free-speech-and-naming-policies-2611/

and inclusion. The application of these policies to people of different political leanings, as well as their enforcement, has been nothing short of challenging.

In summer 2018, Ontario premier Doug Ford declared his commitment to protect free speech in universities and announced that all publicly funded colleges and universities in Ontario would have until January 1, 2019 to "develop, implement and comply with a free speech policy that meets a minimum standard prescribed by the government."[48] Institutions failing to comply with the free-speech requirement could face a cut in funding.[49] The new policy also requires that institutions develop a definition of free speech based upon the University of Chicago "Statement on Principles of Free Expression."[50] Some Ontario universities did not see the need to modify their existing policies, which their administrators deemed to be already in line with these principles, while others hustled to revise their policies to meet the deadline.[51]

Some objected to this provincial directive by arguing that there has been no free speech crisis at all in Canadian universities, which are contractually obligated to protect academic freedom and freedom of expression, and attempts at shutting down speakers became news only because they have been highly unusual.[52] Notwithstanding that free speech policies are meant to protect all speeches regardless of their political content, some questioned the motives of Ford, the leader of the Progressive Conservative Party of Ontario, deeming it an attempt to play to his conservative political base.[53] One called

48. *The Politics of Free Speech*, CANADIAN ASSOCIATION OF UNIVERSITY TEACHERS (Dec. 2018), https://www.caut.ca/bulletin/2018/12/politics-free-speech (last visited Apr. 17, 2020).
49. *The Politics of Free Speech*, CANADIAN ASSOCIATION OF UNIVERSITY TEACHERS (Dec. 2018), https://www.caut.ca/bulletin/2018/12/politics-free-speech (last visited Apr. 17, 2020).
50. *The Politics of Free Speech*, CANADIAN ASSOCIATION OF UNIVERSITY TEACHERS (Dec. 2018), https://www.caut.ca/bulletin/2018/12/politics-free-speech (last visited Apr. 17, 2020).
51. *The Politics of Free Speech*, CANADIAN ASSOCIATION OF UNIVERSITY TEACHERS (Dec. 2018), https://www.caut.ca/bulletin/2018/12/politics-free-speech (last visited Apr. 17, 2020).
52. One example is James Turk, director of the Centre for Free Expression at Ryerson University, who contends that "[u]niversities, along with the conventional media and public libraries, are the principal advocates for, and defenders of, freedom of expression in our society. The university's raison d'être is premised on free expression. This general freedom of expression is bolstered, almost universally in Canadian universities, by contractual guarantees for academic freedom that ensure academic staff have free expression rights in their teaching, research, and more broadly, including the right to criticize the university itself and its administration publicly—an action that would lead to discipline, if not termination, in most other workplaces." *The Politics of Free Speech*, CANADIAN ASSOCIATION OF UNIVERSITY TEACHERS (Dec. 2018), https://www.caut.ca/bulletin/2018/12/politics-free-speech (last visited Apr. 17, 2020).
53. Examples include James Turk and Creso Sá, director of the Centre for the Study of Canadian and International Higher Education at the University of Toronto. *The Politics of Free Speech*, CANADIAN ASSOCIATION OF UNIVERSITY TEACHERS (Dec. 2018), https://www.caut.ca/bulletin/2018/12/politics-free-speech (last visited Apr. 17, 2020).

this directive by the Conservative government "compelled speech" and "a tremendous attack on the free speech and free expression of teachers."[54] According to a convoluted and ill-reasoned argument put forth by a critic, the directive was intended as a "threat" to "stifle dissent" on campus.[55] The critic cited an extreme example of how freedom of expression was used to champion racist beliefs to conclude that free speech advocates would more likely abuse this freedom to incite hatred rather than discuss "real controversies."[56] Not to "stifle dissent," following this warped logic, means that only members of universities who discuss "real controversies" should enjoy free speech. On the other hand, those observing a real free speech crisis insinuated that government intervention should not have been necessary on the ground that the same laws should govern free speech on campus and in the broader society: campus free speech policies based upon laws prohibiting hate speech, harassment, and discrimination would be very simple.[57]

Are attempts to shut down free speech in Canadian universities highly unusual? Even assuming they are, their infrequency does not indicate they are not alarming enough to warrant thorough analyses. The rest of this chapter will critically examine a careful selection of these attempts to shed light on whether free speech is under attack and whether those attacks have escalated to the crisis level on Canadian university campuses. Special reference will be given to the concepts explored in part II of this book. It needs to be emphasized that the following critical analyses are based upon open-source information accessible in the media and that no interviews of any kind were conducted by the author. Moreover, at least at the time of writing this chapter, the author did not know the people mentioned in these analyses on a personal level and was not connected to any of them.

54. Nora Loreto, *Calling Out Ford's Chill on Free Speech*, NAT'L OBSERVER (Aug. 30, 2018), https://www.nationalobserver.com/2018/08/30/opinion/calling-out-fords-chill-free-speech

55. Denise Balkissoon, *Doug Ford's PCs Believe in Free Speech—and Those Who Don't Like It Can Shut Up*, GLOBE & MAIL (Dec. 19, 2018), https://www.theglobeandmail.com/opinion/article-doug-fords-pcs-believe-in-free-speech-and-those-who-dont-like-it/

56. Denise Balkissoon, *Doug Ford's PCs Believe in Free Speech—and Those Who Don't Like It Can Shut Up*, GLOBE & MAIL (Dec. 19, 2018), https://www.theglobeandmail.com/opinion/article-doug-fords-pcs-believe-in-free-speech-and-those-who-dont-like-it/

57. *See, e.g.*, Bruce Pardy, *Outraged Responses to Ontario Free Speech Directive Reveal the Problem the Directive Is Trying to Solve*, SOCIETY FOR ACADEMIC FREEDOM AND SCHOLARSHIP (Apr. 2019), https://www.safs.ca/newsletters/article.php?article=1006 (last visited Apr. 22, 2020).

II. Case Studies

Certainly, even on liberal campuses, conservative speakers are not the only people who have been frowned upon and speakers advancing different ideologies have sparked protests. One example was former child soldier Omar Khadr, who was invited to Dalhousie University on February 10, 2020 to deliver a keynote address at a panel discussion hosted in partnership between the Roméo Dallaire Child Soldiers Initiative and Dalhousie's Open Dialogue Series.[58] Khadr is a Canadian who, as a young child, was taken to Afghanistan by his terrorist father, and captured by the United States military when he was fifteen.[59] In 2010, during his detention at Guantanamo Bay, he pleaded guilty to the murder of U.S. Army sergeant Christopher Speer and four other charges at a hearing before a United States military commission, and agreed to an eight-year sentence.[60] However, the SSC of Canada ruled that the Canadian government's interrogation of Khadr at Guantanamo Bay "offend[ed] the most basic Canadian standards [of] the treatment of detained youth suspects."[61] In 2012, Khadr returned to Canada to serve the remainder of his sentence in Canadian custody, before he was released on bail in 2015.[62] In 2017, the Canadian government publicly apologized to Khadr "for any role Canadian officials may have played in relation to his ordeal abroad and any resulting harm" as part of the settlement of the civil suit launched over the violation of his Charter rights, and announced a $10.5 million payment to him in compensation for damages arising from its mishandling of his case.[63]

Khadr's unusual experience as a child soldier, the suffering he endured on the battleground and at Guantanamo Bay, and his efforts to reform himself as an ex-convict all qualified him to advocate against the use of child soldiers. His speech, without a doubt, must have informed and inspired his audience. His presence did draw a small, peaceful group of protesters, mostly veterans,

---

58. Alicia Draus, *Omar Khadr Makes First Public Appearance, Delivers Keynote Address at Dalhousie University Event*, GLOBAL NEWS (Feb. 10, 2020), https://globalnews.ca/news/6534245/omar-khadr-dalhousie-university/
59. *E.g.*, *Key Events in the Omar Khadr Case*, CBC NEWS (July 7, 2017), https://www.cbc.ca/news/canada/key-events-in-the-omar-khadr-case-1.1153759 (last visited May 5, 2020).
60. *E.g.*, *Key Events in the Omar Khadr Case*, CBC NEWS (July 7, 2017), https://www.cbc.ca/news/canada/key-events-in-the-omar-khadr-case-1.1153759 (last visited May 5, 2020).
61. Can. (Prime Minister) v. Khadr [2010] 1 SCR 44.
62. *Key Events in the Omar Khadr Case*, CBC NEWS (July 7, 2017), https://www.cbc.ca/news/canada/key-events-in-the-omar-khadr-case-1.1153759 (last visited May 5, 2020).
63. *Key Events in the Omar Khadr Case*, CBC NEWS (July 7, 2017), https://www.cbc.ca/news/canada/key-events-in-the-omar-khadr-case-1.1153759 (last visited May 5, 2020).

outside the venue, who called him a "terrorist" and who apparently did not believe that he should have been released or given an enormous settlement, let alone granted a platform.[64] Fortunately, there was no attempt at all to shut down what must have been an enlightening speech, or to cancel this highly educational event.[65]

Interestingly, though, the scale of the protest against Khadr, who was handsomely compensated by Canada's Liberal government, was a far cry from the massive, at times violent, protests sparked by well-known conservative speakers, speakers who may not be deeply conservative but who dared to challenge the left-wing ideologies upheld by Canada's Liberal government and dominating many universities, or speakers courageous enough to criticize the hostile and repressive government of a foreign country from which an increasing student population originates.

Example 1

Jordan Peterson, a professor of psychology at the University of Toronto, has been the target of massive, sometimes violent, protests on Canadian university campuses. In the fall of 2016, Peterson openly criticized the Act to Amend the Canadian Human Rights Act and the Criminal Code (Bill C-16), which introduces "gender identity and expression" as prohibited grounds of discrimination.[66] He argued that the law would compel the use of certain pronouns and infringe on the fundamental right to freedom of expression.[67] His critique of Bill C-16, as well as the culture of political correctness more generally, received

64. *See* Alicia Draus, *Omar Khadr Makes First Public Appearance, Delivers Keynote Address at Dalhousie University Event*, GLOBAL NEWS (Feb. 10, 2020), https://globalnews.ca/news/6534245/omar-khadr-dalhousie-university/; Canadian Press, *Former Guantanamo Bay Detainee Omar Khadr Speaks in at* [*sic*] *Child Soldiers Panel*, TOR. CITY NEWS (Feb. 10, 2020), https://toronto.citynews.ca/2020/02/10/former-guantanamo-bay-detainee-omar-khadr-speaks-in-at-child-soldiers-panel/

65. *See* Alicia Draus, *Omar Khadr Makes First Public Appearance, Delivers Keynote Address at Dalhousie University Event*, GLOBAL NEWS (Feb. 10, 2020), https://globalnews.ca/news/6534245/omar-khadr-dalhousie-university/; Canadian Press, *Former Guantanamo Bay Detainee Omar Khadr Speaks in at* [*sic*] *Child Soldiers Panel*, TOR. CITY NEWS (Feb. 10, 2020), https://toronto.citynews.ca/2020/02/10/former-guantanamo-bay-detainee-omar-khadr-speaks-in-at-child-soldiers-panel/

66. Jordan B. Peterson, *Part 1: Fear and the Law*, YOUTUBE (Sep. 27, 2016), https://www.youtube.com/watch?v=fvPgjg201w0 (last visited Jun. 1, 2020); *see Canada: Senate Passes Landmark Transgender Rights Bill*, GLOBAL LEG. MONITOR (Sep. 11, 2017), https://www.loc.gov/law/foreign-news/article/canada-senate-passes-landmark-transgender-rights-bill/ (last visited Jun. 1, 2020).

67. Jordan B. Peterson, *Part 1: Fear and the Law*, YOUTUBE (Sep. 27, 2016), https://www.youtube.com/watch?v=fvPgjg201w0 (last visited Jun. 1, 2020).

significant national and international media attention.[68] In response to the controversy, his university sent him two letters of warning, one noting that free speech had to be made in accordance with human rights legislation and the other stating that his refusal to use the preferred pronouns of students and faculty upon request could constitute discrimination.[69] Despite this, and a campaign initiated by disgruntled student activists from his and other universities calling for the termination of his teaching position, the university informed him that he would keep his position in December 2016.[70] His book *12 Rules for Life: An Antidote to Chaos*, which he published in 2018 and promoted on a world tour, became an instant national and international bestseller.[71] Its sequel, which came out in 2021, was also a top seller.

Bill C-16, introduced by the Liberal government in May 2016 and passed into law in June 2017, amends sections of the Canadian Human Rights Act and the Criminal Code with the aim "to protect individuals from discrimination within the sphere of federal jurisdiction and from being the targets of hate propaganda, as a consequence of their gender identity or their gender expression."[72] The Canadian Bar Association supported passage of the bill, arguing that it would provide necessary protections for transgender people without posing

---

68. *See, e.g.*, John Semley, *The Jordan Peterson Paradox: High Intellect or Just Another Angry White Guy*, GLOBE & MAIL (Jan. 31, 2018), https://www.theglobeandmail.com/arts/books-and-media/the-jordan-peterson-paradox-high-intellect-or-just-another-angry-white-guy/article37806524/ (last visited Jun. 1, 2020); Jessica Murphy, *Toronto Professor Jordan Peterson Takes on Gender Pronouns*, BBC (Nov. 4, 2016), https://www.bbc.com/news/world-us-canada-37875695 (last visited Jun. 1, 2020).
69. *E.g.*, Tom Yun, *University of Toronto Letter Asks Jordan Peterson to Respect Pronouns, Stop Making Statements*, THE VARSITY (Oct. 24, 2016), https://thevarsity.ca/2016/10/24/u-of-t-letter-asks-jordan-peterson-to-respect-pronouns-stop-making-statements/ (last visited Jun. 1, 2020).
70. *E.g.*, Patty Winsa, *He Says Freedom, They Say Hate: The Pronoun Fight Is Back*, TOR. STAR (Jan. 15, 2017), https://www.thestar.com/news/insight/2017/01/15/he-says-freedom-they-say-hate-the-pronoun-fight-is-back.html; Aiden Currie, *Hundreds Sign Open Letter to U of T Admin Calling for Jordan Peterson's Termination*, THE VARSITY (Nov. 29, 2017), https://thevarsity.ca/2017/11/29/hundreds-sign-open-letter-to-u-of-t-admin-calling-for-jordan-petersons-termination/ (last visited Jun. 1, 2020).
71. *12 Rules for Life: An Antidote to Chaos by Jordan Peterson*, PENGUIN RANDOM HOUSE, https://www.penguinrandomhouse.com/books/258237/12-rules-for-life-by-jordan-b-peterson--foreword-by-norman-doige-md-illustrated-by-ethan-van-sciver/ (last visited Jun. 2, 2020).
72. By adding "gender identity or expression" to the list of prohibited grounds of discrimination in the Canadian Human Rights Act, the law makes it illegal to deny services, employment, accommodation, and similar benefits to individuals based on their gender identity or expression. By adding "gender identity or expression" to the definition of "identifiable group" in section 318 and to the sentencing provisions of section 718.2 of the Criminal Code, the law protects individuals from being the targets of genocide or hate propaganda because of gender identity or gender expression and makes gender identity or expression an aggravating factor in sentencing. Can. Hum. Rts. Act, ss. 2 & 3; Crim. Code, ss. 318 & 718.2.

any risk to freedom of expression.[73] Nothing added to the Human Rights Act or the Criminal Code compels the speech of private citizens, it explains, as long as the use or avoidance of certain words is not intended to promote hatred against certain groups.[74] Hence, the use or avoidance of preferred pronouns as forms of gender expression is not illegal per se and would unlikely lead to criminal prosecution. Yet laws on pronoun use, in Canada and elsewhere, have raised concerns among scholars and commentators who criticize these laws for imposing ideas about gender identity and requiring people to express beliefs that they may not hold or even understand, regardless of the actual risks of prosecution.[75] One should not doubt the importance of these pronouns to some transgender people whose well-being hinges on the recognition of their preferred gender identities, or the importance of civility and respect in society.[76] Yet it may be argued that civility and respect should not be legislated: hate speech may be outlawed, but writing gender identity and expression into the law, let alone dictating that people recognize others' identities and how they should address one another, is legislative overreach. Greeting people is a sign of civility, but legally compelling people to do so is coercive.

It is ultimately beyond the scope of this chapter to debate whether Bill C-16, or laws on pronouns more generally, infringe on freedom of expression. Regardless, Peterson's public remarks about the law, even if misguided and meritless, do not amount to hate speech or discrimination against transgender people. In his YouTube video, he criticized the bill's definitions of gender

---

73. René J. Basque, *Bill C-16, an Act to Amend the Canadian Human Rights Act and the Criminal Code (Gender Identity or Expression)*, Canadian Bar Association, 3 (May 7, 2017), http://www.cba.org/CMSPages/GetFile.aspx?guid=be34d5a4-8850-40a0-beea-432eeb762d7f (last visited Jun. 4, 2020).

74. "The amendment to the CHRA will not compel the speech of private citizens." "Nothing in the section compels the use or avoidance of particular words in public as long as they are not used in their most 'extreme manifestations' with the intention of promoting the 'level of abhorrence, delegitimization and rejection' that produces feelings of hatred against identifiable groups." René J. Basque, *Bill C-16, an Act to Amend the Canadian Human Rights Act and the Criminal Code (Gender Identity or Expression)*, Canadian Bar Association, 3, 4 (May 7, 2017), http://www.cba.org/CMSPages/GetFile.aspx?guid=be34d5a4-8850-40a0-beea-432eeb762d7f (last visited Jun. 4, 2020).

75. *E.g.*, Bruce Pardy, *Meet the New "Human Rights"—Where You Are Forced by Law to Use "Reasonable" Pronouns*, Nat'l Post (Jun. 19, 2017), https://nationalpost.com/opinion/bruce-pardy-meet-the-new-human-rights-where-you-are-forced-by-law-to-use-reasonable-pronouns-like-ze-and-zer (last visited Jun. 4, 2020); Josh Blackman, *The Government Can't Make You Use "Zhir" and "Ze" in Place of "She" and "He,"* Wash. Post (Jun. 16, 2016), https://www.washingtonpost.com/news/in-theory/wp/2016/06/16/the-government-cant-make-you-use-zhir-or-ze-in-place-of-she-and-he/

76. *E.g.*, *What and Why: What Are My Pronouns and Why Do They Matter?* My Pronouns, https://www.mypronouns.org/what-and-why (last visited Jun. 6, 2020); *Talking about Pronouns in the Workplace: About Gender Diverse and Expansive Identities*, Human Rights Campaign, https://www.hrc.org/resources/talking-about-pronouns-in-the-workplace (last visited Jun. 6, 2020).

expressions and identities from the perspective of a clinical psychologist, expressed his fear that the law would be used to shut down discussion of related issues, and asserted that he would not recognize other people's right to determine what he says.[77] Elsewhere, he clarified that he did not rule out the idea of addressing students by their preferred pronouns: what he truly opposed was compelled speech as well as the arrogance and possibly political motivations of some people who might make those requests.[78] Because he only commented on the law and its possible free speech implications, but did not attack transgender people, as some claimed that he did, the warning letters did seem unwarranted, and attempts to shut down his speech by student activists on Canadian university campuses were overreactions.[79] Perhaps he should have heeded his own advice in his bestseller and explained his views more precisely to help his listeners grasp their nuances.[80] Nevertheless, due to the sensitivity of this issue, and the reluctance of some zealous activists to allow the mildest and well-intended criticisms of the law, even the most precisely articulated argument might not have been sufficient to quell their anger or dissuade them from trying to shut down his speech.

Peterson's remarks on Bill C-16 were made in the context of his critique of political correctness. Citing the experiences of some of his clients, he illuminated how the PC culture has led to self-censorship and oppressive, toxic workplaces.[81] He also took a thoughtful and conscientious approach to debunk the assumptions underlying the mandatory "anti-racist" and "anti-bias" training

---

77. Jordan B. Peterson, *Part 1: Fear and the Law*, YouTube (Sep. 27, 2016), https://www.youtube.com/watch?v=fvPgjg201w0 (last visited Jun. 1, 2020).

78. "Peterson told *Vice* on Thursday that he had never actually interacted with a student who asked to be addressed by their preferred pronouns, but he refused to confirm or deny whether he would comply with a request if asked by a future student to do so. Instead, Peterson said the issue is 'complex' and 'cannot be simplified' to a yes or no answer. 'It would depend on how they asked me. [. . .] If I could detect that there was a chip on their shoulder, or that they were [asking me] with political motives, then I would probably say no. [. . .] If I could have a conversation like the one we're having now, I could probably meet them on an equal level.'" Jake Klvanc, *A Canadian University Professor Is Under Fire for Rant on Political Correctness*, Vice (Sep. 29, 2016), https://www.vice.com/en_ca/article/7bmjqg/a-canadian-university-professor-is-under-fire-for-rant-on-political-correctness (last visited Jun. 6, 2020).

79. *E.g.*, Jack O. Denton, *Tensions Flare at Rally Supporting Free Speech, Dr. Jordan Peterson*, Varsity (Oct. 17, 2016) (last visited Jun. 6, 2020). At his free speech rally at the University of Toronto, a group of student protesters tried to drown out his voice, calling him "transphobe" and accusing him of "hate speech."

80. Jordan B. Peterson, 12 Rules for Life: An Antidote to Chaos (2018). Rule 10 says: "Be precise in your speech."

81. Jordan B. Peterson, *Part 1: Fear and the Law*, YouTube (Sep. 27, 2016), https://www.youtube.com/watch?v=fvPgjg201w0 (last visited Jun. 1, 2020).

program at his university.[82] Despite the amount of offense that this critique might ignite, it did not constitute hate speech or discrimination against minority groups. Because even ardent supporters of PC culture may disagree on these programs and initiatives, his university's warning letters likely have had a chilling effect on well-meaning criticisms and suggestions that can help to make it a better institution.

What might have been more concerning was Peterson's project, later scrapped, that aimed to reduce student enrollment in classes that he believed had become "indoctrination cults." He proposed to rely on artificial intelligence to scour curriculums for what he considered harmful "postmodern neo-Marxist" content and put the collected information on a website.[83] This project, which he soon abandoned of his own accord,[84] would likely have made his fellow academics feel intimidated and stifled their freedom of expression and academic freedom. Just as outlawing offensive speech may drive hateful sentiments underground rather than eliminating them,[85] discouraging certain political thoughts in academia may deprive people of serious opportunities to learn and debate them and increase the appeal of harmful ideas to an uninformed public. If allowed to proceed, his project would also likely stigmatize certain traditional disciplines (such as sociology and literature), if not causing them to close—disciplines that have nurtured the minds of many generations, some of which have become intellectually sterile due to the dominance of monolithic narratives but can be reformed by (re) introducing different approaches and content.

Ironically enough, the university administration's later actions implied that it considered Peterson, a well-respected academic who thoughtfully critiqued the law on pronouns and the PC culture, to be worse than the Hong Kong

---

82. Jordan B. Peterson, *2016/10/03: Part 2: Compulsory Political Education: A Real World Case at the U of T*, YouTube (Sep. 27, 2016), https://www.youtube.com/watch?v=f-7YGGCE9es&t=24s (last visited Jun. 7, 2020).
83. *E.g.*, CBC Radio, *Toronto University Professor Says Controversial Website "on Hiatus"*, CBC (Nov. 13, 2017), https://www.cbc.ca/radio/asithappens/as-it-happens-monday-edition-1.4396981/toronto-university-professor-says-controversial-website-on-hiatus-1.4396986 (last visited Jun. 7, 2020). In August 2017, Peterson revealed that he was working with developers to design artificial intelligence software that would scour university curriculums for what he considered "post-modern neo-Marxist course content." He hoped that this could help to reduce enrollments in "postmodern neo-Marxist cult classes" by 75 percent across the West in five years.
84. CBC Radio, *Toronto University Professor Says Controversial Website "on Hiatus"*, CBC (Nov. 13, 2017), https://www.cbc.ca/radio/asithappens/as-it-happens-monday-edition-1.4396981/toronto-university-professor-says-controversial-website-on-hiatus-1.4396986 (last visited Jun. 7, 2020).
85. *See* Jordan B. Peterson, *Part 1: Fear and the Law*, YouTube (Sep. 27, 2016), https://www.youtube.com/watch?v=fvPgjg201w0 (last visited Jun. 1, 2020).

police, who were once reputed to be "Asia's finest" as a branch of the British colonial government, but since the summer of 2019 have used excessive force on pro-democracy protesters and activists at the order of the Beijing-backed government. In May 2020, student activists wrote to Canadian universities, the University of Toronto included, that had published Hong Kong police recruitment advertisements to urge them to take down the ads, noting the police force's brutal handling of peaceful activism and criticism by international human rights groups and arguing that the ad signaled support for an organization that violates international human rights laws.[86] Despite repeated requests, the University of Toronto's career office refused to take down the ad after consulting with its career services partners and finding that the employer and job posting followed all its employment and recruitment protocols and did not contradict federal and provincial guidelines or its own policies—guidelines that are governed in part by "Government of Canada Human Rights," including freedom of expression and peaceful assembly as fundamental freedoms.[87] Its spokesperson said "[t]he University encourages all students to look at their own interests and values as they make career decisions about which positions to pursue."[88]

The university might have aimed to avoid taking a stance on political issues. Yet refusing to signal support for an employer that abuses human rights and facilitating the recruitment of people into such an organization is a moral rather than a political stance. If the career office would not consider advertising sex work for moral concerns, it arguably should not have put up this recruitment ad, or should have taken it down when requested like some universities (such as McMaster University) did. Instead, it made a blatantly bad faith argument by doubling down on the position that the employer and job positing did not violate federal and provincial guidelines or its own policy.[89]

---

86. *E.g.*, Steven Chase, *Canadian Universities under Fire for Publishing Hong Kong Police Recruitment Ads*, Globe & Mail (May 19, 2020), https://www.theglobeandmail.com/canada/article-canadian-universities-under-fire-for-publishing-hong-kong-police/

87. Tiffany Lam, *U of T under Pressure to Remove Hong Kong Police Job Ad*, Now Mag. (May 22, 2020), https://nowtoronto.com/news/hong-kong-police-recruit-universities-canada/ (last visited May 28, 2020).

88. Tiffany Lam, *U of T under Pressure to Remove Hong Kong Police Job Ad*, Now Mag. (May 22, 2020), https://nowtoronto.com/news/hong-kong-police-recruit-universities-canada/ (last visited May 28, 2020).

89. *See* Tiffany Lam, *U of T under Pressure to Remove Hong Kong Police Job Ad*, Now Mag. (May 22, 2020), https://nowtoronto.com/news/hong-kong-police-recruit-universities-canada/ (last visited May 28, 2020).

Certainly, the university could also have pulled the free speech card by arguing that refusing to advertise the position or taking down the ad constitutes censorship. Just as audiences should have the opportunity to hear offensive speakers and decide whether to agree with their views, graduating students should be able to view the ad and decide whether to pursue the job opportunity. However, it would be disingenuous for the university to take a pro-free-speech stance toward the Hong Kong police recruitment ad while applying a different standard to Peterson's expression.

How can one explain the University of Toronto's double standards? Apparently, it does not cost anything to warn or attempt to shut down a controversial professor who challenges mainstream ideologies. Standing against Hong Kong and Beijing authorities, by contrast, takes a certain amount of moral courage. This lack of moral courage in the face of a foreign power, which is unwarranted and will in the long run damage the university's reputation and erode Canada's sovereignty, is something to which this chapter will return toward its end. There could have been other reasons. The administration could have been swayed by the belief that Hong Kong people only deserve "Chinese-style democracy" handed down by the Beijing government, not universal human rights to free speech and assembly enjoyed by Canadians and people in the free world, and that the police suppression of the protesters, however brutal, was legitimate despite its violation of international standards. It could also have been blinded by the belief that all forms of colonialism are bad and societies could not have benefited from this evil institution called British colonialism, leading to their disapproval of pro-democracy protesters and activists for promoting the view that Hong Kong fared better under British governance than under China's authoritarian rule. It could also have perceived that fair-skinned Asians, unlike black people, are low on the oppression hierarchy, and cannot be oppressed by members of their own race/ethnicity who have the same skin and hair color. There is no doubt that given the university's unflinching commitment to equality and social justice, the high caliber of its administrators, and their compassion for the marginalized and oppressed, these explanations would have been highly unlikely: if valid, they betray a racist and ignorant mindset and extreme indoctrination. Wouldn't it be unthinkable that such ideologically possessed (for want of a better term) extremists—and racists—could hold positions of power at one of Canada's most prominent universities?

Example 2

To be fair, it can at times be difficult for people born and having grown up in a peaceful, democratic society to fully comprehend the politics of a foreign city or country and the traumas of state-sponsored violence. Unfortunately, for some individuals who have lived comfortable lives, who may not have experienced major catastrophes, and who have never been shot or teargassed or even suffered a punch, expressing views that deviate from mainstream ideologies is comparable to committing some of the worst forms of violence. According to their mindset, even those who platform or acknowledge these views need to be reprimanded or severely punished.

This happened in November 2017 at Wilfrid Laurier University (WLU), where graduate student and teaching assistant Lindsay Shepherd played two clips from *The Agenda with Steve Paikin*, a current-affairs program produced by a publicly funded channel TVOntario, in her first-year undergraduate communications class.[90] The first clip featured Paikin discussing gender-neutral pronouns with Jordan Peterson, in which Peterson argued against being legally compelled to use gender-neutral pronouns, which he thought were "the constructions of people who have a political ideology" that he did not believe in and an "attempt to control language in a direction that isn't happening organically . . . but by force and by fiat."[91] The second clip showed Peterson discussing the issues with Nicholas Matte, a historian, who told Peterson that he cared not about his language use but "the safety of people being harmed."[92] Following the class, Shepherd was summoned to a meeting with her supervisor, the head of her academic program, and an acting manager from the university's Diversity and Equity Office. She recorded the meeting without their knowledge and later released the tape to the media.[93]

---

90. *E.g.*, Christie Blatchford, *Thought Police Strike again as Wilfrid Laurier Grad Student Is Chastised for Showing Jordan Peterson Video*, NAT'L POST (Nov. 11, 2017), https://nationalpost.com/opinion/christie-blatchford-thought-police-strike-again-as-wilfrid-laurier-grad-student-is-chastised-for-showing-jordan-peterson-video; Aaron Hutchins, *What Really Happened at Wilfrid Laurier University*, MACLEANS (Dec. 12, 2017), https://www.macleans.ca/lindsay-shepherd-wilfrid-laurier/ (last visited Jun. 25, 2020).
91. The Agenda with Steve Paikin, *Genders, Rights and Freedom of Speech*, YOUTUBE (Oct. 26, 2016) (originally broadcast by TVOntario), https://www.youtube.com/watch?v=kasiov0ytEc (last visited Jun. 25, 2020).
92. The Agenda with Steve Paikin, *Genders, Rights and Freedom of Speech*, YOUTUBE (Oct. 26, 2016) (originally broadcast by TVOntario), https://www.youtube.com/watch?v=kasiov0ytEc (last visited Jun. 25, 2020).
93. Shepherd released the recording to the *National Post* as well as two other newspapers. Columnist

During the forty-two-minute meeting, Shepherd was informed that "one or multiple students had come forward" to complain about her, although the identity of complainant(s), the subject matter of the complaints, or the number of complaints were not disclosed for "confidentiality" reasons.[94] Shepherd's supervisor, Nathan Rambukkana, accused her of creating an "unsafe environment" and "toxic climate for some of the students" by playing the clips and maintaining her neutrality toward the issue.[95] When she argued that she presented the clips "in the spirit of debate" to expose students to an issue "already out there" and that "all ideas are valid" in the university, the professor replied that "it is not necessarily true."[96] He suggested that her showing the clips was "problematic" because the students were "very young adults" (albeit eighteen or over) who had not yet developed the "critical toolkit" to examine the issue.[97] Comparing the pronoun debate to whether a student of color should have rights, he argued that the issue was "not something intellectually neutral that is up for debate."[98] He went so far as to suggest that Peterson was "highly involved with the alt-right," and compare her showing the clips in a neutral manner to "neutrally playing a speech by Hitler."[99] The program head, Herbert Pimlott, associating Peterson with the Nazis and white supremacists, said that he "showed a form of charlatanism," and that all his claims and research "lacked academic credibility."[100] Both Rambukkana and the acting manager in the Diversity and Equity Office, Adria Joel, claimed that Shepherd's action caused violence to transgender students by suggesting that transgender identity is "potentially invalid," and as such it violated the university's Gendered and Sexual Violence

---

Christie Blatchford of the *Post* ran the story in the *Post*. Christie Blatchford, *Thought Police Strike Again as Wilfrid Laurier Grad Student Is Chastised for Showing Jordan Peterson Video*, NAT'L POST (Nov. 11, 2017), https://nationalpost.com/opinion/christie-blatchford-thought-police-strike-again-as-wilfrid-laurier-grad-student-is-chastised-for-showing-jordan-peterson-video

94. Paul George, *FULL RECORDING Lindsay Shepherd Interrogated by Wilfrid Laurier University's Gender Police*, YOUTUBE, 4:55–5:20 (Nov. 24, 2017), https://www.youtube.com/watch?v=9Nd32_uIcnI (last visited Jun. 25, 2020).
95. Paul George, *FULL RECORDING Lindsay Shepherd Interrogated by Wilfrid Laurier University's Gender Police*, YOUTUBE, 4:58, 6:20–23 (Nov. 24, 2017).
96. Paul George, *FULL RECORDING Lindsay Shepherd Interrogated by Wilfrid Laurier University's Gender Police*, YOUTUBE, 4:21–23; 6:25–35; 7:50–55 (Nov. 24, 2017).
97. Paul George, *FULL RECORDING Lindsay Shepherd Interrogated by Wilfrid Laurier University's Gender Police*, YOUTUBE, 25:00–40 (Nov. 24, 2017).
98. Paul George, *FULL RECORDING Lindsay Shepherd Interrogated by Wilfrid Laurier University's Gender Police*, YOUTUBE, 5:48 (Nov. 24, 2017).
99. Paul George, *FULL RECORDING Lindsay Shepherd Interrogated by Wilfrid Laurier University's Gender Police*, YOUTUBE, 2:25–28: 9:55–10:00 (Nov. 24, 2017).
100. Paul George, *FULL RECORDING Lindsay Shepherd Interrogated by Wilfrid Laurier University's Gender Police*, YOUTUBE, 34:01, 15, 29–30 (Nov. 24, 2017).

Policy and likely even the Ontario Human Rights Code.[101] The meeting ended with Rambukkana asking Shepherd to send him her lesson plan prior to each class due to what he believed to be a breakdown in communication and not to show any more clips of Peterson.[102] He also added that he had to discuss the matter with other members of the faculty: he was not certain about what else would happen and therefore did not rule out subjecting her to formal punishment such as by the termination of her teaching assistantship.[103]

After the incident was made public, WLU's president and vice-chancellor Deborah MacLatchy and Rambukkana, likely due to public pressure, published "letters of apology" on November 21. MacLatchy said that the incident "does not reflect the values and practices to which Laurier aspires."[104] In December 2017, MacLatchy further issued a statement confirming that there was "no wrongdoing on the part of Ms. Shepherd in showing the clip from TVO in her tutorial," that "[n]o formal complaint, nor informal concern relative to a Laurier policy, was registered about the screening of the video," and that there were "numerous errors in judgement made in the handling of the meeting" that should never had taken place.[105]

What was *problematic*—a word used by the professors numerous times throughout the meeting—was not Shepherd's showing the clips, but the conduct of these so-called educators. Whatever noble intentions they may have had in reprimanding her for showing the clips, they could not justify their fabrication of complaint(s). While she apparently did not give any form of trigger

---

101. Paul George, *FULL RECORDING Lindsay Shepherd Interrogated by Wilfrid Laurier University's Gender Police*, YouTube, 3:45–48; 22:20–40 (Nov. 24, 2017).
102. Paul George, *FULL RECORDING Lindsay Shepherd Interrogated by Wilfrid Laurier University's Gender Police*, YouTube, 38:30–45 (Nov. 24, 2017).
103. Paul George, *FULL RECORDING Lindsay Shepherd Interrogated by Wilfrid Laurier University's Gender Police*, YouTube, 39:00–40:15 (Nov. 24, 2017).
104. Deborah MacLatchy, *Apology from Laurier President and Vice-Chancellor Deborah MacLatchy*, Wilfrid Laurier University (Nov. 21, 2017), https://www.wlu.ca/news/spotlights/2017/nov/apology-from-laurier-president-and-vice-chancellor.html (last Jun. 25, 2020); Nathan Rambukkana, *Open Letter from Nathan Rambukkana to Lindsay Shepherd*, Wilfrid Laurier University (Nov. 21, 2017), https://www.wlu.ca/news/spotlights/2017/nov/open-letter-to-my-ta-lindsay-shepherd.html (last Jun. 25, 2020).
105. Deborah MacLatchy, *President's Statement Re: Independent Fact-Finder Report*, Wilfrid Laurier University (Dec. 18, 2017), https://www.wlu.ca/news/spotlights/2017/dec/president-statement-re-independent-fact-finder-report.html (last visited Jun. 25, 2020). According to the unreleased report by Robert Centa, a lawyer hired by WLU to conduct an independent investigation into the matter, Shepherd did not violate university policies and the meeting involved "significant overreach." Christie Blatchford, *Investigator's Report into Wilfrid Laurier University Vindicates Lindsay Shepherd*, Nat'l Post (Dec. 18, 2017), https://nationalpost.com/opinion/christie-blatchford-investigators-report-into-wilfrid-laurier-universit-vindicates-lindsay-shepherd

warning prior to showing the clips, there was no reason why students should feel triggered by either the clips or a respectful classroom discussion on pronouns and grammar. Further, a teaching assistant who made a good-faith effort to facilitate a discussion should not be held responsible for any rude remark(s) that some student(s) might have made, or the hurt feelings of those who might have felt offended by any such remark(s).[106] The assumptions that the students were too young to watch or engage in the pronoun debate, that the classroom ought to be a safe space, and that the content of the clips made it unsafe and toxic, were nothing short of condescending. Comparing the pronoun debate, which is about language use, to whether a student of color should have rights is an example of false equivalence that is misleading and shows nothing but intellectual laziness. By unfairly associating Peterson, whose speech offended some people, with Hitler, the Nazis, and the alt-right, they were also guilty of abusing these terms and facilitating the loss of their meanings. Both to toughen their minds and to be reminded that the worst atrocities have been committed by extremists on both ends of the political spectrum, they need to watch documentaries about different communist regimes, the Chinese Cultural Revolution, or the recent state-sanctioned abuses in Tibet, Xinjiang, and Hong Kong—no doubt, on the condition that the realities portrayed would more likely enlighten and inspire than emotionally traumatize these adults.

Shepherd was labeled a "provocateur" by some media outlets for recording the meeting and releasing the tape to what is considered a conservative-leaning newspaper.[107] Arguably, her real intent was not relevant. The scandal was caused not by her showing the clips or her secretly taping the meeting, but by the misjudgment of the WLU staff members who deemed the meeting necessary and their problematic conduct during the meeting. It is not rare for professors to discuss lesson plans with teaching assistants—though program heads and heads of equity and diversity offices rarely attend these meetings—and even to dictate what materials to teach in classes. The professors could have told her, albeit rather disingenuously, that the clips she showed were not the most relevant to the course and suggested more "useful" alternatives. Telling her that some ideas that she presented in class were not acceptable and were not up for

---

106. *See* Aaron Hutchins, *What Really Happened at Wilfrid Laurier University*, MACLEANS (Dec. 12, 2017), https://www.macleans.ca/lindsay-shepherd-wilfrid-laurier/ (last visited Jun. 25, 2020).

107. *E.g.*, Mack Lamoureux, *Canadian Conservatives Are Having a Bad Time at the Online Hate Hearings*, VICE (Jun. 4, 2019), https://www.vice.com/en_ca/article/ywyqbw/canadian-conservatives-are-having-a-bad-time-at-the-online-hate-hearings (Jun. 25, 2020).

debate was an infringement of her freedom of expression. It would be disingenuous to say this incident did not also implicate academic freedom.[108] To the extent that academic freedom includes the freedom of inquiry and freedom of teaching, outright denial of the validity of certain ideas also threatened the academic freedom of a budding scholar who, as she planned her lessons, may well be exploring different ideas to decide what topic(s) she should engage in her own research.

In June 2018, Shepherd filed a lawsuit against WLU, all staff members in the meeting, and a student, alleging "harassment, intentional infliction of nervous shock, negligence, and constructive dismissal" caused by their "objectively outrageous and flagrant conduct."[109] Later that year, Peterson filed two lawsuits against the university and all staff members at the meeting. The first one alleged defamation and injurious falsehood by remarks comparing him to Hitler and attacking his professional and personal character.[110] The second one alleged that the university issued a media statement accusing him of using his lawsuit "as a means of unduly limiting expression on matters of public interest, including gender identity."[111] One can only hope that these lawsuits have not distracted any of the involved staff members from their noble duties as educators and, regardless of the verdicts, will remind the public of the importance of freedom of expression in academia.

---

108. *E.g.*, Abigail Curlew, *Laurier University's "Free Speech" Controversy Ignores the Complexities of Academic Freedom*, NOW MAG. (Dec. 18, 2017), https://nowtoronto.com/news/laurier-university-free-speech-controversy-ignores-academic-freedom/ (last visited Jun. 25, 2020).

109. The student was among those whom Shepherd alleged partook in the "continuing abuse and a toxic climate from the university and its representatives" after the incident was made public. *E.g.*, James Jackson, *Jordan Peterson Suing Wilfrid Laurier University*, HAMILTON NEWS (Jun. 21, 2018), https://www.hamiltonnews.com/news-story/8687155-jordan-peterson-suing-wilfrid-laurier-university/

110. In Peterson's words, "I'm hoping that the combination of lawsuits will be enough to convince careless university professors and administrators blinded by their own ideology to be much more circumspect in their actions and their words." Tmcleanful, *Jordan Peterson Details His Lawsuit against Wilfrid Laurier University*, YOUTUBE (Jun. 27, 2018), https://www.youtube.com/watch?v=bPAX61SFbBk (last visited Jun. 28, 2020).

111. Maintaining that their comments about Peterson are not defamatory, Rambukkana and Pimlott nonetheless argue in a third-party claim that they could not have known the statements would be recorded or disseminated outside the meeting. They also maintain that Shepherd had "power and control" over the recording and its distribution and intended for the contents of the meeting to potentially become widely available and discussed. Any damages or injuries that the court may find Peterson suffered would be "attributable to Shepherd and her publication and dissemination" of the recording. Paola Lorrigio, *Two Laurier Professors Sue Former TA Who Recorded Disciplinary Meeting*, CANADIAN P. (Dec. 28, 2018) https://www.ctvnews.ca/canada/two-laurier-professors-sue-former-ta-who-recorded-disciplinary-meeting-1.4233791 (last visited Jun. 28, 2020).

Example 3

The Lindsay Shepherd incident preluded more attempts to muffle dissent, deplatform speakers, and cancel events on Canadian university campuses. In March 2019, some students at Queen's University School of Law started an online campaign against its three-year "Liberty Lectures" series, which was sponsored by law alumnus Greg Piasetzki and organized by Professor Bruce Pardy, a senior member of the law faculty.[112] The campaign letter denounced "the attempt of the 'Liberty Lectures' to co-opt the term 'free speech' as something which is ideologically juxtaposed to promoting inclusivity and diversity" and to invite speakers who "directly targeted minority groups by appropriating and disparaging their demands and overtly rejecting their phenomenological history and identity from behind a seemingly neutral podium of 'academic free speech.'"[113] It also accused the law school of endorsing the lecture series and allowing the series to make the school "an unwelcoming and unsafe place for those already underrepresented in the legal profession and to request from those students that they continually justify their own existence and right to belong."[114]

Without a doubt, all speakers whom Pardy invited had been outspoken and all lecture topics had been challenging and even divisive. The inaugural lecture, entitled "The Rising Tide of Compelled Speech in Canada," was given by Jordan Peterson in March 2018 as part of his book tour. In response to concerns among some professors about this lecture, Daniel Woolf, the principal of the university, defended it in a blog post: "Expressing one's affront to an idea or position is completely acceptable in an academic environment . . . blanket calls for censorship, however, are intellectually lazy and are anathema to scholarly pursuits."[115] An open letter by the concerned professors, which garnered approximately 130 signatures from faculty, students, and alumni, communicated their belief that Woolf's "free speech" defense failed to "adequately [cap-

112. Lucy Sun, *Student Letter against the Liberty Lectures*, CHANGE, https://www.change.org/p/queen-s-university-faculty-of-law-student-letter-against-the-liberty-lectures (last visited Jul. 9, 2020).
113. Lucy Sun, *Student Letter against the Liberty Lectures*, CHANGE, https://www.change.org/p/queen-s-university-faculty-of-law-student-letter-against-the-liberty-lectures (last visited Jul. 9, 2020).
114. Lucy Sun, *Student Letter against the Liberty Lectures*, CHANGE, https://www.change.org/p/queen-s-university-faculty-of-law-student-letter-against-the-liberty-lectures (last visited Jul. 9, 2020).
115. Daniel Woolf, *Informed Respectful Debate Is Central to Academia*, PRINCIPAL'S BLOG (Feb. 10, 2018), https://www.queensu.ca/connect/principal/2018/02/20/informed-respectful-debate-is-central-to-academia/ (last visited Jul. 9, 2020).

ture] the complexity of the nature of the issues at stake."[116] The "debates" to which he referred "take place within the context of a rising tide of white supremacy and hate."[117] Woolf was urged to use "this moment not just to proclaim the importance of free speech, but to acknowledge the objections to the speaker's views, the bases for these objections, and the costs borne by those who are harmed by this speech."[118] Case law indicates that if the university had banned the talk and been sued, the court would likely have deferred to the university's decision to cancel. Woolf allowed the speech to proceed by reiterating his free speech defense. In a faculty senate meeting, he highlighted the importance of diversity in thought and opinion: "I do not accept the notion that one can support freedom of speech, or academic freedom and simultaneously deny the speaker a platform . . . this removes the opportunity for those who disagree to challenge those views."[119]

On the day of the event, an estimated 150 people congregated outside the hall, many banging on garbage bins and chanting "F**k white supremacy" and other obscenities.[120] Not long after the event started, a former student on the upper story of the hall yelled "a f**king lie . . . [t]here's no such thing as compelled speech" at Pardy, who served as the host.[121] Two students then walked onto the stage, showing a large banner with the words "Freedom to smash bigotry," before they were ushered off by an event organizer.[122] Halfway through, some protesters began pounding on the hall windows until one stained glass

116. Sarina Grewal, *Official Open Letter about Jordan Peterson Event Released*, QUEEN'S UNIV. J. (Mar. 2, 2018), https://www.queensjournal.ca/story/2018-03-02/news/official-open-letter-about-jordan-peterson-event-released/

117. Sarina Grewal, *Official Open Letter about Jordan Peterson Event Released*, QUEEN'S UNIV. J. (Mar. 2, 2018), https://www.queensjournal.ca/story/2018-03-02/news/official-open-letter-about-jordan-peterson-event-released/

118. Sarina Grewal, *Official Open Letter about Jordan Peterson Event Released*, QUEEN'S UNIV. J. (Mar. 2, 2018), https://www.queensjournal.ca/story/2018-03-02/news/official-open-letter-about-jordan-peterson-event-released/

119. Sarina Grewal, *Official Open Letter about Jordan Peterson Event Released*, QUEEN'S UNIV. J. (Mar. 2, 2018), https://www.queensjournal.ca/story/2018-03-02/news/official-open-letter-about-jordan-peterson-event-released/

120. Christie Blatchford, *Jordan Peterson v. the New Freedom Fighters at Queen's University*, NAT'L POST (Mar. 8, 2018), https://nationalpost.com/opinion/christie-blatchford-jordan-peterson-vs-the-new-freedom-fighters-at-queens-university

121. Sarina Grewal, *Jordan Peterson Lecture Continues Despite Disruptions by Protesters*, QUEEN'S UNIV. J. (Mar. 6, 2018), https://www.queensjournal.ca/story/2018-03-06/news/jordan-peterson-lecture-continues-despite-disruptions-by-protesters/

122. Sarina Grewal, *Jordan Peterson Lecture Continues Despite Disruptions by Protesters*, QUEEN'S UNIV. J. (Mar. 6, 2018), https://www.queensjournal.ca/story/2018-03-06/news/jordan-peterson-lecture-continues-despite-disruptions-by-protesters/

window was broken.[123] Toward the end of the lecture, protesters blocked the front and back entrances of the hall. While several individuals barricaded the back entrance with garbage containers, one protester yelled "lock 'em in and burn it down!"[124]

The disruptive behavior of the protesters was a stark contrast to those of the host, the speaker, and the attendees, who remained calm, civil, and respectful throughout the event. In fact, one would be hard-pressed to find any instance of hate speech, or any expression that was remotely hateful or even discriminatory in the lecture. Peterson emphasized that his objection to Bill C-16 had nothing to do with transgender rights but everything to do with freedom of expression, adding that he received support from many transgender people who agreed with him.[125] When a student pointed out that people may have different versions of the truth and views regarding their identities, he clarified that the "real issue" was not the acknowledgment of other people's identities but the compulsion by law to do so.[126] Pardy concurred by stressing that all people have liberties and should not be legally compelled to validate others' choices[127]—liberty means nothing other than the freedom to do whatever one wishes without infringing on the freedom of others. Attendees might have adhered to the belief that legislating the use of pronouns is necessary to prohibit discrimination, and still have found value in other parts of the talk. For instance, during the question-and-answer session, Peterson urged the student audience to take control of their voices and write what they think rather than pandering to their professors who might hold strong or even ill-informed opinions that they do not agree with.[128] While remaining true to oneself rather than sacrificing one's

123. Sarina Grewal, *Jordan Peterson Lecture Continues Despite Disruptions by Protesters*, QUEEN'S UNIV. J. (Mar. 6, 2018), https://www.queensjournal.ca/story/2018-03-06/news/jordan-peterson-lecture-continues-despite-disruptions-by-protesters/

124. Hugh Mungus, *Jordan Peterson Protest at Queen's University: "Lock 'Em In and Burn It Down,"* YOUTUBE (Mar. 5, 2018), https://www.youtube.com/watch?v=xPyPSyM3B3c (last visited Jul. 9, 2020); Ian Sherriff-Scott, *Jordan Peterson Protesters Break Window at Grant Hall, Barricade Exits*, QUEEN'S UNIV. J. (Mar. 6, 2018), https://www.queensjournal.ca/story/2018-03-06/news/jordan-peterson-protesters-break-window-at-grant-hall-barricade-exits/

125. Jordan Peterson, *The Queen's University Talk: The Rising Tide of Compelled Speech*, YOUTUBE, 26:00–27:00 (Mar. 12, 2018), https://www.youtube.com/watch?v=MwdYpMS8s28&t=5731s (last visited Jul. 9, 2020).

126. Jordan Peterson, *The Queen's University Talk: The Rising Tide of Compelled Speech*, YOUTUBE, 40:30–42:30 (Mar. 12, 2018).

127. Jordan Peterson, *The Queen's University Talk: The Rising Tide of Compelled Speech*, YOUTUBE, 40:30–42:30 (Mar. 12, 2018).

128. Jordan Peterson, *The Queen's University Talk: The Rising Tide of Compelled Speech*, YOUTUBE, 49:30–50:10 (Mar. 12, 2018).

character for short-term gain may sound clichéd, the importance of this advice often gets overshadowed in an ideologically driven environment, in which courage can falter and even the most morally upright and intellectually honest may be tempted to toe the party line. Indeed, numerous thought-provoking questions were raised by students. One example was why genocides committed by fascists are always condemned, while those committed under communist regimes have been downplayed or even dismissed.[129] Any insight into this troubling phenomenon will not only shed light on why many people like to virtue-signal about the "alt-right" but are hesitant to condemn communists for the atrocities they have committed. It may also enable them to appreciate, rather than denounce, the use of the term "Chinazi" to refer to the Chinese Communist Party—one that combines the worst attributes of the radical left (communism) and the far right (fascism).

If there was any shortcoming in the Peterson-Pardy dialogue, it may be that the host's perspectives largely aligned with the speaker's and the perceived bias that resulted. Arguably, this was compensated by the one-hour question-and-answer session that allowed a dynamic exchange of ideas with the audience. It was both disappointing and ironic that none of Peterson's most vocal critics at the university, including those who attempted to deplatform him, came forward to challenge his views or ask for clarification during this session. Their inaction was likely due to the belief that such dialogues, taking place "within the context of a rising tide of white supremacy and hate," would only lead to conclusions that favor the powerful and oppress minorities.[130] This is a self-defeating attitude, given that the dialogues both on the stage and between the host/speaker and the audience were devoid of academic jargon and holders of this attitude did not provide a better alternative than dialogue and rational debate, an Enlightenment tradition, to approach the issue. The very belief itself was also self-contradictory, unless their perspectives regarding the topic were not derived from dialogue and debate, but born out of an unnamed, superior, and more enlightened method transcending the odious tide. In view of the critics' reluctance to openly engage with the speaker, the student protesters' outright refusal to attend his talk was not at all

129. Jordan Peterson, *The Queen's University Talk: The Rising Tide of Compelled Speech*, YouTube, 1.34:00–35:00 (Mar. 12, 2018).

130. Sarina Grewal, *Jordan Peterson Lecture Continues Despite Disruptions by Protesters*, Queen's Univ. J. (Mar. 6, 2018), https://www.queensjournal.ca/story/2018-03-06/news/jordan-peterson-lecture-continues-despite-disruptions-by-protesters/

surprising. Neither was their attempt to shut him down through violent and illegal means—conduct bearing an uncanny resemblance to that of the Red Guards during the Chinese Cultural Revolution—which unfortunately and astoundingly went unpunished by the university.[131]

In October 2018, *National Post* columnist Conrad Black, along with Joe Black, professor of business history at Queen's University, was invited to give the second lecture, titled "In Praise of Sir John A. Macdonald: Historical Icon Meets the PC Brigade." Pardy informed the faculty and students that the reason for the lecture was the recent removal of references to Sir John Macdonald, Canada's first prime minister, from the law school building.[132] Several professors raised objections, pointing out that it took place several days after the new Indigenous art installation at the building and the Orange Shirt Day that honors survivors and victims of residential schools.[133] The timing of the lecture made it seem like an insensitive and "provocative" arrangement.[134] However, whether provocative was positive (as in thought-provoking) or negative (as in intending to trigger hurt feelings) in part depended on the content of the talk, the values that it offered to the attendees, and whether the

---

131. Ian Sherriff-Scott, *Jordan Peterson Protesters Break Window at Grant Hall, Barricade Exits*, QUEEN'S UNIV. J. (Mar. 6, 2018), https://www.queensjournal.ca/story/2018-03-06/news/jordan-peterson-protesters-break-window-at-grant-hall-barricade-exits/. The willingness of one protester, who identified as "gender-queer" and went by the pronoun "they," to share their feelings toward the event in the university newspaper was a breath of fresh air. As this student recalled, they left the hall before the talk began, upon feeling that the presence of the protesters was not taken seriously and that standing with friends outside the hall was more important. However, by refusing to even attend the talk, they seemingly failed to understand the speaker's argument and was convinced that it was "derived from a consciousness that undermines trans folks' existence." As they put it: "[p]ronouns aren't a weapon of silence and recognizing someone for who they are isn't about legal philosophy. Rather, it's about love." There is no denying that love is a noble sentiment and this student deserved respect for taking the time to communicate through her writing. Yet one must question whether love can or should be compelled. While laws need to be enforced, and civility—in society or on campus—needs to be promoted, the "love" word is often exploited and turned into a tool of oppression by authoritarian regimes. Daisy, *My Experience at the Jordan Peterson Protest*, QUEEN'S UNIV. J. (Mar. 15, 2018), https://www.queensjournal.ca/story/2018-03-15/opinions/my-experience-at-the-jordan-peterson-protest/
132. Raechel Huizinger & Ian Sherriff-Scott, *Liberty Lecture Praises John A. Macdonald, Divides Law Faculty*, QUEEN'S UNIV. J. (Oct. 4, 2018), https://www.queensjournal.ca/story/2018-10-04/news/liberty-lecture-praises-john-a-macdonald-divides-law-faculty/; Ian Sherriff-Scott, *Law School Tense as Liberty Lecture Approaches*, QUEEN'S UNIV. J. (Sep. 28, 2018), https://www.queensjournal.ca/story/2018-09-28/news/law-school-tense-as-liberty-lecture-approaches/
133. Ian Sherriff-Scott, *Law School Tense as Liberty Lecture Approaches*, QUEEN'S UNIV. J. (Sep. 28, 2018), https://www.queensjournal.ca/story/2018-09-28/news/law-school-tense-as-liberty-lecture-approaches/
134. Ian Sherriff-Scott, *Law School Tense as Liberty Lecture Approaches*, QUEEN'S UNIV. J. (Sep. 28, 2018), https://www.queensjournal.ca/story/2018-09-28/news/law-school-tense-as-liberty-lecture-approaches/

manner in which it was conducted was civil enough to deliver these values. For those who had been instilled with the idea of "white guilt" and who believed that no benefits—or positive aftereffects—could possibly be brought about by colonialism, the talk might inspire them without trivializing the suffering that Indigenous peoples went through. Given that the decolonizing movement had been sweeping through many Canadian cities—in fact, throughout the Western world—and what happened at the law school was part of this trend, the event also offered an opportunity to reflect on how far decolonizing practices should go and whether decolonization of a country, a teaching curriculum, or a person is truly beneficial, worthy, or even possible. What if a person growing up in a British colony believes that she cannot be decolonized without being deprived of her very identity or spiritually and mentally "killed"—must this process proceed at the expense of her identity and spiritual and mental well-being? Some attendees might have felt devastated by praise of Canada's first prime minister and thoroughly unconvinced that he deserves any praise. Others might have trouble making up their minds. Some others might have walked away, discomforted but incited, their minds brimming with questions such as the following: Should the beautiful Indigenous artwork coexist with, rather than replace, Macdonald's painting or name? Should Queen's University be renamed if Queen Victoria was found out to be a white supremacist and to have committed racist acts by today's standards? What does a multicultural society like Canada need the most?

In March 2019, University of Pennsylvania law professor Amy Wax was invited to deliver the third lecture, titled "The Perilous Quest for Equal Results."[135] Wax rose to fame in the U.S. due in part to her critique of affirmative action policies at most American law schools and universities, which finds its equivalence in the diversity, equity, and inclusion initiatives in Canada.[136] Criticizing such initiatives, as explained in chapter 5, does not lead to discrimination or hate speech against minorities. Although Wax was not the first person in academia to criticize affirmative action, her negative comments about black students' academic performance at her law school, based upon her perception

135. Queen's University School of Law, *Events: The Perilous Quest for Equal Results*, QUEEN'S UNIVERSITY, https://law.queensu.ca/events/the-perilous-quest-for-equal-results-0

136. *See, e.g.*, Colleen Flaherty, *A Professor's "Repugnant" View*, INSIDE HIGHER EDUC. (Jul. 24, 2019), https://www.insidehighered.com/news/2019/07/24/penn-law-condemns-amy-waxs-recent-comments-race-and-immigration-others-call-her; Colleen Flaherty, *What a Professor Can't Say*, INSIDE HIGHER EDUC. (Mar. 15, 2018), https://www.insidehighered.com/news/2018/03/15/penn-says-amy-wax-will-no-longer-teach-required-first-year-law-courses-after-more

and memory, were not quite necessary to advance her argument.[137] It was thus understandable for students to feel triggered by what felt like personal attacks, and outrage over the remarks was predictable.[138] Numerous critics, though finding flaws in Wax's arguments about affirmative action and other topics as well as her manner of critique, have defended her against charges of racism.[139] Pardy could have invited one or more respectable, mild-mannered American academics to speak on the topic.[140] Doing so might have increased the general receptiveness to the talk, while creating far less noise than inviting Wax did. On the other hand, some people tolerating no criticism of these initiatives might have considered any lecture on this topic harmful, regardless of the speakers' reputations or intent or the substance of their arguments. In this most unfortunate (not at all impossible) scenario, those honored enough to be invited to deliver the lecture might have had their names unjustly dishonored for contributing to an important topic.

Principal Woolf acted properly by not caving in to the pressure of those who sought to deplatform the speakers. Judging from the overreactions of Pardy's lawyer colleagues, some of whom did appear to be ideologically driven and averse to facts and opinions countering their own, whether the law school provided an environment conducive to free inquiry was left in doubt. It is unclear whether all who signed the campaign letter against the Liberty Lecture series were members of the law school or even the university. Regardless, the supportive comments did not reflect well on their writers and on the law school that was supposed to have educated them. One comment, which called for more effort to eliminate "hate speech," insinuated that the lectures contained hate speech and revealed a complete lack of understanding of the legal term.[141] Another comment claiming that there is no "room for continued colonialist

---

137. Refer to chapter 6 for a detailed discussion on why criticisms of affirmative action need not be triggering to individuals.

138. See chapter 6 also for a detailed discussion of trigger warnings and affirmative action.

139. *See, e.g.*, Jonathan Zimmerman, *What's Wrong with the Attack on Amy Wax*, INSIDE HIGHER EDUC. (Sep. 4, 2019), https://www.insidehighered.com/views/2017/09/14/academics-may-not-agree-what-amy-wax-says-should-defend-her-right-say-it-essay; *see also* Christopher DeGroot, *Standing Up for Good Sense: A Defense of Amy Wax*, N. ENG. REV. (Oct. 2019), https://www.newenglishreview.org/Christopher_DeGroot/Standing_up_for_Good_Sense%3A_A_Defense_of_Amy_Wax/

140. Examples include law professor Richard Sander from the University of California, Los Angeles, who authored *Mismatch: How Affirmative Action Hurts Students It's Intended to Help, and Why Universities Won't Admit It* (2012) with legal journalist Stuart Taylor Jr., and Harvard law professor Jeannie Suk, who published an op-ed reflecting on her experience as an Asian American who gained acceptance to Yale University and the affirmative action battle at Harvard.

141. *See* Lucy Sun, *Student Letter against the Liberty Lectures*, CHANGE, https://www.change.org/p/queen-s-university-faculty-of-law-student-letter-against-the-liberty-lectures (last visited Jul. 9, 2020).

perceptions" on campus betrayed an authoritarian mindset that harbors no respect for freedom of thought, rational debate, and the value of persuasion.[142]

One nevertheless should never doubt the sincerity of the campaign letter, which ends with the following earnest statements: "As Queen's Law continues to strive to be a leader in Canadian law schools and legal academia, we ask you to reconsider the series of decisions which made it possible for the 'Liberty Lectures' to exist as they do today. We ask you to be conscious of how and where external funding is accepted by the school, and whether that funding will truly promote academic freedom or simply echo historical prejudice against disadvantaged groups. We ask you to have an honest and balanced conversation about the importance of 'free speech' on campuses. One day, when we are Queen's Law alumni ourselves, we wish to remember our experience of Queen's Law as one which celebrated our diversity and supported us regardless of our differences."[143]

Although there was no countercampaign in support of the lecture series, students who had enjoyed and looked forward to these lectures and worried about their possible cancellation, but who might have been far less vocal about their support, could have responded with equal earnestness: "As Queen's Law continues to strive to be a leader in Canadian law schools and legal academia that produces tough lawyers and critical thinkers, we ask you to reconsider the type of education and learning environment that made some students so convinced that the 'Liberty Lectures' led to prejudice against minorities and made the law school 'unsafe' for them, without even attending the events or appreciating that many students (minorities included) do want to be challenged. We ask you to be conscious of how and where external funding is accepted by the school, and whether that funding will truly promote academic freedom or enhance the formation of 'safe' echo chambers. We ask you to have an honest and balanced conversation about the meaning of 'hate speech' on campuses and in society and the urgency to distinguish it

---

142. *See* Lucy Sun, *Student Letter against the Liberty Lectures*, CHANGE, https://www.change.org/p/queen-s-university-faculty-of-law-student-letter-against-the-liberty-lectures (last visited Jul. 9, 2020). Philip Best, a critic of Aboriginal law and policy, was invited to deliver the fourth lecture in March 2020. It was postponed due to COVID-19. *See* Sydney Ko, *Indigenous Groups, Dean of Law Faculty Express Concern over Upcoming Liberty Lecture*, QUEEN'S UNIV. J. (Mar. 6, 2020), https://www.queensjournal.ca/story/2020-03-06/news/indigenous-groups-dean-of-law-faculty-express-concern-over-upcoming-liberty-lecture/

143. *See* Lucy Sun, *Student Letter against the Liberty Lectures*, CHANGE, https://www.change.org/p/queen-s-university-faculty-of-law-student-letter-against-the-liberty-lectures (last visited Jul. 9, 2020).

from rational, spirited debates and difficult conversations on important matters. One day, when we are Queen's Law alumni ourselves, we wish to remember our experience of Queen's Law as one that toughened our minds and trained us to be better lawyers, thinkers, and human beings, which celebrated the diversity of thought and opinion and not merely of skin color, and which welcomed and supported us regardless of our political leanings, beliefs, and interests, rather than facilitating the view that those holding or exploring different perspectives are 'bonkers,' 'bad guys,' and 'bigots.'"

Not all principals are reasonable and intellectually honest like Woolf. In 2020, the new principal, Patrick Deane, published an op-ed in the university's alumni review arguing that the whole idea of free speech is constrained by Eurocentric assumptions that are "unimaginable except as facilitated by social and economic privilege" and suggesting that the university must be remade according to "the principles of equity, diversity, inclusion and Indigeneity" in order not to perpetuate "systemic oppression."[144] The op-ed thus insinuates that censorship is justified to save minority groups, who are victims of free speech, from oppression.[145] To be fair, Deane may not be aware that free speech is a universal value the importance of which has been affirmed not only in European but also other cultures.[146] However, as a reader wisely stated, the notion that free expression is oppressive rather than liberating is strangely reminiscent of "freedom is slavery" in George Orwell's classic *Nineteen Eighty-Four.*[147] The biggest irony, though, remains that even if Deane may not be well versed in world history, philosophy, or even Orwell's works (which would be strange given his background in literature!), as a Canadian he should have been aware of the fact that many immigrants of non-European descent in Canada have escaped from dictatorships in their home countries to pursue better lives in what is supposed to be a democratic society, of which freedom of speech serves as a cornerstone.

---

144. Patrick Deane, *The Choices We Made*, QUEEN'S ALUMNI REV. (Mar. 2020), http://www.queensu.ca/gazette/alumnireview/stories/principal-choices-we-make (last visited Dec. 22, 2020).
145. *See* Patrick Deane, *The Choices We Made*, QUEEN'S ALUMNI REV. (Mar. 2020), http://www.queensu.ca/gazette/alumnireview/stories/principal-choices-we-make (last visited Dec. 22, 2020).
146. Examples can be found even in Chinese history, although China is unfortunate enough to have fallen under the control by the CCP. Fan Zhongyan (989–1052), a nobleman and reformist in the Sung Dynasty, said it would be "better to die for speaking the truth, than to stay alive by remaining quiet."
147. Calum Anderson, *Letter to the Editor*, QUEEN'S J. (Oct. 13, 2020), www.queensjournal.ca/story/2020-10-13/opinions/letter-to-the-editor-october-13th/

Example 4

Speakers did get deplatformed. One example was Andy Ngo, an American journalist of Vietnamese descent whom the Free Speech Club of the University of British Columbia (UBC) invited to deliver a talk titled "Understanding Antifa (Anti-fascist) Violence" on UBC's Robson Square campus in January 2020.[148] Having paid the booking deposit and having the talk confirmed in November 2019, the Free Speech Club was notified by the university in December that the event had to be canceled due to concerns about the safety and security of the campus community.[149] After UBC refused to rescind the cancellation, the club, with the help of the Justice Centre for Constitutional Freedoms, brought a lawsuit against UBC for its cancellation of the event and "its refusal to defend freedom of expression."[150]

It would be fair to distinguish antifascism, which is a noble cause and nonviolent per se, from Antifa as a protest group, which frequently commits violence and of which Ngo became a victim. Those claiming that people who are "anti-Antifa" are pro-fascist need a serious education in logical thinking. UBC forfeited its duty as a higher educational institution by unilaterally terminating its agreement with the Free Speech Club to host Ngo's talk on its campus, an agreement that obligated it to provide Ngo a platform for what would have been a timely and educational lecture of tremendous importance on this militant protest group that had attacked him physically in the past.[151] In fact, Ngo's book

148. *E.g.*, Henry Anderson & Helen Livingstone, *Free Speech Club Takes UBC to Court for Cancellation of Andy Ngo Event*, UBYSSEY (Jan. 13, 2020), https://www.ubyssey.ca/news/FSC-takes-UBC-to-court/ (last visited May 23, 2020); Jennifer Saltman, *UBC Event Cancelled, Debate Continues about Free Expression on Campus*, VANCOUVER SUN (Jan. 5, 2020), https://vancouversun.com/news/local-news/ubc-event-cancelled-debate-continues-about-free-expression-on-campus/

149. *E.g.*, Henry Anderson & Helen Livingstone, *Free Speech Club Takes UBC to Court for Cancellation of Andy Ngo Event*, UBYSSEY (Jan. 13, 2020), https://www.ubyssey.ca/news/FSC-takes-UBC-to-court/ (last visited May 23, 2020); Jennifer Saltman, *UBC Event Cancelled, Debate Continues about Free Expression on Campus*, VANCOUVER SUN (Jan. 5, 2020), https://vancouversun.com/news/local-news/ubc-event-cancelled-debate-continues-about-free-expression-on-campus/

150. Free Speech Club, *We Are Suing UBC*, FREE SPEECH CLUB (Jan. 13, 2020), https://www.freespeechclub.com/news (last visited May 23, 2020); *also* Henry Anderson & Helen Livingstone, *Free Speech Club Takes UBC to Court for Cancellation of Andy Ngo Event*, UBYSSEY (Jan. 13, 2020), https://www.ubyssey.ca/news/FSC-takes-UBC-to-court/ (last visited May 23, 2020).

151. The Free Speech Club, which did not apply for official club status with UBC's Student Society, has had a tradition of inviting individuals whom the left-wing consider to be controversial speakers, including American right-wing speaker Ben Shapiro, who campus groups campaigned to deplatform but failed. *E.g.*, Thea Udwadia, *Students Call on UBC to Cancel Ben Shapiro Talk*, UBYSSEY (Jun. 19, 2018), https://www.ubyssey.ca/news/student-letters-against-ben-shapiro-event-on-campus/ (last visited May 23, 2020).

Unmasked: Inside Antifa's Radical Plan to Destroy Democracy became an instant national bestseller after its publication in 2021. The university's risk assessment showing that the event could put its students, faculty, staff, and infrastructure at risk was not without grounds, given that Ngo had attracted violent protesters in the past.[152] However, the accusation that Ngo liked to harass minorities was groundless: on the contrary, he was the very victim of Antifa violence, which he did not deserve no matter how offensive his speech might have been to this group or others.[153] Rather than caving in to pressure by extremists, the university should have worked with the Free Speech Club to implement measures to increase the likelihood that Ngo's talk and discussion could proceed safely. It was deeply ironic that a lecture on Antifa violence, for which Ngo's firsthand experience made him a qualified speaker, had to be canceled due to perceived threats by extremists whom the university administrators were too cowardly to stand up to.

How will the provincial court rule on this case? Because Canadian courts have followed a tradition of affirming the autonomy of postsecondary institutions in making decisions, the court may reject claims that UBC breached the Free Speech Club's Charter right to freedom of expression by refusing its space for hosting Ngo's talk, on the grounds that university is not government and extracurricular activities as such fall outside of "government programs."[154] Nonetheless, the Alberta Court of Appeal's decision in early 2020, though not binding on any BC court's decisions, might also have some impact on how the BC court will rule on UBC's refusal to reinstate Ngo's event. Hence, the judge may also be persuaded that UBC's cancellation was a form of governmental action, and may consider that the infrastructure and landholdings granted to UBC or sustained by its funding are designed to serve the core purpose of the university by permitting debate and sharing of ideas in a community space.[155] If so, the BC court may determine that UBC had not established that the can-

152. *E.g.*, James A. Gagliano, *We Need to Pay Attention to the Attack on Andy Ngo*, CNN (Jul. 2, 2019), https://www.cnn.com/2019/07/02/opinions/antifa-andy-ngo-gagliano/index.html (last visited May 23, 2020); Editorial Board, *Antifa Attacks a Journalist*, Wall St. J. (Jul. 1, 2019), https://www.wsj.com/articles/antifa-attacks-a-journalist-1156202136

153. *See, e.g.*, Henry Anderson & Helen Livingstone, *Free Speech Club Takes UBC to Court for Cancellation of Andy Ngo Event*, Ubyssey (Jan. 13, 2020), https://www.ubyssey.ca/news/FSC-takes-UBC-to-court/ (last visited May 23, 2020); James A. Gagliano, *We Need to Pay Attention to the Attack on Andy Ngo*, CNN (Jul. 2, 2019), https://www.cnn.com/2019/07/02/opinions/antifa-andy-ngo-gagliano/index.html (last visited May 23, 2020).

154. *See* BC Civil Liberties Association [2016] BCCA 162; Lobo [2012] ONSC 254.

155. *See* UAlberta Pro-Life [2020] ABCA 1.

cellation of the event affected the Club's Charter right "as little as possible in light of the applicable statutory objectives."[156]

Example 5

Deplatforming academics by terminating their employment or forcing them to resign has also happened in Canadian universities. In May 2019, a group of academics at the University of New Brunswick issued a public letter condemning the views of their colleague Ricardo Duchesne, a professor of sociology, as "racist and without academic merit" and alleging that he abused his status by "[c]loaking these views in academic legitimacy."[157] In response, Duchesne, a mixed-race immigrant from Puerto Rico, asserted his academic freedom and his "right to criticize the mandated ideology of diversity and mass immigration" that was "initiated and supported by privileged white people."[158] In June of the same year, the university announced that Duchesne would retire to pursue his research independently after twenty-four years of service.[159] Although Duchesne, who insisted that he was no racist or white supremacist, declined to answer questions about the reasons for his "retirement," whether he received any financial incentive to depart, or whether he had been told of the results of the university's investigation into allegations against him, circumstances indicated that he was likely forced to resign.[160]

Duchesne's colleagues' allegation that his work violated professional ethics and rules prohibiting discrimination is not without grounds. His statement that European civilization is superior and mass immigration is "downgrading" European civilization is not inherently racist, nor is his statement that the influx of Chinese immigrants to Vancouver had been "too fast" and bad for the city—

---

156. *See* UAlberta Pro-Life [2020] ABCA 1.

157. Joe Friesen & Jessica Leeder, *Academics at University of New Brunswick Criticize Professor for Alleged Racist Positions*, GLOBE & MAIL (May 23, 2019), https://www.theglobeandmail.com/canada/article-academics-at-university-of-new-brunswick-criticize-professor-for/

158. Joe Friesen & Jessica Leeder, *Academics at University of New Brunswick Criticize Professor for Alleged Racist Positions*, GLOBE & MAIL (May 23, 2019), https://www.theglobeandmail.com/canada/article-academics-at-university-of-new-brunswick-criticize-professor-for/

159. Joe Friesen, *Controversial University of New Brunswick Professor to Retire amid Probe*, GLOBE & MAIL (Jun. 4, 2019), https://www.theglobeandmail.com/canada/article-controversial-university-of-new-brunswick-professor-to-retire-amid/

160. *See* Joe Friesen, *Controversial University of New Brunswick Professor to Retire amid Probe*, GLOBE & MAIL (Jun. 4, 2019), https://www.theglobeandmail.com/canada/article-controversial-university-of-new-brunswick-professor-to-retire-amid/

even assuming that they are poorly reasoned or proven to be wrong.[161] Neither would lead to racial discrimination. European civilization is indeed highly esteemed by many and for good reasons, one being that democracy originated in ancient Greece. Rapid demographic changes due to mass immigration do lead to problems that must not be overlooked. Yet his book *Canada in Decay*, which criticizes the undemocratic policy of mass immigration and racial diversification in Canada, goes beyond statements on Europeans' cultural superiority by offering an argument that is at least partially race-based. It aims to debunk official myths promulgated by Canadian institutions by arguing that Canada was founded by Indigenous Quebecois, Acadians, and English speakers and that mass immigration will cause Euro-Canadians to become a small minority in their homeland.[162] However, it is one thing to argue that the culture of the founding Europeans is superior. It is another thing to conclude, as his book does, that the influx of racial and ethnic minorities will lead to the "ethnocide" of Euro-Canadians and Canada's "decay" and that minority immigrants cannot integrate, embrace the strengths of Canadian cultures, and contribute to Canadian society due to their race or ethnicity. As much as he seems to dislike racial politics promulgated by the elites, which is the basis of the multiracial and multicultural policies that he detests, he promotes his own racial politics according to which Euro(white)-Canadians, by virtue of their skin color, are superior to other races and ethnicities, and their dominance is necessary to stop Canada from falling into "decay."

Duchesne has not been able to prove the superiority of the white race or a definite link between race and culture. In addition, whether there is any truth to his argument that Canada is being destroyed by nonwhite immigrants, his work, which falls short of offering any constructive solution to better a multicultural Canadian society, arguably promotes discrimination against Canadians of non-European descent. While freedom of expression entails the right to harbor racist views, and a racist speaker at a one-off event would not lead to real, substantial harm to a university, a professor should not have used his platform—a permanent one no less—to promote racism and discrimination without offering solutions, or touted his work, published by a nonacademic press, as

---

161. *See* Joe Friesen, *Controversial University of New Brunswick Professor to Retire amid Probe*, GLOBE & MAIL (Jun. 4, 2019), https://www.theglobeandmail.com/canada/article-controversial-university-of-new-brunswick-professor-to-retire-amid/

162. RICARDO DUCHESNE, CANADA IN DECAY: MASS IMMIGRATION, DIVERSITY, AND THE ETHNOCIDE OF EURO-CANADIANS (2018).

academic writing.[163] In fact, Duchesne never hides his racial politics in his social media posts, which are consistently dripping with his obsession with skin color and the superiority of the white race. For instance, one of his race-obsessed Twitter posts says that all the world's great writers are whites.[164] This is an unfounded, ludicrous claim coming from someone who is at best a sociologist with no expertise in literature and presumably has not read most works of literature in their original languages. Deplatforming him may seem like a drastic measure. Nonetheless, one cannot help but wonder whether he should have been hired and given a permanent or long-term platform in the first place. Certainly, given that a candidate typically puts his best foot forward and delivers a positive image at the job interview, it likely was impossible for his former employer to foresee the racism and discriminatory content in his works and Twitter posts published many years down the road.

Example 6

Many international students from China easily take offense at criticisms of the Chinese government that contain no hate speech or racism against them. In numerous incidents, they have attempted to shut down criticisms on racism grounds, sometimes through violent or disruptive methods. Unfortunately, Canadian universities very rarely denounced such actions, let alone punished or reported them to the police. Their inaction and complacency have played into the hands of those who habitually pull the race card and appropriate Western liberal narratives of free speech, tolerance, and dignity to suppress criticism of hostile and corrupt governments, including intellectually honest criticism indispensable both to academia and for the democratic governance of Canada.

In early 2019, Chemi Lhamo, a Canadian citizen of Tibetan origin and a longtime advocate of the Tibetan independence movement, was elected the

163. One should also note that Duchesne published his work with Black House Publishing, a nonacademic publisher seeking to publish works that mainstream publishers "dare not handle" and that "freedom loving liberals" "have sought to silence." Although a book should be judged by its contents and not by its publisher, it would be fair to say that books that tackle controversial subject matter should not have trouble finding better publishers if they contain some academic merit. This book you are now reading, which is not without its share of controversial opinions, managed to draw the attention of several very reputable publishers before finding its comfortable and welcoming home at the University of Michigan Press.

164. *See* Duchesne's race-obsessed Twitter account: http://twitter.com/DuchesneRicardo (last visited May 20, 2020).

student president of the University of Toronto's Scarborough campus. Soon after that, her photo on Instagram drew thousands of hateful comments by her fellow students from China, most expressing "one China" and anti-Tibet sentiments while others were downright threatening.[165] An online petition, which demanded that she be removed from the post on the grounds that her political stance and "irrational" criticism of China—"her own country"—made her ineligible to represent the student body, amassed over 10,000 signatures.[166] A former Canadian Security Intelligence Service official for the Asia-Pacific region rightly believed that the campaign against Lhamo was directly supported by the Chinese government as part of its aggressive attempts to conduct surveillance of dissidents overseas and extend its political influence into foreign nations.[167]

Lhamo was, without a doubt, entitled to advocate for Tibetan independence. Her criticism of the Chinese government did not constitute hate speech or discrimination against Chinese. On the contrary, some of her attackers, by threatening her or otherwise causing her to fear for her safety, breached the provincial law prohibiting harassment. Ironically, what was irrational was not Lhamo's criticism of China, but her attackers' allegation that China was her "own country," considering that she was in fact a Canadian citizen. It would be beyond despicable for the Chinese embassy, which denied involvement in these attacks, to have attempted to quell dissent outside its jurisdiction. The death threats were reported, at Lhamo's request, to the Toronto and campus police, who at least attempted to investigate the matter. On the contrary, the university, where the attacks took place, did not publicly denounce the attackers' conduct or issue a formal statement in support of Lhamo: its administrators' inaction at best indicated their negligence, and at worst betrayed their lack of moral courage.

---

165. An example of the former was "China is your daddy—you better know this." Examples of the latter included "Ur [You're] not gonna be the president of UTSC. Even if you do, we will make sure things get done so u [you] won't survive a day. Peace RIP [rest in peace]." "People like u deserve a gunshot. Hope you go to hell immediately." Tom Blackwell, *Tibetan Canadian Student Politician, Uyghur Rights Activist Come under Attack by Chinese Students in Canada*, NAT'L POST (Feb. 14, 2019), https://nationalpost.com/news/canada/tibetan-canadian-student-politician-uyghur-rights-activist-come-under-attack-by-chinese-students-in-canada; *"China Is Your Daddy": Backlash against Tibetan Student's Election Prompts Questions about Foreign Influence*, CBC NEWS (Feb. 14, 2019, 4:52 PM), https://www.cbc.ca/news/canada/toronto/china-tibet-student-election-1.5019648
166. As of June 2, 2022, the link to the petition is still available at https://www.change.org/p/update-on-petition (last visited May 6, 2020).
167. *E.g.*, *"China Is Your Daddy": Backlash against Tibetan Student's Election Prompts Questions about Foreign Influence*, CBC NEWS (Feb. 14, 2019), https://www.cbc.ca/news/canada/toronto/china-tibet-student-election-1.5019648

It was highly unlikely for the Chinese attackers to have been uninformed about Charter values and Canadian university policies. In fact, these attackers, be they formally backed by the Chinese government or not, regularly appropriated the Western narratives of free speech and human dignity in their attempts to shut down criticisms of the Chinese government. Also in early 2019, two Muslim student groups at McMaster University invited Rukiye Turdush, a social worker who escaped from China, to address the well-documented abuses of the Uyghur minority by the Chinese government. A coalition of five Chinese student groups at the university issued a statement decrying this "ridiculous anti-China event," saying that it promoted "hatred" against China and "infringed" the "dignity of the Chinese students."[168] One Chinese student engaged in menacing conduct by videotaping the event and swearing loudly when questioned about his opinions on her talk. This time, the Chinese embassy, which as usual denied involvement in the protests, lauded the students for their "just and patriotic actions" and emphasized that they enjoyed freedom of expression to protest the event.[169] In response to this despotic abuse of liberal narratives, McMaster reiterated the university's commitment to freedom of expression of all people and allowed the talk to go forward, although it fell short of its obligation by failing to denounce the student's conduct or punish him for it.[170]

Apparently, it has been rare for Canadian universities to publicly denounce the increasingly common attempts to shut down criticisms of China, let alone punish violent offenders or report them to the police. When the "Lennon Wall" at Simon Fraser University, set up in the wake of Hong Kong's pro-democracy movement in 2019 to enable people to show solidarity with Hong Kong protesters, was destroyed by Chinese students who disagreed with the movement and the supportive notes on the wall, the university's spokesperson denounced such conduct and stressed the need for respectful dialogue.[171] Yet when similarly

---

168. Tom Blackwell, *Tibetan Canadian Student Politician, Uyghur Rights Activist Come under Attack by Chinese Students in Canada*, NAT'L POST (Feb. 14, 2019), https://nationalpost.com/news/canada/tibetan-canadian-student-politician-uyghur-rights-activist-come-under-attack-by-chinese-students-in-canada

169. Tom Blackwell, *Uyghur Activist Who Sparked Chinese Student Protest at McMaster Worried about Message Targeting Her Son*, NAT'L POST (Feb. 15, 2019), https://nationalpost.com/news/uyghur-activist-who-sparked-chinese-student-protest-at-mcmaster-worried-about-message-targeting-her-son

170. *See* Tom Blackwell, *Uyghur Activist Who Sparked Chinese Student Protest at McMaster Worried about Message Targeting Her Son*, NAT'L POST (Feb. 15, 2019), https://nationalpost.com/news/uyghur-activist-who-sparked-chinese-student-protest-at-mcmaster-worried-about-message-targeting-her-son

171. Xiao Xu, *Hong Kong Tensions Reach B.C's Simon Fraser University as Notes, Posters Supporting Protests Partly Torn Down*, GLOBE & MAIL (Jul. 28, 2019), https://www.theglobeandmail.com/canada/british-columbia/article-hong-kong-tensions-reach-bcs-simon-fraser-university-as-notes/

disturbing incidents happened at UBC, including not only the vandalizing of its Lennon Wall but also the violent disruption of a Hong Kong pro-democracy rally on its campus, the university administration only paid lip service to the importance of free speech by stressing the need for constructive debate, but failed to punish the offenders or report their criminal behavior.[172]

Students from China did manage to shut down a speech on at least on one occasion. In April 2020, during the height of the COVID-19 pandemic, Waterloo University professor Dipanjan Basu posted about China and the pandemic on Facebook. He called China "an expert in producing viruses" and criticized the way it profited off of the pandemic, which was to "[c]reate a problem, hide it, suppress those who talk about it, and then make business out of it."[173] Other posts alluded to the Wuhan bat market, which was believed by some to be the origin of the virus: "How will bat chow mein taste?" "Rat, Bat, Cat, . . .—Thinking Chinese!"[174] Basu soon deleted them and closed his account. A group of Chinese students petitioned online to hold him responsible for "provoking racism."[175] Hong Kong students counterpetitioned to "say no to Chinese denialism" and to "commend" Basu's "bravery and willingness to speak truth to power."[176] The university's spokesperson expressed concern about his use of "racist language," while the university stated that it "does not condone racism in any form and makes every effort to support a culture of acceptance and respect."[177]

---

172. *E.g.*, Salomon Micko Benrimoh & Henry Anderso, *At Rally on Chinese National Day, Students Clash over Democracy in Hong Kong*, UBYSSEY (Oct. 2, 2019), https://www.ubyssey.ca/news/clash-over-deomcracy-in-hong-kong-rally/ (last visited May 7, 2020); Gabriel Robinson-Leith, *Despite Vandalism, Students Erect Lennon Walls for Hong Kong Protesters*, UBYSSEY (Sep. 11, 2019), https://www.ubyssey.ca/news/students-erect-lennon-walls-for-hong-kong/ (last visited May 7, 2020). One student from China poured water over the pro-democracy protesters, while another attempted to destroy their property. *See, e.g.*, Xiaofeng, *Hong Kong Pro-Democracy Rally at UBC*, YOUTUBE (Oct. 1, 2019), https://www.youtube.com/watch?v=CUA1I_jJkjc (last visited May 9, 2020).
173. Carl Samson, *University Professor Calls China an "Expert" in Producing Viruses, Pakistan in Terrorists*, NEXT SHARK (Apr. 3, 2020), https://nextshark.com/racist-professor-china-producing-viruses/ (last visited May 11, 2020).
174. Carl Samson, *University Professor Calls China an "Expert" in Producing Viruses, Pakistan in Terrorists*, NEXT SHARK (Apr. 3, 2020), https://nextshark.com/racist-professor-china-producing-viruses/ (last visited May 11, 2020).
175. Liumen Wu, *Make Prof. Dipanjan Basu Responsible for Provoking Racism*, CHANGE.ORG, https://www.change.org/p/university-of-waterloo-make-prof-dipanjan-basu-responsible-for-provoking-racism (May 12, 2020).
176. Edward Leung, *Say No to Chinese Denialism: Support Prof. Dipanjan Basu for Speaking on the Wuhan Virus*, CHANGE.ORG, https://www.change.org/p/university-of-waterloo-say-no-to-chinese-denialism-support-prof-dipanjan-basu-for-speaking-about-the-wuhan-virus (last visited May 12, 2020).
177. Carl Samson, *University Professor Calls China an "Expert" in Producing Viruses, Pakistan in Terrorists*, NEXT SHARK (Apr. 3, 2020), https://nextshark.com/racist-professor-china-producing-viruses/ (last visited May 11, 2020).

On this occasion, the Chinese students' indignation was partly justified. Because racism is defined as the belief that one race is inherently superior to others, Basu's statements that COVID-19 originated from China and that its government profited from the pandemic are not racist. In fact, distinguishing unfounded prejudices against a certain race from criticisms of their government is not only a good way to fight racism but can also help prevent the race card from being used to shut down criticism of corrupt governments. In addition, as chapter 5 explains, excessive political correctness and the avoidance of potentially offensive statements would thwart the pursuit of knowledge. Basu was entitled to make statements about the origin of the virus even if they turned out to be factually wrong. The other statements, however, might lead to discrimination even if they were not made with racist intent. "How will bat chow mein taste?," if addressed to a random Chinese or East Asian, insinuates that all Chinese eat bats, although this unsanitary, disease-spreading habit is practiced only by some people in China. "Rat, Bat, Cat, . . .—Thinking Chinese!" likewise generalizes the eating habit of some people in China to all people of Chinese descent. Whether the university determined that all statements made by the professor are racist remains a mystery. It could, and should, have turned this incident into an educational opportunity to explain what racism truly means—even though many students from China, who have been taught to identify strongly with their government, may find it difficult to understand that there is nothing racist about criticizing their government or any government.

Example 7

Contrary to the frequently disruptive and often violent protests by nationalistic Chinese students, there have been very few—if any—protests targeting speakers who defended the Chinese government, and no attempts at all to shut down their speech at Canadian universities. Those who might have harbored strong sentiments against the Chinese government, for example, exemplified considerable forbearance and respect at a poorly moderated seminar hosted by UBC. Hence, when a Chinese government official defended the state policy of sending Uyghurs to Xinjiang concentration camps for "reeducation," no suitably qualified moderator engaged this government official in a productive dialogue, and his denial of human rights abuses in his speech, which lacked academic merit and sounded like typical Chinese propaganda, remained unchallenged.[178]

178. The speaker was Yu Jiantuo, an assistant secretary general of the China Development Research Foun-

In an interesting turn of events, the Students Union of McMaster University made a decision in September 2019 that might be accused of intolerance by the nationalistic Chinese students. It decertified the Chinese Students and Scholars Association (CSSA) by revoking all its privileges as a student club, due to its alleged links to the Chinese government, for example, as indicated by reporting Turdush's talk to the Chinese embassy earlier that year. In its statement, the Students Union claimed that the CSSA had "coordinated closely with Chinese diplomatic officials" and "tried to obscure their connections to the Chinese government while simultaneously surveilling and intimidating students on campus who speak out against the Chinese government."[179] In decertifying the CSSA, the Students Union thus aimed to "protect McMaster students from possible consequences they may face for simply voicing their concerns and having beliefs that are . . . legitimate."[180] The CSSA's appeal of its decertification failed miserably.[181]

The McMaster Students Union might seem to have betrayed the liberal value of free speech by depriving the CSSA a platform, especially to Chinese students or the Chinese consulate-generals who have a knack for appropriating liberal narratives to advance their own agenda. What the Students Union did, in fact, was to stop a hostile government from reaching across the Pacific Ocean to threaten the freedom of expression, academic freedom, and safety of all McMaster members. Intimidating its members or otherwise making them feel threatened contravenes Canadian laws. Hence, the university has every right to decertify a student club when its mandates or ideologies are found to violate Canada's human rights laws, which in this case the CSSA clearly and unabashedly did.[182]

---

dation, which is run by the State Council of China. The two moderators were Institute of Asian Research professor Yves Tiberghien and a senior fellow of the institute, Evan Due. Tiberghien did not attend the Q&A session, while Due also served as a consultant of the research institute where Yu worked, making him a highly inappropriate moderator of his talk.

179. Justin Mowat, *McMaster Student Union Bans Chinese Students' Group from Campus*, CBC (Sep. 26, 2019), https://www.cbc.ca/news/canada/hamilton/mcmaster-china-student-association-ban-1.5298882

180. In fact, the Students Union's decision was supported by anonymous testimony by a student of Chinese ethnicity, whose identity was kept secret for safety concerns, stating that the CSSA, "[b]y reporting a Uyghur refugee to a genocidal regime," "sen[t] a chilling message to students on campus: toe the Party line, or you will also be reported, and thus suffer the consequences." Justin Mowat, *McMaster Student Union Bans Chinese Students' Group from Campus*, CBC (Sep. 26, 2019), https://www.cbc.ca/news/canada/hamilton/mcmaster-china-student-association-ban-1.5298882

181. Owen Churchill, *Chinese Student Association at McMaster University Loses Appeal: Remains Decertified after Report of On-Campus Talk to Consulate*, S. China Morning Post (Nov. 5, 2019), https://www.scmp.com/news/china/diplomacy/article/3036309/chinese-student-association-mcmaster-university-loses-appeal (last visited May 12, 2020).

182. *See* Grant v. Ryerson Students' Union [2016] ONSC 5519.

In an opinion published anonymously, a student from China decried the Students Union's decision and its "hurtful and damaging message," which left Chinese students at McMaster all "angry and confused."[183] The student played the race card, perhaps inadvertently, by calling the disbanding of the CSSA "racist" for discriminating against Chinese students on the grounds of their "political expressions, free speech and ancestral origin."[184] Yet the decertification of the CSSA by no means deprived these students of their rights to express their pro-China views and associate with their compatriots; it only aimed to stop the Chinese government from interfering with the freedoms of McMaster members and its effects would be limited as such. Although, as the writer claimed, the belief in an "unified and prosperous" China is not "extremist" or "dangerous" in itself,[185] reporting expressions criticizing the Chinese government to the Chinese embassy made speakers feel intimidated and put their safety at risk. The writer rightly argued that the real test for racism is "how one treats minority groups who do not agree with you and do things that make you feel uncomfortable."[186] It is nonetheless not racist by any stretch of imagination to curb conduct that jeopardizes other people's freedoms and safety and undermines the democratic governance of Canada.

Honestly, a reasonable reader cannot help spotting the hypocrisy of this "proud Chinese student" who chose to make Canada home after "great consideration" despite harboring such pride in the great motherland,[187] and who both embraced Western liberal values and condoned human rights abuses in China. After all, can people honestly say they love their spouses while being sexually committed to others? Do such people have any claim to fidelity, chastity, and integrity? Certainly, it is only human to harbor a certain degree of attachment

---

183. Anonymous, *CSSA-Gate at McMaster: The Scars of Exclusion*, The Silhouette (Nov. 7, 2019), www.thesil.ca/opinion-cssa-gate-at-mcmaster-the-scars-of-exclusion (last visited May 12, 2020).
184. *See* Anonymous, *CSSA-Gate at McMaster: The Scars of Exclusion*, The Silhouette (Nov. 7, 2019), www.thesil.ca/opinion-cssa-gate-at-mcmaster-the-scars-of-exclusion (last visited May 12, 2020).
185. Anonymous, *CSSA-Gate at McMaster: The Scars of Exclusion*, The Silhouette (Nov. 7, 2019), www.thesil.ca/opinion-cssa-gate-at-mcmaster-the-scars-of-exclusion (last visited May 12, 2020).
186. Anonymous, *CSSA-Gate at McMaster: The Scars of Exclusion*, The Silhouette (Nov. 7, 2019), www.thesil.ca/opinion-cssa-gate-at-mcmaster-the-scars-of-exclusion (last visited May 12, 2020); in fact, a clearheaded Chinese student wrote a witty and compelling response by asking this writer to apply the same freedom of expression principle to the "Uyghurs who are suffering in concentration camps for the high crime of not being sufficiently Han Chinese, or the visible minority students who, after Mac CSSA's actions, became fearful of openly criticizing the Chinese government." J., *Having Chinese Diplomats on Our Campus Is Alarming*, The Silhouette (Nov. 14, 2019), https://www.thesil.ca/opinion-having-chinese-diplomats-on-our-campus-is-alarming (last visited May 12, 2020).
187. *See* Anonymous, *CSSA-Gate at McMaster: The Scars of Exclusion*, The Silhouette (Nov. 7, 2019), www.thesil.ca/opinion-cssa-gate-at-mcmaster-the-scars-of-exclusion (last visited May 12, 2020).

to one's country of birth and cultural roots, while racism and discrimination are never excusable. Yet can one truly blame Canadians—those with a heart and a conscience—for feeling wary and distrustful of nationalistic immigrants from China who joyously wave the Chinese flag and sing its national anthem, zealously praise its authoritarian government, and heartlessly and unrelentingly defend its well-documented atrocities in their new home?

The McMaster Students Union showed tremendous moral courage in safeguarding the freedom of expression and safety of its students. Other Canadian universities and their student unions should follow suit should they discover that their student clubs are backed by foreign governments attempting to intervene against their freedoms. This would nonetheless be difficult due to the heavy reliance on Chinese money. In the wake of Meng Wanzhou's arrest by the Canadian government (and the Chinese government's arrests of the "two Michaels" in what seemed to be its retaliation against Canada),[188] the internal documents of a Canadian university, which received substantial funding from Chinese companies, betrayed its serious concern—bordering on fear and despair—over the possible adverse impacts of a deteriorating China-Canada relationship on the enrollment of Chinese students, who were a major source of revenue for the university, and on other funding from Chinse sources.[189]

It would be fair to surmise that should incidents similar to McMaster's happen elsewhere, many Canadian university administrators or student leaders might not act justly and properly for fear that doing so would lead to "racism" charges by Chinese students and declining Chinese student enrollment. To many of these administrators and educators, unfortunately, the feelings of nationalistic Chinese students and a sense of superficial harmony achieved by coddling these cash cows matter more than academic integrity and freedom of expression.[190] Above all, Canadian academics' reluctance to openly criticize the

---

188. In December 2018, Meng Wanzhou, the Chief Financial Officer of the Huawei company, was arrested at Vancouver International Airport on a provisional extradition request by the U.S. Department of Justice for fraud and conspiracy to commit fraud in violation of U.S. sanctions against Iran. Within days, Canadian nationals Michael Spavor and Michael Kovrig were arrested in China and indicted under its state secrets law, in what seemed to be a retaliatory move against Meng's arrest. In late 2022, the U.S. Department of Justice dismissed all the charges against Meng, who left Canada for China after spending more than one thousand days under house arrest in Vancouver. Soon after that, the two Michaels were released from detention and flown back to Canada.

189. Douglas Quan, *Meng Wanzhou Arrest Caused UBC Leaders Concern over Enrolment, Fundraising, Internal Documents Show*, NAT'L POST (Nov. 7, 2019), http://nationalpost.com/news/meng-wanzhou-arrest-caused-ubc-leaders-concern-over-enrolment-fundraising-internal-documents-show/

190. Anecdotal evidence indicated that the university administrators of a graduate residential hall went so far as to monitor residents' social media posts to ensure that their contents would not trigger the

Chinese government after the passage of its National Security Law in 2020, which enables it to assert extraterritorial power over offending parties regardless of their citizenship and place where they allegedly violate the law, may also translate into a general reluctance to confront any attempt, by the CCP or nationalistic-fevered Chinese students, to undermine free speech in Canadian universities.[191]

• • •

If every person has a price, then the price-setter should aim at the highest price. Canadian university administrators and educators should introspect about their role as educators and intellectuals. They must ask themselves: Is it truly excusable to surrender to the tyranny of a hostile foreign government, or trade the long-standing missions of the university, their cherished democratic values, and Canada's sovereignty for short-term profits and a superficial harmony that seems to align with the diversity initiatives trumpeted by Canadian universities? Taking a firm stance against a tyrannical and morally bankrupt foreign regime is a formidable task, considering that campus free speech in Canada is the least protected among all the Western jurisdictions examined in this book. Nonetheless, standing up to an external enemy and resisting authoritarian forces that seek to undermine freedom of expression from within are both crucial to salvage Canadian universities as places of learning and inquiry.

Chinese students who lived there. Amy Lai, *June 4—Reminiscences of a Hongkonger in Canada*, MACDONALD LAURIER INSTITUTE (Jun. 3, 2019), https://www.macdonaldlaurier.ca/june-4-reminiscences-hongkonger-canada-amy-lai-inside-policy/ (last visited May 12, 2020).

191. Amy Lai, *Opinion: Canadian Academics May Fear Reprisal for Criticizing China—But They Must Not Self-Censor*, GLOBE & MAIL (Oct. 22, 2020), www.theglobeandmail.com/opinion/article-canadian-academics-may-fear-reprisal-for-criticizing-china-but-they/

Conclusion

The end is the beginning. This book's introduction cites German poet Heinrich Heine: "This was a prelude only. Wherever they burn books they will also, in the end, burn human beings."[1] Censorship at universities in Western democracies beyond what the laws require, no matter how sound the justifications may seem, and regardless of the politics of the censored expressions, is reminiscent of book-burning in dictatorial and authoritarian regimes.

Recall also the story that the author's friend remembers with disgust about the little girl and her pet chicken.[2] Members in academia who slander their friends and co-workers for harboring "wrong" thoughts, or destroy their colleagues' careers due to their ideological "impurity" or nonconformity, are no less pathetic than the girl who slaughters her chicken to please the Chinese Communist Party. While the girl turns to the red scarf to help overcome her grief and persuade herself that her bloody act is courageous and honorable, many of these adults destroy the lives of others—who may well be decent and law-abiding members of society—often self-righteously and without the slightest remorse.

Part I detailed the origin of free speech in the university setting, addressed the history, definitions, and significance of academic freedom, and clarified their differences while illuminating their mutually beneficial relationship. Erosion of these freedoms throughout history has only jeopardized universities' core functions. Once these freedoms have vanished, the university itself cannot be said to exist as a haven of free speech and academic freedom.

1. This is taken from Heine's famous tragic play *Almansor* (1821) ("Dort, wo man Bücher verbrennt, verbrennt man am Ende auch Menschen.")
2. *See* the introduction.

Part II argued that free speech is a natural right essential to the pursuit of truth, democratic governance, and self-development. The right to speak, which also includes the right to remain silent and arguably also the right to utter falsehoods, is nowhere more important than on university campuses. Although political correctness may help create an inclusive society, banning expressions for fear that they offend protected groups and individuals will discourage free inquiry and frustrate democratic governance, as topics and expressions frequently considered offensive generally would not constitute harassment, discrimination, or hate speech. While the concept of "microaggression" should not be invalidated, recipients of microaggression should exercise their freedom of expression—a core part of dignity—to resist words or acts that they deem to have undermined their dignity. This part also turned to three common phenomena on university campuses. Deplatforming speakers, which has taken different forms, is generally not a good strategy to build an inclusive campus environment. Neither are trigger warnings. Speech deemed "triggering," which has come to refer to anything "provocative," is not necessarily harmful given the pedagogical values of thought-provoking ideas and methods. Ideas and methods of pedagogical values must not be mistaken as personal attacks, while personal attacks against those who dare to challenge orthodoxies must not be justified in the name of peace and harmony. Finally, any safe space should be limited in scope. Turning the entire university into a "safe space," based upon an overly broad concept of violence, may justify the use of preemptive violence against perceived threats to its "safety."

Part III looked at three Anglophone jurisdictions to explain how their laws protecting freedom of expression have not deterred the worrisome trend of (self-)censorship increasingly prevalent over the past decade. Civil debates have been shut down by universities that bowed to pressure from radical groups and fellow academics who wanted no challenges to their ideologies. In some cases, universities sought to terminate academic employment and denied support to members whose rights or safety, or both, were assaulted. By examining whether the suppression of free speech was justified in numerous case studies, these chapters have affirmed many speakers' right to speak without defending their politics or vindicating their opinions. They have also argued that universities must avoid inconsistent application of the free speech principle to different groups, which unfairly privileges the feelings and safety of some groups over those of others.

The chapters have shown that academic free speech is better protected in

American universities than in their British and Canadian counterparts due to its First Amendment, which applies to public universities. Abundant case law also affirms the contractual protection of free speech at American private universities. In addition, despite numerous attempts by university authorities to disinvite speakers and penalize employees for their speech or free expression, pushback against the Chinese government's aggressive campaigns to suppress free speech on American campuses has been consistent and successful.

While the future of campus free speech in the United Kingdom looks more uncertain than in the U.S., the British government's affirmation of the fundamental importance of campus free speech and attempt to pass a new free speech law indicate that it is moving in the right direction. The Canadian government, however, has done little to affirm the importance of campus free speech, which, quite extraordinarily, is not guaranteed by its constitution due to the high degree of deference given to university authorities. Canadian university authorities, by relying upon warped logic and sometimes even sounding like the "Big Brother" in George Orwell's fiction, have actively chipped away at the free speech of their members on numerous occasions. The future of campus free speech in Canada cannot be bleaker.

All chapters in part III, closing with a discussion of the threat posed by the Chinese government and their agents and supporters to free speech on these Western campuses, emphasize that if "every man has his price," university administrators and educators must strive to raise theirs and not concede to foreign tyrannies. Western universities trading their cherished democratic values for money are little different from people claiming to believe in the sanctity of sex while willingly offering it for money. Given that some universities might in fact prioritize money over fundamental values, their action is even more comparable to voluntarily becoming mistresses for material benefits at the expense of other people's marriages. In addition, it is perplexing how some immigrants from China continue to sing the praises of the Chinese government while exporting its authoritarianism to their new homes. This is often analogized, in Chinese, to a widow choosing to break her vow to her dead husband while setting up an archway to showcase her chastity. Unfortunately, such hypocrisy is mirrored in the conduct of many university authorities. Just as those who willingly have sex with people other than their partners or spouses have no claim to chastity, Western universities cannot claim to embrace freedom of speech and inquiry and yet so readily sacrifice it for financial gain.

"If liberty means anything at all, it means the right to tell people what they do not want to hear,"[3] Orwell once said. A quote from an author who remains unknown, and which has been circulating widely in social media, is equally, if not more, compelling: "If harsh criticism disappears completely, mild criticism would become harsh. If mild criticism is not allowed, silence would be considered ill-intended. If silence is no longer allowed, complimenting not hard enough would be a crime. If only one voice is allowed, then that only voice tells a lie."[4] Admittedly, free speech is not without limits, and expressions emanating from an unjust environment may help reinforce the unjust practices and thus harm parties who suffer the injustices. Yet to confer authority on any one party to police free speech and shut down lawful expression it deems too "harsh" would create more harm than good. By conceding to powers that seek to strip away this long-standing value at their discretion, that allow only one voice and that promote what the only voice speaks as truths, society embarks on the path of no return. The university is the last fortress against authoritarianism: the demise of free speech in universities is a death knell to democracy.

3. George Orwell, *12 Essential George Orwell Quotes about Freedom*, PENGUIN BOOKS, http://www.penguin.co.uk/articles/2018/nov/12-essential-george-owell-quotes-about-freedom-liberty.html (last visited Apr. 22, 2021).

4. The original quote is in Chinese. This translation is mine. (*See*: http://www.reddit.com/r/Plato/comments/f0b4ac/looking_for_a_quote_allegedly_from_plato/)

About the Author

Amy Lai is Researcher and Visiting Associate Professor at Freie Universität and the author of *The Right to Parody: Comparative Analysis of Copyright and Free Speech* (Cambridge University Press, 2019). She is the winner of Pen Canada's Ken Filkow Prize for Freedom of Expression, the Heterodox Academy's Open Inquiry "Exceptional Scholarship" Award, the National Communication Association's Franklyn S. Haiman Award for Outstanding Scholarship in Freedom of Expression, and the Voltaire Preis by Universität Potsdam in Germany.